GLENN McFARLANE IS A senior journalist and Associate Editor (Sport) at Melbourne's *Herald Sun*. He has been a journalist for 26 years and has written ten books, including *The Official Collingwood Illustrated Encylopedia*; *The Machine: the inside story of football's greatest team*; *Jock: The Story of Jock McHale Collingwood's Greatest Coach*; and collaborated with Hawthorn star Shane Crawford on his bestselling autobiography, *That's What I'm Talking About*.

GW00507146

THE FAIR DINKUMS

GLENN M^CFARLANE

MACMILLAN
Pan Macmillan Australia

First published 2016 in Macmillan by Pan Macmillan Australia Pty Ltd
1 Market Street, Sydney, New South Wales, Australia, 2000

Cataloguing-in-Publication entry is available
from the National Library of Australia
http://catalogue.nla.gov.au

Typeset in 12/15.5 pt Bembo by Midland Typesetters, Australia
Printed by McPherson's Printing Group

Front cover image and inside cover background full credit: Frank Hurley,
National Library of Australia, nla.pic-an10885587-s12.
Frame image on inside cover and picture section: Shutterstock.
Soldier portraits on inside cover, picture section, and part and chapter headings
(listed left–right as featured on inside cover): Dawn McFarlane, Avis Coles,
AWM DA10176, AWM DA10200A, AWM DA10068, Neil Walker,
AWM P03143.001, AWM DA10168, AWM DASEY0780, AWM P03236.102,
David Rae, Alastair Campbell, AWM DACS0275, AWM H06136,
AWM DA10193, Ellen Bunting, Neil Chisholm, Bellingham family,
AWM P07138.001, AWM DA09629, AWM H06319,
AWM DACS0332, Jeanette Robinson, Ian King.
RSL Virtual Memorial photograph in picture section: Image provided by the
RSL Virtual War Memorial (Durdin Family Collection): All Rights Reserved.
Full image credit: Frank Hurley, No title (Soldiers laying on stretchers) 1917;
gelatin silver photograph; 15.5 × 19.5 cm (image) 16.9 × 21.5 cm (sheet);
National Gallery of Victoria, Melbourne; Presented through the
NGV Foundation by Janine Hinderaker, Member, 2003 (2003.372).

This book is dedicated to my great-uncle, one of the Fair Dinkums, born in the right place at the wrong time; to my grandmother, who lost her big brother; and to my mother, who introduced me to the story.

Contents

'The sort of Australian who used to talk about our "tinpot navy" labelled the Australians who rushed at the chance of adventure the moment the recruiting lists were opened "the six bob a day tourists". Well – the "Tourists" made a name for Australia. . . . The next shipment were the "Dinkums" – the men who came over on principle to fight for Australia – the real, fair-dinkum* Australians.'
'"Dinkum" – Australian for "true."'

— Charles Bean, *Letters from France*

Introduction

'The gods love romance, else why was the youngest
nation on earth tried out on the oldest battlefield
of history?'

THEY ARE CALLED 'THE Fair Dinkums', for it was said that you had to be fair dinkum to enlist after it became clear what a mess the Gallipoli campaign had become. Reports of a successful operation had been exaggerated from the outset, so the extent of the mess – the botched landings, the chaos of that first day – was not yet fully apparent to Australians at home. In its place was guesswork, propaganda or newspaper eulogies about the triumph of cold steel, courage and creativity against the Turks.

The reality was very different. Some of the heroism was unquestionable and the ingenuity undoubted, but the only Australians who had a true understanding of what life was like on Gallipoli at that time were those still there, or those who had been transported home maimed and wounded, or racked by

1

sickness, physical or psychological trauma. To the overwhelming majority of Australians, other than those with a passion for geography or for Homeric tales from an age long past, that stretch of Turkish peninsula remained mostly unknown.

The 152 men who formed the 8th Reinforcements of the 7th Battalion were under no illusion as to what was awaiting them as they prepared to sail off to war on Thursday afternoon, 26 August 1915. These men who became the Fair Dinkums milled around the pier in Port Melbourne, their feet sore and swollen from marching, their eyes scanning the crowd that had gathered for a familiar face as they prepared to walk up the gangway to board the refurbished steamer-turned-troopship, *Anchises*.

They were not the only soldiers on the platform that day. Hundreds of reinforcements from other battalions were also on the crowded pier, leaving on the *Anchises*. The only thing distinguishing the soldiers was the coloured patch of their respective battalions; the Fair Dinkums' was a horizontal brown on red patchwork. The 'Mud and Blood' insignia not only set the Fair Dinkums apart from the other soldiers on the pier that day, but would unite them forever.

None of the Fair Dinkums were aware that earlier in the month four members of the original 7th Battalion – a unit they were sailing halfway across the world to join up with – had fought with such rare distinction in the Battle of Lone Pine that they would eventually be awarded the Victoria Cross. Corporals William Dunstan and Alexander Burton, and Lieutenants Frederick Tubb and William Symons had performed extraordinary feats of bravery during the August Offensive, 1915. Burton's medal would be a posthumous one. The man who recommended the Victoria Crosses was the commanding officer of the 7th Battalion, Lieutenant-Colonel Harold Elliott, better known to his men as 'Pompey'. He had been given the nickname – reluctantly, it must be said – of a famous Carlton VFL footballer, Fred Elliott, who, like the military man, possessed a volatile streak and whose family suggested it came from 'a throwback to Pompeii and Mt Vesuvius'. Pompey Elliott, the military man, was already known for his eruptions, but also for military prowess and his capacity to keep order when the chaos around him became too much. He knew a handful of those Fair Dinkums about to embark and join him and the rest of the 7th Battalion on the other side of the world and, in time, he would come to shape some of their destinies.

The Australia the Fair Dinkums were leaving was very different from the country that had so enthusiastically, almost breathlessly, agreed to go to war the previous August. The 'Originals' – as the first batch of enlisted men were later called – had sailed from the same location just over ten months earlier. These men had left fearing the European War, as it largely was then, would be over before their ships docked in France.

Instead, as the first convoy of ships left Australian waters, the Ottoman Empire came into the war on the side of the Central Powers. The Originals' destination then became Egypt, where they underwent intense training before they joined the British Expeditionary Force and took part in the Gallipoli landings on 25 April 1915. The Fair Dinkums knew they were now headed to Gallipoli after some training in Egypt. And while so many of the Originals who had sailed off through the Port Phillip Bay Heads had a vision of war crafted from folklore passed on from previous generations, or from the well-worn pages of W.H. Fitchett's bestselling *Deeds that Won the Empire,* the men who followed them already knew this was a conflict like none other. They knew it would change their lives.

In four months, they had seen casualty lists and honour rolls for fallen soldiers grow by the day, the week and the month, since news first broke about the Gallipoli landings to the failed August Offensive. For all the misinformation, half-truths and furphies about the state of the war, and despite the fearlessness of the Anzacs – as the Australian and New Zealand soldiers were now being called – inescapable was the constant flow of fatalities and casualties.

Behind each name was a heartache, a mourning family. And behind each casualty list was a collective push for more men to enlist to not only maintain the fighting, but to somehow drive the Anzacs from the ravines, gullies and roughly carved trenches and dugouts of Gallipoli all the way to their objective, Constantinople. The Fair Dinkums, and those at Port Melbourne to see them off, had no idea that, at the official level, the hopes of the Dinkums achieving their objectives at Gallipoli had long since been extinguished, though the campaign raged on regardless, like a nightmare without an awakening.

IT WAS SO DIFFERENT when Australia first went to war. Europe had been destined for armed conflict for many months – some would attest, for years. The assassination of Archduke Franz Ferdinand, heir to the Austro–Hungarian throne, and his wife Sophie, provided the trigger. Ferdinand had toured Australia in 1893, yet the consequence of his bloody passing in Sarajavo on 28 June 1914 was lost on most Australians. A series of intricate treaties between some of the oldest powers of Europe complicated the matter. France was bound by its treaty with Russia, which left Germany and Austria–Hungary ready to go to war against them. For a time, the Central Powers figured Great Britain would remain neutral, even if the Germans went to war with France or invaded Belgium, which they ultimately did.

They were wrong. The British declared war on Germany on 4 August 1914, and the rest of the Empire, Australia included, followed suit.

The news of impending war set off a chain of excitement in Australia, far removed from the conflict. There were unprecedented scenes in the heart of Melbourne the following day, the *Argus* reporting that a 'strained expectancy' had swept across the city: 'The streets were exceptionally crowded and every corner boasted its little debating society, usually led by some voluble individual, with a more or less approximate idea of the European situation'. By lunchtime, when the news had filtered through that Great Britain – and therefore Australia – had made its position known, every possible reaction was evident in the streets: relief, unbridled enthusiasm, gratification and, in some instances, pessimism.

Prime Minister Joseph Cook, fighting an election that he was destined to lose, told the country: 'Whatever the difficulty, and whatever the cost, we must be steadfast in our determination. We owe it to those who have gone before to preserve the great fabric of British freedom and hand it onto our children'. Even before the official start of the war, on 31 July, Opposition Leader Andrew Fisher had told a gathering in Colac, in Victoria's western district, that if the worst was to happen, 'Australians will stand behind the mother country to help and defend her to our last man and our last shilling.' The words would sit with him forever.

Victorian Premier Sir Alexander Peacock brought a bit of mirth to a gathering at Melbourne Town Hall after the declaration of war on 4 August. Sir Alexander, when confronted by a man who took exception to his comments, heckled back at the interjector: 'Never mind him, he has had too much German lager, or it is a little bit of German sausage that he has not digested'. Then he extolled the virtues of the relatively new Commonwealth of Australia to tackle the task at hand, saying, 'What a fine thing it was that federation had become an accomplished fact! Now Australians were speaking with one voice to deal with their common interests, and not with six voices.'

By the end of 1914, Australia had 52,561 volunteers pass the stringent physical tests to enlist. The Originals were encamped in Egypt as they trained and waited impatiently for their call to battle. With Turkey now in the war, a British plan to force the straits of the Dardanelles and to take Constantinople was seen as the most effective way of ending the threat of the Ottoman Empire, and of striking a telling blow to the Central Powers.

But the plan was far easier achieved on paper than it was in reality. The March naval attacks had had limited success, so it was decided a land attack on the Gallipoli Peninsula was required. In came the Australian and New Zealand Army Corps. The location had a sense of ancient history to it, and Australia, federated only fourteen years earlier, was intent on playing its role.

There was a mythical feel to the stretch of land where the Anzacs fought in 1915, as one soldier penned:

The gods love romance, else why was the youngest nation of earth tried out on the oldest battlefield of history? How those young men from the continent whose soil had never been stained with blood thrilled to hear their padres tell them as they gathered on the decks of the troopships in the harbour of Lemnos that tomorrow they would set foot almost on the site of the ancient battlefield of Troy, where the early Greeks shed their blood, as sung in the oldest battle song in the world.

But Australia was locked in a battle against a foe it barely knew or understood, in conditions unfamiliar and unrelenting, and in an arena where the fingerprints of ancient conflict and crisis stretched back not only through the centuries, but through millennia. As soldier, politician and historian Staniforth Smith wrote:

The gaunt, stark peninsula of Gallipoli is a palimpsest of great historical events. It was at the entrance to the Dardanelles that Agamemnon tied up his ships to besiege ancient Troy. The romance of Hero and Leander still clings to those ancient shores. The island of Lemnos was the first stopping place of the Argonauts in their quest of the Golden Fleece. Gallipoli was the stepping stone between Asia and Europe. The vast armies of Darius and Xerxes crossed the Narrows in their attempts to subjugate the Greeks. Alexander the Great poured his warriors over Gallipoli (or Thracian Chersonese) and across the Dardanelles, for the conquest of Persia and India; and Roman legions thundered by in their efforts to conquer and govern the then known world. It was here that the Turks first secured a footing in Europe. It was on this historic ground that Australians and New Zealanders, coming from lands unknown at those remote periods of time, landed under a hail of shot and shell, and carved in strange hieroglyphics the name of 'ANZAC', the glory of which will remain imperishable.

The Australians landed on that beach early on the morning of 25 April 1915. Back home, as the guns blazed, the snipers pinpointed targets, and men scurried up hills, the Australian community remained oblivious to the happenings half a world away. It took the best part of four days for news to filter back to Australians and Andrew Fisher, prime minister again since 17 September 1914, gave rise to cheers in the House of Representatives when he spoke about the campaign and Australia's role in it: 'Some days ago the Australian War Expeditionary Forces were transferred from Egypt to the Dardanelles. They have since landed and have been in action on the Gallipoli Peninsula. News reaches us that the action is proceeding satisfactorily'.

Less than satisfactory was the trickle of casualty lists in the newspapers that soon became a flood. Some of the Fair Dinkums, yet to commit to signing up or too young to do so, were among those waiting outside newspaper offices, eager to hear the latest reports from the front and to scan the casualty lists for anyone they knew.

It wasn't until 8 May that one of the firsthand accounts of the landings appeared in the *Argus* and other newspapers.

British war correspondent Ellis Ashmead-Bartlett's story set the scene for Gallipoli myths for a century, and his account of what occurred that fateful morning had young men – and some older ones – rushing to join the fight, inspired by his words and the deeds of their countrymen. His pen had its share of flourish, and more than a hint of hyperbole, when he filed:

> The Australians who were about to go into action for the first time, in trying circumstances, were cheerful, quiet and confident. There was no sign of nerves nor of excitement . . . men, who six months ago had been living peaceful civilian lives, had begun to disembark on a strange and unknown shore in a strange land to attack an enemy of a different race . . .
>
> The Australians rose to the occasion. Not waiting for orders or for the boats to reach the beach, they sprang into the sea, and forming a sort of rough line, rushed at the enemy trenches . . . this race of athletes proceeded to scale cliffs without responding to the enemy's fire. They lost some men, but did not worry! There has been no finer feat in this war than this sudden landing in the dark and storming the heights, above all holding on whilst their reinforcements were landing. These raw colonial troops in these desperate hours proved worthy to fight side by side with the heroes of Mons, Aisne, Ypres and Neuve Chapelle.

It mattered little that Ashmead-Bartlett hadn't even been there for the landing. Unlike Australia's official war correspondent Charles Bean, Ashmead-Bartlett didn't come ashore until 9.30 pm.

By the time the Fair Dinkums began walking aboard the *Anchises*, Gallipoli was at a deadly stalemate and the 8th Reinforcements of the 7th Battalion knew what they were headed into. It wasn't *Boys' Own Annual* stuff but a harsh new war where the casualties were not only horrendous, but sizeable in number too.

A reminder of this came the day before the Fair Dinkums set sail. A ship carrying more than 200 sick and wounded Victorians, and a further 200 from New South Wales, South Australia and Tasmania, docked at Port Melbourne shortly after 10 am, to be greeted by the Melbourne public who had come out in force to welcome them home. The *Age* noted that: 'Public feeling was stirred a pitch of intense enthusiasm . . . that stood the test of two or three hours waiting; an enthusiasm that lasted as long as there was a motor car with a soldier in it in sight'. Hundreds of cars decked out in Australian and British flags had been put at the disposal of the Australian Patriots' League, and the Ascot Vale Military band struck up the patriotic 'See the Conquering Hero Comes' as men came down the gangway, cheered on by family, friends and grateful strangers who made the trip to Port Melbourne to welcome soldiers home.

The reality of a far-off war bringing home men altered forever – some of them scarred mentally and physically for the remainder of their lives – was a common occurrence in the coming years. According to the *Age*:

> everyone was anxious to see the war-scarred soldiers. If a soldier walked or was assisted down the gangway with one end of an armless sleeve tucked into his tunic pocket; if he was minus a leg or showed signs of having had his limbs shattered, or had lost his sight, he was sure of a 'hoy' from the boys up on the decks . . .
>
> Here and there the smiles were watered with tears, for among the troops were a few who were maimed and some whose bandages and general appearance gave a slight indication of the fearful ordeal through which they had come. More than that, some who had gone away with friends had before them the sorrowful task of telling to parents the story of how their sons had fallen.

It was a reception that few received for a homecoming, and theirs was 'a greater glory than that of a sporting champion returned with captured laurels'. The *Age* continued:

> The men, most of them wearing slouch hats but with a few wearing helmets and one decorated in a Turkish fez, were given free railways passes, along with the assortment of goodies passed on by the grateful public. But five 'cot cases' were quietly whisked away to Caulfield Military Hospital, their futures uncertain and their homecomings crushed by the weight of their ailments.

It is impossible to think that the Fair Dinkums were unaware of the return of the hospital ship or the state of the men who had sailed back on it. That was the reality of war. And while newspaper reports about ships sailing out of port with troops were suppressed to ensure any German ships or submarines – 'tinned fish', as they were called – would have no advanced warnings, the return of hospital ships received plenty of news coverage.

The men of the 8th Reinforcements of the 7th Battalion spent their last night in Australia in the Broadmeadows camp. They had been there for a few weeks, undergoing most of their training at Seymour since their enlistment. A meningitis outbreak in Melbourne, and in the various army camps throughout the state, had people on edge. Many afflicted were in isolation either in the camps or at the Alfred Hospital; two of the five people who died the day the Fair Dinkums left Australia were soldiers.

In the days before the Fair Dinkums' departure, unfounded rumours claimed that the Dardanelles had been forced, that the Straits had been penetrated by British warships. False hopes and premature celebrations occurred in towns from Yea to Melbourne, where church and school bells rang, schoolkids were dismissed early and jubilation was displayed on the streets.

★

THE WEEK THE FAIR Dinkums sailed was the 55th week of the war, 124 days since the Gallipoli landings, and the sixty-ninth casualty list had been issued, detailing another 49 deaths and 378 wounded.

The *Daily Advertiser* told the story of Lieutenant Hubert Meager, of the 3rd Australian Infantry Brigade, and his prophetic letter to his mother who lived on the Isle of Wight. The letter had arrived the day Meager was killed on Gallipoli and his message from the grave captured the prevailing mood of the country: 'My Dearest Mother – If I be taken off, do as the Roman mothers did: Keep your tears for privacy and steel your heart. Get a dozen recruits in my place'.

The push for new recruits continued unabated. Ninety-nine were accepted in Melbourne and the country centres of Ballarat and Bendigo on 26 August 1915. The plea to hasten the recruiting came from Colonel Cyril St Clair Cameron, an assistant adjutant general and advisor to commander of the Australian Imperial Force, Sir William Birdwood, who had arrived invalided back in Australia the day the Fair Dinkums sailed. Cameron had been a part of the Gallipoli landings and returned intent on pushing the recruitment drive as strenuously as possible. On reaching Fremantle, he told reporters:

Blood and bone and iron alone *can* win the present struggle, and although Australia has answered nobly to the call, we must double our efforts. As yet, we are only at the beginning of a great struggle for national existence, and the Turks must be wiped clear out of existence before we can hope for any successes that will lead to the final victory . . . Australia has the men. Let us all get in and get the business over. Every available man must get into training, for all will be wanted. They must learn to shoot, to obey, to dig, the last being almost as important as the other two. My message to the men of Australia from Lord Kitchener is simply 'Enlist'.

The Fair Dinkums had already heeded that message and had committed their lives, at least for the foreseeable future. They knew as they trudged up the gangway that the war was not going to be over by Christmas. They knew they would not see their families and loved ones until the enemy was defeated.

They knew they would do it together. Some of them had been mates before they enlisted; others were linked by blood. Many of them had enlisted on the same day; some would have their fate decided on the same day. Most were strangers until meeting in the recruitment lines, or after becoming tent mates at Seymour or sharing a cuppa and a smoke around the campfire at Broadmeadows. But what was ahead of them, and the experiences they knew they were about to share, would link them forever, in life and in death.

PART I

THE DINKUMS

1

How far is it to Gallipoli?

'I am going to avenge Ossie.'

IN ANY WAR, NEW men are always required to replace the
dead. That ancient adage, as old as the ground that the Anzacs
were fighting on and dying for on the Gallipoli Peninsula
throughout much of 1915, did not just apply to the fledgling
nation of Australia. The same was said across the world, new
and old. From the moment the news broke in Australia about
the Gallipoli landings and the Anzac involvement, there was
a rush of recruits from the largest of the cities and smallest of
country towns, all eager to do their bit. Many of the men who
were signing up had no idea where Gallipoli was, let alone how
far it was to the stretch of land that everybody seemed to be
talking about.

They enlisted for reasons even more diverse than what the
Originals signed up for the previous year. Much had to do with
fighting for King and Country, and for many of them that was the
order. In 1915, almost 98 per cent of the four million Australians

had been born here, in New Zealand or in Great Britain. Almost 10 per cent of those living in Australia at the time had been born in Great Britain, which showed how ties to the Mother Country – and the Empire – still tugged at almost every seam of Australian life. There were other reasons too, including a sense of duty, a sense of adventure (though that had been dulled by the appalling casualty lists being posted daily on noticeboards outside crowded newspaper offices), economic reasons (six shillings per day was significantly more than the forces of other countries were being paid), and social pressure, which hadn't been there the year before but had become front and centre of Australian society.

There was even a desire to exact some sort of revenge on the Germans – and now the Turks. The propaganda espoused that innocent civilians were no longer safe; part of that came from the sinking of the British passenger liner *Lusitania* on 7 May 1915, twelve days after the Gallipoli landings, by a German U-boat off the coast of Ireland, which the *Argus* called 'an act of cold-blooded piracy and murder'. The mammoth British ocean liner, carrying 1266 passengers and 696 crew, was torpedoed, rapidly broke apart and sank within eighteen minutes. There were 1191 lives lost, including a number of Americans.

But as the casualty lists grew and the supply of fresh young recruits began to dry up, Australian authorities knew they needed a new process to bring more eligible men forward. The initial requirements for eligibility – that candidates be between eighteen and 35 years of age, a minimum of five foot six inches (170 centimetres) with a chest of 34 inches (86 centimetres) – were so strict that it had ruled many candidates out. As one report in the *Argus* noted:

> Scores of men who had been rejected on account of low chest measurements are taking courses at physical culture schools; short men are trying all known methods, and inventing others hitherto unknown, in an endeavour to increase their height,

while a number of those who have had disqualifying defects removed by operation is legion.

Rejection shattered many of those who desperately wanted to fight. Men left recruiting offices in tears, embarrassed by their exclusion and alienated from their mates who had been accepted. It also placed them in a vulnerable position against those who targeted eligible men with white feathers and abuse. But as the Victorian Government began a series of recruiting campaigns in the middle of 1915, the AIF agreed to relax some of the requirements needed to enlist. By mid-July, when the last of the 8th Reinforcements of the 7th Battalion enlisted, the height restriction was cut back to five foot two inches (157 centimetres), the chest requirements changed, the age limit pushed up to 45, and bad teeth and old surgical scars were overlooked.

Lieutenant-Governor Sir John Madden was accompanied by the federal Attorney-General and soon-to-be Prime Minister Billy Hughes at a special patriotic rally at the St Kilda Town Hall at the end of June 1915 to chase volunteers almost by whatever means necessary. Madden noted the difficulties average men had in enlisting and told the packed crowd:

The worst treatment for enthusiasm was to kick a man downstairs, and that was the treatment they received – about 50 per cent of them were rejected. They were rejected for their teeth and because they had the mark of the surgeon's knife on them. Did the men who fought with Napoleon have all perfect teeth, and was it not fashionable to have the marks of the surgeon's knife on one? The process of the camel passing through the eye of a needle seemed to be easy compared with the task of getting into the Expeditionary Forces. The fighting at the Dardanelles had not exhausted all the valour in Australia. Australia did not want to lose her young men, but they must fight for their country, as it would be they that would possess it later.

Hughes, who was prime minister within four months, was at his belligerent best when he reminded Australians of their duties, 'All present [must] now pledge themselves to do their duty as loyal citizens, and devote all their energies and make every sacrifice to help their King and Country in the Great War.' He described the conflict as:

indeed Armageddon. Half the world was engaged – all the world was involved and 25 million men were under arms. It [is] not a war amongst the soldiery, but a war of nations. Let every young man join that heroic band at Gallipoli, who raised the name of Australians amongst the nations, and had written a story that would never die, while men lived to tell it.

Almost on cue, after Hughes' stirring call, one man came forward and told of how he had four sons at the front. He pleaded with the ladies present to allow their 'brothers' and 'lovers' to join up, explaining that his eldest son had been killed at Gallipoli. He relayed a story of how one stranger had approached him on a railway platform the day he heard news of his son's passing, and said: 'I am going to avenge Ossie [Australia]'. A chorus of cheers followed.

The link to Gallipoli, however far away it was, and however unknown it had been, was stamped thereafter on Australians from all walks of life. As former servicewoman and historian Patsy Adam-Smith's *Anzacs* detailed:

By June 1915, when 10,000 Australian casualties had been announced, the cost of nationhood had begun to be felt. It would worsen ... it was said of the men who rushed to join up when war was declared that they were 'Dinkum Aussies'. The men who joined later, after hearing of the fearful death toll, were called 'Fair Dinkums'; men who enlisted even though they knew the odds were against them.

Historian Ernest Scott's *Australia During the War* agreed:

Some came forward because they realised for the first time that Australian soldiers would actually fight in the war, but most were moved by a sense of tragic necessity, and offered themselves to fill the gaps daily created in the ranks, or to avenge killed mates, or because the war would demand greater efforts, or because a real man could not hold back now.

Among these were the 152 men of the 8th Reinforcements of the 7th Battalion who predominantly enlisted over a three-month period from the start of May to the end of July 1915. They varied in age, religious denomination, marital status and occupation, some lying about their age because they were too young – George Yendle died before he turned eighteen – or too old – Edward Spooner said he was 44 when he was actually 53. The men came from the Church of England, they were Roman Catholics, Methodists, Baptists and Presbyterians. There was even a Salvation Army officer among the group. Only 25 of the men were married; 127 were single. They were fruit growers, foundry workers and farmers; packers, plumbers and painters; bootmakers, bakers and blacksmiths; seamen, salesmen, saddlers and students; miners and mailmen; tailors, tram drivers and tinsmiths; labourers and letter-carriers; clerks and carpenters; hairdressers and hawkers; wireless operators and warehousemen. All left those positions to join the AIF.

The man in charge of the Fair Dinkums was Arthur Hart, a 48-year-old public servant from Eaglehawk, an honorary major responsible for getting the men into fighting shape. It was some task, but men recalled him with fondness decades later, knowing that he did his best to prepare them for what was ahead.

Most of the men came from Victoria – from the inner city suburbs of Melbourne, from the big regional centres such as Geelong, Bendigo and Ballarat, and from small country towns that were little more than dots on the map, but punching above their weight in terms of enlistments. Almost a sixth of them were born overseas, unsurprisingly with the great majority of those coming from Great Britain. But there was also a Frenchman by birth, an Italian and a New Zealander. There were seven sets of brothers but, by the end of their time in uniform, many of them felt as if they were almost kin.

2

Brothers in arms

'I swear that I will well and truly serve . . .'

FREDERICK HOAD WAS THE first of the Fair Dinkums to swear the oath of allegiance, even though technically he was one of the Originals when he did it. It was 18 August 1914, just fourteen days after Australia had declared war and a full year and eight days before he left with the 8th Reinforcements of the 7th Battalion. He stood before a witness and bound himself by words to the Australian Army, reading from the same booklet as other eager young would-be-soldiers, 'I swear that I will well and truly serve our Sovereign Lord the King in the Australian Imperial Force . . . until the end of the War . . . I will resist His Majesty's enemies and cause His Majesty's peace to be kept and maintained'.

Hoad was no raw-boned recruit. The 31-year-old married electrical fitter with the Victorian Railways already knew about the vagaries of war, having fought in the Boer War as a private with the 4th Australian Commonwealth Horse unit more than a decade earlier, returning home unscathed but not unchanged by his experiences. Military was in his blood. His late uncle, Sir John Hoad, had served in South Africa, commanding the 1st Australian Regiment in late 1899, comprising troops from Victoria, South Australia, Western Australia and Tasmania. Sir John was invalided home to Australia on 26 August 1900, later serving with distinction in various military and government roles. He had even acted as a guide to Lord Kitchener on his exhaustive inspection of Australia's land defences in late 1909 and early 1910, and helped plan the universal training scheme that was meant to safeguard Australia's defences before his death in 1911.

Fred Hoad's second war was almost over before it started. He had embarked with the first contingent on the *Hororata* in October 1914, and spent months training in Egypt. But sickness and a case of varicose veins prevented him from doing his duty. By February 1915, he was in the No. 2 General Hospital in Egypt at Mena with countless other Australian soldiers, complaining of 'aching pain in his scrotum after marching and also in his right leg with great congestion in the veins of each' and required surgery to remove some of the veins. Classified as medically unfit, he was repatriated to Australia aboard the *Ulysses* on 21 March. That could have been the end of his story in terms of the war, but even as he was sailing back, Hoad was determined to return. This dark-haired soldier from Malvern, with a tattoo on his left arm and a pencil-thin moustache, applied for a commission to become a 2nd lieutenant almost as soon as he arrived home in Australia, citing his military experiences, which included ten months in South Africa and two-and-a-half years as a lieutenant in the 56th Battalion at home. His disappointment at missing the Gallipoli landings was tempered by a posting to the 8th Reinforcements of the 7th Battalion. Having missed the start of the Gallipoli campaign, he had no intention of missing the end of it.

With Hoad on the voyage back to Australia aboard the *Ulysses* were two other soldiers who were also determined to return; the trio did so as part of the Fair Dinkums. Andrew Kinkaid, a 23-year-old labourer from Northcote, had enlisted as part of the 2nd Reinforcements of the 7th Battalion, signing the paperwork and taking the oath at Bairnsdale in September 1914. His medical noted that his left wrist had a minor deformity but that didn't stop him sailing from Australia early in 1915. He was barely in Egypt long enough to make much of an impression as varicocele (an enlargement of the veins around the testes) quickly and painfully earned him a discharge back to Australia. Captain Arthur Hart, the officer in charge of the Fair Dinkums, approved Kinkaid's return to the battalion and the 8th Reinforcements after it was clear he had been successfully operated on, and was once more fit for active service.

Paul Rodriguez, an English merchant sailor well accustomed to sea voyages, was the other Fair Dinkum. The 21-year-old, who listed his mother in London as his next of kin, was one of the very early enlistments, but was forced to return because of a chronic liver complaint, influenza and various ailments, some of which he had contracted on his sea-faring adventures. He had had an attack of colic on his first journey to Egypt and was admitted to hospital in the early weeks of 1915 with pneumonia and a slightly swollen liver. He was given a light fish diet, kept under close watch, and eventually invalided back to Australia. These three Originals were to become Fair Dinkums.

ARTHUR GEORGE CHARLES HART was the man charged with bringing together the 8th Reinforcements of the 7th Battalion. At 48, he would normally have been considered too old for service. But Hart was a well-known, well-liked and, above all, well-respected member of the Eaglehawk community. He lived in Trelwanob at Victoria Street, Eaglehawk, and was working as a clerk to the courts at the outbreak of war. Having been involved in the civilian services for much of his life, he wanted to assist his country as best as he could. It didn't matter that he was married or had young sons who were eager to enlist themselves. Hart wanted to be of service and when he gained a commission in the army, he was chosen to lead the Fair Dinkums. His AIF application showed the extent of his pre-war service: a private from 1891 to 1893, commissioned in 1893, a captain in 1900. In May 1915 he was in the Broadmeadows camp for a few months of preparation, and from there he became a captain (honorary major) in August 1915, just before he sailed. Hart was a prominent member of the Citizens Forces. Many of the men he commanded came from Eaglehawk and Bendigo; he retained a soft spot for not only the men of the district but also for those who came under his command.

Joseph Bellesini, like Hart, was living in Victoria Street, Eaglehawk, in 1915. His family had long connections to the Sailor's Gully–Eaglehawk region; his late father Andrew Sr operated mining and prospecting companies there before his death in 1897, when Joseph was only a child. It made for a tough upbringing, but by the start of the war, he was in the latter stages of his apprenticeship as a tailor. He loved the work, but there was a greater calling. The nineteen-year-old lived with his widowed but feisty mother, Esther, and some of his ten siblings. One of his brothers, Harry, had already left for the front, and was fighting at Gallipoli with the 22nd Battalion. Another brother, Andrew Jr, enlisted in the middle of May, and Esther was eager to ensure that if Joseph was going to fight, he would at least do it alongside one of his brothers, who might be able to look out for him.

As a railway fireman, Andrew, 28, had long since moved away from home, and enlisted at Cressy in Victoria's western districts. His enlistment papers revealed that Andrew was married and had three young children, but that union 'was under orders of separation'. A strong, thickset man standing at just a fraction over six feet tall, compared to his lighter framed, seemingly more vulnerable brother, Andrew's medical was halted briefly at one stage because of scars on his left ribcage from a dog attack years earlier. He was ultimately passed fit for active service. Joseph was one of the last Fair Dinkums to join up, but he linked up with his brother at camp in Seymour, and later at Broadmeadows, before preparing for the sea voyage on the *Anchises*. Their mother was comforted in the knowledge that two of her boys would go off to fight together, and might even meet up with their other Anzac sibling.

Hart had also come to know the Harris brothers, 30-year-old Oliver and 22-year-old Tom, who were from the Quarry Hill region outside Bendigo. Neither was married and each was keen to do his best for his country. During the week, Oliver was a managing law clerk and accountant; on weekends and in his spare time, he had more than a passing interest in military matters, so it was only natural that he enlisted. He already had three years as a private in the militia, and was a keen member of the Eaglehawk Rifle Club. He took the oath of allegiance on 26 July 1915, more than a month after his brother Tom, a telephone mechanic, had enlisted.

Henry 'Harry' Attwood was in his early thirties and well known in the district. His parents had run the Victoria Hotel in Eaglehawk when he was growing up, and only the screams of his sister in the early hours of a morning in 1900 saved it from burning to the ground. Harry had attended Sydney Flat and Eaglehawk State Schools and, in 1897, won certificates in English, Euclid and Arithmetic at St Andrews College. An accountant who ran his own house and land agency, he put a steady income and a comfortable life on hold to enlist, taking the oath on the same day as Oliver Harris.

Tom Hicks was a letter carrier from the Bendigo Post Office who knew in the bleak autumn and early winter of 1915 the importance of information from the battlefield to the families back home. Some of the letters sent from Gallipoli were cherished and met with a rare delight from those receiving them. But Hicks also knew that telegrams contained news that no one wanted to receive, least of all from the men of God who had to deliver them. One of three brothers to enlist, he knew the dangers, but believed it was his duty to do so. His father, who carried the same name, was well known in the district as the vice-president of the Federated Mining Employees Association of Australia.

Others from the Bendigo area who joined the Fair Dinkums included 32-year-old labourer Walter Tracey, 22-year-old fitter and turner Richard McClelland, 22-year-old mining battery-man Frank Wearne, 25-year-old labourer Ernest Baker (who had moved to Brunswick for work), 22-year-old miner Bertie Harris (no relation to Oliver and Tom), 27-year-old farmer Edward Farrell (a single man but who had been seeing a fair bit of local woman Lucinda Little before his departure), twenty-year-old rubber-worker Ernest Makepeace (originally from Kangaroo Flat but who had moved to Melbourne for work) and 26-year-old miner Les Howe (from Eaglehawk, but who had shifted to Parnell in New Zealand for employment).

In the same week that Attwood was passed fit for active service, the *Bendigonian* newspaper detailed the enthusiastic scenes at the local recruiting office and at the train station as locals prepared to farewell the latest batch of troops for camp and beyond, noting:

Crowds of people ... surging round 80 of the new soldiers, who had just been sworn in ... and were about to leave for camp by the noon train for Melbourne. The military band was at attendance, and enlivened the proceedings with spirited and martial airs. A banner was held aloft by two of the soldiers at the head of the column, bearing the words 'Some of the Bendigo Boys; Will you join us?' It was intended that the new soldiers should march through the streets of Melbourne on their arrival behind this banner. The self-centred people in the metropolis would see that the provinces were doing their share, and Bendigo, not the least.

As the gathering moved from the recruiting office to the station, latecomers in khaki battled the crowds to seek the carriage that had been specially reserved for the departing soldiers. 'From the windows they said their farewells to relatives and friends,' the report continued. 'The gathering gave three lusty cheers for the men at Gallipoli, and three equally hearty cheers for the departing soldiers. In the expiring moments the band played "Rule Britannia" and "God Save the King".'

Scenes like this were being played around the country; indeed, around the world. Five young men from Cobram and Barooga – little towns separated by the Murray River – gathered at the local railway station that same month to bid farewell to their family and friends. Brothers Bertie, almost twenty, and Hugh Knight, 21, had received their father's permission to enlist – no small concession, given they worked on the family's 884-acre (340 hectares) farm, Tarnpirr, on the New South Wales side of the river.

Eighteen-year-old Cobram boys Ray Rohner, a labourer, and Ray Eaton, a grocer, were there, ready for the challenge. Roy Anderson, 21, was a hairdresser and tobacconist of some repute in Cobram, who promised 'a cool, clean shave' and 'maximum comfort at minimum cost', but not even a burgeoning business was going to stop him from enlisting. He had a diary in his pocket, as did Rohner, both keen to document as much as they could of the moments that would change their lives. All five 'striplings' were on the platform on 12 July 1915, preparing to leave for camp, and then for the front. The *Cobram Courier* detailed:

Before leaving the young soldiers went through the trying ordeal of saying Good-bye to all they knew – a task that was made more difficult by the tearful demeanour of lady friends, which was in marked contrast to the stoicism and fortitude of the parents – and each one bore himself in a manly manner, though inwardly they felt that they would sooner face twice the number of Turks. [The president of the recruiting committee] . . . in wishing them God-speed and a safe return felt that they would gallantly do their part to worthily uphold the honor [sic] of Australia and the Empire, and would strive to be generous to a fallen foe, yet ever ready to emulate the heroic deeds of their mates now at Gallipoli.

More than 300 miles (480 kilometres) northwest up the Murray River, two mates enlisted on 14 June 1915. Art Pegler was a 24-year-old clerk in the Mildura butchery, and his friend, Bert Plant, a twenty-year-old blocker, was working in his father's horticultural business. Both men had known each other since birth, and committed to looking after each other while abroad. Pegler's family had originally been from Ireland, and when they arrived in Portland, one section of the family stayed there while the rest moved to Mildura. Plant's father was Scottish, and he came to Australia and to Mildura, believing it to be a bounteous place for growing fruit. It would prove anything but, though the family remained working on the land.

Others had made Mildura their home for employment reasons. One was Giovanni 'Jack' Tognola. He was a long way from home, having been born in Valtellina in northern Italy, not far from the Swiss border. Tognola was 31, and working as a labourer in the large Italian community that had found its base in the region. He had arrived in Cairns in 1904 on the *Orontes,* and worked with his brother Luigi in the Atherton region before moving south. How he came to be living and working in Mildura in the middle of 1915 remains a mystery, as does his reason for enlisting to fight for his adoptive country.

Howard 'Billy' Williams from Surrey was working at the butchery as a bookkeeper. He was 23, had a tattoo of a parrot on his right arm, and a belief that he needed to fight not only for the country he had left, but for the new one that promised so much.

Reg Scowcroft was the shining light in what had been an exceptionally dark life for his mother, Annie, and it almost killed her to think he was signing up. He was her world. She called him her 'Dear Boy', the only son of eight children, who grew up in the small township of Chiltern in the far north-east of Victoria. He was 23, worked as a tailor, and spent most of his time in his home town, but also did some work in the Melbourne suburb of Kew. His seven sisters doted on him and his mother adored him, saying there wasn't a blemish about her five foot eleven (180 centimetres), thickset son. Recruiting officers noted the scars on his right knee, perhaps the marks of an adventurous youth well spent, and recorded that he had been rejected by the AIF once for bad teeth. On 14 June 1915, he was accepted, much to his mother's disappointment.

Annie had endured a tough life. As a young woman, she had been sexually assaulted in the Black Dog Creek Forest near Chiltern, the result of which produced her first daughter, who always went by her mother's maiden name, Denny. Later, she married Thomas Scowcroft, and he accepted the daughter who was not his, and they went on to have seven more children. Thomas died in 1902, aged 47, leaving the large family in dire economic straits. Five years later, Annie married a man named Nicholson, who turned out to be a drunk, and who walked out on the family after a few years. Was it any wonder that Annie had grave reservations about her cherished only son signing up to fight in the war? What if she lost him too?

Phillip Bellingham had the most distinctive handlebar moustache, and wherever he went in Leongatha, the town at the foothills of the Strzelecki Ranges in Victoria's Gippsland region, he was impossible to miss. When he enlisted in the AIF in June 1915, the doctor who gave him the medical noted that the man before him had a 'fresh complexion, brown eyes, dark brown hair [and was] Very hairy'. Bellingham was in his early thirties, an unmarried farmer, and an active member of the Leongatha community. For ten years he had been a member of the town's rifle club and was an excellent shot. In the days after he enlisted, the local paper detailed 'the largest ever meeting held in the Leongatha Hall' for patriotic fundraising and recruiting new soldiers. The shire president told the gathering:

> Gallipoli was . . . simply a series of rocky hills and valleys, and ideal country to defend. That is the difficult country where the Australians are fighting today, and with victory after victory gained, they had Constantinople in sight. They drove the Turks over the hills, and some of the enemy's soldiers that had been taken prisoner had said that if they had tried the same feat as the Australians, not one of them would have remained alive.

Farmers used to dealing with difficult terrain on a daily basis stepped forward, unaware the president had misrepresented what was happening on that far-off peninsula in his efforts to get his fellow Leongathans to enlist.

Bill Batson was always the responsible one. The eldest of ten children growing up in the western district town of Camperdown, that seemed to be his lot in life. But he balanced that with a sense of adventure and a youthful passion for roaming the countryside. He loved learning about the lore of the Indigenous Australians he met in the district, listening to their stories about the land in which he lived. He also had a passion for momentous events. One of those was the tragedy and the heroism associated with the *Loch Ard* shipwreck near Port Campbell in 1878, of which there were only two survivors. Batson was a clerk in the Camperdown branch of the State Savings Bank, having started there in 1912 as a sixteen-year-old. But his sense of adventure and sense of duty won out, and he enlisted in the AIF in June 1915.

The Mills family from the little hamlet of Gordon between Ballarat and Ballan sacrificed much for the war effort from the outset, with seven sons, a grandson and a son-in-law enlisting during different stages of the war. The family's patriarch, John, was one of the area's pioneers, coming to Australia in the 1860s, and his 'Irish fighting blood' clearly pulsed through his sons. John's son Bill and his foster son Gordon were part of the Fair Dinkums, joining up within three weeks of each other. Bill had been a fine athlete, his work as a foreman at a quarry still keeping him superbly fit into his mid-thirties. Most of his life had been spent prospecting and mining in Western Australia, but now home, he was making a living out of rocks in Gillies and Starling's Quarry in Werribee. His ruddy complexion clearly came from a lifetime's hard work. At eighteen, Gordon had already been rejected once before because of unsatisfactory teeth, but this lorry driver was not about to let the family down. His dodgy teeth were finally given the all clear.

Walter McAsey enlisted in March 1916, but deserted within three months. Born in Yea and spending much of his early life in Kilmore, perhaps his desertion had something to with his marriage, which took place between his enlistment and his disappearance. Regardless, for a time, this 28-year-old labourer was a wanted man. He went missing on 15 June from Seymour and a warrant for his arrest was out within ten days. His evasion skills on the field were well known in his time with the Delatite Football Club, but he hadn't seriously intended to abscond. He was found, and resumed his training.

Lochlan Morison, a native of Hamilton living in Maroona, near Ararat, enlisted in February 1915, and the medical officer gave particular detail to his assessment, noting: 'Scar of appendicitis operation, right testicle undescended, all front teeth artificial'. But, as Morison went about his training, there was a new issue to deal with: he developed measles and any thoughts of an early departure were gone. That delay brought him to the Fair Dinkums. His return from Broadmeadows was followed by the worst kind of news. His brother Jack, one of three siblings to enlist, died of wounds suffered at Gallipoli. That only made Morison more determined to do his bit, for his fallen brother, as much as anything else.

Sometimes little dots on the map threw farewells so heartfelt and warm for their young men that they put even the biggest metropolis to shame. In Moyston, nestled between Ararat and Mount William in the Grampians Ranges, the town gathered in mid-July 1915 to send off 27-year-old Frank Vanstan. The local rifle club handed him a silver-mounted wallet, trusting that the tutelage he had received would stand him in good stead when he confronted the enemy. Frank's brother had already done that, as part of the Gallipoli landings, and had only been saved from a bullet because of a tin of bully beef that protruded from his kitbag that fateful day. Was it at all surprising that Frank felt the compulsion to enlist? And as the night stretched into the early morning in Moyston Hall, there was dancing until 3 am, patriotic songs, toasts and a fervent desire for Frank and his brother's safe return.

There was dancing, too, at Harkaway Hall, near Narre Warren, as five new soldiers, including twenty-year-old orchardist Robert Haysey, became – for a night – the toast of that little town. Each of the men received an inscribed gold medal as well as a pocket wallet for good measure. The chairman of festivities praised 'the sacrifices the men were making in answering the call of their King and Country' and said the recruits were 'not only worthy of a hearty farewell now, but also of a great welcome on their return, and provision for their future by the country'.

In Warragul, 21-year-old joiner Reg Palmer came forward, as did 25-year-old driver Arthur Robinson from Talbot, just north of Ballarat. Ron McLean was 'a son of the soil', having spent time on the land in Nunga in the far reaches of Victoria before enlisting in Ouyen. The 23-year-old became close mates immediately with Peter McLarty, a 28-year-old labourer from Mitchellstown, near Nagambie, as well as another farmer, 21-year-old Henry Pluck from Oaklands in southern New South Wales. Nineteen-year-old coach painter from Ballarat, Dugald Walshe, was another to come forward to enlist.

Twenty-one-year-old labourer George Henry Rae, sometimes known as 'G.H.', was a powerful specimen capable of using his bulk and, occasionally, his fists to make his presence known. From Gapsted, near Myrtleford, he had 'piercing blue eyes, enormous hands and walked like a cat, soundless'. Even as a young child, he resented his puritanical upbringing and rebelled in every way possible. If his father detested alcohol and cigarettes, G.H. had only one answer. As his son would recall: 'He indulged in all current vices, or at least all those available to him. He made his own way drinking, brawling; he was known as a dangerous foe, especially in the grip of John Barleycorn'.

The tiny town of Lindenow, in the far reaches of the Gippsland lakes, was rightly proud of its local band, which was the envy of the district. But take out the solo cornet player, and it leaves a hole, which was what happened when 22-year-old Ernie Williams enlisted. As one local journalist lamented:

> The war has struck the band world heavily, volunteers from various bands leaving their ranks much reduced in consequence. From the Lindenow band five members are now with the colours. The band farewelled Mr E.G. Williams . . . with hearty and suitable speeches and three cheers and the footballers' war cry.

Williams didn't go alone. His brother Wilfred, known as 'Billy', was also a member of the town's band. He joined up two days after Ernie, ready, willing and able to work together again on a much bigger mission.

Geelong, too, produced its share of Fair Dinkums. Two of them had been rejected in the initial rush to enlist, but were given the khaki uniform when requirements were relaxed. One of them was 30-year-old Louie Kenshole, who came from one of the region's pioneering families. His father, George, had come to Australia – and Geelong – in 1852 and was 'one of the oldest and most respected residents in south Geelong'. Louie stood only 160 centimetres – five foot three inches in the old measure – and was initially deemed too short for the task ahead. But he persisted. Although he was married, this saddler kept going back until they took him. And when the medical officers gave him the tick, they duly noted the tattoos on his forearms – a roughly scrawled image of a ballerina on the right and a milkmaid on the left.

W. 'Cedric' Smith, a 27-year-old construction engineer, was also from South Geelong. He had been knocked back due to varicose veins, but was accepted after some medical treatment. With 22-year-old painter Charles Congdon, who lived in Geelong's main thoroughfare, Moorabool Street, Kenshole and Smith joined the 8th Reinforcements of the 7th Battalion in the second half of July.

Hairdresser, tobacconist, billiard-hall proprietor and local football selector Bill Walker had been well and truly adopted by the people of Tocumwal. He was a well-liked, convivial, knockabout bloke and his customers at the shop he ran in the town loved his company. He was almost 30, married with three kids, and had made the Murray River town his home after moving there with his wife, Olive, from Melbourne. If he hadn't been bitten by the bug of serving his country, he might have ended his days there a town legend. That much was unknown when the residents gave him a farewell in the main bar at F. Beasley's Hotel, downed a few glasses with him, and wished him luck as they toasted a safe and swift return home again. Someone else would have to give them a short back and sides, at least for now.

James William Campbell, who went by the name of Bill, had been in Germany – of all places – the day that war broke out in August 1914. Incredibly, almost breathlessly, he managed to get out of Berlin on a train two hours before the paperwork of war doomed a generation, returning to the sanctuary of England as soon as he could. He was 21 at the time, and knew the consequences would not be good if he had stayed in Germany. He had been on a once-in-a-lifetime youth tour of Great Britain, France and other parts of Europe when he and about twenty other Australians happened to be in Germany the day that diplomacy was extinguished and war became reality.

Born in St Kilda and raised in Melbourne, Campbell took on the role of a station hand at Binya Station, near Griffith, in New South Wales as a teenager. He did it tough there. On his first day on the job, he was assigned to ride a letter into Narrandera, and on the way back, the horse threw him and he broke his jaw. But it toughened him up. Weeks after his 'escape' from Berlin, Campbell and some of the others on the youth tour tried to enlist in the British Army. He missed the cut, but that did not deter this resourceful young man. He took the first boat he could back to Australia, put his affairs in order, and joined the Fair Dinkums by the middle of 1915. Campbell intended to return to Berlin.

BILL SCURRY LIKED TO know how things worked, and had an inquisitive mind. Both attributes stood him in good stead for much of his life, though sometimes put him in the path of danger. He was rising twenty in mid-1915, and employed in his father's architectural modelling firm Wardrop, Scurry & Co. He loved the work, but his part-time passion was soldiering. It made the blood surge through his veins, like when he was having a kick of the football during a tight match with his local side, the Ascot Vale Rangers, on Saturdays. Scurry had already been commissioned in the 58th Infantry, the Essendon Rifles, where he had met, trained with and come to revere Pompey Elliott. Scurry was at the Moonee Valley racecourse less than two weeks after war had broken out, part of a military demonstration for Governor-General Sir Ronald Munro-Ferguson, before more than 15,000 people. He was listed in E Company during the presentation of the colours, his bond to Elliott already entrenched over the previous eighteen months.

Elliott had told his men his thoughts on war and the discipline it demanded in mid-1913, saying:

> Do not think of war as a time of glory, honor [sic] and distinction; but as a time of bitter hardship and sorrow unto death. You will then accept any distinction that comes to you as you would a lucky win in Tattersalls not due to any pre-eminent merit on your part, for there are hundreds just as brave and devoted to their duty as you. They lie rotting on the field – you are alive.

Elliott had instilled a pre-war ethos into the 58th Infantry, which took in Ascot Vale, Moonee Ponds, Flemington and Essendon. For Elliott, discipline was the elixir of good order and service in any form of military operation, 'the root of which lies in the enforcement of every order, however trivial it may seem, and so induce the habit of obedience which men cannot throw off, no matter how great the strain is to which it may be subjected'. When war came, Elliott and his men of the 7th Battalion had their chance to prove their worth.

When war was declared, the curly, fair-headed Scurry immediately sought a commission in the AIF, but was deemed too young. For a period, he worked in the AIF Depot at Broadmeadows but, frustrated by his lack of opportunities, he took off from the camp. He decided to enlist with his workmate and friend Arch Wardrop. Bill's childhood friend, Alf 'Bunty' Lawrence, joined a little later, as part of the 9th Reinforcements.

It was said the man in charge of the Fair Dinkums, Captain Hart, 'winked at the desertion', knowing Scurry's potential and what he could bring to the 8th Reinforcements. It was a decision that Hart never regretted. Scurry was engaged to be married, and the betrothal gave him a feeling of certainty in a world seemingly gone mad.

Arthur Swift and Forrest 'Bill' Usher were also members of the 58th Infantry, who were for a time aligned with Elliott, before Pompey left with the first convoy of soldiers. Eighteen-year-old Swift was a clerk. Usher was 21 and, for a time, a guard on the gates of Government House. From Moonee Ponds came Hugh McKenzie, a 21-year-old wool classer; George Loughnan, a 31-year-old clerk from the pioneering McCrae family on the Mornington Peninsula; and twenty-year-old tinsmith George Moore.

They called red-headed Alf Layfield the 'Smiling Boy', such was his outlook on life. The eighteen-year-old tinsmith from Coburg, one of the working-class suburbs of Melbourne, had a genial disposition. He was fiercely loyal to those around him, and to the things he loved – the Collingwood Football Club, tickling the ivories, and the factory crew he had come to know and love. But those had to be put aside when it came to what was happening on the other side of the world. He had to be there, whatever it took, even if it meant leaving his beloved parents Ada and George, his brother George Jr, and his sisters Ruby and Pearl, the latter only starting school the year that he left Australia. He never thought about not returning.

'Stan' Beattie, also from Coburg, was only a year older than Layfield when he signed up in May 1915. He was a painter, and his freshly inked tattoos – the Union Jack, a wild duck and heart and arrows on his left forearm; the Australian coat of arms and a swallow on his left breast – showed the link between his home and the land of his ancestors. Building contractor Les Martin, a 27-year-old married man, enlisted from nearby Northcote.

Two members of the Fair Dinkums used aliases when swearing to 'well and truly serve our Sovereign Lord the King in the Australian Imperial Force . . . So Help Me God'. The first was a young labourer from the Brunswick Brick Works. He said he was Walter Wilson, 23 years, taking his surname from the street he lived in, when he was actually Walter Day, 'Wally' to his mates. The reason for his deception was simple. He had tried to enlist under his real name and had been rejected. So he gave an alternative name, and got his brother to sign a letter purportedly from his mother. He owned up to the ruse two days before sailing off to war on the *Anchises*, and at the Broadmeadows camp changed his will to make his wife, Inez, the beneficiary. The statement was witnessed by Arthur Hart, and Wally Day finally became a soldier.

The other new soldier used an alias for different reasons. He called himself John Sydney Shaw, the middle name derived from his birth city. His real name was Waldemar Mortensen, born in Marrickville, New South Wales, in September 1887. His was a troubled upbringing, which partly explained his assumed name. His father, Peter, was horrifically killed before his tenth birthday, 'crushed against a truck by a fall of clay and stone whilst engaged in excavating'. Three-and-a-half years later, this state schoolboy was charged with stealing a pound from William Owens' purse and faced Windsor Court. Mortensen owned up to the theft, telling the court 'I took it . . . and changed it at Mawson's Store and every day spent a bit'. The storekeeper remembered the boy buying a shilling's worth of marbles and a melon. He even asked to buy some cigarettes. The court sent Mortensen to the training ship *Subraon,* which housed more than 200 children in a reformatory for wayward boys. He later worked on stations in country New South Wales, on ships that travelled the world – 'to the Americas' – and became estranged from his mother. When he came to Melbourne to enlist in June 1915 he didn't want his past to get in the way of his future. Nor did he want his mother, Olive, to know of his whereabouts.

There was also another reason. He was unsure of his father's background, and if he had any German blood. So Waldemar Mortensen joined the AIF as John Sydney Shaw. It was only his mother's persistence in tracking down her 'lost' son that saw him reclaim his birth name.

At least three Fair Dinkums were under the required age when they joined up. The youngest, at fifteen, was George Yendle, an apprentice solderer desperate to be a soldier. Standing at 168 centimetres, with blue eyes and fair hair before the recruiting officers, he kept a straight face, saying he was eighteen when asked. He had with him a letter purporting to be from his mother, Matilda, though it is not known if she had actually scrawled the words. Part of the letter reads: 'Dear Sir, I freely give my consent . . . His elder brothers are at present serving on the sea. May God bless and protect one and all'. In chasing his father's consent a few days later to further satisfy recruiting staff, he had another letter from his mother explaining there were economic as much as patriotic reasons for his joining up at such a tender age:

> Dear Sir, the signature underneath is George's father's. His eyesight is so bad, so please excuse it. He does not in any way support me or my little ones, it is my dear boy who supports me, and may God bless him. He thinks if he enlists he will be serving his King and Country and also providing for me.

Bill Wain turned sixteen a few weeks before the *Anchises* sailed. Born in Perth in August 1899, he had long lived in Melbourne with his parents in Elsternwick, and worked as an apprentice baker. He, too, had to somehow get his parents' permission to enlist. His baking days were at an end; he was a soldier now, and if it all worked out, his life would be a military one, in war and peace.

At the other end of the spectrum was Bill Mudge, who was in his early forties. He was born in country Victoria, but lived in North Melbourne. He shared a tent at Seymour with Layfield, and the boys in that section respectfully called him 'Dad'. Training was hard work for Mudge in the camp, but the married wickerworker was confident he could cut the mustard when it mattered.

Lincoln Street in Richmond was doing its bit for recruiting, particularly the Murcutt family. Five of the seven Murcutt sons saw overseas service; one became a musketry instructor in a training camp in Western Australia. Another was rejected because of his defective teeth, and died a broken man in Nhill, far from the guns. Bruce Murcutt, the youngest, had no intention of waiting until his eighteenth birthday; there was no time to spare. The seventeen-year-old convinced his father, William, and mother, Eva, that everyone else was putting their age up to fight. When he signed up on 14 June 1915, he was armed with a letter of parental consent, even though he looked like he was barely out of school – which he was. The apprentice bootmaker was only a thimble or two over 160 centimetres (five foot three-and-a-half inches) and was not quite 50 kilograms (7 stone 10 pounds). But as soon as he was handed a uniform and read the oath, he became one of the 'fighting Murcutts' of Richmond, no matter what his birth certificate detailed.

His mother said, 'The fighting spirit is in the family all right. I must say that I never tried to dissuade them from going, but I am sure they would have overcome my objections if I had. They were determined to enlist.'

Service to the community was an admirable family trait. Bruce's father had been a policeman in the Gippsland region and in Richmond for more than twenty years before working for J.C. Williamson. His eldest brother, Joseph, served with honour in the Boer War when Bruce was a child, and had been a bodyguard for the Duke and Duchess of York – the King and Queen by the time of World War I – at the opening of Federal Parliament and during the Federation celebrations in 1901.

Bruce knew he had a lot to live up to. Newspaper reports in *Punch* and the *Herald* detailed his family's exploits, promising grandiose things that most seventeen-year-olds could hardly hope to emulate. Their proud parents forecast that the six Murcutts – leaving aside the son who had been rejected – would 'prove a tough proposition, under equal conditions, for the best six Turks that could be marched out from Constantinople to meet them'. Sadly, the Gallipoli campaign had never been played out in equal conditions, and by the time one of these stories rolled off the presses, the Murcutts and the rest of the Anzacs were preparing to evacuate the land they had come to conquer.

The Murcutt connection extended to one of their neighbours from Lincoln Street, nineteen-year-old blacksmith assistant, Henry Stephens, who joined up with Bruce on the same day. Stephens had been rejected once before for defective eyesight, but managed to get his way through the test and into a soldier's uniform.

Wally Day wasn't the only member of the Fair Dinkums to come from Brunswick. Malcolm McQueen, 30, was a native of Romsey, but lived there with his mother in between time spent seafaring on ships around Australia and the Pacific. His latest posting was on the *Chillagol*, from which he was discharged on 2 June 1915. Within a fortnight he was in the AIF.

Hairdresser Lawrence Black – married, 21 and also from Brunswick – enlisted with Day. He had been involved in the 60th Infantry, and there was every reason to think that Black would be a good soldier when put to the test. From the same suburb came Harold Grange, a few months short of his nineteenth birthday, working in a relatively new industry at the Tarrant Motor Company as an apprentice body-frame builder. His manager wrote to the commanding officer at Victoria Barracks assuring them they would keep Grange's position pending his return. Grange's grandfather had come from Bradwell, Essex, during the 1850s, and his policeman father William gave his consent for Harold to enlist in late July 1915. Harold was a resourceful young man with a hardy soul. Having attended Brunswick State School, ill health saw him sent to the Dandenong hills to recuperate. So that he didn't repeat a year at school, he transferred to Bell Street School in Coburg, even though it meant a six-mile (10 kilometres) walk to and from school each day. It was good practice for what lay ahead; quiet and reserved, he already possessed a hard edge that war would sharpen even further.

Two Tasmanians who called Melbourne home did not know each other until they joined the Fair Dinkums. The first was Bertie Charles Sydney Stedman Southwell, a 32-year-old student at Melbourne University. He was born in Launceston, a member of the school cadets, and lived on the family farm outside Devonport. He spent a considerable amount of time studying, reading biographies, newspapers and the classics, including Roman and Greek histories, and had a passion for fly-fishing in some of the best rivers in Tasmania.

Southwell spent time as a Master at Haileybury College, though by 1915 he was studying for a Bachelor of Arts at Melbourne University. His son Alec said, 'He had a high sense of duty . . . He probably thought it was his duty to enlist, and he did.'

Bespectacled, with brown hair, Southwell set his books aside, knowing that events on the other side of the world would one day be history, and he wanted to be a part of it.

So, too, did Spencer Smith, who was born in Goulds Country, Tasmania, the seventh of fifteen children from a mining and industrial family. His family background summed up both sides of Australia's rich history. As one of his relatives, Dianne Pierce, would detail, two great grandfathers on his father's side were convicts: Benjamin Smith from Essex was transported to Van Diemen's Land in 1842 for seven years for stealing a fork, and Joseph Bottom received the same punishment for a burglary in York eleven years earlier, spending part of his sentence at Port Arthur before being pardoned.

On his mother's side, Smith's family were free settlers, making life on the land as farmers. Smith moved to Melbourne a few years before the war when his father took a job helping to construct and service Luna Park in St Kilda. When he enlisted in June 1915, he had a readymade nickname – 'Gunboat'. A well-known American boxer at the time was Edward 'Gunboat' Smith. In the lead-up to the war, and a year into it, Gunboat was considered one of the best heavyweight boxers in the world. So it was no surprise when the Fair Dinkums bestowed the nickname on eighteen-year-old Smith, who was also handy with his dukes.

Ern Makepeace, the twenty-year-old rubber worker, and Henry Dickson came from the backstreets of Carlton, and joined up within weeks of each other. Dickson was a year younger than Makepeace and, like his father before him, a plumber.

Daniel Von Ende was also living in Carlton at the time, though he had been born in Wedderburn. The nineteen-year-old messenger might have had a German-sounding name, but he carried it through the war, only changing it afterwards. Ben Joyner, an eighteen-year-old blacksmith, was born in South Melbourne but living in North Fitzroy when he enlisted. Wal King, one of four brothers who enlisted, was a native of Albert Park, but living in Abbotsford and working as a salesman when he joined the AIF on 14 June 1915. He was a decent lump of a lad, standing at 185 centimetres (six foot one) and with blue eyes and dark brown hair. Like his brothers, he was an athlete who loved nothing better than physical pursuits, playing sport and being active. The four King brothers enlisted directly opposite to their birth order, with second-youngest Wal the second to enlist after seeing his youngest brother, Henry, off to war from Sydney. But Wal was the only family member of the 8th Reinforcements. Their father, William, a proofreader at the *Argus*, was frequently caught between his professional and personal life as he read countless reports of battles and casualties and rolls of honour each day, wondering with trepidation and self-interest if any of his sons would be listed.

Harry Windley and Robert MacKenzie lived close to each other, and the link between them lasted until their dying days. Windley was from South Melbourne. He had attended Dorcas Street State School and made his living as a steward. He was only eighteen when he joined up. MacKenzie was a year older. A dental assistant from Albert Park, he was born and attended school in Goodwood, South Australia.

Alf Mercer, a labourer who lived in King Street, West Melbourne, enlisted at the same time, as did wool classer Bill Henderson, a 31-year-old recently married man from Punt Road, South Yarra, who had served in the Boer War alongside Fred Hoad.

Men also came from the western suburbs of Melbourne, including the Roberts brothers from Seddon. Five years may have separated blacksmiths Tom, 28, and Ernest, 23, but they were as close as brothers could be. They lived with their mother, Elizabeth, and the rest of their family, and were well-known citizens of Melbourne's west. Tom was a swimmer and rower of some note and worked at the Newport workshops, while Ern worked with Sunshine McKay. The pair enlisted in June 1915.

Two days earlier, Bill Anderson, an eighteen-year-old clerk, enlisted, and the three young men from the same street resolved to fight together. They were afforded a fitting farewell from their family and the residents of Seddon. Harold Blakey from Footscray had joined up the same day as the Roberts siblings. Just before he went into camp with his battalion and departed on the *Anchises* this 21-year-old packer married his sweetheart.

Errol Forster Woods' family had power and influence, but the 25-year-old wireless operator from Toorak was content to become a private with the AIF. Given his background, he could have chased a commission with the AIF or elsewhere; as one newspaper said, 'for half a century [Errol's father William]

Forster Woods was conspicuous in the business of Melbourne', a leading member of the Melbourne Stock Exchange, and eventually its chairman. Errol's mother, Clara, was the daughter of James Service, Victoria's twelfth premier, who had arrived in Melbourne from Glasgow in 1853, where he established an importing and wholesale business as well as a successful political career. Service's first short stint as premier coincided with the capture of Ned Kelly in June 1880, and during his second term, from 1883 to 1886, he espoused the belief that Australia needed to be federated.

Service's grandson, Errol, had far more interest in engineering and wireless transmission than he did in politics or business, though the government was interested in his expertise. Before the war, it was thought that his service in the wireless field, then in its infancy, would prove as important to the community as his father's and grandfather's contributions. One report said: 'Errol Woods, at 18, had the first licence [another report suggested it was the second] and transmitting and receiving set in Australia, and before enlistment had put up what stations there were in Australasia, New Guinea and Suva'. But the desire to do what most men of his age were doing – going off to fight – meant that he put aside further ambitions to join the 8th Reinforcements of the 7th Battalion.

Eric Phillips and Frank Whelan were residing in Prahran when they stepped forward. Phillips, 22, had been born and bred there, and was an electric tram driver when he enlisted on 23 June 1915. A native of Ballarat, twenty-year-old Whelan was a labourer. From nearby Burnley came twenty-year-old tinsmith Fred Mann, who had married soon after enlisting.

Three Fair Dinkums came from Hawthorn – eighteen-year-old clerk Clarence Lay, 21-year-old clerk Frank Dixon, and 24-year-old labourer Ralph Bond. Bond was working in Hamilton at the time of his enlistment and had signed up in front of the secretary of the Hamilton Rifle Club.

Percy Brunning wasn't meant to be a crack shot, but he was. If the blasted recruiting officers couldn't see that, then they had even more questionable vision than he did in the bung eye that came from a childhood accident. As such, he had been rejected by the AIF before, but determined it wouldn't happen again. Brunning's family had run the biggest – and best known – nursery in Melbourne out of their St Kilda base, and he worked there, honing his target-shooting skills in his spare time. A friend recalled:

> Rats had become a real pest [at the nursery], so each morning at six, he would go down to the sheds, turn on a tap and wait for the creatures to come out for a drink. It was while they quenched their thirst that, sitting on a box, he'd ping them off and by such practice developed a facility for marksmanship.

When faced with the obstacle of the AIF eye test, which proved more formidable than the rats, Brunning 'had someone to school him in the procedure of the eyesight test card, and having learnt that by heart, was able to circumvent to secure a place in the AIF', where his sharp-shooting and canny ability to hit a target were well respected.

WAR CORRESPONDENT ELLIS ASHMEAD-BARTLETT'S claims that the Anzacs who first scaled the cliffs of Gallipoli were a 'race of athletes' crafted from a sun-drenched, hardened land did not take into account the significant number who were overseas born. Almost 20 per cent of the Anzacs who enlisted during the course of the war came from elsewhere, with the overwhelming majority from Great Britain. That was almost on par with the number of Fair Dinkums born outside of Australia: almost 30 of the 152 men of the 8th Reinforcements of the 7th Battalion, came from England, Scotland, Wales and Ireland.

One came from France, another from Italy, and there was even a New Zealander among them. Nearly 700,000 people had been admitted to Australia between 1908 and 1913 in the lead-up to the war and, in accordance with the fledgling federation's restrictive 'White Australian Policy', 599,000 were from Great Britain. A high proportion of eligible males enlisted to fight for their old country in the distinctive uniform of their new one; others saw it as a chance to somehow wangle a trip home to see the relatives they had left behind. Some of these men proved to be remarkable soldiers – resourceful, courageous and committed.

Auguste Pierre Lafargues had been fascinated by Australia since childhood. From his classroom in the picturesque French port city of Bordeaux, he fixed his attention on that great southern land on the map, looked out the window and dreamed big dreams. He would go there one day, he told his mother. Australia wasn't even officially a nation when Lafargues was born in 1890, and yet from the time he was a small boy, he endeavoured to find out as much as he could about that country on the other side of the world. He could never explain the attraction or power of his obsession, but it was as strong as anything he had experienced in his life. So much so that family folklore has it that little Auguste – he was diminutive, even later in adulthood – was not yet ten when he found a ship that was leaving his hometown for Australia, and stowed away in one of the lifeboats. He waited until the ship was far enough offshore before revealing himself. His daughter recalled tales of how the ship's captain took the young boy under his wing, and hosted him in his own home whenever they were not at sea. Australia had a population of almost four million at the time; France, more than 38 million. But Lafargues saw his future in that far-off land, even though it was so removed from everything he knew. It was, literally, a new world. Other documents suggest he had come to Australia in his teenage years.

They called him 'Gus' in Australia, with Auguste becoming only a name used in official documents. He lived for a time at Irrewillipe, not far from Colac, in Victoria's western districts. He tried to enlist early in the war, but was rejected because of his height (he was 160 centimetres, or five foot three). By June 1915, with the restrictions relaxed, he had another crack. He had already shown an acceptance of his new land; in 1912, at 22, he became a naturalised British subject of Australia.

The opportunity to prove his loyalty to his new country came when he was working as a timber hewer – backbreaking work that prepared him well for what lay ahead – and overheard fellow workmates discussing how they were going to enlist at the end of their shifts. While he hadn't been born in Australia, he felt Australian. He had come to know the place and loved it, and felt it was worth defending. Better still, if the war panned out the way he hoped, he might even get an all-expenses paid return to his homeland to see his mother and his two surviving brothers after one of the toughest years in France's history. He enlisted in Telangatuk East, near where his hewing gang had been felling trees. The local newspaper was there to witness it:

> The brave deeds of our boys at the Dardanelles [has] filled the patriotism of five young fellows in this district, and they have joined the colours. Four of them are strangers and have been engaged in sleeper cutting . . . [including] August [sic] Lafargues . . . a Frenchman who has already had two brothers killed in the war.

Gus wanted to avenge their deaths, but more importantly, he wanted to prove himself to the country that had adopted him without any expectation.

Giovanni Tognola from Italy and Wilfred Williams from Sussex, England, were a part of the group of bush dinkums who enlisted together in Mildura. Their pathways to Australia had been very different, but their shared desire to enlist brought them together in that remote country Victorian town, and later still, aboard the *Anchises* with the rest of the 8th Reinforcements of the 7th Battalion. Initially Italy was expected to join Germany, Austria–Hungary and Turkey, given their past relationships. However, the Italians remained unaligned for the early part of the war before moving towards a pact with Great Britain, which was ratified the day after the Gallipoli landings. Tognola had been naturalised by the time he decided to enlist in the AIF. The recruiting officers perused his papers with more than a passing interest the day he signed up, but had no hesitation ratifying his entry into the army. He was still unmistakably Italian, as his features, accent and broken English attested, but from the moment he put on the uniform, he was no long Giovanni. He was Jack Tognola of the Fair Dinkums.

Walter Judd was the very model of a Salvation Army officer. He liked to help people, particularly those in need. He was 27 in 1915, and was married to Louisa with two children. Born and raised in Masterton, about 200 kilometres from Wellington on New Zealand's north island, Judd had come from a family of nine, though the reasons for his move to Australia are clouded by almost a century of time. So, too, are his reasons for enlistment. He joined up on 20 May 1915, and listed his home address as Darlinghurst, Sydney, though the transient nature of his work meant that he travelled extensively. A photo of Judd and his wife exists from around the time he joined. In his Salvation Army uniform and cap, he almost looks at peace with the world as he knows it.

Circumstance brought Milton Clews out to Australia from the family's home in Littleover, Derbyshire. His father had passed away, and his mother later married a Methodist preacher. With a furniture-removal business failing, his stepfather initiated the move before the war. Milton arrived in Australia in 1913 and worked as a packer. He came to board with the Curnick family at 64 Hoddle Street, Abbotsford, where he crossed paths with another English boarder, Fred Bayles. Bayles, 30, had been among the early intake of Australian soldiers in the 7th Battalion. Clews, 23, enlisted on 10 June 1915, saying proudly in a letter to his sister, Emily, that: 'You will see that we are going to reinforce Fred Bayles' Battalion, the 7th, which got cut up pretty badly at Gallipoli'. He had no idea then that Bayles was already dead, killed in action in the ill-fated attack on Krithia at Cape Helles on 8 May 1915.

A later letter from Clews from the Seymour training camp explained: 'I was very sorry to hear that poor Fred [Bayles] has been killed. I can hardly realise it yet. I'll have to avenge his death now, something to spur me on'. Clews was presented with a pocket diary by his good pal William Curnick on 4 August 1915, about three weeks before his own departure. In the front of the diary, Curnick had scrawled simply, 'Good Luck'. That pocket book diary remained Clews' constant companion for the duration of the war as he noted the good, the bad and the exceedingly ugly happenings around him.

George Barber knew he might need some of that luck, even though he had come to rely on his tentmates at Seymour as if they were part of his own kin. He was twenty, employed as a groom and fancy leathergoods worker, having come to Australia a few years earlier from Vauxhall on the banks of the River Thames in London. He had become exceptionally close with his mates in the Fair Dinkums, particularly with Wal King, Errol Forster Woods and Bertie Harris, and felt they would always have his back. But you can't be too careful when you are going to war.

Edward Mason Spooner had falsified his age to enlist. He was believed to be 53, but claimed to be 44. A closer inspection might have revealed the true extent of Spooner's background. His hair was listed as a mix of light brown and grey and in the photo taken at the time, he wore the downcast frown of a man who knew the path ahead would be difficult. He was born in South-ampton in 1862 and trained as a carpenter, coming to Australia before the birth of his son, James, in 1890. What possessed him to join remains a mystery; he was at an age when most men were ambling towards retirement and prepared to follow the war through the pages of the *Argus*. James, who had previously been in the Royal Australian Navy for two years, enlisted five weeks after him, putting Edward as his next of kin, even though the Brunswick address he gave for his father might as well have read Egypt or Gallipoli. James sailed on 23 November, two days before Edward landed on Gallipoli. It wasn't until the following year that father and son fought side by side.

You could never mistake David Warwick's background. His thick Scottish accent was evidence enough – and he did like to talk – but when he had his shirt off, the tattoo of a thistle with hands clasped around it, and the words 'Scotland Forever' on his right forearm, marked just where his allegiances would always lie. He was from Annan, in the south of Scotland, and had come to Australia in 1912 in the hope of a better life.

Donald McCallum was another Fair Dinkum who came from Scotland, having left Glasgow with his parents and family as a child to work on the farmland at Allansford in country Victoria. A third Scotsman, George Craven, had also been raised in Glasgow before moving to Australia.

Timothy Brennan loved the sea. Born and raised in Cardiff, Wales, he had been a stoker on ships for much of his life. He had been a member of the British Naval Reserve in Bristol, and later part of the Naval Reserve in Victoria after his arrival in Australia. He was 38 and single when he enlisted in Melbourne on 26 May 1915. It didn't worry him that he had another long sea voyage ahead of him – he was looking forward to it.

Bob Billington was originally from Wales too, from the northern town of Holyhead, which served as a major sea port across to Dublin. He had sailed to a new life in Australia five years earlier, and was working as a labourer when he enlisted in Maribyrnong on 21 June 1915.

Lawrence Flynn, too, was no stranger to travel. Flynn had sought warmer climes in the years before the war because of a consumptive cough and a sickness that would not yield, no matter the remedies or the rest he had. A native of Ireland, he had chased the sun in Florida and in various parts of Mexico to try to shake whatever it was that ailed him. Somehow he managed to keep his health issue from the recruiting officers when he enlisted at the Heywood recruiting office on 22 June 1915. Other than noting that he had 'two scars over his left eyebrow', Flynn was passed fit when medically assessed for a second time at Portland the next day.

Jim Ostler, a 28-year-old factory hand, had no recollection of his brief childhood in Leeds, as he had been only two when his family migrated to Australia. Marriage didn't stop him fighting for the life that his adoptive country had afforded him. Carpenter Robert Royle, a native of Liverpool, had also arrived in Australia early in his life with his family. Married, he had specialised in boat-building when he enlisted.

Albert 'Barney' Allen had come from London in 1912 to work in a grocery in Sea Lake in Victoria's wheat-belt region when he enlisted on 6 May 1915. He was swept up in the excitement of the town, with the local newspaper extolling the virtues of its young men. The *Sea Lake Times* mused:

> War has brought to light virile qualities which peace, and the luxury to which it gives birth, had obscured. Young Australia has displayed a keen desire to fight the battles of the Empire, and better, has shown heroic courage in action ... One by one, and oftentimes in groups, the flower of our young manhood is enlisting for active service in defence of the Empire. The sinking of the unarmed neutral liner, *Lusitania*,

with nearly three thousand noncombatants on board is a clear indication of what a justice-loving people could expect under the rule of the 'Mad Men of Europe'.

Allen, a Cockney lad of 21 years, was suitably inspired and wondered if he might get the chance to see his father again in Battersea on his war travels. Thomas Littlemore was also 21 and working as a grocer in Ascot Vale, having made the trip to Australia from Norley, a small town in northern England, in Cheshire. John Lee, a groom from Chiswick in the heart of London, was another of the 'new' dinkums to have settled in Australia before the war.

Alf Honey was an apprentice baker who found his calling in Maffra, far removed from his labouring life in Cornwell. But the increasing toll the war was taking on the country he had adopted, not to mention on his native home, convinced him to enlist. After all, both of his parents were dead and he had no living guardian in Australia. He was twenty when he enlisted on 1 May 1915, and originally slated for the 7th Reinforcements of the 7th Battalion. But a bout of venereal disease delayed his departure, and he was sent instead to the newly opened Langwarrin camp, which initially housed German internees and until August 1915 was looked on as a 'prison' hospital, where:

The men were herded behind barbed-wire enclosures, and two hundred militia men were employed as guards. The accommodation was miserably unsuitable; the round tents then universally used were old and leaking and unfloored, and in wet weather, damp and muddy. For bedding, the men only had blankets and rubber sheets and they were dressed in oddments of uniform and plain clothes. The small medical staff found it impossible to treat the men adequately . . . Recovery under such conditions was difficult and slow – in some cases impossible.

Honey did recover, though, and his return to health coincided with the Fair Dinkums' preparations. He left the camp that few Australians ever talked about, a place that had seen 7242 patients pass through its doors from early 1915 to mid-1920. The official history records how 'more than 6,000 patients discharged from Langwarrin went overseas on active service; they won 400 decorations, including a V.C. [Victoria Cross]', Honey among one of the decorated.

Michael Thomas's arms gave more than a hint of the things that meant so much to him. Like Brennan and Rodriguez, he had taken to sea at an early age, seeing it as his escape – however temporary – from the harsh streets of Liverpool, which was nestled on one side of the Mersey River, into the Irish Sea and then out to the oceans of world. His hometown was the registered port of the ill-fated *Lusitania,* as well as the ship that was thought unsinkable, the *Titanic,* which sailed to its doom from Southampton. The Liverpudlian had a dancing girl on his left arm and a ship and hands reaching out across the sea on his left forearm. On his right forearm was a lion with clasped hands and the words 'True Love'. Five weeks after the *Lusitania* went to her icy grave in the North Atlantic Sea, taking almost 1200 souls with her, 26-year-old Thomas walked into a Melbourne recruiting office halfway around the world and enlisted.

He wasn't the only Thomas among the Fair Dinkums, though the pair were not related. In 1915, Albert Thomas was a 31-year-old labourer, originally from Shropshire in the west Midlands, having made the journey across the sea some years earlier. It was a boat of a different kind that would land him and some new pals in hot water before year's end. But all that, and more, lay ahead for Albert Thomas and the Fair Dinkums.

3

Aboard the *Anchises*

'"A blasted old tub", such a cruel name to call
our noble ship.'

IN MANY WAYS, BERTIE Southwell was different from the average Fair Dinkum. It wasn't simply because he wore glasses, or that he was still a student, even though he was in his early thirties. It was all that, and more. So much of the difference came from the fact that he was well read and versed in an educational sense, which was unusual in 1915.

Still, he managed to fit in as best as he could, and proved to be a diligent and popular soldier. The one thing he loved was order and direction. The army gave him both, and he thrived on the experiences. Southwell would have been one of the few men aboard the *Anchises* to understand how fitting it was to be headed to one of the most ancient theatres of war on a ship bearing the name of a Trojan War protagonist. Everyone aboard knew the name of the revamped steamer was *Anchises,* but for the purposes of the war, it was known as HMAT (His Majesty's Australian Transport) A68.

Southwell was a reader of the classics and Greek mythology. He knew the ancient city of Troy had fallen at the hands of the resourceful and relentless Greeks, and may have even been familiar with Virgil's epic poem, the *Aeneid,* which detailed how Aeneas had fled the besieged and burning ruins of Troy, carrying his elderly father Anchises and his son Ascanius. In this twentieth-century conflict, three 'sister ships' of the 74 converted transports that ferried Anzacs to the various battle fronts through-out World War I bore the names *Anchises, Aeneas* and *Ascanius* after the three generations who had survived the siege of Troy.

In 1910, almost a decade after federation, it was announced a 'new line of steamships' would be built to meet the increasing demand on the route between Australia and Great Britain. Messrs Alfred Holt and Co from Liverpool stated the Australian passenger service would be served by 'three twin-screw streamers . . . specifically built for the service, each of them over 10,000 tons, registered and designed to carry 250 to 300 passengers'. The first was to be the *Aeneas,* followed by *Anchises* and *Ascanius.* The ships were built in Belfast, and were said to have incorporated everything in comfort and safety to ensure they were 'practically unsinkable'. (This was two years before another Belfast-built ship, whom the builders and operators professed to be unsinkable, sailed on her maiden voyage. Her name was *Titanic.*) The three ships were boasted as having:

> the Marconi system of telegraphy . . . as a further means of providing for the safety of passengers. The fare has been fixed at the moderate sum of from 40 to 45 pounds, from Great Britain to Australia, or vice versa. The time occupied by the old steamers was 42 days, but the new service will complete the voyage in 39 days, and will travel via Cape Town.

At the launch of the *Aeneas,* one-time Australian Prime Minister and then High Commissioner to London, Sir George Reid, said the new steamers brought the two hemispheres closer together and hoped that peace in the new nations could provide an example for the troubles of the old world. He told those in attendance:

> It was the descendants of Irishmen, Scotchmen, and English-men who were building up the nation which I represent – a nation entirely free from the subjects of controversy and the painful historical recollection that existed [in Great Britain and Europe]. [My] best wish was that the same harmony, the same brotherly feelings, the same characteristics might at no distant date characterise the population of these sister islands.

Holt's Blue Funnel line saw the *Anchises* undertake its maiden voyage in early 1911, which met with positive reports from those aboard, who enjoyed its modern conveniences, including electricity and heated rooms, and those watching the ship steam through the waters.

By 1915, the *Anchises* was a regular and much loved fixture in Australian ports. But the dark shadows of war cast a gloom across the oceans of the world, with the fear of submarines (U-boats) paralysing much of the shipping trade. On 23 April, the steamer sailed into port at Liverpool. She was then requisitioned for the Commonwealth, and later slated to be a part of the tenth convoy of ships to leave Australia for Egypt in August 1915. From 9 to 14 August the *Anchises* was refitted as a troopship at the Cockatoo Island dry dock in Sydney harbour. At that stage the men who would sail on the *Anchises* were in their final throes of training at Seymour and Broadmeadows, their date with the ship less than a fortnight away. They had no idea which ship they were sailing off in or their precise destination, though most of the rumours factored in a likely stopover for training in Egypt – as the Orig-inals had done – before moving on to Gallipoli, Constantinople, France and ultimately Germany.

The Fair Dinkums trained for most of the day and bonded around campfires at night in the wettest winter for years. When Governor-General Sir Ronald Munro-Ferguson inspected the Seymour camp in mid-July, he noted 'the good order and admiration of the camp, and the discipline, and the soldierly appearance of the men'. The metropolitan newspapers campaigned to provide better housing facilities for the men than in leaking tents, prompting an equally strong defence from the local newspapers saying that everything was being done to keep the new soldiers comfortable. The *Seymour Express* claimed:

> *The Age* has been doing its best to belittle the ground and make it appear that the authorities made an egregious mistake in removing the camp to our town. The only drawback and inconvenience from which the men have suffered has been the incessant rain which had made the place damp and uncomfortable. This has been the most severe winter Seymour has experienced for years.

New dinkum Milton Clews wrote from the Seymour camp on 20 June:

> I think in six weeks' time, we shall be on the water. I'm just about broke into camp life now, and like it fairly well. There's a decent bunch of fellows in our tent, and we are well in with the cooks as we get plenty to eat. Bread, jam and stew. The camp is situated amongst the mountains, and there is plenty of climbing. We are up at 6.30 for roll call in the dark, but knock off at 4.30, so we have plenty of time to ourselves. There's concerts and boxing every night at the stadium.

The men were inoculated against various diseases that might come their way on their travels, including enteric fever, but there was a meningitis outbreak in a number of the army camps that claimed some. By 5 August, amid flying rumours, Clews was predicting a move to Broadmeadows.

The boredom of camp life frustrated some, including Lance Corporal Harry Attwood, who wrote to his sister in mid-August 1915, saying:

I am at Broadmeadows and when we are quite settled I think it will be better than at Seymour. The blessed shifting about is getting monotonous. It's the third [move] I have had and in consequence haven't had a letter or package from Bendigo or anywhere else for nearly a fortnight . . . We expect to sail from Australia on the '26th' of this month . . . We are still in isolation on a/c [account] of the outbreak of meningitis. I have not seen a case yet, or do I know of any chap – still some have without doubt been sent out of Camp. We were dosed up with Eucalyptus last night . . . I have had to work pretty solidly and am feeling tired today. Drilling is not so hard, but digging, erecting and carrying tents is pretty solid – when followed by a 6-mile march . . . Remember me to all folks who would be interested.

Attwood finished the letter with his signature and '8 Reinforcements, 7th Battalion'.

There was a flurry of activity in the camp on 24 August 1915. It was the day that 'Walter Wilson' became Wally Day, Fred Hoad became a 2nd lieutenant, and Harold Grange and Bertie Harris were among the last of the 8th Reinforcements of the 7th Battalion to finally arrive at camp.

The Fair Dinkums' last day in Australia – Thursday, 26 August 1915 – started early, as always. There was much to do in readiness for departure. For Robert Bruce, that meant having to retake his oath after his paperwork was lost. Roy Anderson made the first entry in his diary, noting the names of the men he had left Cobram station with a few months earlier – Ray Eaton,

Ray Rohner, as well as the Knight brothers, Hugh and Bertie. He also included two other names of men he had come to know and like – Gus Lafargues and John Lee. He documented that the men left Broadmeadows at 10 am, made the journey to Port Melbourne, then boarded the *Anchises* sometime between 2 pm and 2.30 pm.

A large crowd had gathered on the pier to farewell the hundreds on board – the 8th Reinforcements of the 6th, 7th, 8th, 11th, 12th and 16th Battalions and the 3rd Reinforcements of the 21st, 22nd, 23rd, 24th and 28th Battalions. Families knew this could be the last chance to farewell their sons, grandsons, fathers, brothers, cousins, uncles and nephews. Girlfriends and wives stood among the throng, desperate for a last kiss or a wave that often did not come. With the large crush of soldiers crowded on the decks – and everywhere else – of the ship built to house 300 people but carrying almost thrice that figure, it was near impossible to recognise familiar faces, though Private Ray Rohner noted in pencil in his diary he had managed to see 'a great friend on the pier . . . Goodbye to Bill R'. Most of the family members or friends who had come to say goodbye went home disappointed. Clews said in a letter to his sister, 'Was very sorry to hear you wasn't [sic] able to see me at Port Melbourne, but you knew I was somewhere there. I happened to be right up in the Crow's Nest when she left, as you would have hardly recognised me. There was certainly a big crowd there.'

There were cheers and congratulations, and more than a few tears on land and on board as the *Anchises* eased her way from the pier at around 4 pm. The mass of streamers thrown by well-wishers fell away as the ship moved further out into the bay. Aboard, there was a sense of excitement and unease: excitement that the journey was finally underway after the monotony of training, drilling and turning civilians into soldiers, unease from the uncertainty of the challenges that lay ahead. There was the journey, and the fear that a German cruiser or U-boat may be lurking somewhere in the Indian Ocean. That's why there was no press coverage of the departure, with a scan of the Melbourne newspapers from the time making no reference to the *Anchises*. There was also the none-too-small matter that the 152 men of the Fair Dinkums – plus the hundreds of other reinforcements aboard – were sailing into a new kind of war that none either understood or could even imagine.

JUST OVER A YEAR earlier, it was at the Port Phillip Heads that a shot was fired from Fort Nepean's coastal batteries at the fleeing German cargo steamer *Pfalz*, fewer than four hours after war was first declared in London. It was acknowledged as 'the first shot fired in anger in the British Empire at the start of World War One', with millions more to follow over the next four years.

It was a beautiful, clear August night by the time the Fair Dinkums sailed through the Heads at about 8 pm. Clews noted in his diary that it was 'a fine night', but his next four days of diary entries mentioned rough seas. Rohner said after initially passing through the Heads that the sea was 'very calm'. Anderson was sick from the outset, and the constant rocking and rolling of the ship was too much for him. His next entry was short and to the point: 'Food good, sick soon after sea, in bed'. He went to bed in his overcoat, boots and all of his clothes to keep warm. While some of the men revelled in their first night on board, and made new acquaintances, others endured their first night of seasickness.

The weather closed in on the second day, and as the Fair Dinkums awoke to their first full day on board, Rohner noted: 'Very dull. Hailstorm about 8am, a little rain. Light swell in the ocean. Afternoon heavy swell to rough. Waves over deck, very rough all night. Very windy'.

The men of seafaring experience could only laugh at the parade of greenhorns lined up over the side of the ship, bringing up the contents of whatever they had managed to eat. The first enemy they confronted was not 'Johnny Turk' but seasickness. By day three, Anderson had recovered from seasickness, as the ship sailed through the Great Australian Bight on its way towards Fremantle, where it was scheduled to pick up a contingent of West Australian soldiers. He was back smoking again by day four and part of some high-sea hijinks after being served tripe '[it] was rotten. We held a burial service and buried it at sea'. The excitement of seeing a whale was noted, to accompanying roars of approval, as some men took wagers on when the first whale or shark would appear.

Corporal Bill Scurry had a busy start to his onboard life. But he took the time on 29 August to send the first epistle to his mother while the ship was not far off Albany. He recalled how he had spent the first night alone on guard as the sergeant who was meant to be in charge was so seasick that he could not function. For a time, Scurry thought the sergeant was:

too easily [sick] for me to think very much of him, so I was left alone in my glory. Then all the men got sick. I called up one relief, there were six men, not there. One Pte [Robert] Fraser, I went to look for him, and found him full length on the floor with his head in a fire bucket, muttering something about 'a blasted old tub', such a cruel name to call our noble ship. Well, it ended up no sleep all night, and nothing to eat for 24 hours . . .

Oh, my Mother, my heart bleeds for the poor sufferers even now . . . The anguished faces, the haggard looks, and green, purple and yellow skins all form themselves into a picture of misery never to be forgotten. And the noises, they sounded like unto the anguished sighs of a million jilted lovers in conjunction with a battalion of rusty lorry brakes.

Wal King had spent the first night aboard in the guardroom where 'everyone was sick'. In a letter to his father, he detailed:

I can tell you I don't know how it was that I was not sick as you know what a poor sailor I always was . . . I finished guard at 11 o'clock on Saturday, and it was only a great bit of luck that we got off so early. Saturday afternoon, we had physical exercise on the upper deck and it caused a great deal of amusement so we were all feeling a bit grogie [groggy] on it. We had a Church service on Sunday morning, Major Hart acted as chaplain, and acted it very well. We are going to have our first concert tonight and we hope to have a good time.

Like the rest of the men on board, King had been told to give little or no indication of where the ship was headed and what the weather conditions were like. As such, he added: 'We are not allowed to say anything about . . . where we are or where we are going, [so] you must not expect much news at present, but I will write you a long letter shortly and as often as possible. I remain your affectionate son, Wal'.

Alf Layfield stopped smiling for the first few days, and those who had known him since Seymour knew something was wrong. He was as crook as he had ever been. Layfield wrote to his mum that:

I was very bad. It was funny to see the chaps running to the side of the boat. I will not laugh at anybody getting sea sick anymore. The boat rolls a bit, but I am getting used to it. We get fed pretty well on the boat, this morning we had liver and bacon for breakfast, we get three-course meals and plenty of it.

He had been frustrated by the lack of physical exercise in those early days, and longed for more action, but until anyone got their sea legs, that wasn't going to happen. Layfield explained their sleeping arrangements: 'We sleep in hammocks over our tables, but I sleep on the floor. I would sooner sleep there. We have tables to have our meals on, about 18 to each table'.

There was excitement in the pre-dawn of 2 September 1915 when the *Anchises* arrived safely at Fremantle harbour. Many of the Fair Dinkums, as well as many of the hundreds of other men on board, were still sleeping in hammocks slung across tables, though the commotion woke many of them. And when daylight broke, the anticipation of reaching land again was the talk from one end of the ship to the other. But no one other than the officers were permitted to land, though it didn't stop some wags diving into the waters before being admonished. Rohner recorded with clear disappointment: 'Not allowed to get off the boat'.

Anderson wasn't impressed by the Fremantle waterway, noting, 'Harbour very poor, only three ships and a lot of Coal tugs. Very sandy. Swan River, nice big stream. Parade on boat. Boys selling fruit and paper. Township built on hills, very scattered. Can feel the weather getting hotter every day. Strange but true, never saw a motor car.'

If the farewell from Port Melbourne had been heartfelt, with thousands coming to see the ship off, then the experience at Fremantle was no less overwhelming. When the *Anchises* sailed out of port at about 6 pm, followed for a time by countless motor crafts, Clews rated it 'a bigger crowd' than what had seen the ship off in Melbourne: 'We got a great send-off from here . . . just on leaving a fireman fell overboard and one of the soldiers dived in and rescued him'. Several hundred West Australian reinforcements had come aboard, making an already tight squeeze on the ship even more so.

It was the same on most of the transport ships. R. Hugh Knyvett, a soldier on a different but equally crammed journey, explained later:

It is marvellous what quantities of men a troopship can swallow. There were a thousand men on our ship, and we wondered how we could possibly move about, for we marched 'tween decks, and seated on benches ranged alongside deal tables; and when all were aboard there was not room for a man more.

There was sadness coupled with nervous tension as the lights of Fremantle and other towns on the Western Australian coast began to fade from sight at about 6.30 pm. That was the last sight of Australia many men would see for years; some never saw it again, and yet others returned changed forever by the experiences of war. Now, the Indian Ocean was all that stood between the *Anchises* and the east coast of Africa, before the ship headed for the Red Sea. No one aboard the ship knew what lay ahead.

The further the ship sailed, the hotter the weather. There were lifebelt drills to remain prepared for anything that might arise on the high seas. Still, they saw nothing, and by the end of the first week in September the tropical rains started. One day, it rained for twelve hours.

On 6 September one of the men aboard – not one of the Fair Dinkums – was shot through the leg as the soldiers practised drilling. The men were expected to keep their guns clean and in good order.

Ralph Bond, one of the 8th Reinforcements of the 7th Battalion, spent the first few days after Fremantle in the ship's infirmary with the onset of gonorrhoea. On 14 September, Anderson duly noted that the ship had 'Crossed the Equator, Neptune not aboard'.

No one on the *Anchises* knew it, but around the same time something happened that delayed the Fair Dinkums' quest to reach Gallipoli quickly. The original 7th Battalion, which had fought with such distinction on the peninsula from the landings through to Krithia and Lone Pine, was exhausted – in body and numbers. They desperately required a rest, and when that opportunity came in mid-September, the men left Gallipoli for respite on Lemnos Island. They did not return for two months, by which time the Fair Dinkums finally joined up with them.

Pompey Elliott, who had helped turn the 7th Battalion into a disciplined force of men capable of rising to almost any challenge, was himself broken down. He had left Gallipoli a few weeks before the 7th, battling pleurisy, and was sent to convalesce for two months in England. Elliott could easily have won laurels himself, but consoled himself with the fact that the men he had trained had risen to the occasion in the hottest of battles. Elliott wrote to his wife, Kate, at the time, saying:

> I have had such a lot of letters from the boys, many of them crippled for life and not one complaining, but all glorifying in having been one of the 7th. This to me is far above any personal award, for I got to feel for the Regiment and the men in it as I feel for you and my wee bairnies.

That was the pressure and expectation the Fair Dinkums had to live up to when they finally got the chance to go into battle.

On 18–19 September the men spotted land for the first time since they left Fremantle earlier that month. It was Cape Guardafui, the eastern-most tip of Africa, which led into the Gulf of Aden. Rohner noted in his diary: 'Sighted Africa . . . First foreign country seen. Had sports on board'. Anderson gave a better description of the landscape, though noted how short of supplies the *Anchises* was: 'Rough mountainous coast . . . saw whale, many porpus [sic] and several ships. Food getting scarce, drinking water bad. Passed through the Gates of Hell around midday'.

Scurry told his mother about the plentiful and unusual sights to be seen, writing:

> We are now in the Red Sea and it is hot . . . the last few days have been the most eventful of the journey. We saw nothing until

we practically passed Aden, but now we see lots of shipping. One ship we passed yesterday being particularly interesting, being a large cargo boat with no funnels. It runs by motor or oil . . . I thought I was drunk when I saw it first. I have been presented with a new job. I am now Quarter Master Sergeant Acting . . . I still continue on a humble 6/- [but] money doesn't matter as long as we are getting near the star . . . We are within a few days of disembarking.

On the same day that the Bellesini brothers, Andrew and Joseph, first caught sight of the African coast, their sibling, Harry, died of horrific injuries to his head, wrist and back on a hospital ship off the coast of Gallipoli. They were meant to be joining him on the peninsula. Instead Harry, who had not long turned 22, was being lowered into the waters of the Aegean Sea. He had only been in the firing line for a week, and written to his mother, Esther, the day before, telling her he was all right. His brothers did not know of the family's sorrowful loss for some time to come.

As the Bellesini brothers and the rest of the Fair Dinkums made their way up the Red Sea towards the Suez Canal, it was inescapable that they were edging closer and closer to their date with the enemy.

4

This strange land of the Pharaohs

'We just get up, work and go to bed again. Between that,
we live in sand and eat stew.'

EXTENDED SEA VOYAGES HAVE unified strangers since
the beginning of time. When the reason for such journeys
concerned sailing off to war, that only magnified the bond
between men. Such was the lot of the Fair Dinkums spread
out across 32 days and thousands of nautical miles during
late August and most of September 1915. The combination
of onboard training and drilling, and the incessant banter
and camaraderie within the strict military discipline, mixed
in with a touch of laissez-faire larrikinism, brought the men
closer than they could ever have imagined. While there were
hundreds of other reinforcements aboard the *Anchises*, something about their cramped living confines and the constant
company of old mates and new pals helped to define and
distinguish the men who were serving under Major Hart's
command. Everything else that came in the months and years

ahead only built on those ties. Those 32 days, and perhaps for a few days afterwards, were the only time that the Fair Dinkums were truly together, all 152 of them.

From the moment the *Anchises* docked in Port Suez in late September, and the men were finally back onto *terra firma*, fate played a hand against keeping them together. Sickness, an Australian military reorganisation, shrapnel, shells and sorrows of unimaginable proportions conspired to divide these men against their better wishes. But regardless of how long they were together as the Fair Dinkums, the overwhelming majority carried that sense of belonging and brotherhood until their dying days. Hugh McKenzie, who won a Military Cross three years on, was still extolling the virtues of that sea voyage six decades later. After the death of a close mate – a Fair Dinkum – he wrote with unbridled pride about 'that gallant *Anchises* mob of reo's [reinforcements]'.

Roy Anderson had one of those matter-of-fact personalities and it translated to his diary. The detail and order were there. Always. On the day that the ship arrived at Port Suez, he penned: 'Drew into wharf. Niggers on shore. [We] cleaned up [the ship]. Tommies in charge of ship'. He made a note that after barely seeing a ship the whole way between Australia and the Red Sea, there were at least 50 anchored in the Suez harbour. Ray Rohner described the bustling activity as 'very pretty . . . Lots of boats . . . Natives came out to meet us in their boats'.

The Fair Dinkums may have reached their destination for the moment, but the *Anchises* still had further to go. The ship was preparing to sail through the Suez Canal to the waters off Gallipoli. The Fair Dinkums would be there in time, but there was more training to undertake and preparations for battle in the searing sands of Egypt. In contrast, the *Anchises* was heading towards the front without delay. Unknown to some of the soldiers on board, the steamer had been carrying arms to aid the increasingly crumbling Gallipoli campaign. Milton Clews knew about it, writing back to his sister in Melbourne that, 'The *Anchises* had a lot of ammunition on board and went strait [sic] to the Dardanelles'.

Wearily, but with a hint of expectation and excitement, the men stepped off the *Anchises* at 11.15 am on Sunday, 26 September 1915. Eager to stretch their legs after such a long journey and curious to explore, they were afforded neither opportunity. By 12.30 pm, they had embarked on a train journey, crammed into carriages with wooden planks for flooring, little room for movement and less cause for comfort. But as tired and uncomfortable as the soldiers were, it was impossible not to be captivated by the sights on offer. The journey stretched on for hours, with the men none the wiser as to where they were headed or why. As the train rattled uneasily along the tracks, they were able to see the many contrasts that was Egypt – little townships of seemingly immense poverty and limited sanitary safeguards alongside much bigger, more impressive cities that would hardly have been out of place back home. Scorching sands stretched as far as the eye could see, broken up by the occasional oasis of greenery and cultivated crops, which seemed incongruous to what had come before. On and on it went, the uncomfortable nature of the third-class ride. Roy Anderson called it 'very rough' and Wal King compared the carriage to 'a dog box'.

Alf Layfield, who had rarely been out of the metropolitan radius of Melbourne in his eighteen years:

> enjoyed the train ride very much . . . it was very interesting. You will see nothing else but sand for miles, then you will come to a town, then everything looked nice and green. The people grow a great deal of maize . . . [homes are] made of mud. The people are very dirty. The fowls, the donkeys and the people all sleep together.

Clews was similarly intrigued by the:

> wonderful sights on the way . . . some of the towns we passed
> through would make you smile, being little better than a
> collection of pigstys [sic], but in larger towns there are some
> very pretty buildings with towers. All the way on either side
> of the railway maize and cotton grow in abundance, also date
> palms and pomegranates.

Ray Rohner was more intent on recording the industry of the
locals, noting, 'Very rough journey, saw many pretty sights.
Many natives begging along [the] line. Some selling fruit,
lemonade, dates, great camels, donkeys, and some lovely horses.'
Bill Scurry called it a 'dream desert ride':

> Just outside the town we struck some Indian regiments whose
> guards all turned to salute the train . . . and the corporals
> nodded their heads and smiled at our wild cheers as we sailed
> past. Then we saw a section of the Camel Corps. The camels
> were resting in the sand, somebody said they were grazing,
> but I have my doubts. Then, suddenly, we ran through
> beautiful green fields with maize by the acre, none under
> five feet high, and some a great deal over. Everywhere, too,
> were date palms, towering up and here and there a field of
> cotton sometimes with piles of fluffy white balls stacked up
> on the edge. The people, too, are strange. It seems wonder-
> ful to me that they should have lived so for thousands of
> years all in their dirty little mud houses, with the same style
> of diets, and the same unclean habits as they had when the
> Bible was written.

As exhausted as they were by the travel and the crowded
carriages, the men never forgot their first foray into a world so
starkly different and challenging from their own back home.

Scurry was just a month short of his twentieth birthday when the ship docked, and the eye-opener of sailing into Suez stayed with him forever. And if it was different for him and the Fair Dinkums, he couldn't help thinking what his father back home in Melbourne would have made of it, a thought that was still with him when he wrote to his mother soon after disembarking. Scurry mused, part-seriously and partly in jest: 'I've tried to give you and Dad a fair idea of the place, but no way let Dad ever come here . . . he'd walk about with his eyes all over the place, and get trodden on by a camel, for sure'.

Bill Mills had a similar theme in correspondence with his father, saying: 'Cairo is a place to open one's eyes'. One of the oldest nations in the world was playing host to men from one of the youngest, and it was nothing like any of them had imagined, despite the many warnings they had received before stepping off the ship. Some failed to listen, and paid the price. Many of them listened, including Scurry, whose engagement back home was more than enough to keep him well away from the many temptations on offer. The men looked on the varied aspects of Egyptian life – as well as the landmarks dating back millennia that they had first read about at school – with a collective sense of awe, wonder, incredulity, bemusement, unease and, for some, disgust.

The unrelenting sun, still a considerable force in Cairo in September, had gone down by the time the train clicked into its destination, the soldiers relieved to be at the end of such a long journey. It was now almost 8 pm, and the seven-hour trip had delivered them to Zeitoun, on the outskirts of Cairo, and not far from another camp near Heliopolis. Still, they had to march a mile and a half to reach camp. Scurry, as the quarter-master acting sergeant, had to issue blankets and arrange the accommodation when they arrived, while the other men went to the canteen and had 'a pint and eggs and steak'. The men were assigned wooden huts – 'long sheds of pine . . . very flimsy structures, but just the thing for their purpose, as it never rains here, and they are beautifully cool'.

The thing that struck Scurry on that first night in Egypt was just how much sand there was. In a letter home he explained, 'Everywhere is sand . . . nice coarse, hard sand, it is without a lot of flint in it. I'll bring a haversack full home with me.' His head swam with all the sights, the buildings and the construction he had seen on the train journey. This architectural modeller had an eye for how things were made, and was intent on seeing as much as he could while in Egypt, making as many observations as he could either in his letters home or his diary.

The Fair Dinkums had the sleep-in they desperately needed the following morning. Thereafter, their wake-up call was 5 am. But on this first morning at Zeitoun, the men were allowed to extend that through to 7 am. Parade was from 10 am to midday, and then came a route march of 6–7 miles (9–11 kilometres). That afternoon on the march, the men were 'shown a big obelisk, a great high affair of solid stone which Moses built when he brought the Israelites to the promised land'. It was moments such as these that drilled into the men the history of this ancient place. One New Zealand soldier, Ormond Burton, observed of the same region:

From the very dawn of history, this has always been a greatly travelled way. Moses the Hebrew, the hoplites of Alexander, the legions of Rome, the hosts of the Saracens, Napoleon and the Army of Egypt, all have tramped this dusty road. Great captains, mighty leaders, great conquerors, they and their marching men came and went, and still the rich land brings forth its teeming abundance; still the patient 'fellaheen' plough with the ancient share which was known to their forefathers – men of a hundred generations back; in the same fashion they guide the running water into the rightful channels, and three times a year gather in the harvests. Every yard of that journey was crammed with interest.

By day's end, the exhausted men returned to camp for their dinner, a quick chat about what they had seen and most were relieved when it was lights out.

Wal King, the thickset salesman from Abbotsford, had a welcome surprise that second day. By chance, he ran into his younger brother Henry, who had been slightly wounded at Gallipoli and sent back to Egypt to recuperate. Wal had seen Henry off from Sydney when he left Australia, and could barely believe he was able to see him so soon after arriving. Henry had been considered 'the black sheep' of the four brothers, and lived as hard as he could in his early years. It was said the other three of the King brothers were 'non-drinkers, non-smokers and all very straight down the line. They weren't women chasers . . . Henry got the lot'. But from the moment Wal clasped his large hands in a shake with his brother on foreign soil, he noticed the difference in him immediately. He seemed somehow less impulsive. Privately, Wal wondered how his own experiences would change him, and the men around him. He wrote to tell his father, William:

> The most pleasant surprise of all was meeting Henry the second day I was here. I can assure you Dad that it has done Henry the world of good, he seems to be a different chap altogether, and is looking exceedingly well. You have no need to worry about Henry's wound, as it is very slight and he is just about well again.

King had a special concern for the men who had been closest to him, particularly those who had shared tents with him in Seymour, and pledged to remain with George Barber, his closest mate, for as long as they could manage it. King told his father in a letter that his mates: 'Earny [Ernie] Williams and Tom Littlemore . . . have gone to the school of instruction. They joined the Machine Gun school'.

King had no such compulsion to nominate himself, noting: 'They say the average machine gunner only lives a fortnight when fighting. I thought I would stay where I am'. English-born Barber was still with him, and King said, 'I hope we will stick together until the end'.

Barber's sister back in England had complained that he never sent her postcards from his time in Australia, so he figured he needed to do so now, even though he was in Egypt. Barber asked King to get his father to send some Australian postcards of 'Sydney Harbour and Sydney itself and also some of Melbourne and Victorian views' to his sister.

Military life on the ground could be monotonous and mundane. Rohner noted this with pencil precision in his diary: 'Drill hours: Reveille at 5am. Fall in at 6am. Knock off at 9am. Fall in again at 10.30am. Drill till 12 o'clock. Fall in at 4.30pm [then] drill till 6pm'. Scurry felt the same, recording, 'We just get up, work and go to bed again. Between that, we live in sand and eat stew.'

It was solid work in difficult conditions. Clews talked of how 'very hot it is in the sand', which took some getting used to. Layfield kept smiling as he endured the hard work, his pale skin and red hair feeling the effects of the sun's powerful rays. He figured:

Broadmeadows was only play to what it is now . . . We have to be up at five now, and then we fall in at six, have three hours' drill, then we have breakfast, fall in at ten till twelve, then we are free till four, we have two more hours, then we are finished for the day, except when on guard. We were trench digging the other day.

There was an unexpected bonus, which compensated in part for the hard work. He explained: 'We get fed much better than we did before . . . the Egyptian Government allows about eight and a half a day for food, besides what our Government gives us'.

He saw the funny side to the badgering and bartering the soldiers encountered from the local merchants, as well as the gaggle of young children eager to sell them everything from fruit to ancient antiquities which, for the most part, looked decidedly more modern than the sales pitch intended. Layfield recounted to his mother:

It's funny to see the niggers selling things, they will ask you about five times more than it is worth. If they ask you for two piastre, you will think about half a piastre . . . The Niggers say: 'Australian good, plenty money; English no good, no money.' The children have just as much sense at the men. You can't walk along without a dozen kids asking you to clean your boots. If you stop, they will start to clean your boots.

It took the Australians some time to get used to dealing with the local currency, and some of the more questionable vendors.

'The Arabs would rob you right and left, if you let them,' Clews warned of the need to stay alert.

There were countless hours of training, including sharp-shooting on the rifle range at nearby Abbassia, route marches through the sand, and guard duty in the Cairo heat to help keep the order. Lance Corporal Harry Attwood was already a dedicated soldier, and sometimes that dedication got him into a bit of bother. Once he was leading a group of men through the desert in the blackness of night. He explained, writing with a smirk on his face, in a letter to his niece:

We soldiers get plenty of work, sometimes having to drill or march at night. On Friday, at 6 o'clock, we set out across the sand intending to be back before 9 o'clock, but owing to a mix up it was after ten – I was scouting across the sand ahead of the main body of men, and in the dark fell into a small trench and getting out, stepped into another.

Fortunately, there was no harm done, and he was alone when he fell, so there was no ribbing. He could see the funny side of moments like this.

But when it came to the war, there was little room for mirth, given the casualties that continued to arrive from the front. Attwood did what he could to find out about the men of Bendigo, whom he had known in peacetime, and was eager to join at Gallipoli. As he deduced, the news was far from good: 'I have heard lots of news today about boys I used to know in Bendigo. Some are hurt and one or two killed'.

There was still plenty of exploring to do when the soldiers were afforded time off. Rohner engaged in practice-marching on the last day of September, but got the chance to head into Cairo that night. He was unimpressed with certain parts of the city: 'Saw many pretty and bad sights. Saw some of the dark streets. Much evil'. Nor was he impressed with some of the immorality on offer in the backstreets of Cairo, or with the lack of self-control shown by some of the Anzacs. Several Fair Dinkums contracted venereal diseases, including nineteen-year-old Dugald Walshe, which later cost him a trip to Gallipoli. Others missed out for various reasons. As the *Official History of the Australian Army Medical Services* recorded:

> Venereal disease constituted the foremost, and in many respects, the most important cause of disability from sickness [in Egypt]. Preventative measures were practically confined to moral suasion and the provision of counter-attractions. The circumstances under which these diseases had hitherto been treated were peculiarly unhappy, the staff inadequate, the conditions deplorable, methods and equipment rudimentary.

Clews was disappointed by the more salacious sights of the city. In an early letter, he promised to tell his sister 'all about Cairo and the Pyramids and other things in this strange land of the Pharaohs. It is truly a marvellous place'. A few days later, he wrote: 'Cairo is a larger city than Melbourne . . . all nationalities being represented. All the traffic goes on the right side of the street instead of the left. Parts of the city [are] very dirty and smells something awful but in the main streets and squares are some of the finest buildings in the world'. A fortnight later, he added: 'You get sick of Egypt, and stinking, glittering, wicked Cairo, it makes you think a lot more of your own country, but this place is as dirty, except in the main parts of the city. [But] Heliopolis is . . . the Toorak of Cairo'.

But it wasn't only venereal disease causing problems in Cairo and its surrounding camps. Layfield might have let his parents know on countless occasions that he was 'fit as a fiddle' and 'in the pink of condition', but not so some of his mates and one of his superiors. The troops had been warned not to buy fruit from Arab locals by the roadside, with some of the produce believed to have contained 'smallpox'. There had been:

> a lot of sickness in our company; three [are] in the hospital with appendicitis and several are in with disintry [sic]. [Dysentery] is pretty bad over here, the sand is the cause of it. It gets in your nose and down your throat. Our Officer is in the hospital with Diphtheria and it makes it very awkward for us.

Rohner was one of those struck down. The day after he and the men returned from the rifle range, his diary entry for 7 October 1915 read: 'Went to the hospital at Heliopolis with dysentery'. Such was his sickness that he missed a fortnight of entries, finally adding on 21 October, 'A man died in ward with dysentery'. He was soon well enough to be back perusing the pyramids and marvelling at the Sphinx, taking 'a small piece of the latter' as a keepsake. Several of the men contracted mumps, which may have been 'brought by the transports from camps in

Australia', while other cases of influenza, meningitis and general sickness caused discomfort and displeasure.

But it was the medical case of 'Old' Bill Mudge that affected the Fair Dinkums as much as anything else in those first few weeks in Egypt. He had been a father figure to many of the young men from the 8th Reinforcements of the 7th Battalion. His health issues impacted particularly on Layfield and the tent mates from back at Seymour, where Mudge's wisdom and wise words had helped them settle into a soldier's life. Almost from the moment the *Anchises* docked at Suez, Mudge was on borrowed time. In camp back in Australia he had 'noticed a pimple on the inner surface of [his] lip . . . whilst on transport [it] became painful and larger on arrival in Egypt'. Doctors became increasingly concerned as the pimple turned out to be much more – it was cancerous. Layfield alerted his parents back home about how 'Old Mudge has been in hospital ever since we have been there with a Canser [sic] in the throat . . . he has got another one on the lip'. At a medical board of enquiry on 30 October 1915, it was determined that Mudge would be shipped back to Australia, his time in the AIF as good as over. The doctors noted: 'Whilst in hospital it become larger and more painful . . . [it] was excised and microscopic examination showed the ulcer to be epithelioma [an abnormal growth that would be a malignant carcinoma]. The operation broke down and was again excised'. Mudge's war was over before it began. His wife was notified of his immediate return from Egypt, and a few days before the Fair Dinkums stepped foot on the shingled beach at Anzac Cove, he was sailing back to Australia for the fight of his life.

The one thing the Fair Dinkums could not have mistaken was how grave the Gallipoli campaign appeared when they arrived in Egypt. All you needed to do was look in any of the hospitals with its wards full of soldiers of many national-ities, and at those Anzacs who had been wounded – seriously and otherwise – or rendered incapacitated with sickness. Many were casualties of the disastrous and failed August Offensive which occurred a few weeks before the *Anchises* departed Melbourne.

Bill Mills knew all about it. He wrote home to his father, John, in Gordon in country Victoria, saying: 'Went to mass, held in Sisters' Covent, a lovely place. A nun gave me a rosary, The hospital is full of wounded'. The frustration of the Fair Dinkums was that they were waiting and waiting, while some of the other reinforcements who had shared the journey with them from Australia were already on their way to Gallipoli. As Layfield explained in early October:

> A couple of companys [sic] that came over on the same boat as us are going to the front in a couple of days, but we won't be going for a while, our Battalion is back from the front resting. I don't think we are going to the Dardanelles, we might be going to Greece. I'm not too sure. I want to see as much as I possibly can, but wherever we go, we have to go to Lemnos Island for the third stage of training. Seymour was the first. Egypt is the second and Lemnos [will be] the third. I believe you can hear the guns going off from there.

Scurry, too, was impatient, but understanding of the long preparations in Egypt. He expressed that to his mother:

> We do not know when we will get orders to move forward. The Battalion, we are told, is resting at Lemnos Island, and we have heard some 'latrine whispers' that they are going to go to Salonika [Greece], but we take that for what it is worth, and we'll know where we are going when we get there. We are told the Colonel [Scurry's former Essendon Rifles chief Pompey Elliott] is wounded again ... but we are not sure of that either.

King was more confident that the powers-that-be would be sending the men to Gallipoli sooner rather than later, saying, 'The 7th Battalion has been resting for a few weeks . . . but has been ordered back to the front . . . so you may depend we will be there very soon'.

In the meantime, the men were intent on exploring Egypt as much as they could. Scurry was desperate to visit the Great Pyramid of Giza. Fighting forces for centuries had gathered near them, and the young Anzacs were no exception, as the Originals had been before them. Scurry's letters home came not only from a loving son, but from an architectural modeller with a passion for construction. He and his workmate and friend Arch Wardrop took delight in going inside the Pyramid of Cheops, the oldest and most substantial of the three pyramids, dating back to around 2560 BC. Scurry was intent on charting it all with words and a series of markings he made on the letters he sent home. He was nothing if not detailed and ordered. Those qualities, and more, would serve Scurry well in his time in uniform.

Scurry could barely believe how these wonders of the ancient world were still standing in the twentieth century. He detailed:

> We went through a small entrance after having taken off our boots, and down a downward incline for about fifty or sixty feet. The walls and ceilings were of granite, and the floor of limestone, very hard and so smooth and slippery that hollows are made in it for your feet. . . . we went along into the King's Chamber. The chamber is a fairly large room lined with granite in the far end, of which is the coffin . . . at the end of the coffin, some of the flags have been removed revealing the cavity in which the King's jewels were found.

Scurry continued with almost a sense of wonder at the view before him:

Then we went up, we seemed to be going up all day, but this time [we] went right up to the top. We could see way over the flaps to the Nile with the waving maise [sic] between miles of it, and further on the huddled city with its domes . . . and high above it the great frowning Citadel. Behind that was the first outline of bare desert hills.

In contrast, the seedier side of the city and the nightlife held little appeal for him. The first time he went into Cairo the guard who escorted them 'probably had a wrong idea of what we wanted to see . . . In the end, I got so disgusted that I lost myself in my return to get out'. Scurry had a sweetheart back home, and a marriage promise for his return. He didn't need the gratification that others sought.

He was much more complimentary of some of the architectural wonders, particularly those in nearby Heliopolis:

Heliopolis is a better class suburb of Cairo about three miles from our camp and it contains the pick of the modern buildings, or should I say, the newer buildings. The main street consists on the left side of about three or four buildings, each one with heavy granite pillars supporting the true Oriental arches while above the windows and balconies have the rounded arches of the Turks. On first entering the street and the eye strikes along the row of pointed arches, it reminds me of a Gothic cloister, only the pillars are too heavy. The buildings are chiefly made of a sort of free stone, which is quarried from out in the desert. At the far end of the street is the Palace Hotel, now the No. 1 Australian General Hosp. I had to go there on duty the other day and never have I been in such a place.

He went on to describe the beauty and the architectural work of the Palace Hotel. In the next letter home, he detailed Ghezireh Palace, which was the No. 2 Australian General Hospital.

He explained to his mother that she had no need to be alarmed that he was at a hospital, saying: 'Don't be surprised at the address, but we are only here for a week, protecting sick men. If we behave ourselves well we may be able to stay longer, if we are not called to move forward in the meantime'. When he was there, Scurry was camped inside the gates of Ghezireh Palace, which had been built in 1869, having been:

> originally built for a harem, but before the war it was used as a hotel to accommodate tourists who came up to the Casino opposite. The building is right on the banks of the Nile, standing in about twelve acres of what was once beautiful gardens, all the garden beds are now covered with tents. At night the palace is particularly wonderful, when at ten o'clock pm, I leave this little Eden with a relief for the posts, it's fine to look back and see the bright circle of light. Then I relieve the No. 1 post, and march them up the drive, facing the dazzling lights of Cairo, shining across the broad swelling river, right round the hospital till I come to the big iron gates at the park entrance. Here I take the sentry off and lock the gate for the night. I thought as I did it last night that it was almost a presumption for me to be the master of these gates. Big, strong iron monsters, that take my whole weight to move, and then only very slowly. Gates that were there . . . years before I was born and yet who I am to say who shall come in or go out, but I suppose I will have to do lots of peculiar things before I get home.

The Fair Dinkums first encountered captured Turkish and German soldiers in and around Cairo. Layfield saw some 'through the bars of a window. The German officers were very clean, but the Turks didn't look too clean, although they were treated well. They had good food to eat and cigarettes to smoke, so they weren't doing too bad, were they?' Ever a compassionate soul, he found it difficult to reconcile how some of his fellow soldiers were taunting the prisoners of war, who had attracted an audience. He detailed to his mother, 'One of our chaps was laughing at them, another chap told him he shouldn't do that, he said it was a shame because they have to fight for their Country just the same as we do. I think he was quite right, don't you Mum?'

Layfield was part of the group charged with keeping order, mainly with some of the Anzacs who got out of line on the drink or in the seedier parts of the city. He explained:

Every night about five o'clock we used to go into Cairo on picquet, first of all we would go to the soldiers' home and wait for call outs. It was amusing to see the Natives rushing up to us . . . [and saying] soldiers had bought something and would not pay for it, or that somebody was drunk in their shop. When we would get there, there was nothing wrong . . . About 8 pm we would walk through the filthy back streets of Cairo where our soldiers are likely to be. It would nearly make you sick in some places . . . it's a wonder some of us don't die with fever. About half past nine, we would hunt [soldiers] out of the hotels. If we had a big burly MP with us, he would only have to give a rap on the door with his cane, [and] nearly everyone would get up and go straight away, but if we had a little meek and mild sort of chap, he would say 'Come on lads, it's half past nine', [and] no one would move until he'd had another drink or something. It is very seldom I ran anybody in. If we did, it was their own fault . . . Sometimes when we were walking through the streets of Cairo, some nasty fellows would yell out 'Cold Feet', or 'How is [sic] your feet?' when they saw the red and white arm band. But they don't know they might have to be on the same job themselves.

Layfield liked to be liked. He was a young man, noted for his smile, his red hair (which won him the nickname 'Ginger') and his devotion to duty. He knew that he had to do what he was asked, even if it earned him a few jibes in the Cairo backstreets.

King's company also got to see plenty of Cairo when acting on picquet duty:

> Another of our duties was to raid the moll-houses and arrest every soldier we caught after half-past nine. Sometimes they were carrying a little more beer than was good for them. Perhaps they would talk [of a] fight, but I can tell you they always came off second best ... The party I was with were stationed in the part known as the 'Wassa' [the Haret el Wasser district], absolutely the lowest part in Cairo. I have heard experienced people say it is the lowest part in the world.

Having already met the youngest of his brothers, Henry, King also met up with a second sibling, Ted, during this time, and was pleased to hear another one of the four, 'Brom' (Bromley), was back in Australia and ready to make his trip across the world. He had an enjoyable afternoon with Henry before his brother was sent back to Gallipoli, visiting many historic places, including:

> the exact spot where the Pharos [sic] daughter was supposed to have found Moses in the Bull Rushes [sic]. Then we went to the well or something like the well by which they measure the depth of the Nile. I saw so much that I have got them a bit mixed up ... we saw the cave which the Virgin Mary concealed herself in her flight from Egypt to the Promised Land. I have not seen the Pyramids yet but I hope to get there ... [I] think I could spend 12 months just looking round this place.

The Fair Dinkums didn't have much time left for exploring, though, as King explained in a letter home to his father, 'I think our company will be going to the front ... It may be some time before [you] here [sic] from me, as we are not allowed to write very often from the front.'

As October headed into November, the talk around the camp was that the move would soon come. The Greek island of Lemnos was to be the first port of call, where they were likely to meet up with the battle-hardened 7th Battalion, already famous for their fighting exploits, but resting since the August Offensive. From there, it was a short trip of about 50 kilometres across the fabled waters of the Aegean Sea onto the shores of Gallipoli.

5

Off to the front

'We're off at last . . .'

TWENTY-TWO-YEAR-OLD GEORGE BARBER HADN'T accumulated a lot in his life, but whatever he had, he didn't want it to go to waste if something happened to him. He was one of several members of the 8th Reinforcements putting their affairs in order before final word came through for when they were leaving for the front. It was coming, though none of them knew exactly when, and Barber wanted to be ready for all eventualities. So, at the start of November 1915, the former Londoner wrote a will that left all his earthly possessions to his sister who lived in Hoxton, London. He signed the typed document in the presence of two Fair Dinkums whom he had come to know and trust. One of them was Oliver Harris, who had worked as a clerk with solicitors Tatchill, Dunlop, Smalley and Balmer in Eaglehawk before enlisting.

The Fair Dinkums had no idea that the Gallipoli campaign was already on borrowed time as they awaited confirmation of their departure from Egypt after six long weeks. It had been since the failure of the August Offensive, the moment that was meant to change everything for the better, but ultimately doomed Allied hopes of pushing inland or breaking free from the prison that the peninsula had become. That failure, which cost so many lives, took place while the men of the 8th Reinforcements were still in Australia.

The very day the Fair Dinkums had set sail, on the 124th day of the Gallipoli campaign, Australian war correspondent Charles Bean had forecast the difficulties that would come to the Anzacs on the peninsula by the time these Fair Dinkums were there and ready to fight. Recuperating from minor wounds received during the ill-fated August Offensive, Bean knew that the real hardship for the Anzacs would come with the approaching winter. While it would soon be spring in Australia, it was autumn at Gallipoli, and Bean knew that a Turkish winter posed significant problems.

By the time the Fair Dinkums reached Egypt for further training in late September, there were already enough people in high places in Britain eager to bring about an evacuation of Gallipoli that it became a real possibility, although the average soldier – even those on the frontline – remained unaware of the military machinations that were bringing the campaign to a grinding halt. Still, there were frontline Anzacs who dared to believe the hopeless situation they found themselves in was somehow salvageable, even though outside forces were conspiring to bring about a rapid conclusion to the Gallipoli campaign.

British war correspondent Ellis Ashmead-Bartlett, who had eulogised the Anzacs in his initial reports of the Gallipoli landing, had long since lost faith in the commander of the Mediterranean Expeditionary Force, General Sir Ian Hamilton. When Australian journalist Keith Murdoch gained permission to visit the Anzacs at Gallipoli in September 1915, the London *Daily Telegraph* journalist persuaded Murdoch to carry to London a secret letter Ashmead-Bartlett had written for British Prime Minister Herbert Asquith, detailing how the August Offensive was 'the most ghastly and costly fiasco in our history since the Battle of Bannockburn . . . the muddles and mismanagement beat anything that has ever occurred in our military history . . . my views are shared by the large majority of the army'. Murdoch was eventually detained at Marseilles, and Ashmead-Bartlett's letter was confiscated.

That set off a chain of events that further accelerated doubts about the campaign, both in Great Britain and Australia. Ashmead-Bartlett was expelled from Imbros and took his grave concerns home to England. Murdoch returned to London where he put together from memory some of the claims, adding a few of his own, in the so-called 'Gallipoli letter', which he had prepared for Australian Prime Minister Andrew Fisher. The letter, as Les Carlyon noted, 'circulated as a state paper in Westminster' and, while 'larded with factual errors and the author's sense of his own importance, much of it was also true' that 'helped expose the incompetence of the high command at Gallipoli'. Murdoch wrote of the disconnect the Australian troops had with their British counterparts:

Oh, if you could picture Anzac as I have seen it, you will find that to be an Australian is the greatest privilege the world has to offer . . . for the general staff, and I fear for Hamilton, officers and men have nothing but contempt. Sedition is talked around every tin of bully beef on the peninsula, and it is only loyalty that holds the forces together . . . I hope I have not made the picture too gloomy.

Murdoch was gloomy, but praised the Anzacs who were still fighting to win.

It was at that time, though, that the powerful forces in Great Britain concluded that the campaign was no longer a winnable one. The War Cabinet was wavering in its support. As a result, Hamilton sent one of his staff officers, Guy Dawnay, to London to meet with Lord Kitchener and further explain the situation. But it did not go well for Hamilton. Dawnay expressed how dire the situation was – to Kitchener, the Cabinet and the King.

Responding to whispers from Westminster that an evacuation was again on the agenda, Hamilton forecast in October casualties of around 50 per cent, which would have been catastrophic. On 15 October itself, he was told he was being replaced, in a telegram from the British Secretary of State for War, Field Marshal Lord Kitchener. Hamilton was replaced by General Sir Charles Monro, who seemed more inclined to consider plans to evacuate the men from the peninsula – and, God willing, with a minimum of casualties.

On 2 November 1915, Monro pushed on with the prospect of recommending a full evacuation to Kitchener, explaining that:

> On pure military grounds, in consequence of the grave daily wastage of officers and men which occurs, and owing to the lack of prospects of being able to drive the Turks from their entrenched lines, I recommend the evacuation of the peninsula. [They] have done splendid work in the peninsula, but they do not possess the opportunity or time, as they now stand, to create this force into a reliable fighting machine. Hence I think that loss of prestige caused by withdrawal would be compensated for in a few months by increased fighting efficiency.

It was decided Lord Kitchener had to assess the Gallipoli situation for himself to further determine the course of action.

The Fair Dinkums, eager to leave Egypt and do their bit, knew nothing about the proposed evacuation, other than the decision to replace Hamilton. As far as they were concerned, Gallipoli was still very much worth fighting for. News came through on 6 November, four days after Monro's recommendation to evacuate, that had Alf Layfield, the soldier from Coburg, almost bursting with energy and enthusiasm. Here was what they had all been waiting for since they disembarked from the *Anchises:* they were to move out to Lemnos early the following day, and from there, onwards to Gallipoli.

In a short letter to his mother, written in haste from the camp at Zeitoun, Layfield said:

> We're off at last . . . we are tired of this place. I am sending some Christmas cards with this mail. If I get a chance, I will have my photo taken on Lemnos Island. We shall be there for awhile. We have to get up at three in the morning. I suppose we will be leaving about five. We will have another sea ride, a couple of days run, I think.

There was not a lot of sleep in the camp that night, just as there hadn't been on the last night before leaving Broadmeadows. Men spoke in hushed tones after lights out, others penned final letters to their families, and more than a handful followed Barber's earlier lead by putting their affairs in order, just in case.

The men were afforded 'very short notice . . . [we] only knew on the Sat afternoon that we were to leave on Sunday morning at 3.30 am', according to Milton Clews. A number were still ill in hospitals or on sick parade and could not make the trip. Anderson noted in his diary on 7 November: 'Left Zeitoun by train to Alexandria, fine delta land. Products maize, cotton and fruit. Very fast trains. A very big sea port at Alexandria'. The train rolled into Egypt's largest sea port in the early afternoon and awaiting the 8th Reinforcements of the 7th Battalion was the *Royal George*, an 11,000-ton passenger steamship now conscripted to ferry soldiers to war. On this occasion, she was charged with ferrying the Fair Dinkums to the next and final stage of their training. Lemnos was the jumping-off point to

Gallipoli, but they had to get there first, which was no guarantee on these seas.

Bill Scurry, who had been so descriptive about the pyramids, was equally so charting the next stage of their journey. He explained how:

> Our ship is painted like a man of war and can do 21 knots so it would need a pretty smart submarine to have got us. But there were none smart enough, and the hills of Lemnos loomed more and more distinct on the horizon until at last we were right in close to the shore. Then we sailed along a barren and apparently uninhabited shore, till we suddenly turned a point and saw the beautiful smooth harbour before us. First was the line of drums marking the top of the net across the entrance, and then the port I have never seen such a sight in my short life before. There were lines of grey warships, dreadnoughts, cruisers, destroyers, submarines, which we could not see and a thousand smaller things like mine sweepers, lighters and that tribe.

Here was the campaign that brought together hundreds of ships in an effort to win the Gallipoli Peninsula.

There had been drama almost from the time the *Royal George* left Alexandria. Men were understandably nervous about the prospect of facing enemy submarines, joking about the danger of 'cigars', the term for enemy torpedoes. Clews noted that a soldier fell overboard and drowned.

They had every reason for concern. The *Royal George* had 'picked up two boatloads of sailors', according to Clews, from a ship that 'had been torpedoed the day before, so we had to keep a sharp lookout for submarines all the way. We had to carry lifebelts about with us all the time, but I am thankful to say that we got through safely at last'. Clews met someone on board who had known his fallen friend, Fred Bayles, whose death he had promised to avenge: 'He says [Fred] was killed the first week that he landed, so he didn't have much of a chance'.

Anderson's diary gives more detail about the ship torpedoed on 8 November 1915, the British cargo ship the *Den of Crombie*, which was carrying general cargo before being hit by German submarine U–35, about 112 miles (180 kilometres) off Crete. He wrote:

> When out at sea two days in Mediterranean Sea [we] picked up the crew of the Den of Crombie . . . We had no escort for the first four days, then picked up a couple of destroyers which took the lead. On guard duty looking for submarines. Life belts on all day and night armed with 50 rounds of ammunition. Food very rough, cabin very small and stuffy at bottom of ship.

Wal King found a postcard of the *Royal George* when he was aboard and to pass the time and to distract himself wrote to his father to tell him he was well: 'I have left Egypt but I am not allowed to tell you where I am. I am not in the firing line yet, but expect to go there any time now. Hoping you are quite well'.

For the first time, some of the men realised danger lurked in the waters. The trip from Australia was nothing like this: fear almost from start to finish, with lifebelts worn or carried almost at all times. There was much relief when the *Royal George* steamed its way into an exceptionally crowded but picturesque Mudros harbour on Lemnos after four days. Hundreds of vessels were in the harbour, which gave the Fair Dinkums their first real indication of the scale of the Gallipoli operation. The men were eager to come ashore, anticipating a meeting with the men they had come to join, the battle-hardened 7th Battalion, who were still resting, their return to Anzac postponed because of worsening weather conditions. But there was more waiting in store for the Fair Dinkums before they saw battle.

★

IT WAS IN CAMP on Lemnos that the Originals, including Major Geoffrey McCrae, received welcome news that four members – Corporals William Dunstan and Alexander Burton, and Lieutenants Frederick Tubb and William Symons – had been awarded the Victoria Cross for gallantry at Lone Pine. Their return date to Anzac Cove had been delayed by a diphtheria outbreak, which meant quarantine, more training and a series of sports carnivals to keep the men physically sharp.

On the same day that the Fair Dinkums sailed into Mudros harbour another ship arrived, carrying Lord Kitchener himself, en route to Gallipoli. He spent time looking over the operations on the island, preparing to make his assessment on Anzac Cove, though the 7th Battalion men who saw him knew nothing of the sharp turn that the campaign was about to make. Major McCrae said of the man with the most recognisable face in the military: 'He praised us and congratulated us on the work done at Anzac. He struck me as a most genial old man, not the ferocious man he is pictured. Afterwards the senior officers of the Brigade were introduced to K of K [Kitchener of Khartoum]'.

At Gallipoli, Kitchener received a rousing reception from the Anzacs, who were more usually wary of putting too much faith in the top brass, but nonetheless mesmerised to see, in the flesh, the man from the recruiting posters. But the real purpose of his visit – even if those soldiers lauding him didn't know it at the time – was to effectively seal the evacuation of the peninsula. On 15 November, as the Fair Dinkums remained under anchor, Kitchener sent a private telegram to Asquith, saying:

Careful and secret preparations for the evacuation of the peninsula are being made. If undertaken, it would be an operation of extreme military difficulty and danger; but I have hopes that, given time and weather, which may be expected to be suitable until about the end of December, the troops will carry out this task with less loss than was previously estimated.

AS THE MEN OF the 8th Reinforcements waited impatiently in the harbour for word that they could soon join the 7th Battalion, one of the Fair Dinkums tried to speed up the process. Ray Rohner had been one of many to come down with dysentery in Egypt, which meant he couldn't leave with his Cobram mates for the front. He missed the original departure by a few days, and sailed into Lemnos on the *Argyllshire*. He noted in his diary on his second day at sea: 'Supposed to be a submarine following us. Great excitement on board. The gun at the aft of the boat was following the supposed sub all over the place, but nothing came of it'. Just how lucky they were came to light the following day – 15 November 1915 – when they found the crew of another ship in the water. Rohner added:

We picked up the crew of *Orange Prince* which was torpedoed 11 o'clock in the morning. This caused great excitement. About 3.30pm, the vessel went down with 300 bags of mail for the troops in Gallipoli. All of the crew were saved excepting for three stokers. The *Orange Prince* left Alexandria a few hours before us. If we had been a few hours earlier, we would most likely have gone down, too.

Rohner realised how fortunate he and the rest of the men aboard had been. It had been an eventful voyage, and it wasn't over when the *Argyllshire* docked in the crowded and chaotic harbour just after midnight:

We were laying to when a big hospital ship dragged her cable and the wind was so strong that it carried her [into] us. She rammed us but did no serious damage. She broke one of her life boats and the gangway. Then again, at 5.30pm, a French cargo boat whilst steaming into port missed our stern by about two foot.

Rohner was also praying for the Fair Dinkums, including the Cobram–Barooga boys – Ray Eaton, Roy Anderson and the Knight brothers, Hugh and Bertie – and hoping to catch up with them sooner rather than later.

Robert Haysey, the 21-year-old orchardist from Narre Warren, was one of many frustrated by his extended stay on the *Royal George*. He wrote home to his family, and had his letter picked up by the *Essendon Gazette,* saying: 'We left on 7th November in the *Royal George,* and reached Lemnos four days after. They kept us on board another 11 days; then dumped us ashore' on Lemnos, at an Anzac Depot camp.

The following day they finally met up with and joined the men of the 7th Battalion. It was a critical moment for the Fair Dinkums. They had carried the Mud and Blood colours for months, but knew they hadn't earned them yet. Meeting up with the men who had given their battalion such a glorious reputation in a relatively short period of time was an experience. The Originals had already served with rare distinction, yet the Fair Dinkums still had to prove themselves and were about to tested like never before. Acceptance from the veterans would be earned in time, but it was going to happen at Gallipoli, and elsewhere – certainly not at Lemnos. Trust was no simple feat, as the Originals were always sceptical of reinforcements as a rule. You had to prove yourself in battle – no other correspondence would be entered into.

Finally connected, the old and new guards of the 7th Battalion were ready to head to Gallipoli, even as its end date as a battle-field ticked away. Bill Scurry and the men around him didn't know that the powers-that-be had already agreed to evacuate the peninsula. These Fair Dinkums were among the last new men to land there; as far as the 7th Battalion was concerned, only the 9th Reinforcements came later.

If the Originals waited for actions to tell the true worth of these new reinforcements, Scurry had confidence in his fellow Fair Dinkums, and expected them – and himself – to rise to the challenge. In his last letter to his mother before departing for Gallipoli, Scurry wrote, 'We have just got orders to move to Anzac in a few days' time, so then we will be right into it.' For a man as determined to make an impact as he was, there was never any doubt about his capacity to make that happen.

PART II
THE
DIGGERS

PART II

THE
DIGGERS

6

The Peninsula

'We lived like cave men in holes in the ground.'

THE GALLIPOLI THAT THE Fair Dinkums were sailing towards on 25 November 1915 was a very different beast from the one they had imagined, expected or even read about in the newspapers at home and abroad since their enlistment. Gone were the flies, with frost and frostbite their replacements. Gone was the scorching sun that caused untold sanitary issues for soldiers, buried behind dark skies, gloomy clouds and lashing winds off the Aegean Sea, alongside snow and storms. Gone, too, was the belief that this campaign could be swiftly executed in favour of the visiting team, as some of them said in football parlance. Not even the most optimistic of men believed that was possible anymore in the short to medium term.

The weather turned bleaker the longer November wore on. And as the Fair Dinkums edged closer to the stretch of land the Australian soldiers now called 'Anzac' or 'The Peninsula', with waves smashing against the sides of the transports, conditions changed faster than anyone could have envisaged. As one soldier said, 'Without warning, winter came down upon us. No one guessed he was so near.' The 8th Reinforcements of the 7th Battalion had endured a cold snap at Lemnos, where not even the crowded harbour could offer sanctuary from the miserable conditions. These worsened as they made their way across the waters, and still more after they landed on Gallipoli.

Major Alf Jackson, who had been with the 7th Battalion since being handpicked by Pompey Elliott after war had broken out in 1914, captured on camera one of the moments when the Originals sailed off with the Fair Dinkums: the old alongside the new, the experienced alongside the raw, against a background of ships on choppy seas. The men were huddled together, their packs on their backs, crammed in for a lack of space and to keep warm against the biting chill. Some gave the impression of being battle-hardened soldiers who had done this before, and God willing, would do so again. Others seemed nervous and tense, unsure of what to expect or how to deal with what was to come. Some had their eyes out to sea, watching the crashing waves. A few offered faint smiles to Jackson's camera. All of them knew the magnitude of the task ahead, especially those who had been to Anzac Cove before. The Originals had already survived the worst that Gallipoli had thrown at them, and knew that training could never hope to replicate what happened on the battlefield.

Not all of the Fair Dinkums made that trip to Gallipoli. Some were still recovering in Egypt from various illnesses and ailments; quite a number had taken sick either on the way to Lemnos or once they arrived. Boer War veteran Fred Hoad was one of them, struck down with pleurisy on the *Royal George*. Frank Dixon came down with mumps, as did one-time local footy star and brickmaker Alf Fairbank, while Clement Livermore had enteric fever six days before departure. Gordon 'Gordie' Mills was sent back to Egypt when he exhibited signs of gonorrhoea.

The sea journey from Lemnos to Anzac Cove was plagued by terrible weather. Having left Mudros at 9 am, and sailing on throughout the day and into the night, the men moored offshore near Anzac Cove at 10 pm. Some went ashore; others did not get their footprints on the beach until around midnight. It was pitch black, other than the small lights and occasional fires that penetrated the darkness. Despite their restricted vision, the Fair Dinkums realised how difficult the terrain had been, having heard accounts of the original landing five months earlier. The teeming rain ensured an uncomfortable night for all.

Milton Clews had no opportunity to write in his diary that night, exhausted by the journey and loathe to bring it out in the driving squall. But when he filled it in the following day, he explained the other thing that had greeted them that night: 'one shell fired at us from "Beachy Bill"'. The new arrivals were new chums to shelling, but well acquainted with the term 'Beachy Bill', the Anzacs' term for a nearby, well-hidden Turkish battery with a penchant for unloading hell upon the beach. If the new men wondered why there was nothing going back the other way, they were told of an edict from Australian Brigadier General Cyril Brudenell White, who had devised a plan to halt artillery and infantry fire for a few days. These were called 'Silent Stunts' and were designed to prepare the Turks for periods of inactivity. There was method in White's message, though none of the reinforcements were able to grasp it at that moment.

On that cold, miserable first evening on Gallipoli, 'the [7th] Battalion bivouacked in the familiar surroundings of Shrapnel Valley', located on the road up from the beach which gained its name for a reason – there had been plenty of shrapnel flying around the area since the landings. This was where most of the Anzacs had first been introduced to war as they moved from the valley to the ridge. It was the Fair Dinkums' initiation for the first two days.

It was very different terrain from what Narre Warren orchardist Robert Haysey was used to. He explained in a letter home how 'the boys got ashore and charged those cliffs and gullies . . . things were very quiet . . . we reached four terraces cut out of the hill at the top of the gully'. Haysey said the group:

had some narrow squeaks on [the] second day from shrapnel. Third night, it rained; poured for two solid hours. I just sat on my blankets, with waterproof over my shoulders, till it was over; then found a dry hole to finish that night. Next night it snowed on the mud and we got word to shift. I got into a terrible mess . . . cold and snow and mud. Got into some old dug-outs within a few hundred yards of the firing line that night. The snow froze, and my boots in the morning were as stiff as a board. I had to spend 15 minutes with [an] entrenching tool handle on our feet [sic], frozen with mud and snow; and also our boots suffered. I never felt mine during the daytime for three days.

The men who had been to Anzac Cove before could hardly reconcile themselves with the different conditions that winter had brought to the battlefield, unprepared as they were for the cold weather. As one Anzac on Gallipoli noted:

This was the worst enemy those battered troops had yet encountered. Hardly any of the boys had seen snow, and now they were [almost] naked in the bitterest cold . . . In those open, unprotected trenches, in misery such as they had never dreamed could be, the lads from sunny Australia stood to their posts.

Snow wasn't the only new thing that the men saw for the first time. Some of them, including Clews, watched as 'an aeroplane flew over us and the Turks fired a few shells at it. They kept on firing on the beach and I saw a shell burst at the top of one of the cliffs about two hundred yards away'. Getting accustomed to the shelling and shrapnel took time, and some never got used to it.

In a letter he wrote to his sister, Emily, Clews explained:

[We] are just getting settled down and used to shell fire. As I'm writing this, they keep whizzing by overhead. We've had very cold weather since we arrived, first came rain, then snow and frost, and that's not nice when you've not got a home to go to . . . We get little time at present, it gets dark so early.

On the third day, a storm of almost unprecedented proportions hit the Gallipoli Peninsula, and lasted the best part of three days:

gale force winds whipped up the seas, hail hit the hillsides, and rain poured down the hills towards the beach. The howling winds built up to a cyclone – and then turned into a snow storm. By the end of the three days the settlement had been badly damaged, and many of the earthen structures had been washed away. Trenches and dugouts filled up with filthy water, carrying everything from bodies and body parts, to assorted rubbish (including human waste) – and was sure to spread more disease. The storm seemed the final catastrophe for the troops.

On 28 November, the temperature gauges stayed below freezing point. For the men of the 8th Reinforcements, it was a harsh initiation as they were left to bivouac in the open.

A small portion of rum was passed around the men, but not even that could warm them up. It was like nothing any of them had ever experienced before, and sickness followed for many.

Commander of the Anzacs, General William Birdwood, conceded at the time:

For the troops in the trenches there were three days of sheer agony. We were entirely unprepared for such an emergency, the possibility of which had never been foreseen; consequently no precautions against frostbite had been taken, nor were additional stocks of warm clothing available. A terrific thunderstorm was followed by twenty-four hours of torrential rain, during which men got soaked to the skin. Then came an icy hurricane; the rain turned into a blinding blizzard; then heavy snow, followed by two nights of bitter frost.

For the Fair Dinkums and the rest of the troops, the only small consolation was that the trenches, the dugouts and other flimsy structures gave 'some measure of protection from the surrounding hills'. Down the peninsula at Cape Helles, some helpless British troops were battling and drowning in flash floods.

Australian war correspondent Charles Bean explained that the conditions on the Gallipoli Peninsula meant that men were more exposed to the elements than in France. After the storm and the blizzard brought the snow, Bean wrote: 'Once wet our men can never get dry again – while the troops in France they go back after four days at the front to sleep in a house and get a warm bath and dry clothes'. He further voiced concerns in his diary: 'The authorities haven't prepared against the winter; they haven't made a harbour; they now find they can't expect to land water or stores as they would have wished (with piers and boats wrecked) their water condenser is holed and it is bitter tonight'.

On that same day, 28 November, the Fair Dinkums were on the move, shifting up the line to Victoria Gully, and spent the next two weeks employed on fatigues. A lack of drinking water had become critical; the men had their 'water ration cut back to a quarter, and biscuits cut to three-quarter ration . . . a partial solution to the lack of drinking water was adopted, where the men chopped off ice and melted the pieces to obtain extra water'. Conditions were so wild that it was considered too dangerous for the water transports to be brought to the beach. There was 100,000 litres of water remaining, but it was evaporating faster than anyone could have imagined. It left a dire situation where 'men were issued with a cupful of water in the morning and another at dusk . . . nothing during the day'. The shortage was critical, with Clews saying:

> One day I was 24 hours without a drink, but hope we'll get plenty soon. We've had very cold weather, rain, frost, snow and no dug out to go in but today is fine and we're getting settled down a bit. The Turks shelled our position for 3 hours on Monday morning killing and wounding several hundreds of our chaps, but we had our turn when . . . the warships gave them a severe bombardment. A Taube [German plane] flew over us this morning and fired a machine gun, but it was very soon put to flight. Have seen all sorts of shells burst by now, pretty close too.

Some of the Fair Dinkums left behind on Lemnos finally made it across to Gallipoli in early December, including Major Arthur Hart. Fred Hoad was also fit and well enough to fight again, and eager to see his first combat since the Boer War.

Bill Scurry was very pleased to see two very different soldiers land on Anzac Cove at the end of the first week of December 1915. The first was the 7th Battalion's commanding officer, Pompey Elliott, who had returned to the peninsula after months away in England recovering from pleurisy. Scurry was glad to see the man he respected so much return.

At the same time, the 9th Reinforcements of the 7th Battalion arrived, among them one of Scurry's closest mates, Bunty Lawrence. The pair would soon combine to play a key role in one of the most fabled designs of the Gallipoli campaign.

Ever the architectural modeller, Scurry drew for his mother the little dugout that he was living in during this time, saying:

We lived like cave men in holes in the ground. We had our waterproof laced over the opening just leaving enough room to [get] through. The ceiling was very artistically decorated with roots, having a very natural effect and furnished in a nice cove cornice, to keep the dirt from falling. No doubt the ceiling was very pretty. The kitchen was the front part of the dugout, under the waterproof sheet. Here, we kept our rifles, equipment, boots, etc, while we were in bed. The climax was reached when some sturdy youth commenced on a dugout next door, for an officer. This dugout was to be constructed on palatial lines, but they got too ambitious and came too close to us, so that when one of our chaps leaned against the wall, he fell right through on top of the landlord. The next day we had to shift to a new position, so we left our mansion and have not seen it since.

Sadly, the flow of men off the peninsula was far greater than the trickle of troops coming onto it. The adverse conditions were a factor, as the elements were at that time as lethal as the lead from the Turkish side of the trenches. As the whole operation headed towards evacuation – though none of the men knew it at that time – there was a tendency to ship out those who were unwell rather than wait for them to recover on Anzac Cove. Among those who left early were Salvation Army officer Walter Judd (rheumatism), sixteen-year-old Bill Wain (rheumatism), Syd Davies (breathing difficulties and heart issues), Henry Wood (haemorrhoids) and Bertie Harris (sickness).

Sickness had separated Ray Rohner from his Cobram–Barooga mates since Egypt, but he hoped to rejoin them soon. He managed to make it across to Lemnos, but on landing was immediately taken to the No. 3 Australian General Hospital with 'bad feet', and then on to a convalescence home. He did not join the men until the last few days of the month. By then, the 'shindig' they had all sailed halfway across the world for was over. The men were not told nor could they understand the altered military strategy of the Anzacs. Since their landing, there had been no more talk about the great leap forward or advances; it was all about containing the lines wherever possible.

AFTER MORE THAN A fortnight on Gallipoli, the Fair Dinkums and the rest of the battalion were finally moved further up to the frontline. The tension and fear accelerated; the closeness in the group accentuated. A history of the 7th Battalion detailed how:

> the endless fatigues ended on the morning of 11 December, when the battalion moved up to Silt Spur [a small spur off the southwest corner of 400 Plateau, in between Bolton's and Sniper's ridges] and relieved the 5th and 6th Battalions. The unit's ability to quickly carry out a relief was demonstrated on this occasion, as the relief was completed in less than two hours.

While Rohner convalesced on Lemnos, Roy Anderson, one of his Cobram mates, was settling into his first day on the frontline, later writing in his diary, 'Not seen a Turk or fired a shot to date.' A day later, he excitedly noted he had 'Fired first shot' and a day after that, 'Saw six Turks'. The Unit Diary detailed that snipers had been active all day, while the enemy was relatively quiet.

The battalion, and in particular its headquarters, were subject to some shelling from the enemy the next day. As historian Ron Austin wrote:

> the enemy was generally quiet, and the flurry of enemy broomstick and mortar bombs that fell on the trenches during the night failed to inflict casualties or cause any damage. The troops soon adjusted to the daily routine of sniping,

however on the following day the enemy landed 15 shells in the positions, but the only damage done was to three boxes of stores in the BHQ [Battalion Headquarters] area. Similar levels of activity occurred on the next few days, with sniping being carried out each day, and trench development occurring each night, when more barbed wire was laid to curb the ineffectual, enemy bombing forays.

Some of the Fair Dinkums slipped seamlessly into their roles; others were shaken and wondered how they would ever get through. Most were caught somewhere in the middle.

Alf Layfield settled into the discipline and the rigid demands as best as could be expected. He was one of a group of ten men assigned to bomb-throwing in the trenches. His good arm and aim may have been fashioned on the cricket field, but it was also well suited to the battlefield.

George Rae wasn't as genial. Unlike Layfield, who was in a bomb-throwing sap, Rae was on sniper duty with a group of other men. He may have only been 21, but seemed older, and as tough as old teak, or at least the rock-hard biscuits in their packs. A labourer from Gapsted near Myrtleford in country Victoria, Rae could be impulsive and came to the military with his fair share of vices. He got himself into trouble early in his time on Gallipoli, receiving a short detention and seven days' forfeited pay for disobedience and not setting aside his rifle when taking off his equipment. But he was almost without fear in the frontline, and less forgiving of those around him who failed to show the same dash and daring. He had no hesitation in telling them they were 'cold-footed' and had no sympathy for those less inclined to put their heads near the top of the parapet in the trenches. He told them so, and even wrote about them in his letters home, telling it as it was. Being at Gallipoli only convinced him that volunteers were the only way to go rather than compelling unwilling men to enlist:

Anyone that has to be hunted out had far better stay at home. I know which I would pick for a mate to go into the firing line. Give me one that enlisted of his own free-will. I saw enough . . . on the Peninsula. One instance, a lad of 18 years was my mate in a trench. There were two of us in each parapet. We take it turnabout; one snipes for half an hour, and then the other. Well I finished my turn, and told him to go on. He wasn't game to put his head over. I began to wonder how he was going to shoot, but I soon found out. He put his rifle up over his head, not taking aim and just banged away. You can imagine how many bull's eyes or Abduls he would get in a day. It doesn't matter what you do (so says a cold foot) you are running a big risk, but it is all in the game. I reckon the man that gets his mark is worth a hundred of those who poke the rifle over their heads, and pull the trigger. There are numerous cases that would open your eyes, but I will leave them for the tongue when I get back. I have seen a lot of soldiers' letters in the papers saying what certain fights and charges are like. Take no notice of them for they are mostly lies. Perhaps nine out of every ten never had a foot on the Peninsula.

Given the Anzacs had been ordered to scale back their resistance and wondering why they weren't giving more back to Johnny Turk, enemy activity was only moderate in early to mid-December. That meant sickness posed as much of a danger to the Fair Dinkums as shrapnel or shelling. While there were still some deaths during this time, there were none among the 8th Reinforcements of the 7th Battalion.

Married bootmaker George James, 34, was one of the few Fair Dinkums to be wounded on Gallipoli. James had injured his shin in Egypt in October, but recovered to make Gallipoli. It was there, on 12 December, the second day the battalion was in the firing line, that he copped a bullet in the same leg, smashing the tibia. He was repatriated off the peninsula, his war over two weeks after arriving at Gallipoli. By the end of the next month, he was shipped home.

Four days after James was wounded, another Fair Dinkum made it to the front page of Melbourne's leading afternoon newspaper, the *Herald*, under the headline 'North Richmond Brothers Defend Empire's Cause'. It was a story on the suburb's Murcutt brothers, with a photo of them, including seventeen-year-old Bruce, who had lied about his age to join the 8th Reinforcements of the 7th Battalion. The newspaper described the Murcutts as:

> typical strapping Australian sons, fine riders and great rifle shots. Three of the young Murcutts have already made cold meat of dozens of Allahites. One of them writes to say that he has been hit eleven times by pieces of shell but has not yet missed a day's work. The whole male family are natural born horsemen and as, with the rifle, they are reputed to be able to remove the eye of a mosquito at anything under 550 yards (or something to that effect). It would seem that a regiment of Murcutts would pretty soon clear the Gallipoli Peninsula.

The incredulous story about being one of the brothers being hit eleven times might have been an embellishment of the letter he sent home, as newspapers often sought to over-dramatise something that didn't need hyperbole.

Readers in Melbourne had no idea that the peninsula was about to be cleared – but not in the manner that any of them hoped for, or desired.

7

Drip-rifles and departure

'I hope they won't hear us marching down the deres [gullies].'

BILL SCURRY WANTED TO make a difference, an ambition that burnt within from the moment he enlisted and only magnified when he landed on Gallipoli. He was eager to learn and eager to lead those around him whom he had come to know and care for. In a letter written in early December from the roughly crafted dugout he shared with fellow Fair Dinkums Phillip Bellingham, Bob Billington, Frank Whelan and Robert Haslem, as well as with his mate from the 9th Reinforcements, Bunty Lawrence, Scurry excitedly detailed:

> Here, we are right into it. At least we are on the Peninsula and have been here for nearly a fortnight. We all had to revert to ranks on joining the Battalion, but I have since received one stripe and hope for greater things soon . . . We were expecting Colonel Elliott back and he came last night, and nobody's sorry. The life's not too bad here. We get lots to eat. Bully [beef] and

115

meat biscuits mostly, with bacon for breakfast. Last night we had a pudding, a bonza. It's called the Haslem Pudding after the man who made it.

Robert Haslem was a 22-year-old labourer from Chiltern who had sailed on the *Anchises* with Scurry.

'I'll give you the recipe,' Scurry informed his mother:

Some meat biscuits put in a bag and whacked with a bit of wood till they are pounded up small, then soak them, and add a few raisins, then wrap up in a cloth and boil and eat with jam and condensed milk [if you can get it]. The result is just the pong and we ate largely and much. When we had finished, we all had a wash in the pudding water. It worked out to one mess tin full each, but we had a wash and enjoyed it, the last one only dating back twelve days.

Improvisation and ingenuity had been an integral part of the Anzac experience since the landings on 25 April. So it was fitting that the move towards evacuation also included its fair share of Australian resourcefulness. Scurry had only been on the peninsula for a short time, but came to play an unlikely, almost incredible, role in the preparations for the most successful moment of the entire campaign.

There had been speculation for months that an evacuation was in the wind – a cold, chilling wind, it must be said. But while the word had passed around the trenches and dugouts almost as much as disease had, few of the Anzacs thought it was likely, nor wanted it to happen. If they left, wouldn't it mean that the thousands buried under Turkish soil had died in vain? Then what were all of their struggles and sacrifices for?

These were questions none of the Anzacs wanted to contemplate in the dark days of late November and early December. Behind the lines, the men thought that getting through winter was the most important challenge ahead of them. Not even the brief, much-talked about appearance of Lord Kitchener at Gallipoli in mid-November convinced the Anzac mainstays that the campaign's days were numbered, though there was an interminable stalemate that showed no sign of abating. A note thrown from the Turkish trenches into the Anzac lines near Lone Pine in late November, as detailed in Les Carlyon's *Gallipoli*, summed up the frustration on both sides of the conflict, 'We can't advance; you can't advance. What are you going to do?'

Few people, it seemed, had answers to that question. And with the Turks now having access to new howitzers capable of unthinkable damage, and the prospect of getting even more, something had to give sooner rather than later.

In the early days of December almost as many rumours flew about as Turkish shells, most of them about the pros and cons of evacuation. The men of the 8th Reinforcements could barely believe the talk, given they had only been on the peninsula for a handful of weeks. Many of the Originals did not want to believe such talk either, as that would mean leaving behind fallen mates.

Scurry was curious about what was happening, an inquisitive-ness that soon turned to outright suspicion. This was heightened when two of his Fair Dinkum pals, Haslem and Whelan, were sent to the beach to destroy rum stores. What they told Scurry on their return made him conclude that the trench talk about evacuation might not have been the usual hot air, since 'down at North Beach the Machonacie [sic, Maconochie, a meat and vegetable stew] ration was being handed over ad lib . . . so final was this information regarded that no one bothered to seek official confirmation that evacuation was intended'. Scurry kept his counsel, but wondered how he could make a difference when the time came for evacuation. He wanted to be prepared, and hoped that the Fair Dinkums could play a role.

Thirty-nine-year-old Cyril Brudenell White, born in St Arnaud in country Victoria, a meticulous military man and chief of staff to General Birdwood, had earlier been asked to devise a secret plan for evacuation. But even he was unsure if it would ever be enacted. He worked on his plans in his dugout, coming up with a multi-pronged strategy to have the Turks believe that the Anzacs were bedding down for the winter. The initial part was 'the Silent Ruse'. So, on 24 November, at 6 pm, the ploy was that 'all infantry and artillery fire from the Anzac lines should cease for [three] two days, this rule to be broken only if the Turks attacked, or if a specially important target showed itself . . . Thenceforward shorter periods of silence were repeated almost every night along the Anzac line'. It was designed to make the Turks believe 'the Anzac troops had withheld their fire because they required a quiet time in order to improve their trenches against the winter'. White, it was said, 'proposed that no attacks be launched against the enemy; the Turks must be lulled into thinking the Allies were digging in for winter; advance trench lines would be manned; there must be no visible shrinking of the perimeter'.

On the proposed evacuation dates, White envisaged a gradual withdrawal of troops almost under the noses of the Turks. As Ross McMullin's *Pompey Elliott* detailed:

Anzac and Suvla (but not, initially, Helles) were to be evacuated. From Anzac there were more than 40,000 men to be withdrawn. Some had already left. Under the [White] scheme . . . there was to be a series of gradual daily withdrawals until about half the overall number had gone. The remainder, just over 20,000, would then be taken off over two successive nights. During this final phase, the climax of the operation, Elliott would become the rearguard commander of the right Anzac flank, while the 7th [Battalion], as the 2nd Brigade's last remaining Battalion, would be safeguarding to the very end an important sector near Lone Pine.

For much of early December, even Elliott was unaware of what exactly was happening. One of his first letters to his wife after arriving back at Anzac showed how unsure he was of the rumours, and whether they were fact or furphy. On the morning of 12 December 1915, a week before the intended final departure date, he confessed in a letter: 'I don't quite know what is in the wind'. By that same afternoon, Brigadier General John Monash of the 4th Brigade learned of the evacuation deadline as if it was 'a thunderbolt from a clear blue sky'. In his diary, he expressed concerns, fearful both of the potential casualties and the men's reaction:

> It is of course an absolutely critical scheme, which may come off quite successfully, or may end in a frightful disaster . . . I need not say that I feel very unhappy . . . I am almost frightened to contemplate the howl of rage and disappointment there will be when the men find out what is afoot, and how they have been fooled. And I am wondering what Australia will think at the desertion of her 6000 dead and her 20,000 other casualties.

Monash had understated the deaths and the casualties, but not the message, smart enough to deduce that many of the men left on Anzac could be rebelliously reluctant to leave. But the evacuation was already running to its conclusion, with Monash adding: 'The secret is known so far to only a small handful of men . . . already we have stopped the further arrival of stores, mails, reinforcements, munitions, etc'.

The secret became commonly known within days. Unofficially it had spread to the men, and there was, as expected, much resistance in numerous quarters. They couldn't help but notice the changes to what was going on around them. New piers were constructed to help facilitate troop movement, stores were destroyed, reinforcements were no longer brought ashore, and soldiers who reported in sick no longer had to convince the medical staff to earn a passage away to recuperate. The official order for evacuation was forwarded to the men on 16 December, but most knew days beforehand. The wording showed how concerned the 'brass' were about the men following orders they didn't particularly want to. It also gave a hint of the peril if the Turks were to discover the secret:

> The Army Corps Commander wishes all ranks of your division to be now informed of the operations that are about to take place, and a message conveyed to them from him, to say that he deliberately takes them into his confidence, trusting to their discretion and high soldierly qualities to carry out a task, the success of which will largely depend on their individual efforts. If every man makes up his mind that he will leave the trenches quietly when his turn comes, and see that everybody else does the same, and that up to that time he will carry on as usual, there will be no difficulty of any kind, and the Army Corps Commander relies on the good sense and proved trustworthiness of every man of the Corps to ensure this is done. In case by any chance we are attacked on either days, the Army Corps Commander is confident that the men who have to their credit such deeds as the original landing at Anzac, the repulse of the big Turkish attack on May (19), the capture of Lone Pine, the Apex and Hill 60, will hold their ground with the same valour and steadfastness as heretofore, however small in numbers they may be; and he wishes all men to understand that it is impossible for the Turks to know or tell what our numbers are, even up to the last portion of 'C' party on the last night as long as we stand out ground.

Knowing they were now leaving brought another problem. Who would be the last to leave?

Australia's war correspondent Charles Bean didn't want to be among the last men left. He knew that the mail service had been curtailed, but ever diligent, he wrote a final letter to his parents that he later sent, expressing:

> I don't actually want to be in the last lot to leave the beach, because the risk of being killed or cut off is too great . . . it is an adventure – no one can foretell the ending. It depends largely on the weather. Tonight we have ideal conditions – a cloudy sky covering the half moon; but a very smooth sea. There are three more nights to go.

Others were desperate to volunteer to be there until the end, particularly the remaining Originals, who felt tied to this strip of land. This attitude may have been best summed up by one man from the 14th Battalion, who said, 'I came here with the first, and I'll be here with the last.'

The Fair Dinkums were among the last men to land on Gallipoli. As fate would have it, along with a little Elliott intervention, many of them were among the last to leave. Elliott was believed to have requested that he and his 7th Battalion see it out to the end. As Elliott's biographer McMullin said:

> Since the evacuation would be a gradual withdrawal, obviously the last men to leave would be at most risk. Nevertheless officers in every unit were inundated with fervent pleas from men desperate to be in the rearguard. The principle governing selection was supposed to be about suitability rather than insistent volunteering, but it was rumoured 'Pompey' had nominated himself, and probably his battalion as well, for a leading role. This is plausible. He developed something of a reputation for offering men under his command for difficult tasks. Both Elliott and his battalion did end up with important rearguard responsibilities.

Once the evacuation was confirmed, Elliott ensured the secrecy of the plan was adhered to at every step. He told his men, among them the Fair Dinkums, that no one was to openly discuss what was happening, lest the Turks become aware of the Anzacs' intentions. Men were threatened with court-martial if caught putting the operation in any jeopardy.

Elliott later explained:

When the question of the evacuation of the Peninsula ceased to be a secret, I called in the officers and the NCOs [non-commissioned officers], informed them of the intention to withdraw, and of the vital necessity there was for devising some means to deceive the enemy during this period from the time the last man left the trenches until he entered the boat. I told them about an hour would be required, and therefore what was needed must be capable of being constructed in considerable numbers from materials readily available on the Peninsula, and that it was as much their concern as mine, since any of them might be chosen to form the rear party.

Scurry sensed his chance. And with it, he changed not only the evacuation schedule for a number of his Fair Dinkum mates, but also part of the strategy associated with the planning, and created a piece of Gallipoli folklore that will live forever.

Scurry's mind had been swimming with ideas from the moment Elliott called for some good old-fashioned ingenuity to devise a plan to deceive the enemy and get as many Anzacs off the peninsula as possible safely. He set his mind on making the old 'Colonel' from the Essendon Rifles proud of him.

'It occurred to me that if we could leave our rifles firing we might get away more surely,' Scurry said later.

At that time, I don't think anybody dreamed that we could all get away. The sand of the hour glass was the first germ of the idea. If the sand could be made to trickle from above into a container attached to the trigger, the increased weight would finally release it. Next day, I started on that idea, but it wouldn't work. The sand wouldn't run, and the trigger wanted a jerk to pull it. The jerk was easily got over by the cartridge box full of dirt, but water was the only thing I could think of to replace sand. But water was more easily thought of than obtained. In fact, one used sometimes to do a lot of thinking about it. Apart from tea in the morning, our daily ration was a pint per man, and all our meat ration was bacon and bully – either in a stew or a lump. My day's issue only got me far enough in experiments to show me that there was something in it.

Scurry needed to find more water, mindful that he had to do it quickly as the metaphoric sand was slipping through the Gallipoli hourglass.

While working on his invention, Scurry was interrupted by an old school friend, who offered to help. Scurry said:

In a blind sap . . . I had rigged up all the gear . . . an old school pal, Pte A. H. Lawrence – we called him 'Buntie' [Bunty] – had found me at work that morning and scrounged about for tins, bits of string, and packing case wood. If one thought such common things were easy to get, a full record of the prayers, entreaties, bargains, lies and thefts of 'Buntie' on that day would have convinced him otherwise. Then we struck for water, and no issue till evening, so I went to my Platoon Commander . . . and asked for permission to go to the beach for salt water. Naturally, he asked me what I wanted it for, and, afraid my half-finished affair would be laughed at, I lamely said I wanted to wash some things, and was, of course, refused. When the water was issued I hurried back to the 'Workshop' as soon as duty in the line would allow, and got to work again. Before long, 'Buntie' appeared with more string, and put a water bottle *full* down beside me. 'You can have that, I've got plenty,' he said, and went away. The salt bully used to make our mouths sore in those thirsty days, and 'Buntie's' would some-times bleed at the corners, but he had given me every drop of water he had – the whole of his two days' ration. The only reply that I have ever been able to get from him when I have spoken about it is a laugh.

It was a sacrifice Scurry never forgot. With three pints of water now at his disposal, he could test his invention. It worked to the point where he was happy to take his idea further, and he told his platoon commander about it. Then came 'a comic item' when the drip-rifle was tested at AIF headquarters. It ended up being funny, but there were a few worrying moments for the inventor of this unusual device. He recalled:

We had fixed up a rifle to fire out to sea across a path of about 60 yards in front, and set it for five minutes. More than four and a half [minutes] had gone when two Diggers strolled along the track carrying a large wooden cross. They came steadily on, heedless of the shouts of everybody present, and it looked as though they might need the burden for themselves. I scram-bled over to the rifle, but saw the drop weight wobble on its little perch, and 'Crack'. They could not have been more than three or four yards over the line of the bullet, and for all I know they're still running.

Scurry was forced to wait and see if his invention would be given the green light for production. For a time, he was 'dis-appointed, but got some consolation out of watching some wags steam the labels off "bully", pierce a couple of holes in the tin, and replace the label. They hoped that Abdul would eat it, and become indisposed'. Just when Scurry feared his idea might be overlooked, a runner came and told him 'to remain with "C" party [Die Hards] to work with the rifles, which were to be fixed – twelve on a Battalion front. "Buntie" obtained permission to remain and help with the job'. So, too, did a number of the 8th Reinforcements of the 7th Battalion, who chose to stay until the end.

Elliott was proud of his young rising star, recalling that Scurry's:

first proposal was simply that the upper tin should be filled with water and should be so placed as to allow the water to trickle slowly into the lower tin, which latter was attached by a string working over an arm to the trigger. When sufficient water had accumulated in the lower tin the weight would pull the trigger. This idea worked excellently when used with a well-kept rifle. I accordingly paraded Scurry and his apparatus to General [Harry] Chauvel, 1st Division, who arranged for Scurry to give a demonstration before all the senior officers on the Peninsula. As only damaged rifles could be used for the purpose on the evacuation, Scurry was on the occasion of this demonstration supplied with one picked off the dump at Brown's Dip, and the pull being stiff with rust, the apparatus failed to work. It accordingly became necessary to re-adjust the device so as to make the lower tin fall with a jerk and ensure that any old trigger would be made to work. Hence the final arrangement of the apparatus . . . the fact remains it was a youngster fresh from Australia who thus first perfected an idea which I myself put forward to help solve a difficult problem.

And so a member of the Fair Dinkums – a young man with ambition and ingenuity – won the ears of influential men on Gallipoli, even though he had barely been in battle for more than two weeks. According to a history of the 7th Battalion, Scurry 'demonstrated his invention to General Birdwood and his staff on 17 December, [and] it was agreed that 60 of the delayed-action rifles be manufactured, for use during the evacuation'. Charles Bean was on hand to take a photograph of the 'contraption'.

While the device was Scurry's, he insisted that his mate Lawrence share the recognition, as Bunty had sacrificed his water rations to help in its development. Lawrence recalled almost 70 years later that the device:

> was made from Maconochie ration tins and signal wire. The timing device was water dripping from one tin to another. We demonstrated the device to General Birdwood and his staff, and in due course we were relieved of all other duties to construct as number of these rifle contraptions in the Silt Spur trenches. We were also given the doubtful privilege of remaining behind with the last party, and pour the water into the tins so as to start the timing devices.

The night of the evacuation – a remarkable night under a 'gleaming moon' – was one that neither man ever forgot.

On 18 December, the penultimate full day of the Anzac campaign, there were about 20,000 men left, including most of the Fair Dinkums. General Birdwood released his special order to the nervous, expectant men left on the peninsula, urging them to look to the future rather than be locked in the previous eight months of the campaign. The order asked of them:

> In carrying out our present operations, we are undertaking what no soldier ever likes . . . a withdrawal from the front of the enemy. In the present case, however, I know that none of you will feel in the least disheartened, because we all know we have never been beaten, while by the tenacious hold we have kept on the Gallipoli Peninsula, we have retained the best fighting troops of the Turkish Army in front of us and prevented the Germans carrying out their plans of using them as they wished elsewhere. We cannot therefore think that our

losses and hard work here have been of no avail, for as Lord Kitchener informed me, when recently visiting our trenches, he was himself satisfied that we had fully played our part. We must remember, then, that in withdrawing from our present position we are simply carrying out the orders of the government, who after full consideration have decided that we can be better employed in fighting elsewhere; and I know how much all the ranks will look forward to getting to grips with the enemy again wherever we may be sent.

Birdwood insisted silence must be maintained to the end to ensure the operation's success. Only a few months earlier, Sir Ian Hamilton had forecast the prospect of 50 per cent casualties for an evacuation. And even now, there were fears that there could still be considerable casualties, despite the exhaustive planning and preparations undertaken, especially by Brudenell White, and the ingenuity of men such as Bill Scurry.

Birdwood's order continued:

Remember that in the final retirement silence is essential . . . those in the front line to the last will, in their turn, quietly and silently, leave their trenches passing through their comrades in the covering positions to their place of embarkation in the same soldierly manner in which the troops have affected their various magnificent landings on the shores of this peninsula during the last eight months. To withdraw in the face of the enemy in good order, and with hearts full of courage and confidence for the future, provides a test of which any soldiers in the world may be justly proud, and that [the troops] will prove themselves second to none as soldiers of the Empire, I have not the slightest doubt.

Elliott had left the day before the final night, much to his eternal frustration. His impulsive nature and adherence to order

was such that on the penultimate day he remonstrated with a
drunken soldier who had consumed a sizable portion of the rum
he was meant to be emptying in a different manner. As one of
the Originals recalled:

> Pompey had occasion to speak to an 8th Bn [Battalion] man who
> told him to: 'Go to b—— I'm not one of your 7th'. Whereupon
> Pompey went for him, but slipping, overbalanced and falling
> down the steep bank, (injured) his ankle. That sent him to the
> beach, to the hospital ship and later, hospital.

When the Anzacs' last day dawned on Gallipoli, there were
about 10,000 men in the sector, endeavouring to look as if they
had five times as many men. It wasn't easy, but the ruse appeared
to be working. Monash noted:

> The last day on Gallipoli ... last night's move passed off
> smoothly and without incident, everything satisfactory and
> well ahead of time. The weather today is absolutely perfect for
> our purposes, perfectly calm air and sea, cloudy, foggy and dull
> with a very light misty drizzle so that everything in the distance
> is dull and blurred. During the morning the Turks treated us
> to a prolonged and heavy bombardment of the beaches, but
> [it] was not intense enough to indicate that they had any suspi-
> cions, it is probably only the usual morning 'hate', but they are
> a little angrier than usual.

If the deception could be maintained for the next 24 hours,
the remaining troops, including a significant number of the Fair
Dinkums, might just get away with their lives. Part of the orders
for each of the battalion included the following:

> All movements will be made expeditiously and in absolute
> silence and the utmost care will be taken to maintain the

appearance of a normal night. No lights or smoking will be permitted and all orders will be given in an undertone. The word 'retire' must not be used. Troops will embark with 150 rounds per man, iron rations and water bottles filled. Socks are to be distributed for use by men in the firing line. These are to be drawn over boots.

Every precaution was taken to ensure the enemy was not engaged, and had no concept of what the Anzacs were aiming to achieve.

On this, the 239th and last day at Anzac, many of the Originals tended to the graves of their fallen friends. The crosses that marked their resting places were spruced up; anything that resembled a flower was placed on them and many one-sided conversations were had. Guilt mixed with loss, from men who had endured more than they could have imagined only a year before.

The Fair Dinkums felt out of place. They had seen men die in the 24 days they had been there, but nowhere near the appalling numbers from earlier in the campaign. And other than a few close scraps, some stray bullets and sickness, all of them had pulled through so far.

General Birdwood came ashore on the last day to oversee some of the preparations and to provide morale to the remaining troops. One soldier, casting an eye over a series of crosses signifying the graves of men who would never be leaving, said to Birdwood: 'I hope *they* won't hear us marching down the deres [gullies]'.

Scurry and Lawrence worked feverishly to ensure their contraptions were ready for operation, and enlisted other Fair Dinkums to help them, including Percy Brunning, the St Kilda nurseryman, tailor Reg Scowcroft, Wally Day from Brunswick and Milton Clews, who had promised months earlier to avenge the death of his friend Fred Bayles. Others helping out included a bomb-throwing team with Alf Layfield and Bill Mills. Many of the remaining men on the peninsula and most of the Fair Dinkums knew of the drip-rifle. Scurry had been a relative newcomer to the campaign, but had made his mark. They figured if his contraption worked, he might even play a part in one of the most significant evacuations in modern military history.

Monash made a note in his diary, saying, 'We have a clever device for firing off a rifle automatically at any predetermined time after the device is started.'

According to the 7th Battalion's unit diary, at around 5 pm on the last day, as darkness fell, the first of three waves of soldiers (A party) took their leave. A group of six officers and 224 other ranks left in five-minute intervals, overseen by Major Arthur Hart. The B party, a group of four officers and 90 men, were next, and started leaving at 9.35 pm. The final party, known as C, were scheduled to move swiftly but silently from the trenches after 2 am. After the second-last batch left, there were only around 1500 men remaining, and here came the greatest danger. Any hint of the evacuation to the Turks could potentially see the thin line of Anzacs overrun in a matter of minutes, and the exit from the beach would be as bloody as the landing. A touch of luck, some strict adherence to the plans, and the pluck and bravery of the remaining men all combined to ensure that nothing was left to chance and that things ran to plan.

The 7th Battalion rear party consisted of 106 men. One of the last men left near Silt Spur was Percy Brunning, who recalled the tension of the night for the remainder of his life:

I was posted alongside one of the famous 'Bill Scurry rifles' during the night of the evacuation from Anzac ... I was instructed to fire an occasional round, and the Bill Scurry Rifle would take over after we had withdrawn. Cosy with my feet muffled with strips of blankets, I actually fell asleep with my face resting on my rifle butt when I was awakened by the patrolling sergeant 4 Pl D Coy. His sharp reminder that I could be shot at dawn for such a serious offence sure kept me awake . . .

Never mind that if Brunning was still on the Gallipoli Peninsula by dawn, there was a fair chance he would be shot anyway – by the enemy – as the rest of the Anzacs would be gone. Word came through just after 2 am that it was time to leave the line. At five-minute intervals, men departed in darkness, determined not to do anything that would unduly raise suspicion.

Scowcroft was there. Seven months later, when he was once more in mortal danger, those who knew him recalled that 'he was one of the one hundred picked men who were the last to leave Gallipoli on evacuation'. Apprehension was everywhere. Wally Day never forgot how 'we had to bind our feet . . . reek [ammonia] into our cloth and hold it on our mouths. If anyone coughed or looked like coughing, a gun would be held to your head'.

Six of Scurry's drip-rifles had been set up in the area, with a total of 50 strategically placed along more than 400 metres of the line. In between departure intervals, Major Jackson instructed Scurry to head off to pour the water into his drip-rifles. As nervous as he had ever been, far more than before a big footy match for the Ascot Vale Rovers, or when he had first came ashore on Anzac Cove, Scurry and his mate Bunty Lawrence set off on their mission.

Their role in Gallipoli folklore had begun. As *Our Dear Old Battalion* detailed:

Scurry set off to the right, while Lawrence went left towards Lone Pine to add water to the jam-tins. By this time the underground trench to Lone Pine was in total darkness, but the fire steps where the rifles had been set up had fortunately been marked with luminous paint, and cans of water had been left to fill the jam-tins.

Scurry had thought of every possible detail. He even ensured that the drip-rifles would be next to useless to the Turks after the evacuation. But there remained the fear of being isolated from the few remaining men on the peninsula as he went around adding water to the drip-rifles, a feeling that was still with him years later when he recalled:

The 7th 'C' party was divided into eight sections. The section on each flank where 'Buntie' and I were posted was to retire first, and so on, until the line was empty. At the time when the last men would be moving down Lady Galway Road we were to start operating the rifles moving towards the outlet. On the left, where I was posted, the Turks were fairly close, so we had the drip set longer there, and after I saw the men leave the rifle pit on the flank, I stood alone in that black tunnel for 15 minutes. White moonlight through the entrances to the rifle possies made it all the more gruesome, and it was a very frightened lad who at last started to fill the water cabs. Lt. [James] Bowtrell-Harris was waiting at the head of Lady Galway, and I knew when he silently followed me out that 'Buntie' must be clear, and we found him with the rest of the 'C' party under Major [Alf] Jackson, outside the tunnel and we started. Orders were to move smartly, but not to run, and it took considerable self-control to stick to the latter part. I wondered then, and often since, if any unfortunate 'Jacko' [Turk] got hit with one of those bullets [from one of his drip-rifles], as it would have been the depth of stiffness.

They made the journey down to North Beach, the last group of the 7th Battalion that had served with such distinction since the start of the campaign, arriving at around 3.15 am. Lawrence would forever have vivid recollections of that walk to the beach:

down a maze of tracks and past empty dugouts which a few days before had been so alive. We all had several thicknesses of blanket under our boots to ensure that movement was sound-less, and our fixed bayonets were covered with strips of hessian so that they would not gleam in the moonlight. The walk took about an hour, I think [it was actually less than that] and we neither saw nor heard any movement or sound save our own. One solitary officer was stationed at the pier when we arrived. Apart from the sound of occasional Turkish rifle and the crack-ling of a fire burning about 50 yards from the beach, the night was still and silent.

The thing that stuck with Scurry from that night was not the precision of the operations or his part in the final moments of the campaign, but the 'the moon gleaming on those little white crosses we were leaving down in the valley . . . it hurt, hurt hard to do it [leave]'. But he said:

> The discipline of our fellows was perfect. Nobody had any sense of failure, or defeat. The boys were as quiet as ghosts while we moved down in the moonlight to the beach. The only regret we had was when we passed the graves of those who we had to leave behind. We would have liked to have taken them with us.

Within minutes, Scurry and Lawrence and the rest of the men were aboard a small double-decker craft, 'The lower deck was full so we berthed on the top one. About three more small parties of about a dozen men arrived within minutes and at 4am we cast off.' It was one of the last boats to leave Anzac, with Lawrence observing:

> Dawn comes very quickly . . . and by the time we were a quarter of a mile out to sea, the beach and the pier behind us were clearly visible, and our transport *Abbassia* just as clear further out waiting for us. The big gamble had paid off, and how simple it looked in retrospect. It could have been a

peacetime military exercise – one of those 'nobody knows who wins' because there is no enemy. But how close to disaster was it? The very night after we left, the weather broke, and Gen Birdwood was to later pine that had it happened at the same time the previous day, 3000 men would still have been there the following morning, while it is not clear to me how the other 7000 would have got off. And we know from Naval reports that at 7.15 on the morning of the last phase, Turkish shelling had stopped and Turks were swarming over our Anzac defences.

Explosions planted near the Turkish frontline at the Nek were set off and lit the night sky with a ferocity that Monash, watching from out on the water, noted: 'and so ended the story of the Anzacs on Gallipoli ... [the evacuation] was a most brilliant conception, brilliantly organised, and brilliantly executed – and will, I am sure, rank as the greatest joke in the whole range of military history'. As Carlyon said: 'It was certainly a masterpiece. At 4.10 am it was complete. An hour later the Turks were still shooting at ghosts. There had only been two casualties: one man wounded early in the evening, another hit in the arm by a spent bullet as he left the beach'.

In time, decades down the track, some questioned how much the Turks knew of the Anzacs' plans. Debate also focused on how effective Scurry's drip-rifle had been in the swift and successful ruse on the enemy, and whether it deserved its place in Gallipoli folklore. But what can never be denied, or even debated, was the symbolism of Scurry's ingenuity, the pride his fellow Fair Dinkums had in him, and what the unusual contraption meant to the men who had served on the peninsula. Scurry had wanted to make a difference, and on that measure, he had done that, and more. As Lawrence, Scurry and the rest of the rear guard sailed away, they knew that none of them would ever be the same again.

A sense of adventure and duty drove the original Anzacs to enlist. The Fair Dinkums had no such illusions. Despite appalling casualty lists coming out of Gallipoli, propaganda posters asked young Australians to help their mates. It was a call to arms only the bravest would answer.

Top left: The first stop for the Fair Dinkums was Seymour Camp. There the 152 reinforcements, including 18-year-old Alf Layfield (front right), forged the first bonds that would endure for the rest of their lives.

Top right: The Fair Dinkums sailed to war from Port Melbourne on 26 August 1915 aboard the *Anchises*, receiving a heartfelt farewell from family, friends and well-wishers. They knew as they trudged up the gangway that they would not return until the enemy had been defeated.

Greetings from Egypt

Above: Arriving at training camps in Egypt en route to the Dardanelles, the Dinkums detailed their experiences in postcards home, speaking of wonders in an ancient land far removed from their own.

Left: The Fair Dinkums sailed across restless waters to Gallipoli on the night of 25 November 1915 for the first time, alongside the 7th Battalion 'Originals' returning to the peninsula.

Above: Anzac Cove in the month the Fair Dinkums began their time in the trenches.

Below: A snow-caked White Gully four days after the Dinkums arrived at Gallipoli. Frostbite from freezing winter conditions posed as much threat to the Diggers' health as the enemy.

MELBOURNE, THURSDAY EVENING, DECEMBER 16, 1915.

NORTH RICHMOND BROTHERS DEFEND EMPIRE'S CAUSE

Pte. HAROLD MURCUTT

Sgt. F. C. MURCUTT

Pte. BRUCE MURCUTT

Pte. W. C. MURCUTT

Pte. JACK MURCUTT

Pte. J. W. J. MURCUTT

In Richmond, they called them 'the Fighting Murcutts', but in France they were brothers fighting for their country. This extraordinary family of seven sons and seven daughters provided six Anzacs. Bruce was one of three under-age Dinkums to enlist. Days before the Gallipoli evacuation, Melbourne's *Herald* claimed: 'The whole male family are natural born horsemen and . . . with the rifle, they are reputed to be able to remove the eye of a mosquito at anything under 550 yards.'

AUSTRALASIAN POST, 6 JUNE 1963 / COURTESY OF THE SCURRY FAMILY

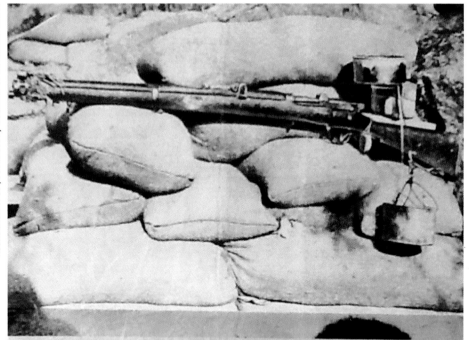

L: The rifle is the one issued to a had to leave it on Gallipoli, but the magazine.

W: Captain W , M.C., D.C.M., improvisation thousands of alian lines.

His "GHOST RIFLE" saved the Anzacs

★ THE young Australian soldier was feeling pretty scared. It was that kind of night. Cold, with a pale moonlight filtering through the firing slits into the covered trench where he was working — alone.

He was writing a unique chapter of Australia's war history — and earning himself a Distinguished Conduct Medal in the process. But he was unaware of these things.

He had thoughts only for the job in hand. Get it done and get out — quickly! And quietly . . .

The young soldier was Lance-Corporal Bill Scurry, of 7 Infantry Battalion AIF. He was 20 years old.

The date was December 19, 1915. A raw night, the air bitter with the hint of the frigid conditions which would soon grip the Gallipoli Peninsula.

From the Turkish lines there came spasmodic fire, with here and there a shot fired in return from the Anzac trenches dug deep into the high ground overlooking the beach.

That had been the pattern of events for many nights, but this night was different.

Men were moving quietly down the slopes, walking with muffled boots on the freshly-dug earth of the trenches. Walking in silence. There was no conversation, no jangling of equipment, no unnecessary haste.

The evacuation of Gallipoli was in its final stages, with the Turks unaware that the great operation had even begun!

Careful planning and absolute

disciplined co-operation had been necessary to deceive the Turks. The shambles which would inevitably have followed if the Turks had realised the situation does not bear thinking about.

Now it was nearly over. Soon the last soldier would have reached the beach and been taken out to one of the waiting ships that for some time after the last one had left, the Turks would continue to notice the sporadic rifle-fire from the deserted positions.

Continued on page 1

Australasian POST, June 6, 1963—Page

Nineteen-year-old Dinkum Bill Scurry signed up for war wanting to make a difference. The ingenuity of his drip-rifle – a self-firing mechanism that tricked the Turks into believing the Diggers were still in the trenches – ensured the last AIF soldiers evacuated Gallipoli with barely a casualty. The device helped win Scurry a Distinguished Conduct Medal and a unique place in Anzac folklore. Commander of the 7th Battalion, 'Pompey' Elliott, hailed Scurry as 'a military genius'.

ALF LAYFIELD

GUS LAFARGUES

BERTIE SOUTHWELL

BILL SCURRY

FRANK DIXON

PERCY BRUNNING

BERTIE KNIGHT

EDWARD SPOONER

JOSEPH BELLESINI

REG SCOWCROFT

ROBERT MACKENZIE

WALDEMAR MORTENSEN

BILL BATSON

WALTER JUDD

BILL WALKER

FRED HOAD

GEORGE RAE

BILL CAMPBELL

LES WOOD

MILTON CLEWS

PHILLIP BELLINGHAM

ROY ANDERSON

RAY ROHNER

WAL KING

Left & top row: Dinkum Bill Campbell was determined to record as much of his war experience as possible, capturing Egypt's bustling waterways in late 1915 and early 1916 with his own camera.

Below: As AIF casualties mounted, sustaining an all-volunteer force became increasingly difficult for Australia's small population. Despite propaganda posters like this, recruitment had slumped by mid-1916. Prime Minister Billy Hughes staged conscription plebiscites on 28 October 1916 and 20 December 1917, hoping to compel citizens to serve. The nation voted 'No' both times.

Above: As commander of the 7th Battalion and later of the 15th Brigade, Brigadier General Harold 'Pompey' Elliott shaped the Dinkums' destinies. A Boer War veteran, his military prowess and capacity to keep order was legend. Here he surveys his men in Alexandria, Egypt, from his beloved black charger 'Darkie'.

Below: Official Australian photographer Frank Hurley's iconic image from the Western Front shows the 7th Battalion near Ypres, marching to the front trenches to relieve their brother diggers. Their comrades' attack the previous day secured Broodseinde Ridge and furthered Australia's advance.

Left: Allied medics and German prisoners tend to the wounded on the Menin Road, 20 September 1917. The Ypres offensive was the end of the road for many Fair Dinkums.

Below: Bill Scurry's serious eye injury from an exploding German 'Rum Jar' bomb would have stopped lesser men, but he was determined to continue serving. Scurry (front left) was an instructor at the 1st Anzac Corps School, where this photo was taken in 1918, but he yearned to return to the frontlines. He got his wish before war's end.

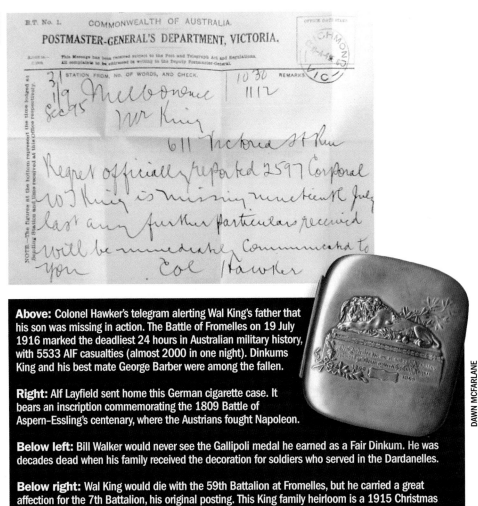

Above: Colonel Hawker's telegram alerting Wal King's father that his son was missing in action. The Battle of Fromelles on 19 July 1916 marked the deadliest 24 hours in Australian military history, with 5533 AIF casualties (almost 2000 in one night). Dinkums King and his best mate George Barber were among the fallen.

Right: Alf Layfield sent home this German cigarette case. It bears an inscription commemorating the 1809 Battle of Aspern-Essling's centenary, where the Austrians fought Napoleon.

Below left: Bill Walker would never see the Gallipoli medal he earned as a Fair Dinkum. He was decades dead when his family received the decoration for soldiers who served in the Dardanelles.

Below right: Wal King would die with the 59th Battalion at Fromelles, but he carried a great affection for the 7th Battalion, his original posting. This King family heirloom is a 1915 Christmas card, naming the locations on the peninsula where the battalion served.

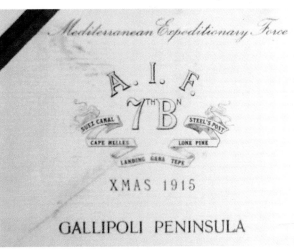

Above: The men of the 7th shared a bond that lasted the rest of their lives. This 1919 reunion was one of many to reunite the surviving Fair Dinkums and keep alive the spirit of lost mates.

Below: Bill Scurry's contribution to the Fair Dinkums legend didn't end with his famous drip-rifle. His many honours included the Military Medal, a Distinguished Conduct Medal and an audience with King George V. A greater prize was won on the ship home where Scurry met Doris Barry, an Adelaide nurse. They married in 1920 and were together until his death in 1963.

8

Birth of the Pup Battalion

*'I'm still in the old 7th . . . I'm glad in a way, but in a
way I'm not – all my mates have gone to the 59th.'*

BEFORE THEIR TIME ON Gallipoli the Fair Dinkums were
a group of inexperienced soldiers eager to prove themselves to the
battle-hardened 7th Battalion. After the evacuation, they became
a rusted-on part of the unit that Pompey Elliott described, with
admitted bias, as 'the best regiment in the Australian army'. They
had performed as well as could be expected in the three-and-
a-bit weeks they had been on the peninsula, and for eight days
had been in the line of fire. One of them had produced a device
that assisted in the successful evacuation – some later boasted that
Bill Scurry was 'the man who fooled the Turkish Army' – and
a number of the Fair Dinkums were in the last boats that pulled
away from shore.

The evacuation of Gallipoli was everything the landings
were not – thoroughly planned and exceptionally executed,
with only a handful of casualties. Brudenell White's meticulous

planning, and the soldiers who carried out orders and operations with discretion and devotion ensured its safe conclusion.

More than 8000 Australians were killed as part of the Gallipoli campaign, but those who survived it were more unified than ever. If the Fair Dinkums had been close since their enlistment and training, their experiences further solidified that bond. They pledged to stick together. As Charles Bean wrote of the Anzacs who had returned from Gallipoli:

> They were a military force with strongly established, definite traditions. Not for anything, if he could avoid it, would an Australian now change his loose, faded tunic or battered hat for the smartest cloth or headgear of any other army. Men clung to their Australian uniforms till they were tattered to the limit of decency.

Having thought for much of 1915 that they would be spending Christmas on Gallipoli, the soldiers instead found themselves back on Lemnos. Those who had been evacuated earlier by relief transport had already set up base at Sarpi Camp, and on arrival Scurry and the rear party, including Milton Clews, marched out to join the rest of the 7th Battalion members. Clews wrote to his sister to tell her that he had survived Gallipoli and was spending Christmas on Lemnos:

> Well Emily, I got safely back from the Peninsula, only being there about five weeks [it was just under four weeks], but I only had 8 days in the firing line. I suppose you'll have all heard about the evacuation by the time you get this letter. I can't say anything about it except that we [were] in the last batch to leave, being in the firing up to the last hour, but I'm pleased to say we got away without any casualty. We left for Lemnos the same night and when we got there we received a big mail, not having had a letter for about a month. I got four

letters from you . . . also two from mother and several letters from England.

Clews devoured the news from home, and tucked into the hearty meals now on offer. He relished having a decent wash, since water was a premium at Gallipoli, 'We couldn't get any [thing] to drink, or even enough for a shave. When we had the snow, we used to fill our water bottles with snow and ice, and let it melt. That's all over now, though we can get plenty of water here, and plenty to eat.' This new dinkum from Derbyshire posted home a battalion Christmas card that showed 'all the battles printed on and our colours in the corner'. The Mud and Blood colours meant something now – and they would forever.

There were many reunions on Lemnos. The Mills brothers from Gordon near Ballarat thought they would be fighting side by side on Gallipoli, but nineteen-year-old Gordie's venereal disease, likely contracted in the back lanes of Cairo, meant he never made that trip. He wrote to his father about how he was now well and that 'Brother Bill is back from the Peninsula – he never got a scratch'. Nor did Bill let on about his brother's condition when writing home. Now back in the relative safety of Lemnos, he told a friend in his hometown of the short but not insignificant role the Fair Dinkums had played at Gallipoli.

'Saw a bit of the real thing while I was in the trenches; the Turks did not throw oranges at us,' Mills wrote.

They were out for game and very often got it; but were soon paid back with interest. They fight very fair anyhow. I was one of the last to leave the trenches. I was a bomb thrower in a party of 15. It was 2.30am when we left the trenches. The worst part was to see our comrades' graves as we passed. Jack, my brother, was killed on the 9th of last August. I think George has met the same fate. I cannot get any word about him. Paddy is here – have not seen him yet.

His pride was evident when he wrote to his father:

The evacuation of the peninsula by the Australian army was a
clever piece of work. I was one of the last to leave, as I was one
of the party of bomb throwers who helped to cover the retreat.
Not a mishap; in fact I don't think 'Allah' knew anything about
it for a couple of days. We were well back on Lemnos Island by
that time.

The death of his brother, Jack, in August, while serving with
the New Zealand Army, affected him deeply: 'I was sorry to
hear of poor Jack's death. I couldn't find out anything about him
at the New Zealand Base – they are not nearly as good as our
own. Gordie is well. I am keeping well, only my teeth are going
bung on me'.

Besides letter-writing and catching up with mail they had
not received for a month, the Fair Dinkums settled quickly back
into camp life, taking the opportunity to have some welcome
respite from training and reorganising new reinforcements.
But with the down time came some officers' worry of sliding
standards and discipline. As such, the superiors kept a keen eye
on anyone who looked like deviating, even slightly, from the
required behaviour or getting themselves into trouble.

Three of the Fair Dinkums learnt the hard way about
the crackdown the day after the last group arrived from the
evacuation in the early afternoon of 21 December 1915. A group
of seven privates, six from the 7th Battalion and one from the
8th, converged around a blue boat owned by a Greek fisherman
that was moored on the edge of Mudros. Three of them had
been part of the 8th Reinforcements of the 7th Battalion – a
bush dinkum (23-year-old hairdresser George Wood), a city
dinkum (eighteen-year-old Harold Addison, an electrician
from Glenferrie), and a new dinkum (Bert Thomas, originally from Shropshire, but of late, a labourer from Ascot Vale).

From his tent in the distance, General John Forsyth saw the men loitering around the boat and decided to act. As court-martial documents reveal, Forsyth called out to an officer, Captain Alfred Derham, that something needed to be done to bring the men into order. Derham went down to the beach and called the men ashore with Forsyth saying: 'At the time . . . most of the men were in the boat and it is my belief that the remainder were handling the boat and if not actually handling the boat, they were quite close to it'.

The men were charged with the unusual offence of 'when on active service committing an offence against the property of a resident of the country in which [they] were serving'. Each of the men pleaded 'not guilty' and denied interfering with the boat. When Captain Derham was called as a witness at the court-martial that followed, he admitted he had been keen to simply warn the men, but that General Forsyth urged him to wait until the men were engaged in the act. He documented:

> I said to [General Forsyth], 'Shall I call them back?' He said: 'No, wait until they get in the boat', or words to that effect. I then waited in the vicinity of the beach until all the men concerned had gathered in or around the boat and had pushed the boat a short distance, namely about 2 yards towards the deep water. I then went down to the edge of the beach and called out to them to come ashore, which they did.

One of the men explained they had planned to take the boat out to the harbour to go aboard a ship to get stores, though only one could produce a pass signed by Major Arthur Hart allowing them to be absent from the camp. Four days before the end of the most eventful year of all of their lives, Wood, Addison and Thomas were found guilty at a court-martial and had to forfeit 90 days' pay. All were shattered by the stain against their name, their frustration only alleviated in mid-February the following year when the penalty was quashed due to 'irregularities in the conduct of [the] court martial'.

The arrival of the Christmas billies from Australia were well received. A few of the billies had maps of Gallipoli enclosed with the message: 'This bit of land belongs to us'. That was enough to bring a moment of reflection for some. Clews sent season's greetings back to his adopted home:

> We got our Xmas billies and plum pudding here and they were all right after the bully [beef] and biscuits we'd been getting on the peninsula. I can tell you what I got in my billy – two tins of tobacco, chewing gum, a pair of socks, cocoa, writing paper, [a] book, [a] game, chocolates, safety pins, etc, a very useful assortment. We are also getting a plum pudding between two.

Layfield apologised to his mother for his delay in writing:

> I suppose you wonder what is the matter with me not writing, but it is not my fault. We were not allowed to write. The last letter I wrote to you was from Gallipoli. I thought we were going to have Christmas on Gallipoli, but we left a week before and went back to Lemnos . . . We got our Christmas billies . . . full of useful things, we have chocolate and lots of things sent to us. We get as much tobacco as we can smoke. I never felt better.

He had rarely been away from home a night before enlisting, and now he had just spent his first Christmas away from his family.

The men enjoyed Christmas Day off – a 'fine sunny day' – by taking part in a church parade and a march past General Chauvel. It was a day to remember, and while they celebrated away from the guns, they hoped and prayed their loved ones on the other side of the world were having as peaceful and prosperous a time of it.

The conditions at Sarpi Camp were 'luxurious', according to Bunty Lawrence:

> We now had an unlimited water supply, one which allowed us not only to bathe and shave, but to boil the singlet that had been the habitant of so many uninvited guests. We were also having hot meals – even bread and butter – and by army standards were being well fed. Our chores by day were few, and we could sleep the sleep of the just in tents warm and dry. We had been paid, and although there was little opportunity for spending, there was always the two-up school to attract custom. But the big thrill was the mail from home – the first in six weeks – and then the Xmas billy with its 'blind date' letter and sometimes a photo of the lovely girl who had packed a billy for no one in particular.

The excitement in the tents on the presentation of the billies 'could only be likened to a family of kids on finding that Santa had been. One of the chaps who had done quite well at the two-up school bought two beaut cigars, and with his mate proceeded to celebrate, lighting them up with a 1 pound note'.

Christmas Day was especially good for Robert Haysey, who began to recover from pleurisy in time for his pudding on 25 December. He had been 'dumped' at the hospital after the evacuation, where 'I was very bad for five days', he recounted. 'My temperature was 103.4. On Xmas Day, I started to get better; had some nice presents from Australia, and was lucky to get a sixpence out of the sister's pud.'

Others were not so lucky. A host of the Fair Dinkums were too sick to celebrate Christmas, bed-bound in hospital with various illnesses from Gallipoli. Some of them never fought again, other than against the influenza, rheumatism and heart conditions brought on by the campaign, or the paratyphoid that plagued them for the rest of the war and, for some, the rest of their lives.

Roy Anderson recorded in his diary on 23 December: 'Ray Eaton, R Rohner, H Knight in hospital influenza'. Rohner hadn't made it to Gallipoli due to his illness, Eaton had first experienced sickness on Anzac but took ill again with enteric on Lemnos, and Knight had fallen sick. By the end of the next month, Anderson was also taken ill with enteric fever and influenza. They were not the only ones: joining them were Hugh McKenzie (rheumatism), Frederick Mann (para-typhoid), Wilfred 'Bill' Williams (rheumatism), George Woods (influenza), Walter Leigh (influenza/heart condition), Harold Addison (tonsilitis), Syd Davies (heart disease), and Richard McClelland (influenza).

Scurry received plenty of attention after the evacuation for his drip-rifle. While ambitious, he was a modest young man, and only when he felt it was appropriate did he write to his family about the moment that changed his life, saying, almost in passing: 'There are a couple of newspaper cuttings enclosed which you might like to see where I am accused of ingenuity. Sounds funny, doesn't it'. He also sent home the:

> magazine from my rifle, which I left on the parapet at Anzac. It was a good rifle, but I had rigged it for an experiment so I did not take it down. The rest left there were old rifles, well smashed about the sights and nose caps and with magazines taken out, so that they would be of no use to the enemy. I would like you to keep it as a curio, and to remind me of things when I get home.

He had no doubt he would make it home. He couldn't really explain it, he just knew. Besides, he was engaged to be married, and Scurry was nothing if not a disciple to discipline, order and responsibility.

Scurry, Lawrence and two other Fair Dinkums used the second half of their 'day off' to explore the island of Lemnos:

One day while there we had a holiday, 'Buntie' and I, and two other chaps went for a climb. The island is a hilly sort of place. The highest peak is called Turks' Head and is about nine miles from the place where we are camped. On the way up we went to a Greek church just outside one of the villages . . . Round the back of the church is a small stone building full of the bones and clothes of the inhabitants who were victims to a Turkish massacre, needless to say we have seen enough skulls lately, so we passed on our way. We climbed up a pretty stiff hill on the way, and sat on the top, in the shelter of a little prayer house, and boiled our billy. When we sat down in the sun and ate sardine sandwiges [sic], I forget how to spell it, but I mean sardines between tips of bread. Then we had some tinned peaches with condensed milk on them, and cocoa to wash it all down. A terrible war, isn't it!

The first day of 1916, for all of the hope and optimism it was meant to bring, produced a miserable wet afternoon that the men hoped was not an omen for the year ahead.

'Very wet,' recorded Roy Anderson. But it did bring with it an order that the battalion would be on the move the following day, with news of a return to Egypt not especially celebrated by the troops who had grown weary of its scorching sun and searing sands.

The men went aboard the *Empress of Britain* along with the 8th Battalion, almost 1000 British troops, and the headquarters of the 1st and 2nd Divisions in the early morning of 4 January, sailing for Alexandria. Clews scrawled assiduously in his diary, 'It is a fine big boat and there's 5000 aboard.' Rohner, thankful to be back again with the Fair Dinkums, noted the precautions in place on the water: 'All lights out at 6 o'clock. No smoking between 5pm and 7am'. There were fears of enemy vessels in the water, or worse still, enemy submarines, with Scurry glad that after having 'made our mad dash across the water' that they had encountered 'no tinned fish . . . so here we are on sand again'.

So it was with a sense of relief that the journey ended safely in Alexandria not long after breakfast on 6 January. After dis-embarkation, the men of the 7th Battalion were whisked away on trains to the little town of Tel-el-Kabir. Men with a feel for military history, including Scurry, knew of the location, which was a little under halfway between Cairo and the Suez Canal, as it had been the site of the famous battle between the British and the Egyptian Army in 1882. Some of the trenches could still be seen from that long-gone battle, which killed 57 British troops and almost 2000 Egyptians.

There wasn't much else to do, but engage in training. Wal King explained: 'We are camped in a much quieter place than Zeitoun now and there is no going into towns like Cairo at night'. In the same letter home, he expressed a view that the Anzacs had little time for their British equivalents, saying: 'What has surprised me perhaps more than anything else is the British Tommy. He is not greatly as big as our chaps and by his appearance, not nearly as able to stand the hard chaps that our fellows can stand. Our chaps don't think as much of the Tommies'.

When noting before the Gallipoli evacuation that Austral-ian soldiers did not have 'the slightest confidence in Kitchener's army – nor have our officers – nor have I', historian Charles Bean had made the same observation of the differences between the Anzacs and the Tommies:

> the truth is after 100 years of breeding in slums, the British race is not the same [as] in the days of Waterloo . . . the only hope is that those puncy narrow-chested little men, if they come out to Australia or N.Z., or Canada, within two genera-tions breed men again.

Tel-el-Kabir was hardly a comfortable initiation for Rohner and his mates. On the first night in camp, they were 'sleeping out in the open' when a horse managed to get loose and trampled 'over the top of us'. Fortunately, no one was injured, but it didn't help that it rained the entire night. The next month saw plenty more rain, with Layfield saying the 'outlandish place' in which they were based was prone to rapid dumps from the sky with barely any warning:

> When we first came to Egypt they used to say, 'Oh it never rains in Egypt', but we have had any amount of it lately. The other day we were out about a mile and a half from camp and it came down all of a sudden, we were wet right through. The rain don't give as much warning as it does in Melbourne.

Twenty-eight-year-old Waldemar Mortensen had fought at Gallipoli as John Shaw to cover up his past and to also try to mask his heritage that sounded a little too German for its own good (it was actually Danish). His estranged mother, Olive, was desperate to track him down from the other side of the world. As Mortensen was settling into Tel-el-Kabir, Olive was pleading with Australian Army officials to locate her son. On 7 January 1916, she wrote:

> I have reason to believe [John Sydney Shaw] is my youngest son. [His] Father served in the Sudan Contingent but are death [sic]. Please if anything should happen to him would you kindly inform me as I am his widow mother would be so grateful [sic]. [I] have not seen him for the last 7 years as he have [sic] been a seafaring man. He is of Danis[h] Parent [sic].

She followed up with countless other letters, explaining:

> I never thought it necasery [sic] to explain the nationality to my boys until now, in fact all the family . . . (we) have relations

145

all over. I leaf [sic] it to the Military to do as is right as I do not understand but pray that God will bless him to do right in his duty he has undertaken.

She persisted with her correspondence, determined that the next time her son went into battle that he would do so under his real name.

The return to Egypt was not without its share of danger. It was feared that, unburdened by a battle on the Gallipoli Peninsula, the Turkish Army could strike at the Suez Canal or elsewhere. General Birdwood 'expected a powerful attack within six weeks', so there was little surprise when word came through late in January 1916 that the 7th Battalion was on the move again. On the first day of February, the Fair Dinkums took a train across the desert to a camp at Serapeum on the east bank of the canal. The day before departure, the unit diary stated:

> The month has ended after an experience which we have not had for a long time and that is a complete battalion working at full strength. The keen but good natured rivalry between companies in regards to the keeping of their respective lines in order was grand, and the true comradeship that existed between the officers, the NCOs and men with their field training and camp life showed that . . . everyone tried 'to do his bit' for the honour of the Regiment, Brigade and Country.

A significant amount of reinforcements from Australia – those who never had the chance to go to Gallipoli – boosted the numbers, though sickness cut through the ranks, with many of the Fair Dinkums already slated for an early departure home because of illness, including Fred Mann, the twenty-year-old tinsmith, who was struck down with paratyphoid on Lemnos. A medical board hearing in Heliopolis on 21 January 1916 decided to send Mann back to Australia to recuperate. Even as he was departing for Australia in early February, he told his mates he would be back.

The rewards for his hard work were starting to come for Scurry. 'My rank is now Sergeant, but the Colonel has given me a hint there is a star on the horizon, so that's alright,' he wrote home. 'I will probably be making a new allotment soon, that will mean more money to be banked.'

By the very next letter, he could add, 'On parade I was called up to the General, and the little star is on its way, in fact, you can now address the letters to 2nd Lt Scurry B Coy 7th Battalion, and it does not matter how often you write them.'

The one thing he couldn't tell his parents was where he and the Fair Dinkums were based, but he gave more than a few hints:

We are now on the [Suez] Canal somewhere between Port Suez and Port Said, but exactly where I can't say. We are in a very sandy desert about half a mile on the Asiatic side of the canal, to which we occasionally go for a swim, which is a great thing. How long we will be here, and what we have to do, I don't know, but the sand is very sandy and we eat it in large amounts. When I get home they will be able to chip me off like a waste mould and find a cement cast of my inside. The work is going on very well, I have a class of the junior NCOs of the Battalion and am also a scouting instructor so that I am going pretty hard all the time, being out at night with the scouts and working all day with the NCOs class.

Part of the scouting included becoming acquainted with the stars of the northern hemisphere. In a letter to one of his sisters, he explained:

I do not know where we would be without some knowledge of them when we are away out in the desert, miles from anywhere. Nearly all the stars here are new to us . . . but there are a few which appear above good old home also . . . All these stars are named from Arabic mythology and the men who named them were either drunk or they had a very good imagination. The Arabic name for Orion is 'El-Gubba', meaning the tyrant. When you see him up in the sky, you can think that somewhere in the desert, that same Orion is helping brother Bill to find his way about.

Eaglehawk's Harry Attwood had a chance meeting with General Birdwood one day in February 1915 while digging trenches near the canal:

While on the bank, General Birdwood passed and asked me if I thought I was at Anzac digging trenches again. I think I saw him smile. I answered him, saying 'Oh no, there is nothing flying about overhead'. He cheered me by saying 'there might *soon be* something?' I suppose we will soon be in the midst of it before very long.

Still, he relished:

a few good swims in the Suez Canal. No other chance of a wash – only a water bottle full each day for washing, shaving and drinking. Of course, the canal water is salt and one couldn't use soap. To look across the sand and see a great ship apparently steaming through it seemed strange at first, but we got used to it. Sometimes in the night when the ships mostly went through we heard Australian cooees. For about eleven weeks we have been camped in the desert sands, and a very poor time it has been – most uninteresting and at periods the work was stiff.

Scurry looked to the positive side of things as best as he could, noting:

We are seeing quite a lot of country. We know what the Suez
Canal looks like now, in fact, we had several swims in it, which
were very pleasant. It certainly is a most wonderful piece of
work . . . The camp here is a very fine place. All the men live
in tents, not more than ten in each one, and have huts for their
mess . . . The crowning blessing of this place is that there is an
abundance of water. There are showers rigged up and good
chance for the men to give themselves a good clean-up. I don't
suppose you really know what a lot [of] this means but I can
tell you it is a very great deal. I often think of the nice boils
I used to have on Friday nights and how hot I'll make them
in the future. I'll fill the house up with steam. The camp
roads are very good, and as we are right on the railway to
Cairo, there are plenty of canteens, where they can get pretty
nearly anything.

As much as he longed for word of an impending departure,
Clews didn't mind the work on the canal. He told his sister:

At present I am engaged with about 30 others in pulling traffic
across the canal on a punt. It is pretty heavy work but I would
rather have it than drill. Well, Emily, I think we will get a
trip to France before the war is over, also I hope to [get to]
England. We see plenty of big boats on the canal which livens
things up a bit. Also we're able to get a swim.

For Layfield, the desert was starting to get him down. His
frustration came from the fact that some of his tent mates from
training camps in Australia had shifted to other companies, and
one of them, Old Bill Mudge, had already been shipped back
home for cancer treatment. He lamented: 'All those chaps that
were in my tent at Seymour are separated into different companies now, there's only [Malcolm] McQueen, [Tom] Murphy and
myself in the same company, and we're in different platoons'.

That was the nature of war, but there were bigger changes to come as the foundations that held the Fair Dinkums together were shaken as much as Beachy Bill had done in those dying days on Gallipoli.

Shock news filtered through to the 7th Battalion on 15 February 1916 that there would be a reorganisation of the Anzac battalions before the end of the month. It meant that the battalion would be split in two, with half of them forming the newly created 59th, and the rest to stay with the 7th. General Birdwood had been faced with the issue of injecting thousands of reinforcements coming from Australia into the experienced soldiers who had fought at Gallipoli. His solution was:

> to halve the veteran battalions which had served on Gallipoli; one half would remain with the veteran battalion while the other half would form the basis of the new battalion. Then by adding 50 per cent of the reinforcements to each of the old and new battalions, the AIF would be doubled, yet still retain a significant level of experienced officers, NCOs and men in each battalion.

The issue came down to which of the men would stay with the battalion they had fought so hard for on Gallipoli, and which would have to move to the 59th Battalion. News of the forth-coming split impacted deeply on the soldiers' psyche.

That wasn't the only shock. The unit diary from that same day included the stunning news that not only was the battalion being split, it was also losing its commander, Pompey Elliott, who was heading to the 1st Brigade. As it turned out, Elliott would eventually go to the 15th Brigade instead, which would at least take the 59th Battalion – the 7th's offshoot – under his wing.

Elliott's farewell address to the troops not only highlighted his pride in the discipline and determination shown by his men, but also a plea for them to deal with the split with the same professionalism. It read in part:

It is with the utmost regret that I am obliged at length to sever any official connection with all who have served under me in this unit. You have cheerfully submitted to the severest discipline imposed on any Regiment in the Australian Army, recognising that it was imposed from no capricious desire for punishment which is distasteful to me, but with the deliberate intention of making you the best regiment in the army. I have been especially severe on absentees without leave. I have done this deliberately because, in the first instance, an absentee without leave is a shirker on those of his comrades who do his work during his absence, and as such deserves no sympathy . . . It would be boastful to assert that we have become the best Regiment in the Australian Army, but let these facts speak for themselves. Up to date we have, as shown by official records, suffered one hundred casualties in killed and wounded more than any other Battalion – one only excepted, and this we lead by over fifty – yet today there is no Regiment more efficient and ready for service than the Seventh. You have never failed to achieve any task set you, drawn up a reorganisation scheme where for a certain number of the Battalion being transferred to form the nucleus of the 59th Battalion. Though it will be hard for those named for transfer – as it is for me – to sever their connection with the Seventh, I appeal to them to put their sentiments aside and firmly resolve to make the old Seventh proud to tell that the 59th Regiment sprang from this Battalion. Let each regiment give a cheer when it meets the other in the field or on the march, and feel proud to know and recognise each other wherever they meet.

At the stroke of a pen, more than 50 of the Fair Dinkums were moved into the newly created 59th Battalion, the so-called

'Pup' Battalion of the 7th. Besides tearing apart great mates and friendships that had developed and been tested on Gallipoli, the split also had a significant bearing on the rest of the men's lives. The stroke of that pen was sometimes said to have been the reason why some men returned home from war and others didn't.

Wal King and his English-born mate George Barber were among those who were transferred to the 59th Battalion. So was Clews, his diary noting the change. Scurry and the mate he had signed up with, Arch Wardrop, were also on the move, along with Reg Scowcroft, Gus Lafargues and his new mate, Alf Mercer. Among those who went to the 59th were Bertie Southwell, Clarrie Lay, Walter Judd, Frank Whelan, Bill Campbell, Ralph Bond, Alf Honey, Frank Dixon, Walter McAsey and a host of others.

Generally, the powers-that-be allowed siblings to stay together, but best mates were often divided. The decision to split the battalions was 'a shock to regimental pride and tradition' and 'the separation was a wrench, but ever afterwards the new and old battalions, however far apart, were bound together by the strongest feeling'. The men who stayed with the 7th Battalion remained under the horizontal Mud and Blood colours; the new battalion would have the same colours, but applied vertically.

The shock even affected those who remained part of the 7th Battalion. On the day of the split, Layfield admitted he was torn between losing the mates he had served alongside and retaining the identity of the battalion he had come to love. It was hard to explain, but he tried when he next wrote to his mother, saying:

> The 7th Battalion have been split up. Half have gone to make the 59th Battalion, but I'm still in the old 7th. I'm glad in a way that I'm left behind, but in a way, I'm not. All my mates that have been with me have gone to the 59th.

One of the consolations came in the form of a 'very good gift' from the Victoria Racing Club. 'We got a nice tin with 50 Havelock cigarettes and a tin of Havelock tobacco, and a little tin of milk and butter,' he wrote. 'That was for each man, [and] it was about the best gift we have had.'

Clews accepted his move to the 59th Battalion, saying, 'You'll see that I've left the old 7th Battalion, and moved into the 59th. It's part of a new scheme they've got for mixing the old soldiers who've been to the Dardanelles under fire, up with the new reinforcements.'

Scurry headed to the 59th Battalion, but a nostalgic part of him wished it had been the 58th. He had been a part of the 58th Infantry, Essendon Rifles back in Australia, where he had first met and admired Elliott. He explained to his parents:

It is a shame we could not be the 58th again . . . we got pretty close to it, so we must just go on and make it what our old 58th used to be. The 7th Battalion was divided into two portions. One formed the 7th; the other the 59th. Both these half battalions were brought up to strength with new men from Australia, so that now there are a lot of battalions consisting of new and old men, which I think will bring excellent results. We have got a splendid lot of men in our [new] Battalion. The idea of making new battalions out of half old and half new men is in my opinion turning out as a splendid success. It was hard to leave the 7th, of course, but it has been hard to leave lots of things since the scrap started. It was hard to leave home and hard to leave those mounds of earth and crosses in the Gullies at Anzac, but it all has got to be done.

And it made it so much more manageable that Elliott was now in charge of the 15th Brigade, which oversaw the 59th Battalion, with Scurry explaining his delight with the message: 'What ho, that will do me'.

Scurry's mate, Arch Wardrop, initially joined him at the 59th Battalion. But he was soon on the move again. Scurry detailed: 'Arch came to the 59th, he is a Sergeant, unluckily "Buntie" could not come, but some day he will get a transfer if he is lucky'. Wardrop ended up joining one of the new Pioneer Battalions:

Arch is going to a new battalion which is being formed. It will be made of tradesmen of every kind and a number of labourers. The officers are nearly all technical men, such as civil engineers, surveyors, architects, master builders, etc. Arch had got very down as he was not being promoted as quickly as he would like, and it did not help him to get on in the infantry.

But Scurry was clearly getting on, with Elliott ensuring that the young man who had worked with him at the Essendon Rifles, and who had played an important role in the evacuation of Gallipoli, got the advancements he deserved. The young man from Ascot Vale confirmed:

I have got my commission. The one star shines alone once again, but I have hopes to bring it another one for company soon ... The Colonel introduced me to Brigadier General Forsythe [sic] who told me that I have been mentioned in despatches to Army Headquarters over a trigger in the evacuation ... I have got as a batman a man named [Eric] Phillips, who was in my section at Broadmeadows and has been with me all through except when he was in hospital, so I know I can thoroughly depend on him, which is very nice.

Now that the Pup Battalion had been finalised, most of the Fair Dinkums wanted to get back into action, which inevitably meant a trip to France, where the stalemate was far more devastating than what had happened on Gallipoli.

154

George Rae (G.H.) loved a scrap and hated sitting in Egypt waiting for something to happen. He had joined the army to fight, not to waste his time in the sand and sun. So when the rumours began that men were moving out to France by the end of March, a broad grin crossed his face to match his broad shoulders. In a letter to an uncle, G.H. told of how he was:

> still well and going strong. Well, old Abdul is just as far off as ever, and by all accounts they are not likely to get much closer. The notice on our board says the Russians are smashing them all up on the other side. We are moving from here in a day or two, we don't know for sure where, but we have a good idea. I would like to see France, but we are not allowed to tell where we will likely be sent. If we go to —— [deleted by the censors] there will be more than six and nine shells. They say the foundries fly at you there; so it will duck your nut there. When we are out of action, we know nothing, or next to nothing, for fear we will run amok.

G.H. didn't mind running amok, and it was clear that he had little fear. He wanted the chance to take it up to the enemy again – this time, the Germans – and he knew that meant heading off to France.

9

Somewhere in France

*'I think if we are to be killed by shells or bullets we will
never mind what happens. Every man has to be prepared for
it as he never knows what minute he is going to stop one.'*

ALF LAYFIELD COULD HARDLY have asked for a better
nineteenth birthday present, other than for the end of the war. It
was 24 March 1916, and the good news came in the form of an
order to the men of the 7th Battalion: they were to prepare to
leave for Alexandria the following day, which almost certainly
meant they were leaving Egypt for France. The news excited
Layfield, yet brought more than a hint of anxiety. It was *on* again,
only this time on a much grander scale than on the Gallipoli
Peninsula. Layfield valued this first birthday away from home,
not knowing if it would be his last. He thought of his mother
and his family every day, but more so today. He longed to be
home again, but the only way to do that was to win the war in
France. If that meant having the Anzacs do their bit, that was
good enough for the ever-smiling young man.

The splitting of the battalion saw him remain with the old 7th, but so many of his close friends had been transferred – most against their wishes – to the 59th Battalion. Layfield had been disappointed that 'half of our chaps went to make up the 59th Battalion . . . all my best mates went away, that were with me at Gallipoli. But you soon get used to the new chaps. We are just like a lot of brothers in our Platoon'. The wrench had been tough, but they dealt with it. After all, Pompey Elliott had told them that, wherever they were on the battlefield, the two battalions would see each other and give a cheer for what had been, and what was still to come. The difference, at least for now, was that the 7th Battalion was preparing to leave for the Western Front and the Pup Battalion, the 59th, would be staying in Egypt. Mates would not only be divided by battalions, but by the Mediterranean Sea.

There had been talk since the start of March that a move was forthcoming and the news, when it became reality, was received with enthusiasm. One of the men of the 7th said: 'we were all filled with joyful anticipation of the good things to be expected there, among a civilised population, with quarters in respectable billets occasionally, and also with mixed feelings at the prospect of being at last against the Germans'.

Before the men left, they managed a glimpse of Edward, Prince of Wales, the man who would one day be King. Layfield breathlessly sent word home that he had seen the future King when they were on the Suez Canal. The Prince of Wales 'rode cheerily through the camp and was heartily cheered . . . He appeared nervous upon this occasion, and quite boyish compared to the grizzly veterans of Anzac'. Those who saw him that day, and who lived to see the horrors of the next world war a generation later, would have thought it almost inconceivable that this young man would only serve 326 days as King, with his younger brother leading the empire into the next war.

On the afternoon after Layfield's birthday, the 7th Battalion left their Serapeum camp for Alexandria. It was 'a somewhat rough trip in open trucks', which took them past Ismalia and Tel-el-Kabir, and by dawn the following morning they had reached the sea port. Awaiting them was the ship *Megantic,* a 14,878-ton ocean liner that had served the Liverpool-to-Canada route before the war. The remaining Fair Dinkums of the 7th Battalion boarded immediately with the rest of their battalion and the 8th. The voyage was a pleasant change from the monotony of Egypt, though the fear of 'tinned fish' resurfaced.

The ship 'was a very large one and the accommodation exceptionally good, every man having a cabin berth', and the voyage made for an appropriate time for the medical officers to further inoculate the men aboard. 'Everyone was duly punctured, but none rightly understood what disease he was now proof against.'

One of the most exciting moments for the men came when they realised their cabins *actually* had beds. Bunty Lawrence recalled: 'Much to our delight when we got aboard this magnificent ship, we had cabins with real beds and mattresses, something we had not seen since we left home, and mother'. There was, however, one problem: the cabins had their fair share of rodents. Rats aside, this wasn't a bad way to travel, as Harry Attwood attested in letters home to his loved ones:

> I wasn't sorry we left Egypt for probably the last time – I am enjoying the trip better than any holiday I have had, I do believe. The sea is calm and the boat, of course, is steady. The air is cool and fresh. I don't think I could have ordered a better voyage. The ship, too, is a beauty, the best I have been on yet. If we were only on our way home after finishing our job properly instead of only beginning, things would just about reach perfection.

He sat on his bed as he wrote, a lifebelt around him, as the men were told to do in case of emergency:

One does not dare walk about without it [the lifebelt] . . .
I am allocated to a life boat . . . the possibility of a submarine
popping up and [up]setting our pleasant [trip] very abruptly is
ver[y] probable, quite a lot of men . . . constantly watch for a
periscope. Machine guns and guards with rifles are prepared
for instant action. So you see much is done to get out of the
trouble when it comes – in addition the ship takes a zig zag
course which makes the target to a submarine very much
harder to hit. I don't let the thought of this worry me. I haven't
seen a 'tin fish'.

In another letter, he added:

Just a few lines before landing in the danger zone . . . Am still
feeling in good form and able to do my share in the struggle.
The trip across the Mediterranean Sea has been full of incident
+ danger in the shape of a submarine that lurks unseen. We
have to carry our lifebelts with us everywhere we go, some
never get a yard away from theirs. Each man has been allotted
a life boat – 40 men making a load – we have to fall-in in front
of the boats two or three times a day for practice. So far, our
journey has proved safe, a destroyer which hovered around us
this morning for our protection has disappeared as we are close
to our destination. I suppose we must be pretty safe.

After a tense but ultimately uneventful journey, the *Megantic*
entered Marseilles harbour late on the afternoon of 31 March
1916. Attwood acknowledged: 'Almost by magic, it seems we
find ourselves in France, where they eat frogs'. The previous
evening had been rough, and many of the men were seasick,
bringing back unpleasant memories of those first few days on
the *Anchises*. A change came over the soldiers, though, when
they saw the famous French harbour for the first time, 'green
hills rising from the sea to great heights, white houses with

red roof gleaming among the trees, dazzling sunlight dancing on the calm waters of the bay, all combined to make a joyous picture', its beauty tempered, if only marginally, by the realities of war on the wharves where 'the indications of warfare, war material, anti-aircraft guns and German prisoners at war' were sobering reminders that the 7th Battalion was not here for a holiday. There was work to be done – and it would be dangerous work – so the men of the Fair Dinkums had to be ready for whatever was coming their way.

Regrettably, there was little time for looking around. By 7.30 pm they were on a train and ready to depart. This was not as luxurious as it sounded, and a far cry from the stately rooms of the *Megantic*. The men were squeezed into open-aired truck carriages that carried, in large print on its side, a sign that read: '*Hommes 40. Cheveaux (en long) 8*'. Quickly, the word passed around: 40 men or eight horses. Thirty-five men were crammed into each carriage. As the 7th Battalion's first history recorded: 'We soon learned to envy the "chevaux" . . . Each truck bore a grim legend, happily as yet unintelligible to most of us, but one which we were destined to know only too well in the days to come'.

For the best part of three days the men journeyed from southern France to the far north of a country in springtime, capturing the senses of men who had been so used to the sand and sun of Egypt for so long. One said:

At the first sign of dawn, the sides of the truck were let down as far as possible and we drank in the landscape with incredulous eyes. It made the profoundest impression on every one of us. Coming, as we had, from the barren, dreary sands of Egypt, the green fields of France were like glimpses into a new world to us. Eyes which had been long accustomed to the drab shores of Gallipoli, to the parched wastes of the desert, and to the uncultivated wildernesses gazed enthralled at the new scenes which unfolded before us as our train crawled north. Vistas of green fields and orchards, trim farmhouses, clean white roads, wooded hills, and pretty villages surrounded by shapely trees, were opened around us.

The journey from Marseilles to the town of Godewaersvelde near the Belgian border took almost 70 hours, but there was a further march of a little over 18 miles (30 kilometres) for the exhausted troops to the town of La Creche. At the many stops along the way, the Fair Dinkums and the rest of the 7th Battalion could barely believe the reception they had from the French community. In Egypt, so much of their dealings with the locals had been commercial enterprises, wanted or unwanted. But the French women and men (mostly men who were too old, infirmed or too young to enlist) had a very different agenda. Almost to a person, they were appreciative that the Australians had come from halfway around the world to help fight for their country. As one digger recalled:

> How excited those French people were over us Australians! They pelted us with flowers and sweets, and while no one objected to the embraces of the girls, we thought it a bit much when the men as well threw their arms around us and kissed us on both cheeks. French customs are new to us, and some of the boys thought the men were crazy.

Women handed out everything from chocolates to crucifixes sworn to have been blessed by archbishops. 'There was not a young man in the whole neighbourhood, and it was the old grandfathers and grandmothers that worked the farms,' it was noted.

> Our hearts warmed to France ... because she had borne the brunt in the first years of the war ... Many of the French people had hardly heard of Australia, but hereafter they will never forget the name of the land whence came those stalwart boys who marched singing through their country; who went

to war with laughter, and when out of the trenches were ever ready to give a hand with the crops.

What was clear to the Fair Dinkums was the impact the conflict had had: 'The war and what it was costing France was thus early borne in upon us'. In their twelve days at La Creche the 7th Battalion 'met men from English and Canadian regiments, who gave us no very glowing account of warfare on this front . . . we were soon busy training. Gas masks were issued, the P.H. helmet type'.

It was the perfect setting, but on 15 April the battalion 'marched in driving rain and sleet to [Rue de] l'Hallobeau [not far from Fleurbaix and Fromelles], a few miles nearer the line'. Some of the officers and NCOs went forward to the trenches to familiarise themselves and some of the troops went to work on barbed-wire duty behind the lines.

WHILE THE FAIR DINKUMS in the 7th Battalion familiarised themselves with northern France, their mates in the 59th Battalion were still boiling in the heat of Egypt, bored by their activities and desperately awaiting the call-up to France. As the 7th Battalion arrived in Marseilles, the 59th were engaged in a thirst-sapping march across the desert.

Scurry detailed the route march as being from Tel-el-Kabir to Ferry Post, Ismailia to his father:

We left Tel-el-Kabir on Wednesday 29th and marched that day to a place called Mosahmah where we bivouacked for the night. The morning of the first day is to be remembered. It was 106 degrees in the shade, but marching along through sand, you will get the idea of what it is like. Most of the men stood up well, but some had to go under. I had a near go to a sunstroke, although we were all wearing helmets.

Scurry's difficulties came when he tried to carry some of the equipment of the men who were struggling:

> To make it worse, for us, none of our men were allowed to fall out without the written permission of an officer, so that we had to stop and write out a chit for every man who dropped and then came up again which meant that we got very little advantage of the halts along the road . . . I could not see anything just a black smudge, but after a lay down under a palm tree, I was very much relieved and was quite alright for the rest of the time.

The vision of 'Sweet Water Canal' proved the equivalent of a mirage, given the water was unfit for drinking and fear of disease meant the men were not meant to bathe in it. Scurry added: 'Some of the poor devils are not blessed with strong wills, so we had just to supply willpower for them, and keep them out of this inviting cool water'.

On the men marched for three days, and it stretched the minds and bodies of those who took part. One of them, not a Fair Dinkum, admitted some men couldn't help themselves in front of the canal. He recalled:

> Those who took part in the march . . . will not forget it in a hurry . . . by the time we reached the Sweet Water Canal we were panting like dogs, our tongues swollen and hanging out, our lips cracked and bleeding. There were many poor fellows just crazed for the need of a drink, under that awful sun that was like the open furnace-door of hell, with the sand filling every orifice in our faces and parching our throats until they were inflamed. We were warned that the Sweet [or fresh] Water Canal was full of germs and that to drink it might possibly mean death, but most of us were far too gone in the agony of thirst to care whether the drink were our last, and we threw ourselves down at the water's edge and lapped it up like dogs.

On the final day, Scurry was in the rear guard to assist with stragglers. He could not have been more proud, particularly of those Fair Dinkums he knew so well:

> They did it like lions, these men with blistered feet, cramped hands and legs . . . just about two miles from the camp I had [one] chap worse than the rest, the sole had come right off one of his boots . . . his feet were like raw steak. I halted my lame 'uns by the road and went and commandeered a motor ambulance, but they would not get into it, as they wanted to finish the march. The chap whose boots were gone I made ride in the ambulance and the rest marched into camp singing a song to the tune of a hymn. The first line was: Old Soldiers never die.

Scurry could see the irony. After a march in searing heat without sufficient water, it was a wonder that none of them perished.

ALL THE ANZACS, WHETHER in France, Egypt or travelling between the two, paused as much as they could on 25 April 1916. So, too, did the rest of Australia. It had been a year since the Gallipoli landings, and while the Fair Dinkums hadn't even enlisted then, they were connected to that sacred stretch of land by dint of their 25-day stint. The men who had fought there – no matter for how long or what their experience – were forever linked.

The 7th Battalion commemorated the first Anzac Day at l'Hallobeau. The unit was inspected on parade by General Harold Walker. It seemed almost fitting that within a few days the battalion would be marching out to Fleurbaix, and be in the line of fire again, as the Original Anzacs had been twelve months earlier.

The other Fair Dinkums back in Egypt at Tel-el-Kabir with the Pup Battalion were afforded a holiday for Anzac Day.

Clews enjoyed the anniversary of the landings by watching a sports carnival that had been put on for the day, noting 'The weather is very hot here at present'.

Scurry's thoughts that day were with the people at home: 'If you dear people at home only knew it, you are carrying out a part far braver than that which wins VCs + DSOs'.

The men who had served at Gallipoli received a blue ribbon that day, and Scurry wore his as proudly as any of the men. He sent his ribbon home to his mother in the next post, saying: 'You will find the piece of blue ribbon I wore on Anzac Day to show I had been in the mess up. Just keep it as one of these days it might be nice to have the first approach to a decoration I ever wore'.

A few more Fair Dinkums commemorated the Anzac anniversary on ships returning to Australia. Errol Forster Woods, the 26-year-old wireless whiz-kid, may have been on his way home on the *Runic* due to the effects of paratyphoid, but he was already plotting a possible return. He didn't know where or how, but the formation of the Australian Flying Corps and their need for those with wireless skills would help pave the way for his return in the future.

On the same ship of invalided solders were other members of the 8th Reinforcements of the 7th Battalion. Jim Ostler, who had spent time with the Camel Corps, was onboard, battling cerebral spinal meningitis. In February, a cable to his family had described his condition as severely ill. Ostler, too, would re-enlist, though his second stint would last a mere twelve days before he was declared 'permanently unfit'.

Syd Davies, a nineteen-year-old bootmaker at Paddle Brothers in North Fitzroy, was also on the *Runic*, a long-standing heart condition worsened by his time in the services. He was first diagnosed with a heart irregularity a decade earlier and had been troubled by shortness of breath since fourteen. Those breathing difficulties were accelerated by the short time he spent on Gallipoli, and the heart disease meant a one-way ticket home. Ballarat grocer Walter Leigh, who had been 21 when he enlisted, also had heart issues that ended his military experience prematurely. He had mumps before Gallipoli, pneumonia and shell shock after leaving Anzac Cove, and was diagnosed with Disordered Action of the Heart (DAH), which had become known as 'Soldier's Heart' before the first anniversary of the Gallipoli landings. His nervous system was almost in collapse; his time in the service all but over. Luck had deserted Leigh in terms of his time with the Fair Dinkums, though his illnesses and nervous condition probably saved his life in the long run.

Back in Melbourne, where the Fair Dinkums had sailed from eight months earlier, there were services and commemorations that first Anzac Day at the Town Hall, St Paul's Cathedral and even in the streets. At the Melbourne Town Hall, Acting Prime Minister George Pearce, who was in charge due to Billy Hughes' absence in London, said every man and woman:

owed a debt of gratitude to brave Australian soldiers ... the men who made the landings did not wait for recruiting meetings (loud cheers). They did not wait for brass bands, and they did not wait for conscription (loud cheers). We honoured ourselves in honouring the men who had fallen there. Long may their memory live green in the heart of their country.

A 'quiet celebration' of returned soldiers:

strolled about Swanston and Collins Streets in interesting little groups – interesting because the day being celebrated was their day, theirs and their brave fallen comrades. Smiling faces, clear of cowardice, showed how pleased they were to be on their native soil, yet how often during the day must their thoughts have strayed from the busy streets about them to the shores of Gaba Tepe as they saw it first a year ago?

One man outside St Paul's Cathedral told of how his mate Jack, as 'fine a pal as any man could wish for', had been one of the fallen.

It wasn't just in Melbourne. In Camperdown, the hometown of one-time bank officer and now Fair Dinkum Bill Batson, there were commemorations. Reverend Bennett gave a lecture on 'the Spirit of Anzac' at the local Methodist Church: 'We must not only make Anzac a memory and a boast, but a challenge, an inspiration and a compulsion to nobler living and service . . . The Spirit of Anzac should silence the selfishness of our lives'.

Batson's name was the third one read out at the unveiling of a roll of honour for the nineteen volunteers who had been members of the Camperdown Methodist Church. In the towns of Cobram and Barooga, where five young men joined the Fair Dinkums, the anniversary took place at the Mechanics Hall. Former Senator Anthony St Leger:

> rivetted the attention of the audience with a speech which firstly dwelt with the heroism and glorious deeds associated in the famous landing at Anzac . . . and the awful change that would occur if Australia were subjected to German rule; and finally touching on the need for men to uphold the honour of the Empire and to support the glorious deeds of the heroes of Anzac.

At the Quarry Hill State School, on the fringes of Bendigo, which Oliver and Tom Harris had attended as children, parents, students and teachers united in commemorating the moment. When the head teacher, Mr Roach, read out the names of those past students who were serving, a small cheer went up when the Harris brothers were mentioned. One of the visiting speakers predicted that the war still had two more years to run, a far cry from earlier predictions it would be swiftly executed.

A chorus of 'We'll Never Let the Old Flag Fall' echoed through the halls, and one student gave a stirring recitation of 'Anzacs Not in Vain'.

Those Cobram–Barooga boys, who had farewelled their Murray River towns on the same train fewer than twelve months earlier, had been separated by circumstance and ill health. Roy Anderson would write later in 1916, 'I don't know where the other Cobram boys are'.

The Knight brothers were in France, preparing to go into battle, having already had a taste of it on Gallipoli. On the peninsula, Bertie encountered shelling for the first time, and quickly learnt about its destructive nature, writing home that: 'We heard a shell coming and looking down the track we saw it land just near three of our mates, one of whom ran and got the casing of it. He hadn't gone more than 20 yards when another one landed almost in the same place'.

In 1916, Keith Murdoch, the Australian journalist, wrote about shelling and its effects on men: 'The arrival of the first shell is a never-to-be forgotten incident. It is like a man's marriage or twenty-first birthday, or like the death of his mother, or the birth of his son. It is considerably more than the first time he kissed a girl. It startles his very soul'.

Bertie and Hugh Knight knew the shelling in France would be more ferocious than it had been at Gallipoli. The brothers were close in kin and connection, and pledged to fight side by side. They knew the shells they could hear rumbling not too far off in the distance would test them like never before, but resolved to meet the challenge together.

Far from France, three other Cobram soldiers were facing their own trials. Anderson was recovering from enteric fever/paratyphoid, having been diagnosed with it just a month after the Gallipoli evacuation. He spent the better part of three months recuperating, but was determined to head to France as soon as possible. When doctors intimated that he might have earned himself a trip home to get himself right, Anderson would have none of it – he *was* going to France.

By the end of May, he was better, and on the move. In a letter to his mother, he explained how he was heading to England, then later to France, when he and his fellow soldiers received news about Lord Kitchener's death and the battle in the North Sea.

The two Cobram Rays – Rohner and Eaton – were both bound for Australia, their war all but over. Eaton had contracted spinal meningitis/paratyphoid, and by the middle of 1916 was already on the hospital ship *Seang Choon*. Soon after he arrived, Eaton sent a letter to Anderson, wishing him well. In a letter back to his mother, Anderson wrote: 'Glad to hear Ray Eaton and Rohner got home safely and hope they are not sent back again as they are not strong enough for the game'.

Rohner, who had meticulously noted his thoughts and his movements since the time he and the Fair Dinkums sailed on the *Anchises,* would not have many entries left to make. Illness had prevented him from joining the men on Gallipoli, and it would also stop him from following the other men to France. Tachycardia (an abnormal, rapid heart rate) and rheumatism meant he could not do what he so desperately wanted to. On 17 June, he noted with a mixture of sadness and relief that he hoped 'to go home soon'. He set sail on *Karoola* on 5 July 1916, spent a day at Colombo, arrived in Fremantle near the end of the month and finally docked in Melbourne on 4 August, the second anniversary of Australia agreeing to go to war, met by his mother and other relatives. Seven days later, he was feted with a fine welcome home in Cobram and awarded a gold medal by its grateful citizens. His war was over before he saw any significant action, and he would have to follow the fortunes – the good, the bad and the ugly – of the Fair Dinkums from the safety of home.

Rohner and Eaton went on to live long and prosperous lives.

The same could not be said for Irishman Lawrence Flynn. His pre-existing, pre-war consumption had flared once more and he was sent back to Australia, where he would refuse treatment until it was far too late.

THE 7TH BATTALION WENT into the firing line in mid-May 1916, but the unit's first deaths in France came earlier that month when two men – neither of them Fair Dinkums – suffered horrific wounds due to a German fuse cap dropped in Dead Dog Road, near Fleurbaix. Layfield was shaken by the incident, writing:

> Some of our chaps had a bad accident the other day . . . they were told to go off working . . . I believe they were coming home [when] they found a nose cap of a shell, and it exploded while they were examining it. Two poor chaps died, and four got badly wounded.

A week later, Layfield and the Fair Dinkums were in the frontline for the first time on French soil. It was so different – and much more dangerous – than what they had experienced in the dying days of Gallipoli. Layfield told his mother:

> We are in the trenches now. When we first came in, it was terribly muddy, so we had to wear sea boots. They are alright. They keep your feet nice and warm. We are doing A1 here, but I can't tell you too much . . . while we are in the trenches I will send these Field Service Cards. That will be better because while we are not on duty, we like to be sleeping. We don't get much of that.

But the frontline wasn't the only dangerous place to be, as Donald Sheridan, a twenty-year-old mailman from Polkemmet in country Victoria, found out. Writing to a Miss Creek from 'Somewhere in France' on 14 June 1916, he told of how he had fallen out of a tree while attempting to scout the German troops ahead of them:

We have just come out of the trenches after spending six weeks on duty. I had a few narrow escapes while there. I had nine days in hospital through an accident while observing up in a tree. I was trying to pick out a place where the enemy had three big guns placed and all at once the limb I was sitting on gave way and I tumbled backwards and fell a distance of twenty feet. Another day, while I was up a tree observing and trying to locate an aero-plane, I was shifted twice from my position by shells. I had a narrow escape. Another day I was up in a big tank built in a brick house, and almost before I was aware of it, from just behind our firing line twelve shells were put into it before I could get down. So you can see I had a pretty hot time of it. I can tell you I don't want another one like it. The place where we are camped now is well away from the firing and range of the big guns, and I'm not sorry either. I think if we are to be killed by shells or bullets we will never mind what happens. Every man wants to be prepared for it, as he never knows what minute he is going to stop one.

By 24 June, the 7th Battalion had moved back into the firing line at Ploegsteert, not far across the French border in Belgium. The first history of the 7th Battalion highlighted the menacing list of battles that this sector had already seen, saying Ploegsteert was 'of evil reputation'. *Our Dear Old Battalion* recorded: 'The [7th] was now occupying trenches in an area that had already seen much fighting . . . the enemy from time to time bombarded the trenches with artillery and mortar fire, and the disconcerting presence of enemy aircraft and observation balloons flying overhead became a daily sight'.

Some good news was noted in the 7th Battalion's unit diary on 27 June when it was revealed that the inventor of the drip-rifle, Bill Scurry, had been awarded the Distinguished Conduct Medal for his work at Gallipoli. Scurry had been in the 59th Battalion since the split and at around the time the news came through, he had only just landed in France after a journey from Alexandria. He was, again, ready to make his mark in this war, as he had done on the peninsula. A few days later, he wrote to his mother with a mixture of excitement and apprehension:

This one is from France, at last. We had a splendid trip over and no subs were rude to us so we landed in France quite fat and happy. Then came a train journey such as I have never seen before or ever dreamed of having. We started from our port of embarkation way down in the south among the wild hills and beautiful vine and wheat covered, always going north through miles and miles of vines and crops which [were] absolutely ablaze with red poppies and every other conceivable wild flower mixed with glorious jumble[s] of colour. There were cornflowers, fox-gloves, daisies and almost every flower that grows. The soft green grass looked so beautiful after the months of desert that it was only the sense of the dignity of my exalted position which pre-vented me from rolling in it like a kid at a picnic . . . Everywhere we go we are given a great welcome by the inhabitants. All along the line there were crowds of people waving and shouting to us. The carriages all had poppies tied on the door handles and 'Vive la Australie' written all over them. Of course, our chaps were not far behind and had written 'Viva la France' above it, and one wit had gone so far as to write 'Vive La Marmalade', a commodity which we all heartily wish had never been invented.

Far from Scurry's intoxicating train ride, one of the men whom he had sailed off to war with was in the hell of the front-line at Ploegsteert.

Bertie Knight was meant to be celebrating his 21st birthday that day. Back home, his parents had already raised their glasses to him. But, in the madness of war, dates and birth milestones meant nothing. Amid the chaos and confusion, Bertie and his brother Hugh, along with another private, Edgar Chenoweth, were left sheltering in a trench, as shells burst all around them. The noise was almost unbearable; the danger like nothing any of them had ever experienced. A German shell landed in the trench beside the men and exploded. Exactly 21 years to the day that he came into the world, Bertie Knight left it, the first of the Fair Dinkums to be killed. Bertie was buried in the Berks Cemetery Extension, Ploegsteert, about 2 miles (3.2 kilometres) from Messines. The Reverend F.J. Miles officiated at his service.

Bertie's brother, Hugh, did not emerge unscathed. He was badly wounded in the sector, his injuries so serious that he was sent to England to recover before being sent home to Australia within a year, relieved to still be alive but shattered at his brother's death.

It took just over a fortnight for news of Bertie's death to reach the Knights' farm, Tarnpirr, in Barooga. The *Cobram Courier* said 'both Mr. and Mrs. Knight . . . bore the distressing news very well, though each was naturally deeply grieved at the loss of their 21-year-old son from whom they had parted exactly one year from the day on which the news came to hand'.

Like millions of mothers on both sides of the conflict and from all corners of the globe, Bertie's mum was almost inconsolable. But she also felt a deep pride in the sacrifice her son had made for his country. The local newspaper told its readers: 'Mrs. Knight, with true patriotic fevour, said she was proud of the manner of her son's death, and if she had twenty eligible sons she would not stop them going to fight for the freedom of this country'.

10

The ghosts of Fromelles

'The first wave went down like "wheat before the reaper".'

GEORGE YENDLE WAS SCARED, but be buggered if he was going to show it. He was still a month shy of his seventeenth birthday, even if his paybook stated he was almost twenty. But he was long accustomed to acting older than his birth certificate, having done so since his father walked out years earlier, leaving him to help support his mother, Matilda, and the family. In peacetime, he was an apprentice solderer in an inner-city factory, but for this 'boy soldier', it was metal of a different kind that made him uneasy this late July afternoon near Fromelles in northern France.

The town's name barely resonated with him and his mates. Above Yendle roared the biggest artillery force he had not only ever seen, but could have imagined. It shook his small frame and he had to plant his feet firmly to the floor of the breastwork trench to stop himself falling forwards, given the rumble of the earth and the humming of shells through the sky. His ears felt as if they were about to bleed, such was the cacophony of chaos and the symphony of the shells smashing from one direction to the next. He and the men around him were in a holding pattern, waiting in the forward trenches for the inevitable call to charge across no-man's land – and hoping the artillery was softening up the Germans ahead of them.

He looked at the men around him, anxious and excited in equal measure, and caught sight of some familiar faces that gave him strength and hope. Some were Fair Dinkums who had sailed with him from Melbourne eleven months earlier and who, like him, had been sent from the 7th Battalion to the 59th. Those men knew his secret, and pledged to keep it, looking out for the kid forced to grow up long before his time. Some had been with him since he first put on the loose-fitting uniform, and he knew he could count on them as he prepared to dash across the open stretch of land towards the German trenches for the first time. It was Yendle's 21st day in France – four days fewer than he had spent on Gallipoli. He feared this extraordinary day might also be his last.

The noise around these Fair Dinkums as they waited impatiently was almost unbearable; the shudder of earth, metal fragments and other projectiles propelling into the sky came with brute force.

The bombardment from both sides made even the most battle-hardened soldiers shudder; it didn't matter if you were sixteen like Yendle or in your early thirties like Phillip Bellingham. These two men could hardly have been more different; Yendle was the boy from Brighton Road State School in St Kilda, who had left to gain an apprenticeship and lived in Carlton with his mother. Bellingham had farmed most of his life in his hometown of Leongatha, and had been a member of the local gun club for almost as long as the boy had been alive. Yendle was only just getting enough facial hair to shave; Bellingham had the bushiest moustache in the battalion.

Their shared experiences on the *Anchises*, and with the other Fair Dinkums on the sands of Egypt and the gullies of Gallipoli, was enough to bond them. Not that age mattered in the army; it was all about experiences, and these two 59th Battalion members were hopeful that their brief time on the peninsula frontline would stand them in good stead for France.

There with them was Reg Scowcroft, who seemed to thrive on his Anzac experience, and was immensely proud to have been among the last hundred men to evacuate Gallipoli. The 24-year-old tailor from Chiltern had promised his beloved mother – her only son from eight children – that he would take every precaution to return home safely. But he knew all that was out of his hands. He didn't trouble her with the reality, though. She didn't need to know. As shells soared overhead, some landing far too close for comfort, Scowcroft knew that pot luck as much as providence was needed to get him the 400 yards (365 metres) to the German line unscathed. As much as the men believed in what they were doing, they also knew the Germans had the high ground at Aubers Ridge, and were more than likely to have an inkling of the advance. The only comfort the Anzacs had was that artillery damage was meant to take out as many enemy machine-guns as possible.

Wal King and George Barber had been close since they first shared a tent and training back at Seymour. King was a strapping Australian whose sporting prowess and discipline seemed attuned to army life; Barber was born and raised in London before making the journey to start a new life in Australia. Somehow these two men clicked, and stayed together when the 7th Battalion was divided, though Barber was moved to the adjacent 15th Machine Gun Company while King stayed with the 59th.

Barber wrote to King's family almost as much as he did to his own. In the last letter he sent to King's family, he spoke of their commitment to each other and how his Aussie mate had always been there for him:

Wally is billeted on the other side of the road and I am with him every day and he is quite well . . . Wally is now a full Corp[oral] again and this time he is going to keep his stripes and get higher up the ladder and I am sure everyone in his company and also every fellow that knows him wishes him success as he is such a Bonza boy . . . According to the reports we have read out to us every day . . . the war in France is very favourable and we have advanced a great deal and if we continue our advances the war will not last much longer . . . All the tent mates are quite well that was at Seymour with us . . .

But the war wasn't going as well as Barber had intimated.

Other members of the Fair Dinkums waiting with the 59th Battalion that afternoon included Bill Campbell, who had been in Berlin on a youth tour just hours before war was declared almost two years earlier; Henry Stephens (known as 'Rusty'), who came from the same Richmond street as the Murcutts; Frank Dixon, whose cousin Ernie Wilkin was also nearby with the 29th Battalion; Ralph Bond, the 25-year-old labourer from Hawthorn who incessantly twirled his identity disc in nervous anticipation as he waited and watched the firestorm overhead; and Alf Honey, one of the new dinkums who had made the country town of Maffra his adopted home, and was willing to fight for it.

There were also other Fair Dinkums in the 60th Battalion being prepared for the charge at Fromelles. These included good mates Robert MacKenzie (a dental assistant from Albert Park) and John Clancy (a railway employee from South Melbourne). Harry Windley was also from South Melbourne. Southampton-born Edward Spooner was 54, but claimed he was 45, and still active and eager to contribute. Like Yendle, he had lied about his age to enlist, and the last thing he wanted to do was to show he was slowing down. Spooner had been transferred to the 60th Battalion, and his son James, who had enlisted two days before his father landed at Gallipoli, joined the same battalion in Egypt in March 1916. The Spooners were one of only two known father–son Anzac pairs to fight at Fromelles.

The rest of the Fair Dinkums who stayed with the 7th Battalion were about 50 miles (80 kilometres) south preparing for the battle at Pozières, which was scheduled for soon after the 59th and 60th Battalions advanced at Fromelles.

Bill Scurry's good work on Gallipoli, and his close links to 'the Colonel', as he still called Pompey Elliott, had seen him become the commander of the newly formed 15th Light Trench Mortar Battery, which was critical to the Fromelles attack. The man who invented the drip-rifle and won a Distinguished Conduct Medal for it had not been in France long when Elliott called him forward with this new challenge.

'Pick three officers and sixty other ranks, any you like in the brigade,' Elliott told Scurry as he put the young man from Ascot Vale in charge of the battery. Scurry was given the temporary rank of captain. A fortnight later, he hastily put together his core of men and prepared the eight guns at his disposal.

It was an astute appointment by Elliott. Just four days before the Fair Dinkums stood in the forward trenches and watched the frightening sky-show overhead, Scurry detailed his new role and his industriousness to his 'dear old mother':

> Just a short note in a terrible hurry. There has been so much for me to do lately that I have not been able to get a decent sleep, so I can't write much. There is a new address . . . it is now Captain Scurry, officer commanding 15th Australian Light Trench Mortar Battery, 15th Brigade AIF. I've some letters after my name [now].

The letter survives a century on, the evidence of Scurry's haste coming with his farewell vertically scrawled down the page. There was much to do, and not much time to do it in.

★

ELLIOTT WAS AT FROMELLES on 19 July 1916, urging the troops on and keeping them focused. It was what he did best. He had grave reservations about the forthcoming battle, but his men didn't need to know that. On the morning of the battle, he sat down to write to his wife, unburdening himself in a manner that he could hardly do with the men who relied on him:

> I am writing this in the morning and about 6 o'clock this evening we will start a battle, nothing like that is going on down on the Somme, but in other wars it would be a very considerable battle, indeed. I have taken every precaution that I can think of to help my boys along and am now waiting the signal to launch so many of my poor boys to their death. They are all eagerly awaiting the signal, and we hope to so pound the enemy's trenches that we won't have much loss at all.

But as much Elliott believed in the men of the 15th Brigade – among them the Fair Dinkums in the 59th and 60th Battalion – he had the most ominous feeling about what lay ahead. His black mood contrasted against the bright, clear day. It wasn't just that the charge across no-man's land was only a few hours away that contaminated Elliott's thoughts. The rationale – if it could be called that – for the ill-conceived, hastily arranged battle near Fromelles (initially referred to as the Battle of Fleurbaix) was that the British wanted to stop the Germans transferring men to the battlefields down south where the Battle of the Somme had been raging since 1 July 1916. It was believed that if the Germans could be duped into believing this action at Fromelles was part of a wider attack, they would be less inclined to transfer soldiers down to the Somme.

This was effectively take two of an attack that had originally been scheduled for 17 July, called off then because mist swept across the fields on the day of the charge. The planning for the push had been a shambles, as the enemy held the high ground and could see almost all of the preparations from behind the lines, armed also with information from spies who had discovered what was going to happen – and when. From the Germans' elevated position, near the fortified stronghold known as the Sugarloaf, they could see the supplies being brought forward and the preparations unfolding. It wasn't hard to ascertain an attack was imminent, yet the Germans knew it was more of a ruse than anything else. Lost was the element of surprise, so much so that when the first planned attack was aborted, the Australian soldiers noted that the Germans had written a sign in English, saying 'What is wrong? You are running a day late'. Another sign taunted, 'Advance Australians – If you can'. It somehow seemed appropriate that the Anzacs peppered the sign with bullets.

In Elliott's view the almost indecent haste seemed the antithesis of what military preparations were meant to be. This stickler for rules and detail could see the holes in the plan, and what was being asked of his men, and he didn't like it. The lack of planning caused Elliott fitful sleep in the days leading up to the attack, and remained so for the rest of his life.

While Elliott couldn't stop what was to happen, he was damned as if he didn't try to point out the flaws of a disastrous plan to his British superiors. On 14 July – five days before the eventual attack – he had his chance. A liaison officer from general headquarters, Major H.C.L. Howard, had ventured from the Somme to assess the planning for the Fromelles attack. Elliott convinced Howard to go forward with him, highlighting some of his concerns as he gave the visitor a view of the sort of ground the men would have to move across. When the pair were alone in discussion, he showed Major Howard a 'pamphlet' detailing the requirements that 'no attack should be made where the width of no-man's land exceeded 200 yards', which was about half the distance that Elliott's men would have to traverse to reach the German trenches. The wide expanse of no-man's land; the flat, plain landscape; and the poor excuse for a river known as Laies, which was more of a drain than anything else, only served to highlight Elliott's fears. If the German machine-gunners could survive the barrage, they had plenty of fields of fire to halt the expected Anzac charge.

He asked Major Howard 'to tell me as man to man' what he made of the scenario. Howard responded with words that Elliott never forgot: 'Well, if you put it to me that way, I must tell you that it will be a bloody holocaust'. Elliott believed those words meant Howard would return to headquarters and make his feelings known to General Haig or General Haking. While he never saw Major Howard again, Elliott's biographer said: 'Representations to Haig influenced GHQ to appraise Haking's proposed attack more rigorously. Haig indicated that he did not want the attack to proceed unless there was definitely enough artillery and ammunition to enable the enemy trenches to be captured and consolidated'. Even so, Elliott confessed to 'very grave doubts as to whether the attack can be a success', and feared it might be something much, much worse.

Haig's wish for an artillery storm to precede the attack was why Yendle and his mates were barely able to think or communicate in the breastwork trenches on 19 July, the day of the attack. From mid-morning to late afternoon, the bombardment was almost incessant. Some of the men put wadding in their ears to shut out the constant noise. Elliott's 57th and 58th Battalions had been reserved for the main action in the original aborted attack. But after the postponement, Elliott called upon the 59th and 60th as the focus of the assaulting battalions, thrusting some of the Fair Dinkums into the frontline in an attack where odds were stacked against them, and far removed from anything they had experienced before. They 'manned the sector facing the German fortification known as the "Sugarloaf" on the other side of no-man's land, which was as flat as the traditional pancake, and between 400 and 500 yards wide'. The battlefield was described by the men as:

ruined farms and orchards, thus covered with grass and neglected crops tall enough to hide in. No-man's land was covered with shell holes full of water from the River Laies which had long since been converted into an irrigation channel that ran in a straight line across part of no-man's land.

The men were waiting with their full packs, complete with bandages and dressings, iodine, gasmasks, 150 rounds of ammunition in their webbing and a further 50 rounds in their bandolier, ready to attack. The artillery appeared to have softened the enemy, even though some of the range came perilously close to the Anzacs on far too many occasions, forcing men to scream out that they sooner preferred to be killed by the enemy than by their own artillery. Confusion reigned even before the jump-off time.

For seven long hours, the bombardment raged, with the Germans returning fire. The 15th Brigade was to proceed in a series of waves, and their leader, Elliott, farewelled his men with the message: 'Boys, you won't find a German in those trenches when you get there'. Those thirteen words haunted Elliott for as long as blood pulsed through his veins, for as long as anger and sadness tore at his heart. The truth was, and Elliott may have feared it as he said it, while the artillery had caused damage, the Germans had expected what was coming. And as the first wave of men prepared to leap over the parapet and charge towards the Sugarloaf, German machine-gun crews were moving into place with deadly purpose.

After almost three hours of waiting in the forward trenches, and seven hours since the bombardment commenced, the first wave of the 59th and 60th Battalions charged towards their destiny. It was about 5.45 pm, and Elliott's prophecy of there not being a German in the trenches was shot down in an instant. As the men charged forward for what was supposed to be the first serious engagement of Australian troops on the Western Front, the rifle and machine-gun fire from the Germans echoed from the Sugarloaf.

One man from the 59th Battalion described the scene:

> The Germans were thoroughly aware of our intentions to attack . . . Nothing could exceed the bravery of those boys. The first wave went down like 'wheat before the reaper'. When the time came for the second wave to go over there was not a man standing of the first wave, yet not a lad faltered. Each gazed at his watch and on the arranged tick of the clock leaped over. In many cases, they did not get any farther than the first wave. The last wave, though they knew each had to do the work of three, were in their places and started on the forlorn hope at the appointed time.

Another soldier from the 15th Brigade observed that 'the air was thick with bullets, swishing in a flat, crisscrossed lattice of death . . . hundreds were mowed down in the flicker of an eyelid, like great rows of teeth knocked from a toothcomb . . . a valley of death filled by somebody's blunder'.

The Fair Dinkums were among the men cut down. Young and old dinkums, city dinkums, bush dinkums, new dinkums – the machine-guns didn't discriminate, mowing George Yendle, Edward Spooner, Reg Scowcoft and many of their mates down with menacing efficiency. The 60th Battalion 'walked into a fusillade of machine gun and rifle fire that meant that for those who went forward, if they escaped being shot or blown up, were finally stopped by the wire entanglement which had not been cut . . . the battalion was for all intents and purposes annihilated'.

Nineteen-year-old signaller Robert MacKenzie was one who didn't get far. He had enlisted in Seymour, and in the only known image of him in uniform he looks hopefully at the camera with a restrained, nervous smile against a backdrop of intersecting Australian and Union Jack flags. That smile was gone as he set off that early evening of 19 July 1916 with his Fair Dinkum mate, John Clancy. The two pals ran forward together before MacKenzie stumbled and fell after bullets ripped through his stomach. He tried to seek refuge in one of the shell holes that offered limited sanctuary amid the chaos. Clancy, who had been hit in the head, crawled into the same shell: 'Three of us lay there together. A shell came over and buried us. Two of us got out. We dug down to MacKenzie and found him. He muttered a few words and died . . . He was a mate of mine'. MacKenzie's body was never recovered.

In their civilian lives, twenty-year-old steward Harry Windley lived only a mile from MacKenzie's home. In their military lives, they would die in an even closer proximity. It is not known how Windley fell or what became of him after he was hit, only that he was reported missing on 19 July 1916. There had been a glimmer of hope, flickering and faint, when a member of the 60th Battalion hinted early the following year that he thought he may have seen Windley's name on a hospital listing. It was soon discredited, but not before it caused more heartache for his family. His brother, Edwin Windley, who was with the 23rd Battalion, remained in contact with authorities throughout this time, with little success. In 1917, Edwin wrote:

[As] he is not on your Hospital index, I understand that he must still be missing . . . But in Australia they received news saying that he was reported in Hospital somewhere about last Feb or March. If you should happen to hear anything of him I should be very pleased to receive any information which would lead me to communicate with him.

The only communication of note came when Windley and a number of his Fair Dinkum mates were finally pronounced 'Killed in Action' at a Court of Inquiry in the field in August 1917, thirteen months after the Battle of Fromelles. Still, hope had long been extinguished before that final blow to a family helpless and so far away.

Whatever made Edward Spooner enlist, his decision brought him together with his son, James. And it was somehow fitting that both were transferred to the 60th Battalion to fight alongside each other. Neither could possibly have imagined their time together in battle would last minutes, not months.

James was the first to go. He was running out in the open in the charge towards the Sugarloaf when he was struck by a shell. One of his mates saw him fall. He was badly wounded, but there was no hope for him. His mate, himself dodging the growing fusillade, had the compassion to pause for a moment and remove James's pack, knowing there was nothing else to be done to save him: '[I] made him a little more comfortable. We had orders to go back and did not hold the ground'. Like so many others, this son of a Fair Dinkum was never heard from again, and his body remained forever unaccounted for.

It is impossible to know if Edward Spooner knew of his son's fate. There was too much going on, and the seams of planning for this attack had long since frayed. Edward had dealt well with army life before 19 July 1916, not flinching in his short time on Gallipoli, nor protesting too loudly when he developed haemorrhoids on his return to Egypt. Incredibly, he was only a decade away from being eligible for an Australian invalid or old age pension, and here he was, making his advance alongside men more than half his age, until one of the German machine-guns found him. Bullets tore through both of Spooner's shoulders and his back, his legs buckled and he collapsed in a heap on the ground alongside men who were either dying or already dead. Was his son one of them?

Unlike James, who never made it back behind the lines, Edward was afforded a lifeline, albeit a tenuous one, rescued by one of the stretcher-bearers sent out to bring in some of the wounded men. Within four days, he was travelling back to

England, transported across the English Channel on the hospital ship *St Denis*. For a brief time, at the Queen Mary's Royal Naval Hospital at Southend-On-Sea, he appeared to be recovering. But it was temporary. On the last day of July 1916 the 54-year-old suffered a haemorrhage and died. He was afforded what his son was not – a funeral and an ascribed grave – and family members who hadn't seen him in years travelled the 110 miles (177 kilometres) from Southampton to say their final farewells. His wife, Rebecca, had to deal with her grief from the other side of the world, in far-off West Brunswick, having lost a beloved husband and son within a fortnight of each other.

The Pup Battalion went into battle beside the 60th and fared as poorly. By the time the men had made it to halfway across no-man's land, they were confronted by waves of bullets. Men fell everywhere – wounded, dying or dead.

The attack was a complete disaster. Badly wounded men took cover wherever they could, with limited success. But if the attack was flawed and a tragic failure, then the aftermath was just as heartbreaking. By the time night fell across the battlefield, there were so many wounded and dying left stranded and isolated in no-man's land that it was almost unbearable for the men back behind the lines. The screams and forlorn pleadings for assistance were almost as painful as the bombardment that preceded the attack. One of the scouts from the 59th Battalion said:

> All were not dead, but we had no men to help the wounded. We had no stretchers, and those that were alive, unwounded, were so fatigued as to be hardly able to stand upright. But we could not stand the thought of the fellows out there without help. We crawled among them, taking biscuits and water from the dead and giving them to the wounded. We could only reach a few of them, and we crawled back at daylight, cursing our impotence, and fearing what the day might bring to these poor comrades, lying helpless in full view of the brutal enemy.

Some men, like 21-year-old Fair Dinkum Alf Honey, went out to do what they could for the wounded, to bring back those who could be rescued and to comfort those who couldn't. Through that long night Honey went out because it had to be done, not worrying about the personal risk that he encountered, earning this one-time labourer and now apprentice baker a Military Medal. The citation said it all: 'On 19th/20th July . . . Private Honey volunteered to go out to rescue wounded men under heavy shrapnel and machine gun fire. He worked all night and under trying circumstances he again volunteered and went out on the night [of] 20th/21st July, 1916'.

R. Hugh Knyvett summed up the scene the following morning when light followed one of the darkest nights in Australian history:

The sight in our trenches that next morning is burned into my brain . . . if you had gathered the stock of a thousand butcher-shops, cut it into small pieces and strewn it about, it would give you a faint conception of the shambles those trenches were. One did not ask the whereabouts of brother or chum. If we did not see him, then it were best to hope that he were of the dead . . . When the darkness came on the second night, we had organised parties of rescue, but we still had practically no stretchers, and most of the men had to be carried in on their backs. Not all were dead, for in some of the bodies life was breathing. Machine guns were still playing on this spot and after we had lost half of our rescuing party, we were forbidden to go there again, as live men were too scarce . . . There were men who were 48 hours without food or drink, without having their wounds dressed, knowing that the best they could hope for was a bullet . . . there were men there with legs off, and arms hanging by skin, and men sightless, with half their faces gone, with bowels exposed, and every kind of unmentionable wounds.

Fromelles was the most disastrous 24 hours in Australian military history: 5533 casualties, almost 2000 deaths and 400 men taken prisoner. Many of these Anzacs were the ghosts of Fromelles, vanished from sight, never to be seen again.

A century on, they are still missing, among them Wal King. King's father was told many months later the only bit of news he ever received of what became of his strapping 22-year-old sportsman, soldier and son, passed on from someone who was near Wally when he fell. The young corporal had been advancing with his party when he stopped a bullet. Wounded, he was seen attempting to return to the lines when the informant pointedly said, 'We never heard any more of him.'

King had several distinctive features that would have made him stand out from others, if he was indeed one of the wounded who returned or one of the prisoners taken further behind the lines. He had a lacerated arm, which meant that it was shaped differently, and he had an old stitching scar on one side of his head. And a double crown of hair. But there was no trace of this man, one of four brothers at the front, and who had written regularly to his father about his experiences and the pride in his promotions.

Even though King's best mate Barber moved to the 15th Machine Gun Company, both men were involved in the Fromelles attack. Barber, a scout, was shot through the abdomen and thigh, but was one of the lucky few to be brought back. That good fortune was tempered by the serious nature of his wounds and the infection that was forming. The 22-year-old was admitted to the No. 2 Casualty Clearing Station and then transferred on a hospital train to the No. 3 Canadian Hospital. He lingered there as he fought against the infection that had spread through his abdominal cavity and into his bloodstream. Peritonitis and an infection in his left lung effectively sealed his fate.

Seventeen days after he was sliced by waves of bullets near the Sugarloaf, George Barber died, just before the dawn of 5 August 1916. His death was reported in Melbourne's *Argus* towards the end of that month. King's dad read about it before anyone else, as proofreader with the newspaper, and stopped instantly at the name as he checked the page. He wrote to the secretary of the Department of Defence seeking confirmation, unaware at this stage that Barber's best mate, his own son, was already dead.

There was a sad irony about Phillip Bellingham's final resting place on the ruined farmlands in the fields near Fromelles, though its precise whereabouts remain unknown. The farmer from Busket Banks in Leongatha in country Victoria was badly wounded and spent an agonising night in no-man's land. One of the men who had made the charge beside him bandaged Bellingham's wounds and comforted him. That same soldier was buried by a shell, but somehow managed to extricate himself. When he came to, that man knew he had to find his way back to a dressing station. So he left Bellingham where he was, and that was the last that was heard of the 33-year-old. Bellingham was first listed as missing, but unlike so many others, he was at least listed as having been killed in action by 8 August, and his parents were informed at the end of the month. They expressed their grief for their 'dearly beloved eldest son' in the local *Great Southern Star* newspaper, saying he was 'loved by all and deeply missed'.

Ralph Bond was another of the missing. The diminutive 25-year-old labourer seemingly vanished along with so many other Australians and was pronounced dead at a Court of Inquiry in August 1917 while his parents mourned his loss from afar. It wasn't until long after the end of the war that they got at least a part of their son back. Incredibly, in 1924, almost eight years after the Fromelles fiasco, Bond's parents received notification that his body had been found. The identity discs he had nervously twirled during the bombardment in the lead-up to the battle were sent back to the family: 'these mementos, though now somewhat impaired by long exposure, will doubtless be valued by you on account of their intimate association with your son'. Their long lost boy had been found, too late to be saved, but in time to give his family the solace of knowing he had a final resting place. Bond was interned 'in every measure of care and reverence in the Cabaret-Rouge British Cemetery . . . six miles north of Arras, France'.

Frank Dixon had missed Gallipoli after coming down with the mumps and had no intention of missing out on this battle initiation in France. But in the chaotic charge at Fromelles, he was posted as missing, as his cousin had also been. Dixon had not been seen since he said 'goodbye' to Lieutenant Hackworthy and went over the top. Those who enquired after him in the days, weeks and months afterwards believed that 'the machine guns . . . did the damage'. But seven months after the letters dried up, with no word from their missing son, came the most startling news imaginable for Dixon's family and his fiancée. A letter from the National Council of Young Men's Christian Association headquarters in London, detailed:

> After having made enquiries about your son, through our secretary in Geneva, Switzerland, we have received official information from Swiss Army Authorities that Mr. Frank Allen Dixon is a prisoner at Hotel de la Paix at Leysin, Switzerland. I am today writing to your son and forwarding him your letters. I shall also request our Secretary in Geneva to pay him a visit and to also render him possible service.

The message was that: 'Dixon [was] going out every day. Health satisfactory'. It was a remarkable turnaround for the family who had figured the silence from their son meant that he was gone. It was as if he had come back from the dead.

Then came the cruellest of blows. A few months afterwards, a cablegram from the commandant of AIF headquarters in London to the Department of Defence in Melbourne confirmed that Dixon was not a prisoner of war. In fact, he had been dead since that fateful night in July 1916. It read: 'War office states it has been officially ascertained that he is not interned in Switzerland. YMCA report incorrect. No trace, Prisoner of War'.

The news was passed on to his family, who could barely believe they had regained their son, only to lose him all over again. Their loss and heartbreak turned to anger and disillusionment at the misinformation. More pain was to come. Dixon's name was listed for the first time as one of the fallen soldiers in the *Argus* in late August 1917. His mother read the list by chance and saw her son's name. She knew he was more than likely dead, but could not believe the army bureaucracy could be so callous as to officially list his death without first telling the family. She fumed: 'Why did we not have official word before it was published? Please inquire and let us have the word without further delay'.

It hurt her, but not as much as losing her son for a second time. While Dixon's body was never found, his cousin Ernest Wilkin was one of the lost Anzacs rediscovered after more than 90 years, buried in an unmarked mass grave. After extensive research by a retired Australian teacher Lambis Englezos in the early 2000s, mass excavations recovered more than 250 British and Australian bodies. Wilkin was identified through DNA and reburied in the Fromelles (Pheasant Wood) Military Cemetery. His cousin is still out there.

Reg Scowcroft was never found, much to his beloved mother's heartbreak, who could barely believe she had lost her only son. Scowcroft was officially recorded as killed in action by a Court of Inquiry the following August, where it was noted that he was 'presumed buried in no-man's land, approx 5J90 to 5K02.1'. Annie complained bitterly about the lack of information and about the deferred pay that came from being one of the missing, with some army officials wondering if some men had actually deserted. They hadn't; they were dead. Annie persisted, and tried to find out what had happened to her boy. As late as 1920 – four years after his death – Annie wrote to officials:

The late No.2654 RJ Scowcroft, 59th Battalion, was my only dear son . . . the only [information] I got was missing on the 19th July, 1916, and the following year, 1917, I got word to say [he was] killed on that date. That is all I ever got, not a thing belonging to my dear Boy.

Part of Annie's death notice for her son in 1917 summed up her feelings, and the pain of so many parents, wives and children who lost sons, husbands and fathers at Fromelles: 'One of many, but our only one'.

Fromelles was meant to be some of the Fair Dinkums' first foray into a major battle in France. But for the Anzacs left living, it ended with the loss of any remaining innocence, and a sense of resentment at the sheer waste of it all. The resentment was focused on the British staff as much as anything else. So many of their mates were gone, vanishing almost before their eyes as ghosts of Fromelles, gone but never forgotten.

11

The gates of Hell

'We bombarded Hell; you bombarded two Hells.'

LIEUTENANT FRED HOAD WAS desperate to make up
for lost time. He felt he had been travelling more than he had
been fighting over the best part of two years, and saw the 7th
Battalion's forthcoming involvement at Pozières as the time for
him and the Fair Dinkums to get their teeth into a real battle.
This Boer War veteran had missed all but the curtain call of
the Gallipoli campaign, despite being one of the earliest men
to enlist in August 1914. A case of varicose veins saw Hoad sent
home well before the first shots were fired on the peninsula, but
he was already plotting a return to khaki when the news came to
him in Australia about the landings on 25 April 1915, five days
after his thirty-second birthday. He fulfilled that ambition when
he was appointed second-in-charge of the 8th Reinforcements of
the 7th Battalion, crossing the Indian Ocean for a second time in
less than a year. Hoad made it to Gallipoli as the campaign was
winding down, yet still played a role in the evacuation.

Now, this ambitious man with a military pedigree wanted to see how he would fare under the extreme pressure of a campaign on the Western Front. Hoad knew many of the men with whom he had travelled from Australia the previous year on the *Anchises* had just been engaged in battle at Fromelles. He knew it hadn't been a success, but envied them, in a way, for at least getting into the action. If he had known that the battle at Fromelles had been a disaster in planning more so than execution, he might not have been thinking along those lines. But the long months of waiting were starting to wear him down. He just wanted to fight.

On 19 July 1916, as their fellow Pup Battalion soldiers were fighting in Fromelles, the men of the 7th were preparing for their own battle. That day, the Fair Dinkums and the old and new hands of the battalion received pink patches that were to be sewn onto the back of their tunics. The 15 centimetres square cloth patch was meant to assist the identification of the men in the middle of the artillery barrage, though the patch was no guarantee the men wouldn't become a victim of 'friendly fire'.

Early the following morning, Hoad and his men left their camp at Varennes and marched out to Albert, the village that had become the gateway to the Somme battlefields. They bivouacked outside the village, and after a few days familiar-ising themselves with maps of Pozières, from where they were to launch their offensive, they marched through Albert once more on their way towards the most significant challenge of their time in uniform. As they marched through the town, the men marvelled at the leaning statue of the Virgin atop the Basilica of Notre Dame de Brebières, which had become one of the most talked about symbols of the war. The base of the statue had been struck by a German shell in early 1915, and it was left hanging 'like a loose tooth that would come away with one gentle push'. There it dangled, somehow defying all forms of gravity, hanging on more in hope than the rules of physics. There was talk among the soldiers of all nations that war would only conclude when the statue finally tumbled over. To counter that was also speculation that the side who caused it to happen would lose the war. So the statue balanced precariously, almost as if it were holding on for dear life, as guns roared in the foreground, and vast armies of men marched past on their way to the frontline.

While the fight at Fromelles was a relatively short, almost suicidal charge and listed somewhat dismissively as a 'series of important raids', the battle for Pozières was something different altogether. It was where the industrious wheels of the war turned more menacingly, and where the scale of the battle and the bombardments defied logic. The struggle for this once beautiful French town, which would be reduced to rubble and shattered stones, would be one of the fiercest of the entire war. The importance of Pozières was without question: parts of the land surrounding the village contained the highest point of the Somme battlefield, and formed a critical part of the German defensive position. If the plateau and the heavily fortified village could be attained, it would be a significant strategic gain.

British troops had begun their assault on 1 July 1916 when Sir Douglas Haig launched an ill-fated offensive with staggering losses against an almost criminally minimal yield of land. The result was considered one of the biggest disasters in British history. The British troops lost almost 20,000 men, with 35,000 wounded. The carnage cast a stain that could not be washed away. The only consolation for the 7th Battalion was that they were otherwise engaged at Ploegsteert in Belgium at that time.

But within the next fortnight, as the British made more unsuccessful endeavours in and around Pozières, the Anzacs were advised to make their way towards the Somme battlefields. Their pathway towards Pozières was underway, and none of the men who served there – and survived – were ever the same again. One later said it was 'a place so terrible . . . that a raving lunatic could never imagine the horror'.

Optimism was about as rare as silence in the trenches, but Milton Clews, now back with the 7th Battalion, was as hopeful as Hoad that the battle for Pozières might be part of the great leap forward for the Fair Dinkums. He wasn't being delusional. They all knew how onerous it would be to break through the lines at Pozières, but believed such challenges could potentially change the direction of the war. In the weeks leading up to the battle, Clews expressed his relief after the men had come out of a different part of the line relatively unscathed: 'Fritz didn't behave too bad to us this time . . . on the whole our boys were the luckiest, I think'. Clews had already caught on to the Australian slang term – Fritz – to collectively describe the Germans. The word around the battalion was that 'great things are happening at present and that our prospects are brighter than they've been for a long time'. He told his sister he may be 'lucky enough to be home by Xmas after all'.

This was meant to be the 7th Battalion's first significant battle since the attack at Lone Pine at Gallipoli in August 1915, but Hoad's hopes of playing a major role in the battle were dashed – at least in theory – when it emerged that the main attack on Pozières – 'the Butcher's Room', as some were calling it – would come from the 1st and 3rd Australian Brigades. The 2nd Brigade (which included the 7th Battalion) would be held as part of the reserves. The attack would centre on German positions in the village as well as the two main defence lines referred to as the 'Old German' OG1 and OG2.

The Fair Dinkums moved to a valley just south of Pozières as part of the back-up for the other divisions late on the evening of 22 July 1916. It was 8 pm and the French summer meant there was still enough light for the men to get their first extended look at the chaos that was the thoroughfare known as Sausage Valley. Soldiers moved about madly in all directions, many of them carting artillery, ammunition and supplies. Horses and wagons were driven through at relatively high speed. The wounded sought sanctuary and the dying were laid to rest. The grass that had once graced the entire valley had long since been trampled out of existence by the millions of pairs of feet heading to and from the frontline, replaced by a series of rough tracks that threw up clouds of white chalk and clay whenever groups of men passed through. Shells cracked ahead of the valley, pushing puffs of smoke high into the sky, machine-guns and rifles echoed in the background, and the war seemed so close you could almost touch it – or be touched by it. It was like a wasteland of the senses. You could barely see ahead of you as dust hung in the air because of the constant activity.

But worst was the smell, the scent of death that hung in the air. One of the signs the men saw that night read 'To Pozières and Beyond', and as darkness descended, the 7th Battalion watched as the other troops marched off towards Pozières and hopefully beyond.

It wasn't dark for long. The night sky became a ominous kaleidoscope of chaos, lit up by the fearsome fusillade cracking overhead. The battle raged on ahead of the Fair Dinkums. In time, some would become a part of it, though not under the banner of their beloved battalion. Major Arthur Hart, the man who led the 8th Reinforcements of the 7th Battalion to war, was one of the officers stood down under a policy designed to keep some of the key men from imminent danger. It was known as the LOB rule – left out of battle. Such was the danger in which the troops were headed, there was a decision to not put too many officers into the fray, lest they be killed or caught.

The 1st and 3rd Brigades attacked soon after midnight and, according to a history of the 7th Battalion, the town of Pozières, or what was left of it, was taken at 3.45 am, which paved the way for some of the Fair Dinkums to enter the fray. Some men were sent forward to act as reserves and others to assist with the operations. Just before dawn a few members of the battalion moved forward through the ominously named Black Watch Alley, a former German communication trench littered with enemy bodies and more than a few Allied ones as well. The battalion was assisting some of the sister battalions and working under their guidance. Many of the men acted as carrying parties for the troops in the absolute heat of battle, carting the bombs and ammunition required for men in the trenches as well as the sustenance needed to help them carry on the intense fight.

The following day – 24 July – saw the men exposed to German gas shells. For some it was the first time they had confronted such an insidious messenger of doom. Those who survived this and future battles felt the effects of the poison gas thereafter.

Some men, including a few teams of bombers, went to assist the 5th Battalion. Later that night the 7th Battalion was preparing to attack the left flank of the OG1 trench, with the 5th Battalion to take the right side. They moved up to shell-shattered ground and then had to do a right turn to line up facing the OG1 line. In darkness, and in the chaos around them, the men moved their way across no-man's land with little idea if they were headed in the right direction or not, while the Germans launched their artillery.

One of the key moments for the 7th Battalion at Pozières came when part of D Company, containing a number of Fair Dinkums, was called up to work near the OG1 trench just before 7 am on 25 July. One of the officers had been killed by a sniper, and the men had to step over his body to proceed. The men launched bombs all along the trench and built a barricade to try and halt the enemy, holding the area for more than a day. This small band of men never wilted under extreme heat and were exhausted when they were finally relieved the following morning. Several were later rewarded for their courage, including Private Wally Tracey, who volunteered to assist Captain Gus Oates in keeping the enemy at bay while the rest of the men worked on building the barricade. They fought doggedly, throwing grenades as if they were cricket balls until their arms ached, and picked off Germans where they could to allow their mates to keep constructing. He may have looked a nondescript, average soldier, but Tracey packed a serious punch. One who knew him well described him as 'under average height and all his prowess sprang from the strong clean soul of him . . . he was less than average, but a brave man and true'. Tracey earned a Distinguished Conduct Medal for his efforts. His citation praised his:

> conspicuous gallantry in action. He exhibited great coolness and bravery, notably in assisting to build a barricade under intense fire, and in bombing and sniping. His excellent work under most trying conditions was invaluable . . . Tracey endangered his life time and again under fusillades of grenades and sniper fire . . . constantly got the enemy on the run by rushing along the parapet throwing grenades and sniping down on the enemy. With this party, Pte. Tracey did excellent work in bombing and detonating regardless of the great danger he was in. Private Tracey remained with Captain Oates holding the trench while a barricade was built in rear when our attacking party had to fall back owing to lack of detonated bombs.

Maybe it was for men like Wally Tracey that famed British writer and cricket devotee Arthur Conan Doyle penned the words, 'If ever there were born natural bombers it must surely be among the countrymen of [Fred] Spofforth and [Hugh] Trumble [legendary Australian bowlers] [and] it proved at that terrible interval by Pozières Village.'

Eaglehawk's Private Joseph Bellesini had been severely wounded in the same firestorm that had engulfed Tracey. As the exhausted members of D Company were being relieved in the trench, one of the men picked up and carried the ailing Bellesini on his back; he wasn't leaving him there to die. Bellesini's brother, Harry, had been buried at sea during the Gallipoli campaign. Three Bellesini siblings had heeded the nation's call.

Joseph and another sibling, Andrew, had joined up as part of the Fair Dinkums, and Andrew had also been wounded at Pozières. Joseph appeared to have little hope of survival when he was evacuated. His mates prayed this tailor would somehow defy his serious wounds, but the odds were stacked against him: he had gunshot wounds to his left temple, left cheek and left knee. Doctors amputated his leg at the Kitchener Hospital in Brighton after he had been repatriated to England. His heartbroken mother, Esther, also dealing with news about Andrew's wounds, and the grief of losing Harry a year earlier, heard about small progresses and large relapses. By January 1917, Joseph was waiting to have an artificial limb fitted just before his departure to Australia, and Esther dared to dream of seeing her son again.

But four days after receiving news that Joseph was waiting for an artificial limb came the news that he had become dangerously ill once more, and the anxiety of waiting for a ship and his prosthetic limb brought about a relapse. Something had to be done to fast-track his return home. Approval came for him to be sent back to his mother in Australia without the artificial leg. The most important thing was to get him home while his sanity prevailed and while his physical condition held out. For some time Bellesini had been having Jacksonian seizures, a form of epilepsy caused by electrical activity in parts of the brain. The head wounds had brought on these seizures and they increased in frequency. Every time his body shook uncontrollably, a little bit of life seemed to ebb away from him. The muscle contractions, the heaving lungs, and the numbing pain of an amputated leg all conspired against him. On the afternoon of 13 March 1917 – 231 days since the hell that was Pozières – Joseph Bellesini slipped away. He was only 21.

Andrew Bellesini was in England nursing his own wounds when his brother succumbed. He had been separated from his wife when he enlisted but had resumed writing to her. His brush with death at Pozières assisted with the interaction, as well as the loss of a second brother to the blasted war. He had been lucky to survive when a bomb 'ripped my coat and tore the cover off my prayer book'. A bullet passed through his shoulder, splintering the bone. His knee also copped some shrapnel. He explained to his wife:

> I suppose you learned that I was wounded. There were a few thousand casualties amongst the Australians. We had charged the Germans, and were in their trenches when they counter-attacked us, and we had a bombing contest. Our officers were all knocked out, and only privates were left, but we got the best of the Huns. I put a few Germans out before I got wounded, as we were fighting at close quarters with bombs and could see the results. We got the best of the encounter, and driving them back, had to walk over their dead and dying in pursuing the others. I was in the front line for a long time until one dog shot me through the left shoulder.

Waldemar Mortensen was fighting at Pozières under his birth name. He had served all but about ten weeks as 'John Shaw', but concluded that if his life was on the line, then he might as well carry one of the only things he owned – his birth name. By the middle of 1916, half a world away from each other, his mother who had been searching for him finally re-established contact with her son.

But in the madness of Pozières no one knew what became of Private Waldemar Mortensen who served with the 1st Australian Pioneer Battalion. The 27-year-old with a ruddy complexion, light-brown hair and grey eyes vanished from the face of the earth, killed sometime between 22 and 27 July. On 1 May 1916, he was behind the lines at Sailly in northern France and had written the following statutory declaration: 'I, Waldemar Hendrig Mortensen, do solemnly and sincerely declare that I enlisted on 14/6/15 under the name John Shaw, which name

I now declare to be incorrect. The name of Waldemar Hendrig Mortensen, I now declare to be my true name'.

Mortensen regained his birth name just in time to die with it. His body, or what was left of it, was never recovered. Olive persisted with letters to defence officials, trying to locate her son's final resting place, but there was no closure for her. She knew Waldemar had been at 'Black Ally [sic] at Poziares [sic]', but little else about his movements. Still, there was a modicum of peace afforded her when one of the chaplains of the 1st Pioneers informed her that her son had 'died like a man and a soldier only could die'. She would continue to chase more information, without success, for another decade.

Yorkshire-born, Australia-raised George Avery had been with Mortensen as one of the volunteers who transferred to the 1st Pioneers in March. And like his fellow Fair Dinkum, little is known about how or precisely where the nineteen-year-old farrier was killed. He fell on or about 25 July 1916, and was never found. His sister, who lost her husband in the war the following year, received what was left of Avery's thirteen months in khaki in a parcel shipped back from Australia that included a tin box that contained a Bible, photos, cards, letters and a diary.

Some of the Fair Dinkums did some extraordinary things in that first foray at Pozières, particularly those acting as stretcher-bearers. Archie Milne was a 23-year-old married man who worked in a butter factory when he enlisted, far away from the mind-sapping experiences of Pozières of July and August 1916. As a stretcher-bearer, Milne saw the worst of it. Day after day, night after night, he went out with the aim of bringing back wounded and near-dead men. Some survived; others didn't. But he and those like him were determined to give them a chance of survival. Twice he was recommended for a Distinguished Conduct Medal. The first came from three sleepless days and nights from 24 to 26 July. Milne teamed up with Private Alex Hardie to work through barrages of artillery, most notably on the morning of 26 July, when they carried wounded men 'right from the position of the bomb throwers to the dressing stations'. It was exhausting, dangerous work. There was heavy bombing going on around them, and the citation for this recommendation explained that Private Milne worked tirelessly through the day and night, bringing some comfort to those who needed it the most.

Another member of the Fair Dinkums also noted for his selfless courage was nineteen-year-old Tasmanian Spencer Smith. While Milne worked as a stretcher-bearer, Smith also had a vital role in the battle. He ensured that men in the heat of battle had what they needed, rushing forward the necessary ammunition, water and rations to keep the men in the frontline functioning.

The men endured the fiercest bombardment they had ever seen. It stretched on for weeks, a near constant rain of shells from the sky and an ear-splitting cacophony of noise. As the battle wore on, there seemed to be no end to the hell. So many of the Anzacs huddled wherever they could, in shell holes and roughly carved trenches, dodging and missing the artillery as it swept across them like a ceaseless storm. And through it all, the village descended further into ruin, the landscape and earth becoming a barren, scorched wasteland.

Some Dinkums were broken by the experience. Others carried on functioning in a haze that later revealed itself as shell shock. Men suffered from tremors in and out of the lines, and for years and decades after. Good brave soldiers melted with anxiety from what they had seen, heard and felt. Bill Walker, a popular hairdresser, tobacconist and billiard-hall proprietor from Tocumwal, had been in the fierce eye of the Pozières storm, which left its imprint on his body and soul. On 26 July, wounded, he was admitted to hospital at Rouen, and then moved to Etaples. It was from there that Walker was reported absent without leave at rollcall at 6 am on 7 August, and he did not return until 1 pm the following day. He lost two days' pay and was sentenced to 28 days' camp confinement, working in the camp's barber shop.

Then when the morning rollcall was made, Walker was absent again without permission, and did not return when the other barbers retired for the night.

Tom Hicks was:

> in the thick of a fight and carrying despatches under fire on my birthday. Oh, what a birthday! . . . my duty as a despatch runner had to be done, and it was my place to do it, and I am thankful to say that I came through this time alright, although we got badly cut up.

A letter carrier in civilian life in Bendigo, at Pozières, the 22-year-old was a signaller with the 7th Battalion's headquarters. His work in the sector during the first and second stints was noted. During the July battles, he barely had time to rest his eyes, let alone fill in the field card that soldiers scribbled on to tell their loved ones back home that they were fine. Hicks had many close calls; twice he was struck on the steel helmet, which he conceded 'would have put me out if I had no helmet on. One dint was from a shell that burst about 50 yards away, and the other from shrapnel. It's all in the game here'. He was recommended for bravery at the time, the citation reading:

> During the recent fighting which resulted in the centre of Pozières, [Hicks] displayed great bravery by continuously delivering messages both day and night, regardless of the heavy artillery barrage which the enemy put on us. In many cases, owing to the enemy's artillery fire being so heavy, it was considered necessary to call for volunteers to deliver special messages and [Hicks] came forward readily.

George Rae was fearless and expected the same from those around him, without question or qualification. He had been advancing on Pozières on 25 July when he was shot through both feet. He figured he had been 'let off lightly, considering the hail of shrapnel, 12 in [inch] high explosive shells, gas shells, tear shells, machine guns and snipers'. Rae was a part of the 7th Battalion that had been designated to take the trenches in front of the village.

'We took it and we took it fairly easily,' he said. They made the charge over no-man's land and worked their way through 'the Hun's trenches', noting that some of the dugouts were 20 to 40 feet (6 to 12 metres) deep and some had carpets and paper on the walls and electric lights. Rae was particularly surprised to find a piano in one of them. But there wasn't time for anyone to tickle the ivories.

Smoke bombs were thrown down the dugouts to curb any unwanted hosts. Rae thought the German troops emerging from the dugouts were like:

stubborn rabbits that you tried to smoke out of a log and won't come out until it is just about dead. Really, it is funny watching them crawling up on their hands and knees through thick smoke. They look rather downhearted when they see our fellows standing all around them. They are cowards when you get in close quarters with them. They keep firing at you until you get right up to them, then when they see your bayonet, down goes their rifles, up goes their hands and they say: 'Mercy'.

Rae could never tolerate cowards, shirkers or blokes with no go in them. He noted that he and his men were up against soldiers who were among the cream of the German Army, but had no doubt as to which side had the upper hand.

'We had the pick of Germany . . . the Kaiser's crack regiment,' he recalled. 'So you can see what the Kangaroos had to hop up against.'

Rae charged through the first trench, then the second, and was on his way to the third when he 'got stopped', shot through both feet. He hobbled on until he got some assistance, 'I would have liked to have been there for their third trench, for it is great sport getting them out of their dugouts.'

Rae was soon evacuated to England along with fellow Fair Dinkums Percy Brunning, Lochlan Morison, Tom Harris and Frank Wearne, and many of the Fair Dinkums wounded at Fromelles with the 59th and 60th Battalions, including Bill Campbell, who had been 'shot through one side of his belly and through one of his hands'. Before Rae was whisked away to the casualty clearing stations – and ultimately to a hospital in Manchester – he overheard an English-speaking German officer say, 'We bombarded Hell; you bombarded two Hells'.

The 7th Battalion came out of the Pozières line in the early hours of 27 July. Fred Hoad, who had so desperately wanted to see some serious action, wrote in the unit diary just before they were relieved: 'Men tired, but cheery'. He was being overly positive: the men were exhausted and desperate for respite from the bombardment and the bloody battle; all had changed forever, and nothing was ever the same again for them. They were tired, dirty and more than aware of their diminished numbers. According to the battalion's first history, a total of 329 men were wounded and 54 killed. In Albert, they washed and slept, and from there, the battalion marched towards Canaples, which they reached on 30 July. That brought about a week of bivouacking in the open, and meeting up with some reinforce-ments – though not enough to replenish the lost numbers. New recruits to whip into shape was precisely the distraction the exhausted men needed.

But the respite did not last long. By 7 August, the Fair Dinkums were once again marching towards the frontline. The rumours of a move forward had been correct, even though they felt they weren't quite ready to go back again. But the men forced a grin – or a grimace, for some – and dealt with it.

The difficult march took them to Vadencourt Wood. Their mood was boosted by the sight of German prisoners heading the other way, their heads bowed, their war over. It was at Vaden-court Wood that the 7th Battalion came across the man for whom most of them were fighting – King George V. The King, accompanied by General Birdwood, inspected the 2nd Brigade and, despite what they had gone through only a matter of weeks earlier, many of the Fair Dinkums gave an almighty three cheers as he passed. The unit diary noted that the cheers for the King were not as loud as they could have been, for many men only discovered he was in the car after it had sailed passed them.

The first stint at Pozières altered the Dinkums forever. The intensity of the battle, the test they were forced to put their minds and bodies through, and the belief they could match it with the enemy gave some of them a strange, inner strength. Some men cracked; others endured, confident in the belief that no soldier of any other uniform could do as much as they could.

Fred Hoad was one of five lieutenants who was made a captain after the July battle. He knew that time was ticking down on the battalion's return to Pozières – and to Hell.

12

Damn Pozières!

'I can tell you I thought it was my last day'.

IT WAS ALMOST ZERO hour, late on the evening of 18 August 1916, and the Fair Dinkums were about to be thrust back into the chaos of battle near Pozières. Anxiety was in the air, competing for space with the artillery that travelled ominously overhead. Captain Fred Hoad seemed oblivious to the tension, his military background kicking in; he realised the importance of keeping the men calm before the attack, and projecting an image of normalcy in a war where normal barely existed anymore. He walked along the top of the parapet, smoking his pipe, seemingly indifferent to the danger ahead of him and his men. He figured that would give his men their best chance of success, not realising the odds were stacked against them even before the start. He thought of his wife and his children back home. The 33-year-old Victoria Railways employee missed them terribly, but he believed each step along the way, every yard of ground gained, brought him closer to Germany, and a resolution that would ultimately lead him home to Malvern.

There were to be two attacks, the first with other battalions north towards Mouquet Farm. The 7th Battalion would head along the Albert–Bapaume Road towards the windmill beyond the ruins of Pozières. The attack was meant to start at 9 pm, but there were considerable hurdles both in the planning and operation. For a start, headquarters was unaware of the timing of the artillery attack until less than 90 minutes before the attack. Confusion and chaos meant few people knew precisely what was happening, or even what was meant to happen. Enemy shelling through the day had killed many men, and it was almost as bad, Lieutenant Bert Plant observed almost breathlessly, when:

> our artillery started up with 9.2 in [inch] guns and did some bad shooting, putting them nearly all into our trenches, so you could imagine what it was like being shelled by both our own guns and the Germans and a lot of our chaps were hit and I can tell you I thought it was my last day.

Hoad and Plant were told they had to take the German trenches 'at all costs'. That was problematic. As he waited and prepared himself, Plant felt 'shaky as I knew we hadn't enough men to do it. Nine o'clock came and it was as dark as pitch . . . and we waited for our captain [Hoad] to give the word'. Hoad and his men had to leap out into the potholed wasteland in near darkness. Weighed down by their packs and equipment, some of the men had to crouch down and allow their mates to jump on their back to get out of the aptly named 'Jumping Off Trenches'. The distance between the Australians and the German trench may not have been considerable, but the degree of difficulty was.

Hoad tried as best as he could to lead. As Hoad urged his men to go, Plant suddenly felt 'as game as a Lion', emboldened by the men around him. This one-time swimming and diving champ from Mildura charged forward with purpose:

> We had about 500 yards to go to the German line and when we got about half way they opened their machine guns on us and it was *hell*, men were falling all around me but we pushed on, then getting close to the Germans they started to throw bombs at us, so we had to retire.

Plant made it back to the trenches 'pretty well knocked out', but somehow managed to assist the wounded and bandage those who needed it. But for the life of him, he could not locate Captain Hoad. No one knew where he was, which meant he was either dead, wounded or captured. Sensing a breakdown in command, Plant reorganised the men in an effort to make a second charge forward: 'Over we went again, this time I got to the German line'.

But as he made it there, a shell landed to his right flank, blowing him several feet in the air. 'I felt a terrible kick in the side and landed head first in the mud, then I picked myself up and found I had been hit on the hand.'

He took out his handkerchief and wrapped it around his wounded hand to stem the bleeding. His eyes were full of mud and he could barely see, so he instinctively went to rub them with his thumb, but 'it was not there', blown clear off. He made off towards the trench from where he started, but the shock and confusion of what had happened to him made him lose his bearings. If it hadn't have been for 'two Red Cross chaps . . . I might never have got to our lines. However, they set me right and sent a chap with me to show me the way to the dressing station'.

The first three stations he made it to were too busy to assist him. Finally, weakened by blood loss, he found a dressing station where a doctor gave him some morphia and tidied what was left of his thumb with a pair of scissors. Then, sensing Plant was fading, the doctors arranged for a special car to whisk him to a place 'about 16 miles away'. Plant collapsed on the journey and did not regain consciousness for four days, waking up in a hospital at Le Touquet. He spent three weeks there, had 'a little talk' with the Duchess of Westminster and his head stroked at night by one caring nurse who gave him 'a little hint that she would like to come to Australia with me . . . but of course I did not hear her'. From there, Plant was sent to England to continue his rehabilitation.

Hoad was not so fortunate. One witness close to the German trench in that first mad charge had seen the captain stagger for a moment, put his hands in the air and fall to the ground. It was almost at the same moment that Plant and others realised the hopelessness of their situation, and sought to return to their own line to reorganise. Hoad was in no position to do this, having been severely wounded in both thighs. His wounds left him drifting in and out of consciousness. He may have only been about ten yards (nine metres) from the German trenches, but remained unseen by the enemy. In a delirium brought upon by his injuries, and blood loss from his wounds, he grasped his revolver and considered ending it all. But the image of his wife and his children kept him from harming himself:

> it was hell on earth. Had it not been for the thoughts of my dear ones at home, I should not have been taken prisoner. I would sooner have taken my own life . . . more than once I was about to do so, I had my revolver ready, then I thought that there may be a chance that our men would make another attack that night, or the next day, and that I would be found and taken back to our huts. And where there is life, there is hope.

He remained in that position, bloodied and badly wounded, for two nights, until he was finally spotted by German soldiers, who threw a rope in his direction when they realised he could not move. They managed to pull him into the enemy trench. Captain Hoad was now a prisoner of war, one of 4000 Anzacs to be captured during the entire conflict.

Initially, Hoad was 'treated with every consideration and decency'. He managed to inform his captors that he needed water – desperately – as well as medical assistance. It was when seeking help that he encountered his first ill-treatment from the Germans. At the first dressing station to which he was taken, he was 'ruffly [sic] handled . . . all my belongings, money, photographs of my family were taken from me. I had been a prisoner for 10 days before I had my first wash, although my face and hands, and body, was covered with blood and dirt'. At the first hospital he was sent to, his pleas for a drink were refused after an operation was conducted on his legs. Then Hoad was 'supposed to have sworn at the German orderly'. As punishment for his alleged insolence he lost the comfortable bed he had, his food was rationed, and he was sent deep into Germany, to the Grafenwöhr internment camp where he and his fellow prisoners were 'treated without the slightest consideration and decency. I remained there for nearly twelve months and spent many months entirely without other British'. Such was Hoad's isolation that, for a time, he figured he had let down his men, and possibly his family, by being captured. He battled psychological and physical wounds, writing, 'I do feel my present position is humiliating . . . I have not received letters from my CO [Commanding Officer] or brother officers. I feel it very much. Have I committed a crime in being taken prisoner? Don't think me a coward.' Initially, his family and his men feared he had been killed outright in the attack. He had been reported missing, but news finally came through that Captain Hoad had been captured. His fighting was over; his ordeal was not.

Milton Clews was dying even before Hoad and his men made the charge across no-man's land. He had been a diligent diarist, but his diary ceased soon after his first stint at Pozières.

His last entries came in late July 1916: 'We went into the trenches again. We got a hot time ... when we got there, we found dead Germans in most of the trenches, also some of our poor chaps'.

Earlier, he had written to his sister, wishfully thinking he may be home for Christmas. His last postcard, written on 1 August, informed his family back home that he was 'resting at present, having just come out of a hot corner [Pozières] in the firing line. I was very lucky I came through without a scratch. I hope my luck will continue'.

It didn't. On the night of 18–19 August 1916, Clews was helping a group of men dig a trench under heavy fire in what was the battalion's second stint near Pozières. A shell burst near him and he was badly wounded. The stretcher-bearers carried him off towards a dressing station, but Clews died of his wounds. A letter home to his mother from Captain Gus Oates mentioned Clews was conscious and 'talking' when treated. Oates continued: 'He was of very quiet and steady disposition and considered a man of excellent character. He was highly regarded by his comrades who feel his loss very deeply'.

Oates spared Clews' mother the details witnesses gave to the Red Cross. Several noted that the shell had blown his right arm off and that he had died before he reached the dressing station. Nothing could be done for the 25-year-old. His loss was sorely felt by George Wood, one of his mates from the Fair Dinkums, who was also his stretcher-bearer.

Wally Tracey received his recommendation for a Distinguished Conduct Medal in his first stint at Pozières for having kept many Germans at bay in a trench for a considerable time. But in the second phase at Pozières, he received enough shrapnel in his thighs and arms to make this his last battle in the war. The wounds made him dangerously ill. His sister back in Melbourne received news of his heroism, with the caveat that he was now fighting for his life. Tracey was sent from the battlefield across to England, and just as he has fought for his life in the field, he did so when out of the line, too. There were conflicting reports about his recovery, which took the best part of twelve months, and saw him reluctantly returned home. His sister was initially told he had lost an arm above the elbow and later informed that one of his legs had been amputated. Two members of the 7th Battalion who served with him and wrote the unit history detailed that Private Tracey had lost a leg. Regardless of his ordeal and the hurdles ahead of him, this humble man capable of remarkable things recovered sufficiently to have a DCM pinned to his chest later in the year, win a lifetime's admiration from his Fair Dinkum mates, and was fit enough to sail home to Australia the following year.

Other men distinguished themselves too. Signaller Tom Hicks had already been noted for his bravery and resourcefulness under fire in the first stint at Pozières. His efforts on his return earned him the Military Medal. In the trenches northeast of Pozières between 17 and 22 August, he showed enormous initiative in keeping the telephone lines between the frontline and headquarters operating during the height of the battle. He did so under intense fire, particularly on the night of 18–19 August: 'The Battalion's advanced headquarters was situated in an old German dugout in O.G.1 and . . . was on very high ground . . . a target for the enemy who shelled it and trenches in vicinity very severely'. The signal lines for the phone were damaged on several occasions. Time and again, Hicks went out to repair the lines, restoring communication. The longest he took to fix the lines at any one stage was fifteen minutes. He did so at great personal risk each time the line broke, but never once did he hesitate or seek to do something else.

Hicks's next letter home out of the lines explained how difficult the assignment had been, but he believed the first experience at Pozières had been worse: 'We finished up the last go pretty tired; but not so tired as in the other one. It was not so long, nor so deadly on our men'. Still, he added:

You asked me how I like trench life. Well, 'The Dards', as you call them, don't hold a candle to what we have just come away from. Along the front, especially near the firing line, there is not a 10-yard square piece of ground; it's nothing but shell holes. Really, one cannot describe the scene of fighting as it is here. Anyhow, wait till I get back home and I'll have a try, as a fellow will have a lot to tell.

There was little doubt about that, though many of the men who endured the action at Pozières could never explain it to their families back home.

Another Fair Dinkum signaller under notice at this time was 29-year-old Peter McLarty, who carried messages between headquarters and the frontline. Even when the 'communication trenches were destroyed, and the enemy kept up almost a continuous artillery fire, [McLarty] was ready for duty, never appearing to tire. When he returned to the front lines he invariably carried ammunition or rations. His work was consistently good and meritorious during the whole engagement'. While his Military Medal recommendation was not validated, the men he assisted never forgot him. When he died years later, they remembered his qualities in and out of uniform, calling him 'a man much liked for his droll matter-of-factness, as he was admired for that transparently unselfish nature whence sprang that steady devotion to duty, strict adherence to principle and ready helpfulness ever active in him'.

The stretcher-bearers worked as tirelessly as anyone. Archie Milne had been recommended for a Distinguished Conduct Medal in the first stanza at Pozières, and again after the second, which came under dramatic circumstances. He showed 'conspicuous bravery when . . . working continuously with his fellow stretcher bearers until they were killed or wounded'. Twice he carried on his back men who were bigger than him from the heat of the firing line to the dressing stations. On one occasion that he did this, he dropped off a man at the dressing station and promptly fell down in complete exhaustion himself. Someone offered him a drink, but his parched lips had to wait – he had not the energy to do anything. As his citation noted: 'He was practically unconscious from fatigue'.

Light rain fell like tears across Pozières on the morning of 19 August, with the objectives of the mission far from achieved. When the light mist disappeared, there were incorrect reports from aerial reconnaissance that one company of the 7th Battalion – Hoad's B Company – had been seen in the German trenches. The battalion commander, Colonel Carl Jess, knew the information was wrong and argued that the edict to stage another charge would be suicidal; there were enough casualties and deaths, and no need for more. Jess threatened to resign his commission rather than send his men into another firestorm. After much heated debate and threats, Jess told the brigadier that he 'wouldn't be long in letting the public of Australia know who murdered the 7th Battalion'. The order to stage another attack was rescinded to everyone's eternal relief.

By late evening on 21 August, news came through that all men were desperate for – they were to be relieved from Pozières, to be replaced by the 19th Battalion. The long march back to Albert in the early hours of the morning was followed by a move to the nearby town of Warloy. It was there that the men were meant to finally get some sleep, though their place of slumber for the night was restless with rats. There was more movement the next day, but the men remained out of the line as they sought to recover.

On 26 August 1916, the first-year anniversary of the Fair Dinkums' voyage on the *Anchises*, Jess finalised an extensive report about the second Pozières campaign undertaken by the 7th Battalion. He concluded that:

> I do not think that any other Officers, or men under such circumstances, could have fought better, or shown greater

initiative under the extreme circumstances, and though the operation was not the success that was intended, it has enabled us to gain [some] commanding positions . . . as this matter so vitally affects the reputation and record of the 7th Battalion, I have endeavoured to get from all sources accurate information as to actual happenings . . . I would wish to say for the Officers and men that through such fire and without sleep from the morning of the 15th till the night of the 21st inst, no sign of faintheartedness was seen, nor were requests for relief ever made.

Even as Jess signed his name to the report, the men of the 7th Battalion were on the move again, making a five-hour train trip to the border of Belgium, near the trenches at Ypres. For a time, the unit was stationed near the town of Poperinghe, though they were not permitted to go out in the village. Some of the men went against battalion orders, eager for some time in a real town far removed from the rubble that had been Pozières. They went to the trouble of unstitching their battalion Mud and Blood patches and turning them vertically, so they looked like the 59th Pup Battalion's badges. The ruse worked. Major Hart strongly believed he had recognised some of the men who had been out of bounds. But the colour patches looked like the 59th. Hart was either not convinced it hadn't been the soldiers he thought it was, or simply cut the men some slack. The offending men had some fun – and got away with it.

Fittingly, the Fair Dinkums who were now in the 59th Battalion and who had survived Fromelles were not far away from their old 7th Battalion on their anniversary of setting sail. They were at Rue de Bois, between Fromelles and Fleurbaix. Bill Scurry, still leading the 15th Light Trench Mortar Battery, wrote about that 'very eventful day' in a letter to his mother:

We did not think then that by the next Aug 26th I would be a Captain, with a battery of my own. I suppose I shall have grown up quite a lot since then, as I can assure you there is quite a difference in the responsibility of making centre flowers and that of commanding a battery armed with a secret weapon. But don't get the idea that the work is too hard or that I am becoming a nervous break-up, (or should I say breakdown) as such is far from the case, and I have never been in better health before. Even to me who has had a twelve months absolutely crammed with incidents, it seems a long, long exile, but to you it must seem ever so much longer. But cheer up Mum, for I think I can safely guarantee that long before the next 26th August, I will be making the usual row at dear old 70 Middle St [in Ascot Vale].

He finished the letter sitting around a campfire made in an old oil drum, just before a dinner of roast beef, roast potatoes and onions, followed by stewed plums and custard. It was better than what prisoner of war Fred Hoad was served up in his POW camp that day.

The two engagements at Pozières had seen 132 members of the 7th Battalion killed, 444 wounded and four POWs. They were among 22,826 Australian soldiers who fell within:

a few yards of ground . . . a monstrous sacrifice, which tumbled the romances and grand illusions of the past into the dust, when they rarely rose again. After Pozières many soldiers looked back to their boyhood, and saw an unfamiliar world . . . The Australians never forgot Pozières, nor the English staff which sent them there, nor the mates killed, nor the New Army divisions which had failed so often on their flanks, nor a thousand scenes of horror and heroism, nor, most terrible of all, the ceaseless, merciless, murdering guns.

13

The darkest of days

*'One thing that shone throughout – glowed gloriously –
the magnificent spirit of those shivering, mud-caked
chat-infested mates'.*

LAWRENCE BLACK WAS A serial absconder. There was no other way of putting it: the 22-year-old hairdresser had only been on French soil for less than a month when he was first reported absent without leave. It would not be the last time. This episode set a pattern for the remainder of his war. If Black had been in the British Army, his wanderlust could have seen him executed. But Australians could only be sentenced to death if they had been involved in mutiny or had deserted to the enemy. No death sentences were carried out for Australian soldiers in this war – all were commuted to military prison sentences.

There had been no warning signs about Black's behaviour before 1916. A diminutive young man with hazel eyes and dark brown hair, he had served Brunswick's 60th Infantry well for three years and took his equipment back when he signed up for the AIF on 14 June 1915. Working as an apprentice in his father's barber shop, Black married before his departure with the Fair Dinkums on 26 August. He had missed the Gallipoli finale, and was being treated for rheumatism in a Cairo hospital when the Anzacs were evacuating the peninsula. He sailed to France, arriving at Marseilles on 17 May 1916. By the end of that month, Black was back in hospital, admitted to the 26th General Hospital with VDG (venereal disease, gonorrhoea). It's not known if this was the byproduct of his absence not long after his arrival from France, visiting the well-known brothels, or whether it dated back to those houses of ill repute in Egypt. Black spent thirteen days in hospital, but was discharged to duty on 12 June. Six days later, he went missing from Etaples, the little fishing village in northern France that war had transformed into an Allied camp and hospital base. On this first occasion, he was absent without leave for eleven days, and when he returned, he had to forfeit pay for 33 days. The 1st Divisional Base Depot that imposed the sentence on Black figured he had learnt a lesson. They were wrong.

If that had been the end of Black's adventures, it might have made for a nice tale told in male-only company on his return in the pubs of postwar Melbourne. If that had been his last indiscretion it may not have been too far removed from what some other Anzacs might have done, those who could sometimes be easily led, or who felt hamstrung by the army's officialdom. For the Anzac legend, then and now, sometimes leaves sinew off the bones of the men as they were.

But this was not the end of Black's unusual war – far from it, and little of it had to do with fighting the enemy. It was more about fighting the urge to be a free spirit in an age when such behaviour too often ended in court-martial and confinement. The duty Black had been released to after leaving hospital didn't last long. If his previous charge had been absent without leave, his next was on a more serious scale. He was accused of 'deserting His Majesty's service' while on active service. Once more at Etaples, Black left the camp and failed to return, and this time it appeared as if he had no intention of coming back.

Another Fair Dinkum – indeed, another hairdresser – also took off from the same camp on the same day. More than likely, they travelled together. Bill Walker had been working in the camp barber shop, on what should have been a brief respite from the horrors of his experience at Pozières. Unlike Black, Walker had been in the frontline and knew the ferocity of the war. He had enlisted out of a sense of duty, been a good soldier, was a 'crack shot' and a well-liked, popular member of the 7th Battalion.

If it hadn't been for the madness of Pozières, it is doubtful this married man would ever have left the camp that August day. A month earlier, on his departure from the lines, he was diagnosed with shell shock. The strain of war was more than most men could bear: the constant pounding of the guns and the shells crushed the spirit of even some of the fiercest of soldiers, as did having to work while expecting to die any second. The impact of shell shock on the wellbeing of soldiers was an unknown quantity then, and no war in the history of humanity had previously assaulted the mental or physical senses as much as this had. When the commanding officer filed a report on Walker's absence, he assumed the normally reliable man would be back in a day or two.

He wasn't. His name was called at every rollcall thereafter, to be met by a stony silence. Second Lieutenant Walter Chinery knew Walker had no permission to leave the camp. He added that 'the accused' was liable to be called back to his battalion in the firing line at any given time. Perhaps 30-year-old Walker had an inkling that he would have to go back to the front soon, and didn't want to face those guns again. After what he had endured at Pozières, he had every right to fear what might be in store next for him.

Black and Walker had shared a tent at the Etaples camp before fleeing. In the early hours of 23 September, the men were sleeping in a deserted, tiny one-room house in the middle of the field out on the Lefaux Road, to the north of Etaples. The house was hidden behind a large hedge and as the two men, and several other absent without leave Australian soldiers slept, they must have felt comfortable that the cover of darkness and the mass of the hedge would hold their hiding spot. Their slumber was shattered at 3.30 am, as surely as if a stray shell had landed on the little disused home. It was just the rap on the door of the military police, and as they forced entry, the men inside could hardly resist capture. It was over in a matter of minutes. In all, seven Australians were arrested that night, and charged with desertion. Black and Walker knew they were in trouble, but only Walker seemed to accept his fate.

Walker's court-martial took place on 9 October 1916, and the point of contention was whether he had intended to desert or whether he had just been absent without leave. The gap between his decision to leave and when he was caught was not in his favour. But he had been seen in and around camp in the days after, as it turned out. Walker had been observed 'at Reveille . . . in the barber's shop' on 2 September, but no one thought to arrest him. Captain Edward Strahan, who was in attendance when Walker and Black had been captured, told the court-martial he saw: 'Several Colonial troops [in the house], the above named man being one of them. I arrested him and conducted him to my office. Since his arrest he has been detained in the Field Punishment for safe custody'.

As Walker and Black were both married, their decision to leave camp and fail to return had consequences far beyond their own welfare: their punishment meant their wives back home had to endure without the regular wage that the army provided, at least for the period in which they were held. That was hardly ideal, particularly for Walker's wife, Olive, and his children. The sledgehammer of being found guilty of desertion and being sentenced to five years' imprisonment was almost as mind-numbing as the shell shock he had suffered. Within a month, Walker's severe sentence had been commuted to two years' imprisonment, which was still almost an eternity in his eyes. He was sent to Rouen Prison, and stayed there until January 1918, the last year of the war.

Black was less accepting of his fate. He was also given an extended prison term, but took matters into his own hands. A return to Etaples camp from his field punishment camp 'owing to his verminous condition for steam bath and clean clothing' provided the opportunity. He did the rest. On 26 October 1916, Black asked the guard to allow him to go to the 'latrines' and Private Douglas Ellerton, of the 10th Battalion, escorted him. Black disappeared inside while Ellerton waited outside. After fifteen minutes he checked, only to find the elusive Black gone – again. At his court-martial, Black said:

> I had bad diarrhoea ... after being in there for about 15 minutes, Pte Ellerton walks through while I was still there. When I walked out of the latrines, Pte Ellerton was not there. I then walked along the road. I had taken whiskey for the first time in my life that morning and felt stripped. I walked along the road past the pumping station ... I was induced by friends to go away.

Whether it was the whiskey or the carelessness of his guard or his friends' urgings, Black was off once more. This time he made his way from Etaples to Boulogne. The French military police had been informed that 'Australian deserters went to Boulogne and had been gathering in certain houses indicated to the police and were spending money there very freely'. Black was apprehended at an address in Boulogne at about 11 am on 6 November 1916 and handed over to the British military police.

The subsequent court-martial found him guilty of desertion, and he was sentenced to five years' imprisonment. Like Walker, the penal servitude was eventually reduced to two years' hard labour. Black spent Christmas 1916 in a military hospital at Rouen, again battling VD, his past once more catching up with him.

While Black and Walker were evading the military police on 3 September 1916, Bill Scurry's war – and his life – was changed utterly. This remarkable young man was not simply content to have produced the drip-rifle apparatus that had assisted with the Gallipoli evacuation and won him the Distinguished Conduct Medal. On arrival in France, he was given command of setting up the 15th Light Trench Mortar Battery, and 'the Colonel', Pompey Elliott, recommended him for a Military Cross for his excellent work, including at Fromelles. The citation, written by Elliott, read in part:

> Since he has been in command of LTM Bty 15th Inf Bde at Petillon, July–September, 1916, by his courage, energy and ability, he worked a complete revolution on the feelings of the infantry towards his guns. Instead of, as was the case in the beginning, these mortars being disliked as liable to draw unnecessary force upon the infantry, they are now sought out as an aid in silencing troublesome machine guns and snipers . . . From the outset, Capt Scurry set a fine example of self-sacrificing zeal and enthusiasm in regard to the employment of the mortars until he was wounded.

Scurry always had an uncanny knack for knowing how things worked. That's what he was doing on the morning of 3 September 1916 when he was handed a German 'Rum Jar' bomb that had failed to detonate. His task was to work out why it had not gone off. Scurry stripped the unusual pattern of the fuse and tried to reassemble it. A 'small safety block' that was supposed to come out while it was in flight had been displaced, though Scurry had been unaware of this. As he tried to replace the detonator and turn the fuse over, the Rum Jar exploded and he bore the full brunt of the damage.

The bomb ripped at his face and chest, sending fragments flying in all directions. A sharp pain concentrated in his right eye and Scurry's world went black. His right index finger was blown almost clean off, and left shattered, irreparable. The digit was later 'nicked' – amputated. In the frantic seconds after the explosion, Scurry felt his soldier's instincts kick in. As his mates rushed to his aid, this diligent, ordered soldier was thinking about the fuse and what had gone wrong, so that the same would not happen to the next man who came across this unusual German contraption. Most thought Scurry's war was over, but there was no such concession from the man himself. Even as he was being dragged away, all but blind in one eye, and with wounds to his face and body, Scurry insisted he wasn't ready to go back to Australia just yet.

Elliott was crestfallen when he found out what happened to one of his favourite soldiers. He had been deeply affected – and angered – by the Fromelles tragedy, and a matter of months later, he had seemingly lost one of his shining lights. Still, he didn't deny that Scurry could still be useful. His rationale was simple: 'I would rather have him with one eye than a dozen others with two. In my opinion, he is a military genius of a type unfortunately only too rare'. That was high praise indeed from a soldier of his stature.

Scurry's next letter home, six days after the explosion, gave a glimpse of what he had gone through, though typically he kept the gory details from his parents, sisters and fiancée. It was his handwriting that gave it away since the letter was penned in his opposite hand. He apologised to his mother for 'this work of art', and tried to ease her mind. He played down his wounds:

All along I have been looked after splendidly and as I only have my hand and a few cuts on my face . . . no hurry, I am having a good time. Sister would have written this letter for me, but it is practice and I can assure you the sisters have not too much spare time. They are wonderful people and the more you see of them, the more wonderful they are. The orderly wants to put my dinner on this tray, so I must close my left-handed letter.

The one thing he neglected to say was just how close he came to being killed that day. That could wait for another time. That could wait until after the war. There was still plenty to be done.

The reality was that Scurry couldn't write again for more than six weeks since there was too much strain on his damaged eye. Even then, he didn't provide details on what had happened to him, the only giveaway the address at the top of the page – London General Hospital. He spoke about the city, and how he planned to see it all. He promised to chart his experiences as diligently as he had in Egypt the previous year. He detailed the surprise 21st birthday party the hospital had thrown for him in October, complete with cake, flowers and 'all sorts of beautiful things'. The cake made especially for him had an Australian flag on it with makeshift wattle. He was presented with 'a beautiful silver fountain pen' with his initials WCS (William Charles Scurry) inscribed on it. The matron of the hospital played a part in the proceedings, and one of the surgeons was mockingly condemned as a German spy and 'shot with a cracker'. The entire party – comprising patients and staff – went outside for a special photograph, complete with 'absurd hats'.

It wasn't until February the next year that Scurry explained precisely what had happened to him the previous September: 'I did not want you to worry about me at all, and not think I was dropping to bits, because I'm not'. But what he hadn't taken into account were the 'gruesome' details some people back in Australia revealed of his injuries, 'most of which have not any foundation'. He admitted to having 'two *small* pieces of metal in my right eye, quite fixed and unable to do any harm now, and as one penetrated the lens, it was necessary to take the lens right off, so the eye has now only the perception of light'. An artificial glass lens helped with vision, though it was limited. Still, he stressed: 'It never gives any trouble', though the 'strange angle of my bung eye' earned him the nickname of 'Boss-Eye' among his close friends.

The 'Smiling Boy' Alf Layfield wasn't smiling too much through September 1916. The weather was closing in and the incessant rain turned the trenches into mud and slush. It wasn't even winter yet, but the early onset of the cold, damp conditions, coupled with bullets and the barrage, made life difficult, especially when the 7th Battalion were in the firing line. Layfield tried to write as regularly as he could to his mother, Ada, but it was hard when the men were in the trenches and the rain beat down on them. He managed four letters that month.

When Scurry was in England for treatment, Layfield was stuck in a trench near Ypres. The battalion had taken over the Bluff/Spoil Bank Sector from the 2nd Battalion and the Duke of Wellington's Regiment. The tunnellers were working on trench improvements, which stirred up the rats, some of them almost as big as wombats. Layfield didn't mention them in the letters, but detailed the miserable conditions, and how men would often 'sink about a foot in the mud'. During this time, he had to escort parties of men out every third night on 'harassing raids' on the enemy trenches: 'You ought to have seen us when we came back . . . it was pitch black dark, and we were stumbling into shell holes and sliding all over the place'. Still, Ypres wasn't quite the hell Pozières was, and Layfield acknowledged that:

we have just come out of the trenches a few days, but it was good up there . . . different to the place we were in. It was like Heaven, sometimes you would think there was no war on at all, until we opened up with our artillery, then that would start Fritz going, and then it would be pretty warm for a little while. Fritz don't like our artillery, but of course we don't love his [either].

To his father George, he described how 'it is pretty rotten to have to walk through the water nearly up to our knees . . . it's a wonder some of us never died with cold'. He admitted he had been pretty lucky to come out of Pozières 'without a scratch', something that couldn't be said for the landscape, which was scarred beyond recognition. He wished he had seen it before this war. How pretty would it have been! But the shell holes, the mud and the sheer desolation seemed to have made a permanent imprint on the land. The best a soldier could do was to get on with the job, and that's what he intended to do. He didn't envy the 'brass' who were said to have slept in chateaus or those with cushy jobs far from the guns. But he did admit that it 'wouldn't break a few hearts [for them] to spend a few nights, especially if there is nothing doing at all'.

Layfield and the Fair Dinkums made the best of what they had, which wasn't very much. They stuck together, for better and for worse. And that was enough for Layfield. As he proudly penned, 'it's either a bivouac in the open, or sleep in an old farm or something like that, but we are dinkum soldiers'.

The bleakness mirrored the state of the war. The autumn and winter of 1916 was no friend to the soldier, and almost as much of an enemy as Fritz. The Australian troops, who had surprised their British counterparts at Gallipoli with their pluck, daring and ingenuity, had shown enormous resilience in their short time in France. Australia's official war correspondent and chronicler of the campaigns, Charles Bean, detailed how Sir Douglas Haig:

had surprised Queen Victoria's son, the old Duke of Connaught, by telling him that the Australians were among the best disciplined troops in France: 'When they are ordered to attack, they always do so,' he said.

But the losses at Fromelles and Pozières, and the slowing up of enlistments on the home front, had created a serious problem, of which Prime Minister Billy Hughes believed only had one solution – conscription.

So while the 7th Battalion was dealing with the mud near the Ypres sector, Hughes was slinging his own mud in the Australian Parliament, doing everything he could to facilitate a 'yes' vote for the conscription plebiscite to be held on 28 October 1916. It would prove a divisive argument in Australia and also in the trenches as debate raged about the practicalities of sending in conscripts to join volunteers, as the Fair Dinkums had been.

Tom Hicks Sr used his role as vice-president at the Federal Mining Employees Association of Australia to urge the workers to vote for conscription. At a meeting at Charing Cross in the heart of Bendigo, Hicks Sr addressed a large gathering, which included a high proportion of 'ladies', and pointed to the uprising at Eureka in Ballarat 62 years earlier to make his point. He said the 'interests of the workers were at stake in this titanic struggle' and that:

> the time had come for every man to declare where he stood in this great crisis . . . it is an unwritten law amongst miners never to desert a man in a time of peril . . . [and] the workers of Bendigo and elsewhere would be true to their traditions, and fight for freedoms as the miners fought at Eureka. This war must be won, and it was the duty of Australia to do its part as one of the dominions of the Empire.

He urged Australians to think of how future generations would regard them if an unsatisfactory peace with Germany were realised, and called for the protection of Great Britain as she had been 'like a mother in past decades'. With three sons who had fought in Turkey and now France with distinction, Hicks Sr said, 'Australian soldiers had honoured their little nation by their deeds at Gallipoli. Were we going to retain them or were we going to desert them?'

Others unionists argued that Australia was not in imminent danger of being overrun, saying this hardly constituted a need to drag reluctant participants across to fight on the other side of the world. There were divisive debates and rowdy public meetings in Melbourne and towns in country Victoria as citizens fought for the *for* and *against* proposal. Hughes's plebiscite asked one question, 'Are you in favour of the Government having, in this grave emergency, the same compulsory powers over citizens in regard to requiring their military service, for the term of this war, outside the Commonwealth, as it is now in regard to military service within the Commonwealth?'

Australians were divided like never before. Voting was extended to the men who were fighting abroad. They cast their votes a fortnight before polling day. Many of the frontline Anzacs were frustrated by the 'shirkers' who failed to 'do their bit', but almost as many of the volunteers did not want to serve alongside conscripts. It was a difficult question with no easy answer.

On the day that the Australian public voted on the issue, Major Arthur Hart, who had been such a key part of the 7th Battalion, left for England to take up a role as Commanding Officer of the 2nd Training Battalion. At 50, he was the oldest officer in the unit. Hart was remembered by his men as an officer who 'gave loyal service and, in his quiet, effective and efficient way, assisted in no small measure to the maintenance of the organisation of the Battalion'. Many of his battalion were sad to see him go, and some never saw him again.

It was around this time that the 7th Battalion's original commander, Pompey Elliott, came to see the men he had formerly led, bringing with him some of the men of the

59th Battalion, among them some members of the Fair Dinkums. Men and mates who had barely seen each other for months shook hands, threw their arms around each other, and shared a few tales. There were even a few tears shed for fallen friends and missing mates. As one of the men recalled: 'The terrible story of Fromelles was told [to] us in return for our experiences at Pozières'.

Scurry cast his conscription vote from England while he was recuperating from his wounds and coming to terms with a lack of vision in his right eye in the London General Hospital. When news filtered through to him later that Australia had narrowly voted against Hughes's proposal – 1,087,557 'yes' votes to 1,160,033 'no' votes, with only Victoria, Tasmania and Western Australia voting yes – Scurry was surprised. It wasn't so much that he wanted to force men to enlist against their will, but he knew the Anzacs needed assistance. His frustration was magnified by the fact that he was convalescing at a time when all he wanted was to go back to his men. Later he wrote of his disappointment about these:

> fine 'self-sacrificing people' who 'wouldn't sign a man's death warrant' or feared 'Asiatic races'. Don't these people realise that the war is real. I wish they had been with us on that wonderful moonlight night [in evacuating Gallipoli] and seen the moon gleaming on those little white crosses we were leaving down in the valley . . . But there, men's death warrants were signed long before, mainly because the men who should have been helping them were at the theatres or football matches, or at union meetings arranging shorter hours and more pay. Or did they see a brigade we know reduced by more than half in one day, just because, well, never mind why, but had some more been there to help, it may not have been so. And so I shall go back soon, and see my men, who helped me make the little battery I'm so proud of, first standing by working their guns,

while Bosch is searching for them all the time ... It's a most comforting feeling to be in a house in London, and hear people talking about the things Australian soldiers have done and be just feeling proud you are Australian, when somebody will say: 'But fancy the Conscription Referendum', and the pride goes, and this homeland of ours appears a land of mice, and crawling cowards.

Bert Plant, like Scurry, was recovering in England. Also like Scurry, he was now writing home to his family with his left hand, having had his thumb blown off at Pozières. He could barely believe the conscription result, expressing 'surprise at the large number of NO votes' and said he would like to spend six months touring the states and territories of Australia, 'telling people what the actual needs are ... The boys in the trenches need more spells than they get, the reserve being altogether inadequate'.

Plant knew then that his chances of heading back into the trenches was minimal, given his injuries, but he couldn't see why other 'slackers' at home could not be asked – or even told – to contribute more. He was told he would not go back to the frontline, but resolved to fight it. He just wanted to lend a hand – even his forever-altered right hand, if it came to that – because he owed it to his mates still over there. Plant was unquestionably in the yes camp. But there were conflicting thoughts among the Anzacs in the frontline. They voted yes, but far from over-whelmingly. The soldiers' votes for conscription tallied 72,399, while 58,894 were against the proposal. Charles Bean noted that after Pozières there were many Anzacs who were less prepared to force a man to fight against his will.

At home, though, Prime Minister Hughes refused to accept the decision, and was already planning another conscription vote, despite the mood of many in his party. By mid-November 1916, Hughes had had enough and walked out of the party room, taking 21 colleagues with him to form a new government under the banner of a new party. The Labor Party was split, the nation remained divided, and all the while the men in France fought on.

On 1 November, the Fair Dinkums of the 7th Battalion moved back into the trenches at Gueudecourt in appalling conditions. Rain had transformed the trenches into pools of mud and slush. The cold was sapping, and mud seemed to attach itself to every part of a soldier's kit and soul. The appalling conditions around Gueudecourt and nearby Flers were the worst experienced by men in the war, according to Bean. He was photographed in a trench near Gueudecourt, his feet almost cemented into the mud, his arms pushing against the sides of the trench.

George Rae described how 'the further we go, the colder it gets, so I suppose it will be very cold in Berlin . . . The way things are going at present, I think it will soon be over, for we are winning easily'. Few were as optimistic as this hardy soul, and you couldn't blame them. The march into the frontline was wretched, with men slipping off the side of the road into shell holes full of dirty water, mud and often rotting corpses. Layfield lamented that the men were 'up to our necks in mud . . . our clothes are smothered in mud'. For the first six days of November, the men were engaged in various activities in the trenches. Some were improving as best they could the section known as Grease Trench; others were on fatigues.

The conditions tested the resolve of the men who had survived Pozières, the fires of hell from a few months earlier now replaced by the frigidity of a muddy wasteland. It wasn't just the 'trench foot' rotting the men's feet, or the pneumonia-inducing conditions sending so many of them to hospital, or even the German machine-guns and artillery that cut across no-man's land, resulting in more casualties and fatalities. It was all that, and more. The men took to applying chalk to their feet as a precaution against 'trench foot' and were relieved to be issued with sheepskin jackets, which the wags in the battalion joked made them look like 'wooly lambs'. Lambs to the slaughter, no less.

Robert Royle and Tom Littlemore were English-born gunners who moved to Australia to chase greater opportunities. The pair knew each other from the *Anchises* and were fighting in close proximity on 3 November 1916 as part of a group of eight men heading forward to relieve 'some chaps'. They had just got into a trench when a shell exploded around them. Royle and Littlemore were killed, along with two other men. One witness said Royle had been blown to bits. The men of the 2nd Machine Gun Company expressed profound sadness at Royle's passing, for he was well known and liked by all of his comrades and in his regiment. He was buried, and in the chaos surrounding them, a small white cross was erected for him. Littlemore's final moments were not documented. To this day, their exact burial locations remain unknown.

As cruel as it sounds, the dead were at least out of the mess. The living had to endure conditions almost unimaginable to those who hadn't experienced them, while pushing their bodies and minds to the limit. Tim Brennan felt as if he couldn't fight anymore. Broken down by the miserable conditions, this forty-something, usually resolute Welshman turned Fair Dinkum collapsed under the weight of physical and psychological trauma. Brennan had been a stoker on ships, a fireman, a naval reserve man and was known in his hometown of Cardiff and his adopted town of Melbourne as a bloke always up for the fight; diminutive, but determined and dogged.

But he felt beaten. He lost weight. His face became gaunt. His black hair turned grey, as if the war had aged him more than the years that preceded it. Brennan had been a member of the 8th Reinforcements of the 7th Battalion, but had moved to the 59th Battalion, and then to the 60th Battalion. In the first week of November, the 60th were training in poor weather at Flesselles, just outside of Amiens. Eighteen men were sent to hospital on 8 November, mainly due to colds, but Brennan's cough rasped deep within his chest, his head ached as much as it did when shells landed close by, he had persistent diarrhoea and, significantly, he was morose. He was whisked away to a hospital in Amiens, then moved to Rouens, and finally to England, where he was tested for tuberculosis. The result was negative, which fitted his mood, but Brennan was increasingly concerned about what lay ahead for him.

While he was being assessed, some of the other Fair Dinkums who were still with the 7th Battalion were having a much needed respite. They had come out of the lines on 6 November, and a week later, had the luxury of hot baths at Ribemont. It was akin to an early Christmas present or a swag of letters from home. It was like no other bath that many had ever experienced: wiping off the mud, cleansing the blisters and boils on their feet, and washing away some of the memories of the most trying weather conditions they had experienced – even worse than in the dying days of the 'Old Dardanelles'.

Snow fell again that week, just as it had in their brief time on Gallipoli. They fought the rest of 1916 in extremely difficult conditions, spending time in and out of the trenches, dealing with the cold and the mud as best as they could. One of them remarked in December, just after they came out of the lines in time for Christmas:

> The battalion [was] bogged down in mud – almost. It's doubtful if we've been an hour dry the 16 days and nights we've had in this watery waste occupying ditches called Switch Gird Gap, and Grease Trench, Bull's Run, Pilgrim's Way and Goodwin Post. The carrying fatigues throughout those sunless days were bad enough – those down in the pitch blackness was [sic] immeasurably worse. One thing that shone throughout – glowed gloriously – the magnificent spirit of those shivering, mud-caked, chat-infested mates.

Another Fair Dinkum was taken before his time on 17 November 1916. Tom Roberts, 29, was one of three brothers to join the AIF. He and his 24-year-old brother Ernie were black-smiths, and lived with their mother in Seddon. They had fought side by side at Gallipoli, but were separated when they joined different parts of the engineers' section. Ernie had been wounded in September, and was recovering from gunshot wounds to the right shoulder and thigh in St Luke's War Hospital, Halifax, while his brother Tom was with the 5th Division Engineers near Switch Trench, Gueudecourt.

Tom was athletic and well known for his sporting prowess in the Footscray district. He had a bit of dash about him, too, and liked to have a good time. Just before leaving Egypt in May 1916, he had been censured for that very Australian pastime – having a punt – in a camp at Serapeum. He and a few mates were caught because a light was burning in their mess hut well after 'lights out'. The men were playing two–up, and there were no 'cock-atoos' keeping an eye out or guarding against the possibility of being discovered. When they were caught, Roberts and his mates put it down as a moment when the odds went against them. They received fourteen days confined to camp and lost fourteen days' pay. Six months later, far from the sands of Egypt, and in the quagmire of Switch Trench, the odds were once more stacked against Tom Roberts. He was killed in action, and buried where he fell, just under 2 miles (3.2 kilometres) north of Combles. Years later, the Grave Restoration Unit reburied Roberts' physical remains in Guards Cemetery, Lesboeufs. Long after the war had ceased, Roberts' mother – by that stage she was also mourning another son, Albert, who had died in 1917 – received twelve photographs of Tom's grave. It was little compensation for a grieving mother who had sacrificed two sons, but she could take solace in the fact that Tom had a resting place when so many others didn't.

As the year stretched on, and November headed towards a dark, dank close, some of the Fair Dinkums in the frontline were afforded the chance to have some leave in England. Layfield missed out. He desperately wanted to go, but didn't have the £10 to fund the trip or relatives across the Channel who could put him up. He knew his mother and father back home were struggling enough, so he comforted himself with thoughts of a trip the next year.

Les Wood was one of the lucky ones – he was one of those eligible. Wood, now with the 1st Australian Pioneer Battalion, had maternal relatives in Northampton who were happy to accommodate him. He also hoped to catch up with older brother, Harold, who was in the merchant service in London. Les was only 21. Just two months earlier, he had been promoted to lance corporal in the field, and had earned almost two weeks' leave. His excitement was almost palpable as he boarded the ship to cross the Channel. He had been granted leave from 27 November to 7 December 1916. Whether in Northampton or London, both places promised to be a brief sanctuary away from the guns and the industry of war.

The visit with his relatives was good enough, but getting the opportunity to return to London and see his brother again was special for Les. They had a meal together, and talked of old times, not knowing if the war would allow them the same luxury in the future. As they parted, they promised to meet again – somewhere, sometime. The handshake was as hard as it could be, the sentiment unashamed as the siblings parted company, Harold back to the ship that was about to take him away, and Les off into the crowd, ready to spend his final day in London before going back to join the Fair Dinkums.

Harold took one last look at his brother, waved, and then he was gone. For years and decades afterwards, Harold would think back to that split-second for clues. It was a recurring moment in his dreams – a flash of happiness that led to a lifetime of grief. He told those closest to him that he thought he had heard something like an explosion by the time he reached the ship, and later wondered if it had somehow impacted on Les. He would never know, and that was the hardest part. The only certainty was that Les was never seen again after the brothers parted near the docks, and the mystery of Les's disappearance would weigh on Harold like an anchor for the rest of his days. He didn't even know Les was missing until his mother wrote to him many weeks later, explaining that his brother had failed to front up and had been classified a deserter.

Les Wood's pay stopped almost immediately. As the days and weeks passed, it was hoped he might return, but he never did. Like the other Fair Dinkums who simply vanished on the battle-fields at Fromelles and Pozières, Wood was there one moment, and gone the next. But he had disappeared in London, not the frontline, and a Court of Inquiry the following year found he had 'illegally overstayed leave' and was deemed a deserter. Offi-cially, the army continued to contact Wood's mother for several years after the war, informing her of the need to tell them if her son turned up. But those who knew Les – and loved and trusted him – never accepted that he had run away. His mother prayed he would come back one day, but he never did. His brother, the last to see him and say goodbye, not realising it was for forever, maintained something must have happened to Les that day. Was it the explosion, or might Les have been murdered in London, which was why no body was ever recovered?

Harold was heartbroken, and the family mourned for as long as they drew breath. And the men who had lived with Les, and fought beside him for more than a year and a half, could never reconcile themselves with the army's conclusion that he had absconded and left them in the lurch. It wasn't Les's style – something had to have happened to him in London. A century on from Wood's disappearance, he is still classified as a deserter.

14

Mud and blood

*'I only have to think of my pals tramping through the mud
and waters and the discomfort that surround, and I feel
like a deep-dyed shirker – never mind, my luck is in . . .
it will not always be so good.'*

AS 1917 DAWNED AMID New Year prayers, the 7th Battalion's commander Carl Jess felt nothing but admiration for his men, many of them Fair Dinkums, for the way in which they had fought against the enemy and the extremities. And they kept fighting, regardless of the obstacles in their way, man-made or natural. They had been tested like never before, and had emerged as committed to each other as they had ever been, even if there had been more than a healthy cynicism about the British command.

They were not intact, though. So many of them were gone – some forever, some for the remainder of the war. Yet still they fought on. Jess marvelled at their camaraderie and composure under fire, and was inspired by their resilience and respect for

one another in the most trying of circumstances through 1916 –
a year that had begun in Egypt, taken them to the hell that
was Pozières and ended in the cruellest of winters. Jess received
a Distinguished Service Order for guiding the men through
Pozières. He wished he could pin a medal to each of their
breasts, but knew he couldn't. Instead, he recorded:

> Through it all, the mud, the slush, the snow, the enemy shelling
> and the endless fatigue, our men are always cheerful, eager to
> do what was asked, and accepting the casualties and adversities
> as part of the price which has to be paid for winning (and we
> are winning and going to keep on doing so) the great game.

Christmas 1916 had been spent out of the lines, though it
was a tight call. The men spent the one-year anniversary of
the Gallipoli evacuation – 20 December – in the boggy, mud-
covered trenches near Gueudecourt, but there was universal
relief when they were relieved three days before Christmas.

A year earlier they had celebrated the festive season on the
island of Lemnos. This year it was to be spent in the 'cosy huts'
at Melbourne Camp, near Memetz, fewer than 5 miles (8 kilometres) from Albert. A swag of letters from back home had been
amassed for this very occasion, which the men devoured with
the same relish they did their Christmas feast, and the nip of
rum rationed to them. Their Christmas billies were filled with
an assortment of goodies.

Alf Layfield might not have his trip to England, but he could
not have been happier with his new pipe, a tin of cigarettes, a
pair of bootlaces, a mouth organ, a bottle of Hazeline Snow face
cream (at least it wiped the mud away), a bottle of Bovril (extracts
of beef that could be diluted into a hot drink), a box of figs,
chocolates, a packet of chewing gum, a new toothbrush, a bundle
of pipe cleaners, a cigar in a cigar case, an assortment of safety
pins and a letter from a young woman by the name of Dollie

Roberts, from Scotchmer Street, North Fitzroy. He wondered what Dollie was like. He might even look her up after the war. As he sat down to write his festive greetings to his mother that afternoon, he expressed his satisfaction with the day:

> We were very lucky to get out of the trenches for Christmas. We were just like a lot of school children opening the boxes to see what we had in them. Well, dear mother, this is my second Christmas away from home, and I hope this New Year will see me home once more again.

He played the mouth organ, and wondered if he would remember how to play the piano – it had been so long. A piano would have made for a perfect Christmas; that, and being back in the house in Coburg celebrating with his parents Ada and George, his brother Geordie, and his sisters Ruby, and little Pearlie, who was only in her first year at school when he left, and must now have forgotten what he looked like. He hoped not. He acknowledged the 'bad luck' of missing out on getting 'Blighty leave':

> just because I never had the 10 pounds, but I'll be right as soon as my mate comes back from England. I have to have a pound a day to spend. I'll have a jolly good time there, Mum. I might take the train up to Scotland, while I'm there. I wish I had relations in England and Scotland.

Still, as disappointed as he was, Layfield maintained the smile that earned him the nickname the 'Smiling Boy'. He would be twenty in March, and felt as if the war had dragged him into adulthood, as it had with a whole generation of teenagers from around the world. He didn't complain. He just got on with the job.

The Fair Dinkums who had transferred to the Pup Battalion had the same good fortune to be out of the lines for Christmas. They were relieved on 15 December 1916, and 'passed the day in peace and quietness', sitting down for a hearty feast of 'roast beef, sauce, vegetables, fruit, plum pudding, beer, etc. Greatly appreciated'. The battalion's diary described Christmas 1916 as one of rest and relaxation. They talked of good times, and forgot about bad ones. They talked of mates lost over the past year, and moments that changed them forever. They knew there would be more of both in the coming year, but with full bellies and a couple of beers underneath their standard-issue belts, they managed to forget about the war for a day.

The 7th Battalion's Sergeant Harry Attwood was in Scotland at the time, having been sent across to Britain in late November for training, and granted leave to Edinburgh for Christmas. One moment he was 'billeted in the back room of a small farmer's house' in France where he was used to sleeping on a brick floor; the next he was boarding a ship across the choppy Channel for an officer's training school in England. All this happened in the space of two days, and there were some pangs of guilt at escaping the boom of the guns and the misery of the trenches while the rest of the men were still locked in the heat of battle. He made that point to his sister:

> I find myself most happily situated, the contrast with my last place of living is extraordinary. I only have to think of my pals tramping through the mud and waters and the discomfort that surround, and I feel like a deep-dyed shirker – never mind, my luck is in . . . it will not always be so good. However, I will miss the winter's worst. I expect to work hard and if I do well enough, I can hope to be made an officer some old day.

He wanted to look the part at least, and in trying to achieve this, went off to get measured up for a new uniform. The man with the tape measure inquired his name as part of polite conversation, and when he fired back 'Harry Attwood', the tailor reeled back in amazement.

'He replies, why that's his own name', Attwood told his sister in the letter. 'All operations ceased while I was plied with questions. He told me a brother of his by the name of Thomas Attwood had gone to Australia some 30 odd years ago and had a son called Harry.' For a time, the astonished tailor believed he had found his long-lost nephew. He hadn't, but the pair carried on, trying to trace any connection between the two Harry Attwoods. It was a good tale to send home.

Attwood's quest to become an officer didn't get in the way of him seeing parts of England and Scotland in his free time. One of his favourite places was Stratford-upon-Avon, the Bard William Shakespeare's birthplace. He was almost intoxicated by the history in front of him at Shakespeare's house: 'Saw no end of his relics. The town is quaint and interesting. I could have spent the whole day in Shakespeare's town alone'.

Bill Scurry was still recovering from his wounds in England. His right eye would never be the same again, but the rest of his wounds were, at least, improving. Writing home from the Hotel Victoria, he said he hoped to be in the frontline again, though the chances of that happening were about as likely as him shooting in competitions again, since:

> My left eye is quite alright and the right one is coming on well, and will soon be able to see quite well, though I don't think it will ever shoot in the VRA [Victorian Rifle Association] matches again. In myself, I am absolutely well, so the rest is only a matter of time. But I must not strain my peeper . . .

Still, the London fog in the lead-up to Christmas was doing all that, and more. One night after heading to the theatre, the thick fog and eyestrain left him as lost as some men had been on the battlefield. To his mother, Scurry wrote:

> You have heard of London fog, well, there is one in full swing now . . . I went to the theatre last night, to *The Professor's Love Story*,

and on my way there I got into the middle of the road and could not make out where I was. However, I found a policeman standing under a lamp and asked him if I knew where I was. He said: 'I don't know, sir, but I know where I am.' So I replied: 'Well, I'm in the same place as you are, so where are we?'

The policeman sent Scurry on his way to the theatre through the city with directions. He spent Christmas at an estate with other officers, where they got dressed up and:

acted out some silly goat's show, in which I took the part of the village idiot, and everyone remarked how natural I was. Very rude of them, I think. On Boxing Day, all the farm hands and the tenants etc were given dinner in the house and afterwards they all got presents and cake. Another officer [and I] decided we would be parlor maids for the occasion. We got nice clean aprons from the sisters and borrowed some little caps from the maids and adorned ourselves accordingly . . . I do wish you could have seen your only son in his parlor maid's turnout.

Scurry headed back to France on the fourth day of 1917. It wasn't the return to the frontline that he so desired, but he was at least back where war was still raging. For a time in January, he was camped at a new training school on the old trench system from whence part of the Somme Offensive had raged the year before. He expressed excitedly that 'there was not one inch of all our ground which did not teem with historic interest'. All around him he could see:

the old tumbled-in trenches, deep mine dug-outs, broken rifles, heaps of tangled wire covering the shell-torn ground with the white crosses to mark the last resting places of hundreds of brave men – British, French, and German – all kept one reminded that a soldier is the most honourable man on earth.

For a time, he stood before what was left of Pozières, where he knew some of the Fair Dinkums had fought – and died. It made him emotional and proud for 'what men on earth are more entitled to live and use what there is of Poziers [sic] than the Australians who won it?' As he scanned with his good eye, and what vision was left in his other, Scurry couldn't help but be saddened by what remained of the village. There was:

> literally not one foot of wall, and the country round is nothing but a barren waste of holes and rusty, barbed wire but every-where are the little white crosses which one gets so used to seeing all the time, but which mean much more than the finest monument, for each mark the spot where a man fell.

He felt it was the perfect place for young officers to train. How could they not be affected or influenced by all those white crosses, knowing that each represented a life sacrificed, not to mention the thousands of men who had become one with the soil without an official resting place?

> Can you imagine a better setting for our young officers to learn the beginning of their jobs, or our older veterans to come and brush up what they may have forgotten? From a more technical point of view, we had miles of actual battlefield for exercises, [we] could fight again old actions on the same ground as we did two or three times the attack by an Australian Battalion on Mouquet Farm [which had taken place between August and September 1916].

The ghosts of fallen men were only disturbed for a period of time, though, as the training camp was soon shifted north towards Flanders, as the new captain 'couldn't help wondering for the first time whether L. Corp Scurry, who used to sit and make toast with little knots of pals, was not really better off than

Capt. Scurry who would have had to answer then if the train [taking them north] had caught fire'.

By the end of January 1917 Scurry was on the move once more. As much as he played down the nature of his injuries to his family back home, his hand was giving him trouble, and the old wound needed attention in England. The medical board gave him a month's leave. He returned on the same ship, *St David,* which had transported him there after the explosion the previous September.

He was also about to have an audience with the King. George V was the monarch millions of soldiers were fighting for. Most of the Anzacs were now fighting for Australia, and for that ensign of a flag that had fluttered in the chilly breeze outside Scurry's hut in the training school near Pozières. So many of the Anzacs had started out fighting for Great Britain as much as Australia. But the events of the war meant they had so much to be proud of from their own country and their own countrymen, and so much to feel resentment for from the British.

Scurry was only 21 when he first met the King, who was three decades older. The young soldier from Ascot Vale, who had simply wanted to make a difference in this war, 'went to get a pretty little M.C. [Military Cross] pinned on', and 'though [the King] dishes them out by the millions, he seemed to take a live interest in everybody'. Scurry joked that they were 'now on such friendly terms that I'm going to ask him down to Mentone for the weekend when I get home', noting that George V was 'a very nice, old youth, and said some nice things to me'.

A week later, he was back at Buckingham Palace at a colonial officers' reception with 60 others. They strode through the Grand Hall, up the grand staircase and into the magnificent ballroom, which had been converted for the occasion into a moving picture show room. The men were ready for the show to begin, when the King and Queen Mary came into the room. Scurry joked to his mother:

After the movies, we all filed out and we were presented to all the Royal Family. They were very nice to me because I had two medals. I am sure you would have been surprised if you had seen my beautiful bows. None of your little nods and by the time I had passed five of them, I had got quite a backache and a very swollen head. Well, we all went down the Grand Staircase once again, and then into the room where we were all herded on the medal day, and found tea ready for us. We ate as much as we could, and then strolled into another salon. While I was standing talking to the Queen's Secretary . . . in walks all the Royalty again. His Majesty came straight over to us . . . Oh Mother, if you only could see your little Willie with one hand in his pocket and the other . . . discussing current matters with the leader of our race. He is a wonderfully natural man, and during our talk, which lasted about ten minutes, he made me feel very at home. In fact, I might just as well have been talking to any other gentleman.

Scurry also spent some time with the King's mother, Queen Alexandria, 'a very nice lady, but very deaf, and has a strong Danish accent'. But it wasn't all seriousness and stiff conversation. One of the other Anzacs brought a smile to Scurry's face by ducking out of the royal gathering to go on a date with a young woman waiting for him:

we all chaffed him about his cheek leaving Buckingham Palace to go and meet a girl . . . [he] argued that the King would not have worried if he had not been there at all, but the girl would have been very put out if he had been late.

While Scurry met George V in February 1917, Fred Hoad was wasting away in a German internment camp. He was mostly bedridden, still trying to recover from the wounds he had suffered at Pozières before his capture. He felt isolated and, in

251

part, abandoned. He had not received any letters from the men he had fought alongside, and wondered whether it was because he had the ill fortune of being captured. A few things kept him going: one was the thought of his wife, who had endured her own health issues, and his two beloved children. He also knew he had to keep up a strong façade for his fellow prisoners of war, for morale was almost as important as the meagre rations the prisoners received.

Then, there was the correspondence Hoad had struck with a 45-year-old Australian woman, Miss Mary Chomley, who was the secretary of the Prisoner of War Department for the Red Cross. Chomley had originally come from Riddells Creek in country Victoria, but she followed the war to London in 1914, understanding that the work of the Red Cross was going to be imperative in providing the link between the Australian soldiers and their families back home. Her role during the long years of the war, especially for the men who had been captured and became prisoners of war, went a long way to earning Chomley an OBE by war's end, not that she sought that. This persistent woman did it for the sake of the men in captivity, isolated from their family and their mates, and looking for any sort of certainty in a world they could no longer control.

In February 1917, in one of Hoad's early letters to 'Dear Miss Chomley', as he always addressed her, he unburdened himself, saying:

> I am still in hospital. My wounds are slowly healing – it is now going on six months since I was wounded. Quite a lot of muscle on the right leg has been destroyed. [It will be a] long time before I will be able to walk properly, my old wounds are again troubling me.

Hoad kept in regular contact with Miss Chomley, charting the food parcels that were sent to the men in the camp and all the while requesting to see if she could have any sway in getting Hoad moved to Switzerland, where the conditions were more relaxed. The biting winter was bad enough in the frontline, but for Hoad, the freezing conditions and the lack of provisions to keep him and the other men warm made life exceptionally difficult. He tried not to complain, but when he did, at least Miss Chomley listened. He also tried not to give up, but when the mood of his mail became more morose, Miss Chomley seemed to know the right thing to say, most of it centring on the importance of his family back home. Hoad came to rely on her regular letters, even though the diligent Red Cross worker was corresponding with so many Australian prisoners during the war. He was grateful to the woman he had never met, but who was helping to keep him sane, telling her:

> The boys and myself are sorry to hear of your difficulties under which you are working. We all appreciate the kind effort put forth by you in your noble work. I am about the same and looking forward to getting to Switzerland. I don't think I have any chance unless you can help me.

While Hoad was dealing with the cold-hearted treatment of his German captors, his old mates from the 7th Battalion were enduring the coldest French day in decades. The 'Great Freeze' fell on 26 January 1917 as they were encamped at Fricourt Farm. The battalion war diary noted it was the coldest day in France in 21 years . . . but the Germans kept themselves warm by keeping the guns blazing.

The weak rays of the midday sun could offer no comfort – 'that little silver ball . . . that looked so wan'. It wasn't much better in the days after – 'Everything is frozen . . . the morning meal was delayed owing to the difficulty of melting the ice'. Men did what they could to stay warm. In the early hours of 30 January, Layfield sat down beside a fire that gave off some heat, but not much. It was three in the morning, and as he sat with his feet up against the flickering flames, he took the time to pen a letter to his sister Ruby.

'It's a bit too cold to sleep without boots on,' he wrote, 'so I am sitting near a little fire passing the time by writing a few letters.' He spoke of how he desperately wanted to get 'Blighty leave' as soon as he possibly could. 'It won't be long before I go,' he wrote with more than a hint of excitement. His fingers, almost frigid, ached as he put his pencil to the page, but he assured Ruby that he wished they could be used for something other than the war. He longed to play the piano again, something he was exceptionally talented at, but well out of practice: 'I'd like a good rattle on the old keys . . . but I suppose I must be getting pretty stale now. It will be soon two years since I had any practice'. His fingers were now reserved for work and war. In a letter to his mother, written soon after, he took delight that his brother 'Geordie' was starting to learn the violin. He offered up a suggestion: 'Mum, if you like, you can change our piano [for a new one], but don't do it for my sake. In any case, I forget the name of those good pianos'.

That was the last letter Ada Layfield received from her son. By the time she got it, her Smiling Boy was dead, and it arrived almost like a message from the grave. The only problem was that Layfield had no known grave – it had been lost in the chaos of battle.

Ada never got rid of the piano after that. It was her son's, and now he was gone, his music silenced forever. She didn't know much about how he perished, or precisely where, on 25 February 1917, 27 days before what would have been his twentieth birthday. His mates shared some of their recollections, one story coming just weeks before he was cut down. At one stage between his last letter and his last moments, Layfield had found himself in a tiny church in a small, broken-down village. He wandered in and found an old piano tucked away in the corner, and immediately set to work, the music countering the sound of guns that boomed in the background. Soon, a gathering of French locals – young mademoiselles, elderly women and war-weary men too old and broken down for the fight – trickled into the church to listen to something that had long been lost to them too. It was a moment the gentle young man from the other side of the world treasured. The family never knew if the story was fact or folklore, but they so dearly wanted it to be true, because they knew how much the piano meant to Layfield, and perhaps to the people who were soothed by his playing.

The harsh reality of Layfield's death is less comforting, though he died, as he lived, with a smile on his face. Perhaps he was relieved that his battle was over. He was immensely proud to never have been away from the battalion. And he was there with the 7th, as always, when they went into the support lines at first, near Flers, on 13 February, and then into the frontline beyond Factory Corner six days later. By the time of his death, the Germans had retreated from parts of the sector, while still leaving a cluster of troops released to halt the pathway for the British and Australians.

Men all across the line wondered what had happened to the Germans. 'Where's Fritz gone?' some asked aloud. It soon became apparent that they hadn't retreated, but had withdrawn to their new defensive line, which they called the Siegfried Line. The Australians and British referred to it as the Hindenburg Line. It was a stunning new development in a war that had been bogged down in the mud and the madness of manic majors and generals for far too long. The 7th Battalion moved from Bayonet Trench in the late afternoon of 25 February and, as Layfield's A Company moved towards the German trenches, the clatter of machine-gun fire and artillery attack cut across them. Those who survived tried to dig in between Bayonet Trench and Rye Trench, but there were many casualties. The raid caused fourteen deaths, including Layfield's, who never stood a chance against the guns.

Witnesses to Layfield's final moments gave their recollections to the Red Cross. One of his A Company mates said he was 'hit by a machine gun bullet in two or three places' and killed instantly. Another said he had been 'shot dead through the head by a bullet in an advance'. In the fading light many saw him fall, but they made sure to identify him by his disc – number 2605. One private said, 'We were at Le Barque together and about a quarter to a half mile from Ligny[-Thilloy] on the 25th February, when he got fatally hit by a bullet and was left in a shell hole.' Another said:

> I was with him in the advance . . . [he] was buried in the field which was in front of Ligny-Thilloy. His grave was marked with a small cross and his name and all particulars were placed in two bottles, one at the head, and one at the foot of the grave. He was short, stout build with reddish hair and complexion, and of a happy disposition.

One informant said, poignantly, 'Layfield always had a smile on his face, and after he was killed, [I] was told by several men of the Co who saw him fall that he still had just the same old smile.'

Several of Layfield's mates contacted his parents, sharing in their grief. Private Claude Carpenter, who had fewer than eight months to live himself, said Layfield had:

> died a soldier's death, fighting for a just cause of freedom and liberty, also for his King and Country. He was the gamest and [most] unafraid of men in the platoon, and always willing to do his duty, whatever it might have been . . . being one of the most popular and well-liked boys, by those who knew him, I tell you his death and absence is sincerely felt by us all. He was given a decent burial . . . he was buried . . . [near] a trench known as 'Rye' Trench, in front of Thilloy.

His platoon commander, Lieutenant Oswald 'Ossie' Reynolds, described him as a 'fine, clean living lad . . . always eager to serve his country, but never forgetful of home and friends'.

A subsequent letter provided a few more details to his grieving family:

The sad event took place on the night of the 25th February, on a position about a quarter of a mile south of the village of Le Barque, near Ligny-Thilloy. The previous night we had advanced and taken the enemy front line and this night the company advanced over 500 yards over very muddy ground, just a series of shell holes, under machine gun fire almost all the time. All the officers, except two, were put out of action and some NCOs were hit, but your boy got forward to a position . . . leading the section all the way, and winning [the company's] admiration for his fearlessness. It was at this point, just as he was dropping into a shell hole that he received his mortal wound. His body was buried on the spot and a rough cross erected to his memory.

The Smiling Boy was forever gone, his music too.

Within a few weeks, the German strategy became more apparent. The Hun had withdrawn from Bapaume and 'he fell back on his great Hindenburg Line, a prepared position some miles beyond the town'. Left behind were a series of booby traps in the trenches that needed to be carefully navigated, particularly for those diggers with a penchant for getting their hands on German souvenirs. There were also wire entanglements that made it seemingly impregnable, though the hardy souls never saw that as a barrier. They would tackle it when they had to.

When the men of the 7th Battalion came out of the frontline, news came through that the Pozières hell-hole had claimed another of their Fair Dinkum mates, Joseph Bellesini, who finally succumbed to his wounds suffered on 25 July 1916. Another loss soon after Layfield's made it even tougher for men who felt they had seen enough heartache. It didn't look like Joseph's brother, Andrew, was coming back to the old 7th, either. He had joined the Provost Corps, and was recovering from his own wounds at Pozières. Given the Bellesini family had now lost two sons, it seemed only fair that Andrew be kept out of the frontline for his mother's sake. The men never begrudged Andrew a possible ticket home.

One Fair Dinkum heading back to Australia during 1917 was the man who had led them from the *Anchises* to the front-line. Major Arthur Hart, nearing his 51st birthday, could not stand the physical strain any longer. In the early months of 1917, he was relieved of his position as the Commanding Officer of the 2nd Infantry Training Battalion in England. The winter had taken a cruel swipe at Hart's wellbeing and he was in a poor state of health. A report into the state of the training battalion and into Hart's condition concluded that he needed to be replaced and should be sent home. One senior military official observed:

> Major Hart . . . admits that he is in a poor state of health and has been since he came to England, and is unable to do himself justice . . . Major Hart is getting on in years and is too old, if not in the best of health, to be carry out the duties of a Training Battalion Commander.

Hart arrived home in Melbourne in the middle of 1917, and returned to Eaglehawk, where he had enlisted, and received a reception fitting for the commander he had been at the start of his war journey. He was praised for being on the peninsula 'until the last night of the evacuation where he brought off a party of 230 men. He and his men held a line until within a few hours of the final movement'. He was lauded for being just outside Pozières when the shattered town was taken.

But Hart wasn't just there to claim credit for himself. He turned his praise to the magnificent Bendigo and Eaglehawk boys, and specifically named a number of the Fair Dinkums, including Lieutenant Oliver Harris, who was rising up the ranks of the 7th Battalion, Military Medal winner Tom Hicks, Frank Wearne, Richard McClelland, and Les Howe. Hart said the Germans were 'poor fighters at close quarters and easily gave in', which might have been disputed by some of his former reinforcements.

'They did not fight as fairly as the Turks,' he said.

On one occasion during a raid . . . one of the Germans threw up his hand and cried 'Kamerad' [Comrade]. The Australian who was approaching with his bayonet levelled, lowered his rifle, and as he did, the German seized him by the throat. Fortunately, an officer with a revolver was nearby, and the German was shot.

He could not speak highly enough of the young and not-so-young Australians who had been under his care and command. He told the reporters eager to interview him:

[While] it was well recognised that, although the discipline of the Australians was different to that of the English soldiers, they were not inferior to the English. They displayed greater dash and much more resource. They bore what hardships were necessary, always cheerfully, and the spirit of comradeship carried them along very well indeed.

BACK IN FRANCE, THE bleakness of winter began to fade and spring was fast approaching. Mud started to dry, and thawing conditions made things almost bearable. In this scorched landscape where renewal seemed almost impossible, the Anzacs wondered if the change in the weather would finally bring some hope.

The rest of March was made up of training for the 7th Battalion, first at the aptly named Bendigo camp near Bazentin-le-Grand, then at Dernancourt, and also at Buire. At Dernancourt, new open-warfare training techniques were tried, given the German change in tactics. In the last week of March, the men mended the road at Le Sars, but had just as much trouble pitching their tents in the wasteland that was Buire. One recalled: 'Those who were there will remember the difficulty they had finding somewhere on which they could pitch a tent, such being the density of water-filled craters in the gully allotted to us'.

The remaining Fair Dinkums in the 7th and 59th Battalions could sense that war was altering, but were unsure how. They commemorated the second anniversary of the Gallipoli landings about 20 miles (32 kilometres) apart. The 59th were encamped and resting at Mametz, just a few miles east of Albert, near where the 38th Welsh Division of the British Army had attacked during the first Battle of the Somme the previous July. They spent the day competing in brigade sports and then marched past General Birdwood at the conclusion of the activity.

But their respite was short, and they returned to the lines soon afterwards, to play their part in the next phase of the Battle of Bullecourt.

The 7th Battalion were in the support lines in the subsector of Pronville, east of the battle near Bullecourt on 25 April 1917. A message arrived from General Walker for the men who were at Gallipoli two years earlier when the landings had taken place. The Fair Dinkums felt part of the commemorations, since the date had come to be seen as not just about Gallipoli, but of the history that they were still making in France. There wasn't much time for reflection, though. There was work to be done, and artillery and aircraft above causing concern.

Scurry had a reunion of sorts in London on the second anniversary of the landings. He had been out the previous night, and arrived home tired. Another Anzac Day just made him want to be back in France with his men rather than in London. He was deep asleep when the light was abruptly switched on at two in the morning. Initially dazed, he rubbed his eyes before he came across a familiar face. It was Captain James Bowtrell-Harris, who had not only been in the Essendon Rifles with him, but who had been with the 7th Battalion from the start. The two old mates spent Anzac Day together, which started off with 'Bow' receiving his Military Cross at Buckingham Palace, and ending at the theatre watching *Maid of the Mountain*, followed by dinner at the Ritz-Carlton.

Scurry longed to be back in the frontline, but the damage to his eyes meant that was not going to happen. When he caught up with Elliott in England, he was told, 'I should probably be going back to France to do a job behind the lines, well out of the way of "bang noises".' Scurry got word to leave for France soon after Anzac Day, with Elliott making sure he could make a meaningful contribution out of the lines as part of the 1st Anzac Corps School of Instruction:

> You see that by my being sent back to the school, the General has made up his mind that nothing more is going to happen to your little Willie. Of course, I don't like the idea of leaving the battery again much, but the General's wonderfully far-seeing judgment has done so many things, that I know it is absolutely the best course, so off I go to a way back-behind-the-line soldier, but I don't suppose it can be helped.

As the Anzacs fought doggedly in the Battle of Bullecourt through April and May 1917, attempting to break into the Hindenburg Line, Scurry was frustratingly well behind the lines with the 1st Anzac Corps School. On his return to France in late April, he noted:

> I am back in Sunny France, but in a very safe part of it . . . So much for England for a while, for a good while, I hope, for

though I had a splendid time there, I feel as though I am one of the King's 'bad bargains'. It is so long since I have done any real work.

He spoke of how the weather had changed the mood of the men after a woefully cold winter:

The days are getting simply beautiful again, and what with the trees just budding little wee green leaves and the birds singing all around me, if I hadn't had my hair cut yesterday, I'm blessed if I couldn't write a fair story of soul-stirring rhyme or, better still, I could lay back in the nice clean sand and go to sleep like a lizard.

Scurry had no intention of doing so. There was a war still going on, and he didn't give up trying or asking to be back in the fray. In the meantime, he set to work training men and becoming an outstanding instructor, just as he had been a diligent, determined and damned good soldier.

15

The push towards Passchendaele

'I can order them to take on the most hopeless looking jobs, and they throw their hearts and souls not to speak of their lives and their bodies into the job without thought.'

HARRY ATTWOOD WAS GOING back to the 7th Battalion, and he couldn't be happier. Having spent months in England on training courses, being promoted to 2nd lieutenant, and even doing a stint with the 5th Battalion, it just seemed right that he would rejoin his Fair Dinkum mates again. By July 1917 he was back with the 'Old 7th' when great things were happening. This accountant from Bendigo had the feeling the odds were now in favour of the Anzacs, and he wanted to share those experiences with those he knew and respected above all else. His sense of belonging was summed up when he wrote to his sister that month, informing her proudly: 'I've transferred back to my original Battalion after seven months' absence. Of course, I'm very pleased, it's good to see the old faces again'.

He didn't mention the faces that were now memories. Still, there were enough old mates left to make him feel almost at home, and some of them, including the man who had just been appointed the battalion's adjutant, Oliver Harris, had been there the very day he had enlisted in 1915. Attwood's mindset was clear – he wanted to get back into the action. He had the chance to take leave to Paris, but knocked it back with barely a thought: 'I was nearly going . . . but I do not want to be away just now. When our next spell out arrives, I hope to pay a visit – [I] am saving up – and will make the most of the fair days'.

He knew the 7th Battalion were about to take part in a big push and he wouldn't have missed it for all the francs left in his wallet. There was no time to waste, and no time for extended epistles to his sister. In a letter scrawled to her on 15 September, just days before the battalion's next engagement, he apologised for his short missive. The next one would be more detailed, he promised.

Around the time that Attwood was being welcomed back to the 7th Battalion, another Fair Dinkum was taking part in an emotional reunion of his own at an old home in the ancient town of Bordeaux, the port city nestled on the River Garonne. Just a few streets back from the majestic waterway, at 7 Rue Pourmann, a diminutive, dark-haired 27-year-old Australian soldier – looking fairly spick in his newly cleaned uniform – knocked on the front door of the house where he was born. When he left Bordeaux as a young boy, he was still Auguste Pierre Lafargues. Now his mates called him Gus. He had left a French lad, and returned an Australian in all but accent. But one thing hadn't changed – his closeness to his mother, especially since his father's passing. He hadn't seen her for what seemed like a lifetime, and here he was, on a late July afternoon, knocking on her door unannounced.

Lafargues had been in France just over a year earlier, but the killing fields at Fromelles delayed his visit home. In the Aussie vernacular that he had adopted with an amused relish, he was bloody lucky to have not turned up daisies like so many of his mates on the night of 19 July 1916. He had been wounded, cleaned up by the machine-guns, but somehow had survived with injuries to his left arm and legs. From there, he had been repatriated to England on the *St Denis* hospital ship. He didn't return until May 1917, and at the first chance to take leave, he applied to travel to Bordeaux. The homecoming was emotional, their happiness mixed with heartache. Together, they mourned Gus's brothers, who were killed fighting for the French Army. Mrs Lafargues couldn't afford to lose another son.

In Richmond, they called them 'the Fighting Murcutts', but in France, they were brothers fighting for their country. Still, it was extraordinary that this family of seven sons and seven daughters had provided six Anzacs. One of them was Bruce, who had enlisted as part of the Fair Dinkums at only seventeen, and grown up as part of the 7th Battalion, though he would come to spend some time with the 52nd Battalion. Murcutt's father documented one of the most remarkable impromptu family reunions involving the Anzacs during the war. As the *Richmond Guardian* recorded: 'It is doubtful if there is one family in the country with a finer war record than the Murcutts . . . Quite recently a letter home told that the . . . brothers had met in France. Picture, if you can, a meeting such as that'.

Family folklore would have it that all six brothers met on one memorable occasion in France sometime in 1917, and as they parted, wished each other luck for the remainder of the war. Another report said it was only five of them, which is almost certainly the case, as one of the six brothers in uniform appeared not to leave Australia. Just as incredible is the fact that all of the brothers – the seventh was rejected for service – would survive the conflict.

Welshman Tim Brennan fortunately got the chance to see his sister, Norah, before being loaded onto a hospital ship bound for Australia in the middle of 1917. She had made the journey to England from Cardiff to see her ailing brother, who had all but been ruined by his experiences of war. In his forties now, he was a shell of the small but resolute one-time stoker who had once thrived on shovelling coal into the furnace. The bitter winter of 1916 had crushed him. His illness started as bronchitis in November, then developed into something far worse. After being evacuated to England, he underwent many assessments; all the while, his weight dropped. One medical report said the place of Brennan's disability had been 'the Somme', as it had been for millions of young and old men. His cold and persistent headache degenerated into vomiting and diarrhoea. Brennan went to the No. 1 Birmingham War Hospital before being transferred to Harefield Military Hospital on 29 March 1917 in a 'very debilitated state . . . His chest has scattered moist sounds with evidence of some fibrosis'.

Deemed 'unfit for general and home service for six months', he was put on a list for a return to Australia, where it was hoped he would recover. His sister bade him farewell, hoping it would not be forever, but must have suspected otherwise. In early July, Brennan was taken aboard the hospital ship, *Karoola*. Just a month later, on 9 August 1917, Brennan's battle ended. It was found that he had a malignant kidney, which had caused his weight loss and his death at sea. The men on the ship, who had hardly known him, gave him the only form of burial they could offer. He was wrapped up in the sheets from the bed in which he had died, and released into the ocean. The silver watch his sister had given him before he boarded the ship presumably went to the bottom of the ocean with him.

Oliver Harris was exceptionally busy in his new role as battalion adjutant, yet he never ceased to send the people of Bendigo his good wishes whenever he had the chance. He took delight in the fact that some of his letters were published in the *Bendigo Advertiser*, with the local paper saying his words 'written on scraps of paper in the trenches are entitled to rank as first-class literary efforts, in descriptive powers to the work of seasoned war correspondents'. Harris confessed that even in the frontline, 'Dear Old Bendigo is never absent from my thoughts. Today more so than ever, I think of it, for with us it is polling day and I am wondering what Bendigo is doing.'

On the day he wrote these words, Harris was voting in the Australian federal election, where he hoped Prime Minister Billy Hughes – who had come to be known as 'the Little Digger' – and his Nationalist Party would be returned. Harris continued:

If only Bendigonians realise that today, and until the result is declared, both Allied and enemies are concentrating much attention on our city, and wondering what stand we will take. Mr. Hughes fills a wonderful position in the eyes of friend and foe, and our foes in particular will rejoice if Bendigo fails to realise its duty and honour.

Harris thought it incredible that the Anzacs were casting their votes while still in the firing line and under enemy shell fire, but insisted 'we took care to move only a few men at a time to the polling booths, so as to avoid enemy shelling, as we are under direct enemy observation, and he shells immediately his observers notice movements'.

The polling booths also brought a smile to his face. Democracy determined in a dugout, it might be said.

'Imagine roads running through cuttings, we call them "sunken roads"', Harris wrote:

Along these roads for miles, troops are dug in the banks and small dugouts [are] constructed. Usually, for a roof, there is a bit of corrugated iron or old flooring boards obtained from the nearest ruined village, and we are never far from ruined villages. We have today turned some of these little dugouts into polling booths. Usually an old box or piece of board does service for a table. The men are very keen. At 'stand to' this morning I heard groups of them keenly discussing how the vote should go. No attempt whatsoever is made to influence the men. All publications and available information is issued to them direct and from that and from what they read in the newspapers sent them from home they form their own opinions.

Harris was unquestionably for Hughes, and when the news finally reached him in mid–May that 'the Little Digger' had won a decisive mandate over Labor's Frank Tudor, he couldn't have been prouder of 'Old Bendigo'.

Like his fellow Bendigonian Attwood, Harris could sense the changing nature of the war, and hoped his men would be given the chance to play a key role again, as they had done elsewhere. Gone was the long, bitter winter, where Harris had seen:

men . . . wade into trenches and in mud and slush well above their knees. In many cases, while in the front line, it was impossible to have even small fires and consequently most of the meals were cold. An effort is always made to send into the front lines at least one hot meal per day, and special food containers are issued for this purpose. These are filled with hot tea or stew, and strapped on the backs of the men of the carrying party – one container per man.

He sensed the Germans were feeling the strain of the war, though he knew there was still much work to be done: 'The hills near us are strewn with the bodies of dead Huns and I should not think he finds too much pleasure in looking at them. Many are visible to him from his own observation posts'.

But the Anzacs were still under increasing strain from German artillery, though despite the many deaths, there were astonishing stories of survival. Harris was particularly affected by one, when a shell smashed into a section the 7th Battalion were living in. A twenty-year-old from Bendigo who had shared the dugout next to Harris was completely buried: 'I ran out to see what had happened and all I could see of the poor chap was his boots'. The men dug for dear life, knowing that every second may be the difference between life and death for this young man. They managed to drag him out; he had part of his cheek torn off, and a slight fracture to his skull, but he was alive, and rushed to a casualty clearing station.

Major Fred Tubb wasn't a Fair Dinkum; he was an Original. But anyone who knew him sensed a presence that belied his size – he was just over five foot five (167 centimetres) – thanks to this farmer and part-time footballer's powerful forearms. Just over two years earlier, as the Fair Dinkums finalised the last few weeks of their Seymour training, Tubb was at Gallipoli building a legend. It happened at Lone Pine when, on 9 August 1915, he helped to hold ground against a formidable Turkish counterattack, rebuilding a barricade while inspiring the men around him in an act that earned him one of four Victoria Crosses given to men of the 7th Battalion on that one day.

Tubb was badly wounded in the arm and head, and repatriated to England and later Australia. That could have been the end of his story, and it would have been more than enough. But it wasn't. Even one of the women who looked after Tubb during his convalescence in England remarked much later: 'I can still see him now, his whole personality radiating vitality and energy'. Tubb didn't return to France until before Christmas 1916, and study and sickness limited his time with 7th Battalion for a long period afterwards. So the Fair Dinkums could hardly have been more excited, and in awe, when Tubb returned to the battalion in August 1917 for the next stage of the campaign – a push towards Menin Road, which would lead to other battles at Polygon Wood, Broodseinde Ridge and Passchendaele. Attwood, who had read about Tubb's exploits, was pleased to be in the same company. He couldn't wait to get started, and after a sports carnival in September – where Tubb ran in the heat of a foot race but pulled up feeling the effects of a hernia that troubled him – the 7th Battalion prepared themselves for the challenge ahead.

On the night before the battle, scheduled to take place east of the scarred Belgian town of Ypres (pronounced by most of the Anzacs as 'Wipers'), Tubb knew this was going to be his last meaningful battle. One of the men from D Company, which he was in charge of, and Attwood was a part of, recalled the Major telling the men: 'Now boys, this is my last battle'.

The men, who looked up to Tubb almost as if he were super-human, cried out, 'No, Sir!'

To which Tubb replied, 'This *is* my last battle, but you men know what to do and I expect you to carry it through.'

It wasn't a premonition of his own demise, but more that he felt the physical issues he faced no longer allowed him to be a frontline soldier. Those who heard Tubb make his state-ment, including Attwood, knew he would still be giving his all in the attack on the Menin Road. This wasn't just going to be a suicidal front attack, as so many had been in the past. This time the move would be accompanied by serious artillery, and more 'set-piece planning', where a carefully prepared time-table was followed. The 7th Battalion was designated to take the third objective – the Green Line – and the men's helmets were daubed with the colour of their objective. The battalion moved towards their jumping-off points after 11 pm, 'in the inky darkness, through steady rain by a boggy and slippery track', after a pre-battle warm meal and drinks. They were in position by 4.45 am, lying on the ground, waiting for the roar of artillery to kick into action 55 minutes later. As *Our Dear Old Battalion* detailed, the men were heavily packed with what they might need: '48 hours' rations, 2 bombs, 2 grenade rods, 220 rounds of ammunition, 2 ground-flares for signalling to aircraft, and 2 filled water bottles, which made us veritable human camels'.

Ahead of them was the enemy, who held the line in a series of posts, blockhouses and 'pillboxes'. If this was to be his final battle, Tubb had no intention of losing.

Soon after the barrage started at 5.40 am, men from the various battalions swept across Glencorse Wood towards their objectives. The first two – Red and Blue Lines – were reached, though some of the artillery intended for the Germans actually fell on Australian troops, causing a number of deaths. The 7th Battalion moved swiftly towards the Green Line at around 10.30 am. That was reached by 10.55 am, but just as the objective was obtained came a critical blow for the men. Tubb had been mortally wounded after he and his men, Attwood included, were attacking a pillbox manned by Germans unwilling to yield to the assault. There were conflicting reports as to what happened next, though in one account the 36-year-old had been observed 'dancing with delight on top of [the] pill-box, where he was wounded by a sniper'. Badly injured, the larger-than-life character was being moved when a shell burst almost on top of him. The combination of both was too much. Tubb was dead on arrival at the nearest hospital, the gunshot wounds in his back having penetrated his abdomen. The Victoria Cross winner who had seemed invincible, and who was often referred to as the soul of the 7th Battalion, was gone.

Second-Lieutenant Attwood was only a year younger than Tubb, and barely knew him other than by legend. He served with Tubb for only a few weeks, and died on the same day. Attwood was the victim of one of the Allied shells that fell short of its intended target. There were several witnesses to his death. According to one, he was 'killed by one of our own 18 pounders' while he was advancing towards Polygon Wood. One of those with him said 'I happened to be about 10 yards from him and as soon as he was hit, I went and looked at him. But he was killed instantly'.

Another was 25 yards away:

[We] had just gained the new objective and had orders to hold the Block Houses. A shell exploded in the centre of a small party, killing casualty almost instantly, and three other men . . . I saw him move his head and then fall back dead. His chief wounds were through the hips. He was taken behind enemy lines after his death and I do not know where he is buried.

One of the stretcher-bearers recovered Attwood's body, which was taken back across the other side of Menin Road, and buried near Lake Zillebeke. He was only 35.

Shells still cracked overhead and too often came perilously close to the Anzacs. That led the new commander of the 7th Battalion, Lieutenant-Colonel Ernest Herrod, to pull his men back from part of the line. There had been talk of a counter-attack from the Germans, so the men were prepared for whatever might come next. But the one thing they could hardly be ready for was the confirmation that the seemingly indestructible Tubb had died of his wounds. His death cast a pall over the battalion. While the attack on the Menin Road had been successful, and there looked to be more gains, Tubb was gone, and that hurt like hell for so many of the men, including some of the Fair Dinkums. There was continuous shelling, but no serious coun-terattack on the second day of the battle. Before midnight on 21 September, the 7th Battalion was relieved from the line, but there would be plenty more action to come in the Ypres sector.

Lance Corporal Jack Simpson, who was with the 2nd Machine Gun Company, serving alongside the 7th Battalion in the battle, was also killed on 21 September, though his body was never recovered. The precise details of his passing are long since lost, beyond the fact that Simpson, a 22-year-old instru-ment fitter from inner-suburban Melbourne, 'fell in the fight at [or near] Polygon Wood'. Simpson had been promoted to lance corporal sixteen days before his death, and the only items sent back to his parents in Abbotsford were a scarf and a safety razor.

An article on his passing in the *Richmond Guardian* concluded, 'He hath done what he could.'

Twenty-five-year-old Corporal Robert Fraser, an accountant from Ascot Vale, served with Simpson in the 2nd Machine Gun Company, and played a crucial role on 20–21 September, his feats earning him a Military Medal. He had been advancing east of Hogge, when he and those around him came across a deadly enemy barrage. He was wounded severely in three places, including the right foot, but insisted on remaining with his men until he had organised their positioning forward towards their objective. The citation, written eight days later, explained: 'He supervised the placing of five Vickers Guns, and also two German guns. By his prompt action, he was enabled to inflict heavy casualties on the enemy during a counter attack'. As much pain as he undoubtedly was in, Fraser remained with the party through the night, and refused to leave until he could ascertain that all of the positions were consolidated. It was then, and only then, that he accepted he could not continue, and was taken by the stretcher-bearers for treatment. Within a fortnight, Fraser was on the hospital ship, *Jan Breydal,* headed for England, where he was admitted to Reading Hospital.

Stretcher-bearers played an exceptional role in the battles around Ypres. Ben Joyner may have only been twenty when he tended the wounded, but he was industrious as he combed the battlefield, looking for anyone who needed assistance. Men from his own battalion said this one-time blacksmith was the quintessential Anzac, a real character and with a hard edge.

One remarked, 'If anyone answered to the description given the typical Aussie by English war correspondents, in particular – hatchet-faced, devil-may-care, incurably casual – it was he. He remained essentially the same, a likeable fellow even when exasperating.'

Like Fraser, Joyner had been wounded in the battle, but thought so little of his own scrape that he kept going. He was more determined to help those who needed it. He won his citation for work undertaken near Polygon de Zonnebeke, east of Ypres, specifically for displaying 'excellent courage under heavy fire in attending wounded . . . although he [was] wounded he carried on with his work'.

Arthur Robinson, another Fair Dinkum, made a similar mark carrying wounded men through wild storms of fire. Robinson hailed from Talbot in country Victoria, and knew the importance of sticking by your mates. He did that from 20 to 22 September, and was nominated for a Military Medal. He was later bestowed with a Bar for his Military Medal. Like Joyner, he won the award for his work at Polygon de Zonnebeke, and for showing extraordinary courage under fire, collecting the wounded and giving them a chance to fight for their lives. It just seemed to be the right thing to do for this conscientious 27-year-old, who put his own life at risk on countless occasions so that others could survive.

Farmer Henry Pluck, 23, had been wounded at Fromelles the previous year as part of the 15th Brigade Machine Gun Company, and spent a few months in hospital in Newcastle-on-Tyne being treated for shell shock. He recovered, and was back in the frontline soon enough. He was fighting near Ypres on 20 September 1917 when his war ended abruptly. Pluck was 'blown up' by a shell as his world went blank. He recalled nothing until he was taken to a casualty clearing station and then could not raise himself out of bed for more than a week. The shell shock from Fromelles was bad enough, but this one affected him even more. He had constant pain in the back region and recurring headaches. A medical report conducted in the Duxton Ear Hospital in Northampton revealed that dreams had been keeping Pluck awake at night. He also had inflammation of the kidneys and was deemed unfit for active service.

Menin Road was the end of the road for Pluck. He was hospitalised in England and repatriated to Australia early the following year, arriving just before the third anniversary of the Gallipoli landings. It wasn't the way in which the young man envisaged returning, with the war still raging, but he was at home at least, and his hometown of Oaklands, just over the Murray River in New South Wales, welcomed him with open arms. He was one of three returned soldiers given a civic reception at the Oaklands School of Arts where one of the speakers declared the town 'could not do too much to honour these brave men because it was through them, and men like them, that [Australians] were able to enjoy their present liberties'.

Elliott was impressed by what his former battalion achieved:

Our [Australian] boys, particularly the old 7th have made a glorious advance and captured a whole lot of Bosches and driven [them] back a long way . . . That will be another feather in our boys' caps for the British troops have been blocked along this line for about a month. I hope we will do as well when our turn comes, which will be very soon now.

As the 7th Battalion was coming out of the line, the 59th Battalion and the rest of Elliott's 5th Division were preparing to go into battle near Polygon Wood. Having almost been wiped out as a fighting force at Fromelles fourteen months earlier, the 7th's Pup Battalion – or 'Pompey's Pets' as some called the 59th – had made some strong gains in the Second Battle of Bullecourt earlier in the year, but this next phase on the Ypres sector was to be a significant challenge. In a letter home, Elliott sensed the enormity of what lay ahead, saying:

[From] what I can see it's going to be 'some fight' that we're going into . . . the guns are booming like waves on the shore again – drumming to call us to battle and for many of us beating our funeral marches at the same time . . . my poor boys have to face it all time after time, and it is up to officers [even the highest] not to shrink from what their men have to face. But whether we shrink or whether we don't, we must each and all go into it with what courage we can muster.

In the lead-up to the attack, which occurred just before dawn on 26 September 1917, an artillery barrage described by Charles Bean as 'like a Gippsland bushfire' raged as the men went to their fate through a haze of dirt and smoke. The men of Elliott's 15th Brigade – including the 59th Battalion – were attacking a formidable stronghold, which consisted of stripped-back trees, undergrowth difficult to get past, shell holes scorched into the earth and trenches and pillboxes manned by Germans unwilling to yield. Through it all coursed a creek, oddly enough a former riding school, and a significant mound that provided an observational outlook for the enemy. The resistance was considerable, particularly from the pillboxes where machine-gun fire roared towards the Australians. The ground rumbled with artillery fire and the clatter of machine-guns, and parts of the right flank had serious failings, though the men of the 59th Battalion marched on as best as they could, taking possession of whatever ground they could.

Unlike most commanders content to wage their wars from well behind the frontline, Elliott pushed forward in the early morning light on 27 September for an assessment. All the while he was admonishing stray officers who happened to be unlucky enough to cross paths with him. He said curtly to one, 'Your men are up there fighting for their lives, what are you doing?' It's not hard to imagine that officer skulking back in the direction of the battle.

Elliott's presence in the heat of the battle was inspiring. Some would later insist it was the only time they had seen a brigadier in the first line of attacking troops. Elliott could see the chaos of the battle, and sought to make improvements as best as he could. Some of the men, including more than a few Fair Dinkums, couldn't help but go that extra yard, knowing that the man was there himself. Others who hadn't seen him heard about his presence, and information was passed around the troops with relish.

The dirge of dust and fire had subsided for the most part when Elliott toured the battlefield, so he was able to make observations and alterations to help with the push forward. One who was there remarked, 'with mud and slush to our knees, Pompey took short cuts and missed nothing. The boys who looked abjectly miserable when he arrived at the various pill-boxes and shell holes managed to raise a grin when the old man spoke to them'. The morale boost from having Elliott there – a man they unashamedly respected, admired and, yes, feared – was considerable. He took steps to quell confusion and, with the grunt from the diggers, saw to it that the operation's objectives were achieved.

Lance Corporal Dugald Walshe, who started in the 7th, was transferred to the 59th and then the 60th Battalions, almost met his maker a year earlier at Fromelles, but the push towards Polygon Wood had an even more devastating effect on his well-being. He had been severely wounded in the right knee and thigh at Fromelles – badly enough for him to be hospitalised in Birmingham, but not serious enough to stop him from going absent without leave for a day in September 1916, or again for three days early in the New Year.

Other than those blemishes, Walshe worked to his capacity – until Polygon Wood, where the enemy's artillery barrage brought him undone. He was in a support trench on the front-line when he was buried by a German shell that landed near him. The 21-year-old was dug out of the rubble by those close by; surprisingly, he was free of any serious physical wounds. But Walshe did not escape the trauma of being buried alive, and was badly affected by shell shock. For a while he couldn't speak, and was sent to hospital where he began to speak again – slowly at first, and with difficulty. He stumbled over his words and stammered. His hands shook. He couldn't recall how he got from the trenches to hospital. But at least he was alive, safe for the moment.

Elliott couldn't have been more proud of his 'boys', even if his detailed description of the Battle of Polygon Wood – with the flaws of others set out comprehensively and unashamedly – was suppressed by the military chain of command. Of the 15th Brigade, which included the 59th Battalion, he wrote glowingly:

> We had a wonderful battle and a wonderful victory. My boys simply covered themselves in glory . . . many, many have fallen, but we have in the fight stamped our fame on a higher pinnacle than ever. I can order them to take on the most hopeless looking jobs, and they throw their hearts and souls not to speak of their lives and their bodies into the job without thought.

One who impressed was Walter McAsey, a 30-year-old farmer, country footballer and 'a wood chopper of note'. He had deserted within a few months of enlisting in Seymour in 1915, which almost coincided with his marriage, but returned to camp to carry on his soldiering. Now, at Polygon Wood, this signaller with the 59th Battalion won the admiration of those around him with his exceptional bravery and devotion to his duty. According to a history of the 59th Battalion, McAsey's work was acknowledged by his superiors:

> at Tokio Ridge . . . [he] showed great courage . . . he worked as a linesman mostly under heavy shell fire . . . day and night with untiring efforts to maintain telegraphic communication . . . he assisted to lay new cables . . . and did similar work . . . at Polygon Wood.

Edward Farrell was now with the 1st Australian Pioneer Battalion, but still retained pride in the Fair Dinkums of the

7th Battalion he had joined up with two years earlier. He was 33, although he had declared his age to be 27 when he enlisted, and had only recently changed his will. He was also a new father, though he had never seen his daughter, who was born after he had left for the war. It is unclear if he even knew of the child's existence. In July 1917, in the presence of two mates, Farrell revoked his previous will so that Lucinda Little – the mother of the child – stood to bequeath all of his possessions, instead of his own mother. He listed himself as formerly a farmer, but 'now parts beyond the seas as a member of His Majesty's Australian Imperial Force'.

On the morning of 2 October 1917, in fighting that was taking place east of Ypres, he was returning from the front-line. He and his men came 'to a dangerous spot, [and] Corporal Farrell was leading his section, when an enemy shell killed four infantrymen and severely wounded Corporal Farrell'. His injuries included seven different wounds to the head, as well as in the shoulder, leg and hand. He succumbed to his wounds on the same day after being carried back to the 3rd Canadian Casualty Clearing Station. One of the men with him said Farrell 'was most conscientious and fearless, and won the entire respect of all the boys. His quiet and unassuming manner was much admired and had he not been killed, he would have gained rapid promotion'. Any hope of that was buried with him in Belgium, in a simple ceremony.

Back home, Farrell's personal circumstance was much more complex. For the next five years, his mother and the mother of the child he never met squabbled over his personal effects and his medals. Farrell's mum, Margaret, questioned whether her son even knew about the child, pointing out that another child had been born to Lucinda since. She feared 'an injustice to my son', so 'I think I should have these trinkets as all the suffering I have gone through for him, it is only right that his mother should just have preference over others'. And then she added: 'My son, it appears, left a will leaving his money to a young girl, but . . . I could well do with it'. Lucinda argued that she desperately wanted Edward's medals – 'His child and I value those things. His mother would regard it as rubbish – its resting place would be the fire'. There were no winners in this family dispute, which was not uncommon during a time of war, with two resolute women fighting for what they believed was their right, and a son and partner who was never coming home to meet his little girl.

By the early hours of 4 October, the battle-hardened men of the 7th Battalion were huddled next to one another along the tape lined up as their jumping-off point in no-man's land near Anzac Ridge, looking out to their next objective, Broodseinde Ridge. There was an 'ominous hush over all of us as we waited in the thickening drizzle' for the zero hour, which came at 6 am. Forty-five minutes before zero hour, the roar of the German guns rumbled the earth in what was the 'the most savage bombardment yet, the enemy's prelude to his scheduled recapture of some of the ground we held'. The Fair Dinkums never forgot 'the din, the geysers of mud, the vibrations that spread through the level at which we squatted, the opening roar of the barrage just as the Germany infantry were timed to pounce, and the meeting of both attacks'. The driving rain turned the battlefield into a pool of mud.

As the original history of the 7th Battalion summed up: 'Never were minutes more carefully waited, never was time so slow, never was the sound more welcome than the opening of our barrage'. The pounding spooked some of the men. Battalion Adjutant Oliver Harris kept moving through the group, in an effort to keep them calm. He won a Military Medal for this and other work he did on the Ypres sector during this time. While the battalion was waiting and being inflicted with many casualties, Harris 'did remarkably good work re-organising the Battalion under this barrage, thereby not only inspiring the men but setting a good example to all ranks. The successful advance at zero hour was in a large measure due to the good work of this officer'. The men moved towards Broodseinde Ridge and down the slope with the 'enemy retreating as fast as they could before us'.

The 7th Battalion's objective was taken within three hours, but during the course of the day, the fighting and the barrage rolled on.

Two Fair Dinkums never saw the close of 4 October. Spencer Smith had recently received a postcard in the lead-up to this battle. It had a photo of his baby sister – his fourteenth sibling – on the front, with a message 'from' her, in his mother's handwriting: 'To my soldier-brother, I am looking forward to meeting you'. He never got the chance. This twenty-year-old ironworker and part-time pugilist, who had the nickname 'Gunboat' Smith, had already been twice wounded – and survived. But his luck ran out on this day, and he was dead by 11 am.

In the confusion, there were conflicting reports about how it occurred. One mate explained:

He was killed just in front of me in our hop-over . . . on the ridge before Passchendaal [sic]. We were both attached to the 2nd Field Coy Engineers. As we went over, Smith got a big wound over the heart and I picked him up and put him into a shell hole. He would be buried there later.

Another gave a more brutal version:

I saw him killed instantly by a shell at Broodseinde Ridge on the morning of 4th October, 1917. I was about 30 yards from him. His head was blown off. This was in the German line we had just taken. We held the ground. I passed the spot two hours later and the body was still lying there. I cannot say where he is buried. I heard he was reported missing.

Gunboat Smith has no known grave, but the postcard from the sister he never met somehow found its way back to his grieving family.

Gordon Mills had twice been held back from fighting, but when he got to the battlefield, he proved to be a worthy gunner on the Western Front. He had joined up with one of his foster brothers, Bill, as part of the Fair Dinkums. Gordie's war ended near Zonnebeke Mills in the Broodseinde battle, the third family member to make the ultimate sacrifice. His foster brothers John and Pat Mills were killed in 1915 and 1916 respectively. Gordie was listed as missing on 4 October, his father told the news the following month. Soon after, he was declared killed in action, although his body was never found. His family regularly posted in memoriam notices for their 'lost' boys. One, in the *Gordon, Egerton & Ballan Advertiser,* detailed their ongoing pain in 1918: 'They are gone, but not forgotten, and never will be. Released from sorrow, sin and pain, and freed from every care; by angel's hands to heaven conveyed, to rest there forever'.

Sergeant Cedric Smith, another Fair Dinkum now with the 2nd Machine Gun Company, might well have breathed his last that day, but for some good fortune, providence or good old-fashioned pluck. During the heavy artillery attack from the enemy, this construction engineer from Geelong, was buried by a shell. He frantically worked to tear himself out from under the mounds of dirt and mud, and after extricating himself, worked to free seven other mates. As part of the recommendation for a medal he never received, the citation stressed that Smith was under heavy fire the entire time he was dragging the men out. It was a remarkable effort, and even though he was injured himself, Smith point blank refused to leave his men – and wouldn't for five more days. He should have been rewarded with more than just the cheers and good wishes, but that sufficed for him. He wasn't in it for the medals; he was doing it for his mates.

On the same day that Gunboat Smith and Gordie Mills died – 4 October – Bill Batson was writing home to his mother from London, a city that was meant to be impregnable, about the perils of air-raids in the pulsing heartbeat of the British Empire. He explained:

London has been stirring times during this week and last. We had air raids . . . I was at home on Saturday night and did not feel at all happy cooped up, while the air raid lasted (viz 8pm till 11pm) and falling shrapnel did not cheer us up. The planes were flying very low . . . the sound of their engine could be distinctively heard on two or three occasions . . . One of our fellows got one of [the] shells (unexploded) through the roof and into his bedroom.

When Batson, who had been promoted to Staff Sergeant of the Australian Army Pay Corp a month earlier, was out one night that week, he and many other commuters had to take refuge in Victoria Station: 'The place was crowded and people were very nervous. I asked one woman did she feel nervous and the reply was "Yes, but when I look at you big, brave Australians, it makes me forget to be nervous"'.

THERE HAD BEEN RELATIVE success in fighting in the Ypres sector during September and October 1917, but some frustrations were revealed in one history of the battalion:

It is worthy of note that in both these operations the 7th was detailed to capture the final objective, and in both it accomplished everything asked of it . . . [But] it used to gall us a good deal to be unable to follow up a success of this kind. Having reached our objective we were bound to stay there, and not able to exploit our attack as we should have liked.

There were many outstanding feats of bravery. Robert Haysey, an orchardist who was a mate of Ben Joyner, one of the heroes of Menin Road, made a significant contribution as a scout. When some of the runners – the soldiers who relayed messages to and from the frontline – were knocked early in the battle, Haysey volunteered to fill the breach. His extraordinary work on those two days in October earned him a mention by the corps commander and, in time, he would become one of three non-commissioned officers from the 7th Battalion to be awarded the Belgian Croix de Guerre. He was noted for his 'marked calmness and devotion to duty' and 'successfully carried forward important messages under intense enemy shell fire and obtained important information as to the progress of the action'. Art Pegler, the young man from Mildura, was nominated for a Military Medal because of his 'great skills, ability and courage throughout operations' during the push towards Passchendaele. He wouldn't receive it, but would be duly recognised for his courage the following year.

Twenty-seven-year-old Ernest Baker was also nominated for a Military Medal for his work as a scout and a runner. He missed out, but was mentioned in despatches. However, before the Army could send notification of his recognition back to Australia, Baker was dead, hit sometime 25–26 October. Like so many others, he has no known resting place.

Reg Palmer, the 23-year-old joiner from Warragul, also won some acclaim. He came to notice for his work north of Bellewaarde Lake just before dawn on 19 October 1917, when he was leading a group of 30 men. They were in control of nine wagons, carrying slabs to be used in the forward areas. Heavy shelling seriously damaged the road and Lieutenant Palmer worked assiduously and repaired much of the damage. While others around him lay wounded, through constant fire, Palmer carried on, and was as relieved as anyone when the wagons made it back to where they were meant to be.

Signaller Tom Hicks already had a Military Medal from Pozières, to which he would add a Bar at Broodseinde Ridge for his 'great bravery and devotion to duty': 'under heavy shell fire he went out continually repairing breaks in the lines caused by enemy shell fire and under heavy fire successfully carried important messages from Battalion Headquarters to Company Headquarters'.

Back home in Australia, his father Tom Sr was preparing to stand for the Nationalists – of all parties – in the seat of Eagle-hawk, against long-time Labor member Tom Tunnecliffe, in the Victorian state election. A long-time 'Laborite', Hicks had been the vice-president of the Federal Mining Employees Association before his beliefs that Australia needed to expend everything in the war effort saw him expelled by the union's executive. Hicks's switch of political allegiance was a sign of a wider bitterness that was dividing the home front, with people torn between Billy Hughes's push for another conscription plebiscite in December 1917 and the belief that men should never be compelled to fight against their wishes. Hicks campaigned heavily on the pro-conscription banner, but he narrowly lost the poll, despite solid support from his local region. When the result was called in Tunnecliffe's favour, the Member of the Legislative Assembly called for three cheers against conscription. In contrast, when Hicks rose to speak, calling for three cheers for conscription, 'three hoots were given in response'.

It was a debate that tore at Australia's conscience. One letter to the *Argus* in late 1917 showed the depth of feelings from one camp:

We can now divide the Commonwealth into two parties . . . 1): the soldiers and their relatives and all who are making sacrifices for the Empire, and 2): men who are making no sacrifice, but are drawing large salaries – shirkers and traitors. The sooner the people get hold of this division, the sooner shall we put an end to the present tomfoolery.

The arguments on the other side of the debate were just as passionate and vocal.

The level of enlistments in Australia during 1917 were drying up; the flood of two years earlier when the Fair Dinkums had joined up had now become a trickle. That scared the hell out of Tom Hicks Sr, who worried about his decorated sons fighting abroad.

Hughes's question for the second plebiscite was far more straightforward than the first, 'Are you in favour of the proposal of the Commonwealth Government for reinforcing the Commonwealth Forces overseas?' The vote was held five days before Christmas 1917. To the disgust of Hughes and Hicks, the Australian public voted against the proposal for a second time. This time Victoria, the state that had provided the bulk of the men of the 8th Reinforcements of the 7th Battalion, voted no to the proposal, as did the majority of Australia, the difference being 166,588 against Hughes's question. There would only be volunteers for this war.

On the day that Australians voted no to conscription, the 7th Battalion and the Fair Dinkums were in the forward area at Wytschaete, once a nice little village just 5 miles (8 kilometres) from Ypres, but now a shell of what it once was. General Birdwood visited the men on 24 December to wish them good tidings. Almost on cue, it snowed on Christmas Day, but the men were pleased that the sacred day was thankfully quiet, albeit exceptionally cold, and there were no casualties.

This was the Fair Dinkums' third Christmas away from home, and a fourth for the Originals. As the Christmas billies once more arrived, thoughts drifted more and more towards Australia. But the relative peace for Christmas was shattered on Boxing Day when the Germans surprised everyone by 'putting about 300 [gas] shells over covering an area of about 500 square yards' into the reserve company at Denys Wood, connected by duckboards to the main trenches. It was said: 'The Hun celebrated

Boxing Day . . . with mustard gas. There was no wind, and the poison penetrated the dugouts and hung around the wood for days before finally evaporating. Company headquarters was in an underground dugout beneath a pillbox and suffered worst'. Seven officers were badly affected, as were nearly all the men in D Company. Many of them carried the effects of mustard gas suffered here and elsewhere for the remainder of their days.

The 7th Battalion was relieved on the last day of 1917, and arrived at Rossignal Camp to welcome in the New Year. A resolution was shared by the men – this *had* to be the last year of the war. As Bill Scurry, who was frustratingly still with the Training Battalion, wishing he could go back to the frontline, wrote in late 1917, 'Poor old "Fritz" has just about "burst his balloon" now and I don't think it is a matter of very, very long. As far as I am concerned, he can hand in his checks [sic] tomorrow'.

The balloon had been pricked, but more was still to play out before the war was over.

16

Here comes Fritz

'Gentlemen, the destiny of the Empire may rest on what our Battalion does tonight . . .'

THE WANDERING BARBERS HAD served their penance; now they were about to go back into the lines again. Lawrence Black, serial absconder and sometime hairdresser, emerged from the military prison at Rouen in late November 1917, having had the rest of his sentence put on hold. He was back with the unit for just over a month when, three days after Christmas, he fell victim to one of the many gas attacks to hit the 7th Battalion around this time. The poison didn't kill him, but it took him out of the lines again, as he was evacuated to England for treatment.

Black wound up in the Norfolk War Hospital in Norwich, a former insane asylum converted into a military hospital to allow for the constant stream of wounded men coming across from France. He wasn't there long; the venereal disease that had troubled him flared again, and he was transferred to the Australian Dermatological Hospital at Bulford. He was under their care for 33 days. On his release, Black was back to his old habits, missing from the parade transfer at Sutton Veny on 23 March, and although he was back again two days later, his path for the balance of the war was all too predictable. He would go missing, then return. He followed the same pattern from March to June in 1918, and again in August. He had no intention of being in the frontline during momentous events.

Bill Walker was different. The soldier who had fled with Black at Etaples in September 1916, admittedly after suffering from shell shock at Pozières, had two things guiding him when he left prison. First, he wanted to prove to the men he had served with that he was not only a Fair Dinkum, but fair dinkum about what they were fighting for. His desertion had more to do with his shell shock. He wasn't a slacker.

Few people understood how the unmerciful barrage from Pozières impacted on the minds of men. For some, its effects would last a lifetime; old men decades on from war's end would wake up in fitful screams over what they had experienced and seen. Walker wasn't one of them, though what happened at Pozières almost certainly played a role in why this knock-about soldier put down his scissors (at the time he was working in a hairdressing unit ahead of a return to the frontline) and skipped camp with an accomplice who should have known better. Walker paid for that with more than a year behind bars in the Rouen military prison. His other motivation – even more telling than the first – was to ensure his wife, Olive, and his kids (a son, Roy, and daughters, Marion and Eileen) had access to his pay packets again. This one-time barber, tobacconist and billiards hall operator, who had set up his base in Tocumwal, knew there had been no money to support his family while he was in prison. This time he wouldn't let them down. So he swallowed his pride on his release when he was made to serve at the officers' club – not something that would have come easily – and then when he had to spend some time working at the 2nd Australian Infantry Brigade Signal School. The test came when he was due to go back into the frontline. By April 1918, Walker was back with the 7th Battalion and the way things were looking, he and the rest of the men were going to be in for an exceedingly busy period.

After such an exacting time of it in the push toward Passchendaele the previous year, the first few months of 1918 were comparatively ordered for the 7th Battalion as the cold weather hampered activity. Some men sensed, though, that they would more than make up for it as winter thawed into spring, amid the rumours of a new German push.

Roy Anderson was gearing up to be a part of it again, having spent a considerable stretch of the previous year in England, but he was destined for France now. He was the last of the five Cobram Fair Dinkums to play an active part in the war. One of them, Bertie Knight, had been the first 8th Reinforcement of the 7th Battalion to be killed, back in June 1916. Knight's brother, Hugh, was already back in Victoria, deemed unfit for active service due to wounds and shell shock suffered at around the time Bertie was killed. The two Rays – Eaton and Rohner – didn't make it to Western Front, sent home from Egypt due to illnesses. Anderson remained in communication with Eaton and Rohner. One of his final letters of 1917 explained that: 'after two long hard years I have been recognised. Our Colonel has recommended me for a Commission'. He returned to France a lieutenant at the end of the first week of 1918, excited by the prospect of playing a key role in determining who would win the war.

Former Salvation Army officer Walter Judd needed some salvation of his own at the start of 1918. He had endured a very difficult war and was now heading back to Australia, changed forever. Now almost 30, he was going home to his wife a different man, having seen things no man should see, and dealing with the trauma by drinking to forget the pain. Sometimes it worked; mostly it didn't. Judd had served well, rising to become a sergeant after starting with the 7th Battalion, joining the 59th, and then the 5th Australian Pioneer Battalion. But illness saw him spend a considerable amount of time in hospital and he was deemed unfit for active service, leaving England on 11 January 1918, his war over.

Captain Fred Hoad was at last out of Germany, which brightened his mood and his resolve. If he had had to spend 1918 in a prisoner-of-war camp in Germany, he wasn't sure if he could have made it through. The hard work of the Red Cross, and the indefatigable Miss Chomley (who was still corresponding with Australian prisoners on a daily basis) helped to get Hoad transferred to Switzerland on account of his ill health in November 1917. His wounds from Pozières were still troubling him, and he would yet have more surgery in Switzerland.

Writing from the Hotel Cointe in Vevey, Hoad expressed his gratitude and delight at being out of Germany. 'The Swiss people gave us a glorious time – two receptions were given on the way down,' he wrote to Miss Chomley, enclosing a postcard of Lake Geneva. 'I am full of admiration for such great people. Everybody seems pleased to see us and everything is done to make us forget such a place as Germany. I am quite comfortable – this is a most lovely country.'

In a letter written soon after he stressed, 'Mine was not a pleasant experience in Germany . . . The doctor is calling on all men this morning – I am hoping he will let me get up.' Hoad felt secure enough to document his mistreatment at the hands of his German guards. By that stage, his health was slowly improving and he came to be an enthusiastic explorer of the picturesque city and beyond. Now that he was out of Germany, he pleaded with Miss Chomley to send him any Australian papers she could find; he wanted to see what they were saying about the 'Anzac Battalions', particularly his own 7th Battalion. He had plenty of catching up to do, and longed for when he could be back with his men.

Bill Scurry hadn't seen Arch Wardrop, the friend he signed up with in 1915, for so long, their connection lost due to circumstance. So imagine his delight when at Anzac headquarters in London he ran into his old friend. Scurry detailed the chance meeting:

> Who should happen to come out onto the steps but Arch . . . he is on his way back home, invalided. I, for one, am glad he is going home for both the boys [Arch and his brother James, the latter who would become one of the co-designers of the Melbourne Shrine of Remembrance] have been away long enough for Mrs. Wardrop now, and it is quite time one of them got back.

Wardrop was finally going home; Scurry had no intention of doing that until the war was over for good. Besides, he still hadn't given up on what some might have considered the forlorn hope that he might get back into the frontline − even with a bung eye. Not that he told his mother; with her, he gave the party line: 'It is a good thing that it makes my Dear Old Mother happy to know that I'm not right among the bang noise'. But he watched on with considerable interest at the changing tides of war, and swore that he would get back into action, even if the doctors insisted he couldn't. For the time being, he had to be content with training men at an instructional school and reading and dreaming of battles past and present. Some of the books included two volumes on the life of American Confederate General 'Stonewall' Jackson, a Napoleon biography, countless textbooks on musketry, infantry and machine-gun training, and Shakespeare. This proud Australian also had a battered copy of 'Banjo' Paterson's *Man from Snowy River*.

As March turned into April, and the days grew longer and brighter, Scurry mused about the men serving, 'There are all sorts of exciting things happening over here now . . . I thought for awhile that I might have been able to get back now, but I've got no hope, so I must make the best of it.'

Lieutenant Reg Palmer had been mentioned in the Corps Commander's Routine Orders for his 'determination, courage and initiative' on the Ypres sector in October 1917. He was with the 5th Australian Pioneer Battalion, but had never forgotten his start with the Fair Dinkums. On the morning of 2 April 1918, he was having a shave in A Company's mess room. It was around 11.40 am. In the corner of the room a handful of soldiers were playing patience, a card game, while others were quietly working. Hardly anyone noticed one soldier come into the mess room, take off his gear and move towards the Lewis gun that was kept there for instructional purposes. Classes for the use of the Lewis gun were often conducted in the mess, though not usually when men were going about their daily routines. Palmer wasn't aware when this soldier began to strip the gun and attempt to reassemble it. He may have heard him ask another soldier for the names of the various parts of the gun. Then, across the din of men chatting and trying their hand at patience, three fast, violent bursts echoed across the room, shattering the calm. The men at the table jumped to their feet, and saw Palmer lying in a pool of his own blood, shot through the head after the gun was accidentally activated.

In the court proceedings that followed the tragic death, one of the witnesses said:

Without warning I heard a burst of fire from the gun. This caused me to jump from my work and exclaim: 'What have you done?' I then saw Lieutenant Palmer lying on the floor shot through the head. The gun was at one end of the room near a window, the muzzle pointing towards the door. Lieutenant Palmer was previous to the burst of fire having a shave between the door and the muzzle of the gun. I was busy writing at the time and did not see how the gun was fired.

294

Asked if the man who had been stripping and reassembling the gun was familiar with its operations, the witness offered, 'He is just learning as far as I can tell.'

Another witness to the incident thought he heard:

a series of explosions ... On looking around, I noticed that someone had fallen on the floor, whom I discovered was Lieut. R.W. Palmer. He was beyond aid. Shot through the head. I remained there until Capt. Patterson brought the medical officer ... after which we wrapped the body up and moved it outside.

Palmer was buried at the Toutencourt Communal Cemetery, about 20 kilometres southeast of Doullens. The man responsible for the accident had to be consoled and lived with the guilt ever after, later saying, 'I was so absorbed in what I was doing that I did not realise the fact that I was using live ammunition and consequently endangering anyone's life. I have never actually handled a LG [Lewis gun] in the field, and have had perhaps only an hour's training all told.'

That man was severely censured for his carelessness. Meanwhile, a family back in Warragul had to come to terms with the fact that their son had survived the dying days of Gallipoli and the killing fields of France, only to die while shaving in the sanctuary of a mess room. They placed a notice in the *Argus,* which read, 'Sweetly resting in Jesus, With thoughts of home and duty, You sailed across the foam, to fight for dear old England, and for those you loved at home'. His sister, Lilly, added another: 'A life of promise honorably closed, someday we'll understand'. They never did. Among Palmer's belongings sent home to his family was the razor strop he had been using when he was killed.

The 7th Battalion ended a period of relative calm when it went into the frontline near Hollebeke in Belgium on 24 March 1918. It would have been the Smiling Boy's 21st birthday, but Alf Layfield had been dead for thirteen months. Three days earlier the Germans had begun a move that would change the state of the war, at least for the interim, if not for longer. For months there had been talk that the German balloon that had been so limp and lifeless towards the end of 1917 was about to get some fresh air. Russia had been effectively removed from the war after the Bolshevik Revolution of 1917 and their subsequent treaty with Germany had freed up somewhere in the vicinity of 35 German divisions and 1000 guns for transfer to the Western Front. The Americans had come into the war, but had only five untrained divisions in France. More were due soon, but this provided the Germans with an opportunity to strike hard, and General Erich Ludendorff intended to do so in a vastly different manner from what the Western Front had been used to. The Germans favoured new tactics such as the use of tanks and special strike forces that moved swiftly through the lines, known as storm-troopers. There were four main areas of attack, with the main thrust to finally break through lines that had been denied them previously by outflanking the British Army and the French troops.

The 7th Battalion had not encountered much resistance from the enemy near Hollebeke, though there was an unusual number of bombardments up and down the line. Such demonstrations were meant to be followed up by frontal assaults, but nothing was forthcoming. A battalion history written by two men who had served with the 7th stated:

> The Bosche was as amiable as could be desired. One could not suspect him of any mischief as one gazed over his peaceful lines on those sunny March days; while away on the Somme he was massing a tremendous army and advancing by sheer weight of numbers. Our hearts were with other Australian divisions who had left us to join the battle on that front. Our turn was not long coming.

By the time that happened, the Germans had swept through so many of the hard-won Somme battlesites that the Australians were under siege. The 7th Battalion was finally relieved from the British 21st Division, which had: 'met the German onslaught that first day, and told us of the deadly slaughter wrought by their machine gunners, of no avail against the countless masses of the enemy'. When the 7th was relieved from their position in Belgium, they were immediately told to head down to the Somme to help quell the attacks.

Within days, the Fair Dinkums were headed back to the Somme, to be met with hot coffees from the YMCA, drenching rain from the heavens, and the retreat of the villagers. The Anzacs tried to reassure the fleeing Frenchwomen and a scattering of old and infirm men that they were there to stop the Germans, but before they had the chance to put those words into action came the startling news that the enemy had commenced an attack on the northern front near where the 7th Battalion had only recently vacated. The men could barely believe it. The battalion was told it had to go north again – more than 150 kilometres – back to almost where the men had come from in the first place.

The men caught the train north from Saint-Roch station in Amiens, but only after considerable delays and an enemy bombing campaign that saw shells land in the station yard, killing four men. The Fair Dinkums waited nervously for departure, all the while lamenting the damage that had been done to the city that 'we knew it so well in happier days, a sort of little Paris . . . with its magnificent old cathedral . . . and so we sat for hours, in constant dread lest the enemy should renew their bombardment'.

The train did not leave until 1.30 am on 12 April 1918, and all along the route and on arrival were stations smashed by German artillery, burning farmhouses and a constant stream of refugees fleeing the coming German storm. When the men reached

Hazebrouck at 2 pm, some of the locals packing up their worldly possessions opted to unpack when they saw the Australians' hats, convinced that 'Les Australians' would at least stand and fight. When the Anzacs were having a break during a march towards Vieux-Berquin, they encountered a few British artillerymen rushing past on horseback, who said, 'The Jerries are coming in thousands.' One of the wags in the 7th Battalion answered back just as quickly, 'Mind you don't get drowned in the Channel.'

The Anzacs were shocked at the extent of the British retreat, and the speed and destruction of the German advance:

> In a few days the whole of a vast tract of country hitherto peaceful had fallen into enemy hands. It included many districts and villages almost sacred in the minds of the men. There was the area around La Creche, the Battalion's first resting ground in France; L'Hallabeau, where we next sojourned; Fleurbaix where we were first in the line in France and were schooled in trench warfare; the trenches round Ypres, where we had licked our wounds after the Somme; Polygon Wood and Broodseinde Ridge, which had been won by us at great loss in the short-sighted offensive of the autumn of 1917.

The situation was exceedingly bleak as dusk cut across the sky. The men reached Vieux-Berquin and moved to the open field. Just how tense the situation was came when Colonel Herrod briefed them at what was looking to be a helpless cause. The Germans were attacking the nearby town of Merris and headed in their direction, with only the incoming 4th Guards Brigade and the 8th Battalion likely to give any assistance. Herrod looked at his officers, including Fair Dinkum Oliver Harris, and delivered a message none would ever forget, one that highlighted the gravity of their situation, but also the importance of what they would have to do against a bigger, more powerful and advancing enemy. Herrod told his officers that brigade headquarters had insisted that they hold the line *at all costs*:

Gentlemen, the destiny of the Empire may rest on what our Battalion does tonight and until the rest of the Division arrives. There is a wide gap in the line through which the German armies are pouring. Their objective is the Channel Ports. Our order is to dig in and form an army line of resistance, and the Germans are not to cross the line. There are no troops to support us until our own Division arrives, and no artillery is available.

Witnesses later said they thought they saw tears in the colonel's eyes for the task he had to give his men.

As one of the men later documented: 'Without artillery or any other support, we were practically all that stood on that vital stretch of front between a foe flushed with victory and the Channel Ports which were his objective'.

By 5 pm the battalion had moved to the edge of the Nieppe Forest, and it was while patrolling there that Lieutenant Ossie Reynolds finally came across the 4th Guards Brigade. No one knew precisely where the Germans were coming from, but the certainty was the 7th Battalion was holding a line of more than 3 miles (6 kilometres) with little between them and the rapidly approaching enemy.

One soldier recalled the sky was as:

dark as the inside of a cow, and we leaned against the parapet, the rifles cradled into our shoulders and stared into the night until gremlins danced before our eyes and we saw phantoms that were not there. About midnight our hair stood on end when a cry rang out of no-man's land 'Stand To'.

A town nearby, Merris, fell and the Germans were said to be preparing for a mass attack that could come at any minute or any hour. In the early hours, to the relief of all, parties of the 8th Battalion and other sections of the 2nd Division began arriving. But the men had worrying times after that anxious night watching shadows and expecting the might of the German Army to come storming across the fields at any stage.

Amid this uncertainty, Bill Walker was back in the fold, so much so that he was now manning a Lewis gun. He had regained the trust of those he served with, his desertion forgotten. He was also relieved that his family back home was now getting the financial support it so desperately needed. Six months ago, he was still a prisoner. Now here he was, on the edge of the Nieppe Forest, ready to try and stop the advancing Germans. The expectant mass attack didn't come, however, though pockets of resistance came and went. The Germans launched considerable artillery on the 7th Battalion line and beyond.

The precise details of what happened next to Walker are unknown, though on 14 April he was wounded while manning the machine-gun. The wound was deep in his thigh, and serious. He was whisked away to the nearest casualty cleaning station, but died at 8.50 am on 16 April 1918 as the situation around the Nieppe Forest was being stabilised. His wife, Olive, was forwarded the bad news, and those who knew him in Melbourne and Tocumwal toasted the likable larrikin. Olive mourned him and never married again. Walker may have cost her more than a year's pay when he was locked up, but his death at least granted her a pension and, in time, the Prahran Council gave war widows the opportunity to live in small but new houses in the aptly named Victory Square. Olive and her children lived at No. 13, where she and fifteen other widows had to pay the nominal rent of 1/- per week. But nothing made up for losing a husband and a father. In death, the army quashed the unexpired portion of his sentence; Walker had proven himself in battle, and nothing that had happened before mattered anymore. He was buried in Ebblinghem Cemetery, 'four and three-quarter miles west-north-west of Hazebrouck' in Plot 1, Row C, Grave 8. Two generations later, his grandson found the small well-kept cemetery – which was created only out of the German Spring Offensive – where Walker was finally at rest.

Bill Walker and Fred Mann had sailed to war together, and while their paths took divergent twists and turns, both died on the same day and came to rest in the same cemetery only a few feet apart from each other. Mann, 22, was with the 5th Battalion, and might well have died an old man in Melbourne, but for his dogged persistence. He had sailed with the 8th Reinforcements of the 7th Battalion in August 1915, but on his return from Gallipoli, had been afflicted with paratyphoid. His war could have been over.

But Mann wasn't prepared to accept that, even though he was married. He sailed home from Egypt in February 1916, but by the end of the year he was in France, as a part of the 21st Reinforcements of the 5th Battalion. Mann was in the general vicinity of where Walker was when the German advance looked like overrunning the Anzac troops in mid-April, near the village of La Motte and on guard duty in the early hours of the morning outside a farmhouse billet. The men inside heard the smashing of shells, and one of them inside the building detailed the chaotic scene:

> We were . . . behind the lines in the reserves. There were about 20 of us detailed for gas duty in a farm house. They were bombarding us a good deal which kept me awake . . . I heard him cry for help; he was brought in [and] a bit of shell had gone through his thigh. I noticed it was a very big wound and he bled a great deal. He was bandaged up and someone got a stretcher and took him across the road to the D/S [dressing station]. The next I heard . . . I was told his grave was just outside with a cross.

Mann's wife, Aileen, placed a death notice in the *Argus* on behalf of her and their two children, Helena and Willie. It read: 'No useless coffin enclosed his heart/No sheet or shroud around him/He lay like a warrior taking his rest/With his military coat around him'.

George Rae had also been wounded by German shells on 14 April, but survived. It was the third time he had been wounded, and 'the closest shave I have had'. He explained to his father: 'We were all lying in the open when a shell landed about three yards away on my right, smothering me with dirt and smoke, and giving me a blow from a piece of shell on my right ear and entering my neck just behind the ear'.

It could have been worse. The two men next to him were killed instantly, one blown to pieces in front of him.

'So how on earth I got on so lightly when I was the nearest to the shell, I don't know,' he said. 'Anyway, if I don't get a worse knock than this time, I won't grumble.'

Rae wasn't much for grumbling, anyway. He liked the switch to open warfare that the German Offensive had brought; it gave him a chance to kill the enemy at close quarters, and he had no qualms about that.

'I like it much better than the trenches, as you can have an open go at your man,' he said. 'They are fine targets coming across ploughed fields in broad daylight. A man is a very poor shot if he misses. In any case, if you miss the one you aim at, you have a 100-to-1 chance of hitting some other fellow.'

Even wounded, he sensed the Germans would not:

be able to keep going much longer by the way we are mowing them down as they come over. They have gained a lot of ground and fresh towns, but at an awful cost. At one place one of our divisions [Anzacs] fought five picked German divisions on their own and fought them to a standstill, holding every inch of ground.

Rae was a hard nut, and didn't normally allow himself to become sentimental. But seeing the French residents driven from their homes made him sad – and angry. He told his father:

The people in Australia have no idea of the suffering of the French people. It is awful to see them deserting their homes and going for their lives, leaving everything – absolutely everything – their goats tied up, pigs in the yard, rabbits in their cages, cattle yarded, horses stabled, and everything in the houses . . . I saw one poor cockey with a handcart packed with things, his poor old wife, or mother, sitting on the top, crying like a little child, and the shells were falling in the fields everywhere.

The 7th Battalion, and those other forces now around them, had effectively stopped the German pathway through the Nieppe Forest. But almost a week on the men were still engaged and had to deal with artillery attacks and aerial droppings from planes. They also had to try and accommodate the local community, some of whom had neither the intention nor ability to pack up and leave in case the enemy arrived. Lieutenant Roy Anderson and his men came across an unusual situation when they found a number of elderly Frenchmen and a woman unable to flee their small home in the face of bombardments. Instead of leaving them there, Anderson arranged for stretchers to carry the men out and the woman was able to leave of her own volition. The house to which they had been confined was destroyed by a German shell the next afternoon.

Anderson, though, was about to be dealt a savage blow himself. The young man from Cobram, who had assiduously kept a diary through the early part of his war journey only to let it lapse for much of his time in England and France, was seriously injured in an artillery shell attack a few days later. One of the men who was witness to the incident said:

That night we moved forward to a trench on rising ground and had not long occupied it when a shell fell on the edge of the parapet and Lt. Anderson was critically wounded; four of us carried him to a temporary dressing station in a hut. It was a hard carry and he was in agony.

Anderson was standing against the wall of his dugout when a shell burst 12 yards (10 metres) away. He received wounds to the head and back and was immediately sent from the battlefield to hospital, then transferred to England where a medical board rendered his wounds too serious for further service.

The last of the Cobram-Barooga five was repatriated to Australia, arriving at Cobram station in late October 1918. The local community came out in force to welcome him home, including a few of the men he had sailed with. The *Cobram Courier* documented: 'Roy was given a hearty greeting as he stepped on the platform, cheer following cheer from delighted friends and acquaintances, and as he was motored home more hand-waves and greetings followed from the bystanders'. It was noted that he looked well after 'three years of soldiering and the only seeming effect of his wounds is a loss of a little avoirdupois [weight]'.

The 7th Battalion and those who had fought with them won praise for their cool heads in what was undoubtedly a crisis, and for their willingness to plug the considerable breach in the line before Nieppe Forest. The unit's monthly summation praised the frontline soldiers, saying: 'The spirit of the men is admirable, notwithstanding the Hun Offensive'.

Bill Jamieson, who was there, wrote many years later about the achievements:

Less than 700 men of an Australian infantry battalion, with no artillery or other support behind, and some fragmentary [maybe hypothetical] resistance in the void before, worked with a desperate will, establishing an effective chain of cunningly concealed posts. After 41 hours, the 8th Battalion arrived to take over the northern half of our 'Army Line'; thus more than doubling the strength of the defences with which to meet the assault that, fortunately for us, did not eventuate until early on the morrow. What an eerie night that was with distant farmhouses going up in flames, and menace gathering closer, unseen yet nonetheless felt. When enemy contact was made, it was the 8th's bad luck to take the brunt of the attack, sustaining heavier losses than the 7th. But beyond that 'Army Line' no German Army went, and the Channel Ports were saved.

One of the guard's officers, Oliver Littleton, summed up the moment when he wrote of the Australians fighting near Hazebrouck:

> These magnificent troops advanced down the road, sometimes in the rather unconventional form of artillery formation, and most of them carrying some unconventional equipment. They were superb, and their language, learnt on the sheep stations of their country and matured in a hundred engagements and patrols, was like the battle cries of other days.

A FEW DAYS AFTER the 7th Battalion's remarkable work up north, Pompey Elliott and the 15th Brigade, among them members of the Fair Dinkums who were serving with the 59th Battalion, despaired when Villers-Bretonneux fell through the hands of the English on 24 April 1918. Elliott wanted to have a crack at getting the town back under Allied control, and was finally granted the chance with a surprise night-time counterattack. Elliott's men worked with the 13th Brigade on their assault, with the 59th to advance towards Hill 104 on the northern side of the town. According to Elliott's biographer:

> Their splendid morale and determination were reinforced by the realisation that it was the third anniversary of the original Anzac Day, and they had an opportunity to commemorate it

with a special exploit. The sporadic shellfire and obstructive wire they encountered on their way forward did not deter them. They pressed on . . . The 15th Brigade charge swiftly overcame all resistance in its path. By dawn on the anniversary of Anzac Day it was clear that this daring counter-attack had proved a triumph.

The 59th Battalion's unit diary recorded with great pride: 'Final objective was reached and our line established along the road . . . considering this was a night operation over strange and difficult country the result was a brilliant success. Through-out the men advanced with a dash and courage worthy of the Battalion'.

Never mind that Elliott fumed with indignation that others were now claiming that the audacious attack on Villers-Bretonneux had been their idea, not his. He stated quite clearly to those closest to him that:

> It was entirely to preliminary training that our very substan-tial victory was due. Now some people are calling it the most brilliant feat of arms in the war – we are supposed to have utterly ruined 3 Divisions, from each of which we had a large number of captives and killed more – and are endeavouring by all means in their power to claim the credit of it. Some who opposed my request in the beginning are now unblushingly trying to usurp the credit.

As frustrating as it was, the men of the 59th Battalion and, indeed, the men of the 7th Battalion played a major hand in helping to stop the German advances in different locations. It is fitting that today, almost a century on, Villers-Bretonneux still observes Anzac Day and the contribution Australian soldiers made in protecting or liberating their town with the message 'N'oublions jamais l'Australie' (Let us never forget Australia).

17

Saving Private Bellesini

'I shall go back tomorrow and say to my countrymen:
"I have seen the Australians. I have looked in their faces.
I know that these men . . . will fight alongside of us again
until the cause for which we are all fighting is safe for us,
and for our children."'

PRIVATE ANDREW BELLESINI WANTED to come home. His mother Esther desperately wanted him back, too. So, through the long, eventful year that was 1918, the Bellesini family set in motion a campaign that went to all corners of the globe, and to some of the highest offices in the Australian Government, in an effort to win his return. Two of Bellesini's brothers were already war victims – Harry, killed at Gallipoli and buried at sea in 1915, and Joseph, who died in England in 1917 of his wounds suffered at Pozières many months earlier.

Andrew almost died at Pozières in July 1916, having survived bullets through his shoulder and knee, and a bomb that ripped his coat off, tearing the front cover off his prayer book. He didn't know if he believed in God anymore after what he had seen, but at least the prayer book – likely given to him by another brother, Louis, who was a Roman Catholic priest – provided a protection of sorts. Andrew's mother wanted to ensure the son named after her late husband wasn't going to be the third member of the family to make the ultimate sacrifice in this war. She was prepared to fight to ensure that he didn't have to fight any longer.

She also had her hands full caring for Andrew's three young daughters, who had come to live with her in Eaglehawk because their mother Alice had been confined to a psychiatric hospital in Royal Park since the middle of 1918. Though they were estranged when he signed up, Alice wanted Andrew home too, and his absence had triggered her mental breakdown. Esther believed only Andrew's return could release her daughter-in-law from her mental demons, provide her grandchildren with a father after so many lost years, and prevent another of her sons from being taken. She was determined not to accept no for an answer.

The campaign to save Private Bellesini began at the start of 1918. Andrew's wife Alice claimed that he had told her that, in his role with the Provost Corps, he often had to pay for his own food and clothing. When pressed to provide evidence to support this, Bellesini backed away from the comments and said that his wife had exaggerated them. His captain in the Provost Corps also filed a response, saying Bellesini had never made a complaint about his clothes or rations.

As Alice's condition worsened, Esther took up the fight. She consulted the family doctor, and got Dr T.E. Green to write to the secretary of the Australian Commonwealth Department of Defence, Tom Trumble – the brother of former leading Test cricketer Hugh Trumble – to urge Andrew's return. Dr Green stressed that the soldier had already provided good service for the best part of three years and that two of his brothers would not be returning, making it more important that Andrew was able to do so. Trumble referred the matter to the Australian army officials in London, though they quickly sent word that, given the parlous state of enlistments at home, the only way that Bellesini could be returned was if he was deemed unfit for further service. He wasn't, so he had to stay.

That led Dr Green to the offices of Prime Minister Billy Hughes, detailing how Bellesini's wife had become almost incapacitated due to his absence. He reiterated Bellesini's claims about his clothes and his provisions, though the army was quick to scotch any suggestions that the soldier had been denied clothing and food. Again, the response was negative.

The indefatigable Esther wasn't going to be deterred. Private Bellesini had now been promoted to lance corporal, and she approached a barrister to take the family's claims to the Minister of Defence, George Pearce, in a more formal plea. The letter read:

> Mrs. Esther Bellesini . . . has consulted me with reference to her son, Lance Corporal Andrew Bellesini [AIF], No.2563 . . . Lance Corporal Bellesini's wife, who is the mother of his three children, has lately shown strong symptoms of insanity and I believe these issues have been brought on by his absence, and by the fact of her hearing of her husband being wounded. My client thinks that if her son was returned to his wife that she would probably recover . . . I think under the circumstances the request for his return is a reasonable one . . . [to] help to prevent the further development of his wife's insane symptoms.

By the middle of the year, the officer in charge of the police station at Eaglehawk confirmed that two of Bellesini's brothers had been killed and that Andrew's three young daughters – aged six, four and three – were being raised by his mother. He concluded:

This appears to be a distressing case as the soldier's absence is believed to be the cause of the deranged mental condition of his wife, necessitating the care and responsibility of the children to be thrown on the soldier's mother ... the children are well cared for by their grandmother, who is a very respectable and capable woman.

Esther Bellesini was all that and more, as she plotted her next move in the campaign to get Andrew back once and for all.

In late April 1918, at around the time the 7th Battalion was digging in around Hazebrouck to repel the German advance, Bellesini was working at Le Havre. The Australian administrative headquarters at Horseferry Road, in London, ruled that Bellesini was fit for service, and 'it is not proposed to return him to Australia'. The news saw Alice's condition deteriorate even further. Esther's solicitors insisted in July that she had 'become deranged in mind through his absence. Please let me know if any effort has been made to get this man back as his relatives are much alarmed with his wife's condition and if she were assured that her husband was on his return, she would probably recover'. Accompanying the claim was a statement from a medical superintendant from the Hospital for the Insane at Royal Park, which detailed her condition: 'Suffering from acute mania, restless, excited, exulted, races around the Living Court in a wild way, at times talks fairly coherently, but generally on irrelevant matters. Bodily health good ... could obtain no further information from her as to the possible cause'.

A counter-claim from army officials saw a report from two doctors at the facility who declared 'on the position of Mrs. Bellesini's mental condition ... neither ... considers there is any reason to believe that the return of her husband from the war will materially affect the course of the disorder'. So the Department of Defence ruled again on 27 July 1918 that Andrew Bellesini 'is not recommended [to return] on grounds of the health of his wife. As the man himself was fit for general service on 30/4/18, it is not recommended that he be returned on account of his own health'.

Some mothers would have accepted the finality of the letter. Not Esther Bellesini. She needed her son.

WHILE THE BELLESINI CLAN was digging in, the Fair Dinkums were involved in a tactic known as the 'Peaceful Penetration' by mid–1918. There was renewed confidence in the ranks after the rousing repulse of the German Offensive. Now, as historian Charles Bean explained, the Australians were intent on annoying the hell out of the enemy at every opportunity:

[The] troops began to pester the enemy, trying to waylay his patrols and cut out his posts – to wage, indeed, a cease-less 'private war' on the Germans opposed to them. This was supplemented by a series of set attacks, generally planned to capture sections of the new front line from the Germans before they had fully established it . . . the Diggers called these tactics 'Peaceful Penetration'.

The troops made sudden, sporadic raids on the enemy as they waited for the inevitable major offensive that had been long forecast. The men remained resolute, even though the war was now edging towards its fourth anniversary. In June 1918, the 7th Battalion's Colonel Herrod highlighted the confidence of the men he was commanding:

Notwithstanding continual service in the forward area, the men remain wonderfully keen. The patrol work of the Battalion was exceptionally fine. Constant contact was kept with the enemy posts . . . the morale of the Battalion has seldom been higher than at the present moment.

The Australian divisions now had an Australian-born leader, with General John Monash taking over in what was an exciting appointment for most of the troops. Monash, the son of Jewish immigrants, proudly wrote home to his wife of his role:

> My new command comprises a total at present of 166,000 troops, and covers practically the whole Australian field army in France ... for all practical purposes I am now the supreme Australian commander, and thus at long last the Australian nation has achieved its ambition of having its own Commander-in-Chief, a native-born Australian – for the first time in history. My command is more than two-and-a-half times the size of the British Army under the Duke of Wellington, or of the French Army under Napoleon Bonaparte, at the battle of Waterloo.

Monash's meticulous battle planning, as well as the support use of tanks – long derided but now demanded – to assist the advancing infantry became the template for the balance of the war. This was used to stunning effect when two brigades of Australians, assisted by some of the fresh American troops, took the village of Hamel on 4 July 1918 in 93 minutes. Aided by British tanks and air supplies dropped from the Flying Corps, the concerted attack worked like clockwork.

French Prime Minister Georges Clemenceau personally thanked Monash, expressing the gratitude of his nation:

> We knew that you would fight a good fight, but we did not know that from the very beginning you would astonish the whole continent ... I shall go back tomorrow and say to my countrymen: 'I have seen the Australians. I have looked in their faces. I know that these men ... will fight alongside of us again until the cause for which we are all fighting is safe for us, and for our children.'

Monash's message to all Australian soldiers had the men of the 7th Battalion marching with a powerful feeling of expectation in the early hours of 8 August 1918. They had heard Monash's message from the officers on a short break by the side of a crowded, darkened road on a march between Pont Camon and their intended destination of Lamotte Brebière, a desolate point on the Somme. While the men rested, the officers produced electric torchlights to read Monash's aspirations for the battle ahead. Men came in close together so that the words were audible, some put their arms around each other, others listened with a silence rarely afforded in such a gathering.

Oliver Harris, who only two months earlier was awarded the Military Cross for his exceptional work near Ypres the previous year, sensed the men's determination. Some thought Monash's words 'vague but inspiring', but no one was unaffected by their bold vision, even the wags.

Monash's message read, in part:

For the first time in the history of this Corps all five Australian Divisions will tomorrow engage in the largest and most important battle operation ever undertaken by the Corps . . . I entertain no sort of doubt that every Australian soldier will worthily rise to as great an occasion, and that every man, imbued with the spirit of victory will, in spite of every difficulty that may confront him, be animated by no other resolve than a grim determination to see through to a clear finish, whatever his task may be. The work to be done tomorrow will perhaps make heavy demands upon the endurance and staying power of many of you; but I am confident, in spite of excitement, fatigue and physical strain, every man will carry on to the utmost of his powers until his goal is won; for the sake of AUSTRALIA, the Empire and our Cause. I earnestly wish every soldier of the Corps the best of good fortune, and glorious and decisive victory, the story of which will echo throughout the world, and will live forever in the history of our homeland.

Under the cover of darkness in the middle of nowhere, Monash's words illuminated a belief that an Allied victory was almost assured. The men resumed their march to Lamotte Brebière, arriving at around 4.30 am, just after the Allied artillery kicked into action what was the first phase of the Battle of Amiens, with the 2nd and 3rd Divisions rolling forward.

The success at Amiens had given the 7th Battalion great hope for the future as they waited for their next move, which came a day later near Lihons. General Ludendorff would later write in his memoirs that:

> August 8th was the blackest day of the German Army in the history of the war. This was the worst experience ... The Emperor told me later on, after the failure of the July Offensive, and after August 8th, he knew the war could no longer be won.

The stunning success of the operations at Amiens would come to be seen as one of the most important moments of an interminably long war. What Monash and his officers had done with their painstaking planning, and what the Anzacs had done on the frontline, was to help bring a slow, almost claustrophobic and deadly four-year war towards a climax out on the fields, rather than in the trenches. In the space of just over 400 minutes, the Australians pushed forward 7 miles (11 kilometres) and captured many thousands of prisoners as well as significant German weaponry.

Pompey Elliott's 15th Brigade played their part, and were there when the 7th Battalion went into action a day later. The 59th was able to overcome the 'stumbling block' of Harbonnières and with the assistance of tanks, an Australian flag was fluttering in the light breeze of the village before lunchtime. Elliott's men did remarkably well, though 'Old Pompey' had been shot in his rather ample backside by a stray German bullet. His biographer said: 'The upshot was an unforgettable spectacle – the brigadier perched on a prominent mound, survey-ing the battlefield intently and dictating messages uninhibitedly, with his trousers round his ankles and underlings fussing over his behind'. One of the Originals maintained that it was one of the sights of the entire war, and there was no doubt that day that the Germans, if they had known, would have considered Elliott and his men pains in *their* backside.

Some of the Fair Dinkums in the 59th Battalion who took part in the battle at Amiens on 8 August 1918, and in subse-quent fighting, were badly injured, though most served with absolute distinction. 'Barney' Allen, the Cockney grocer who had set up shop in Sea Lake, had been preparing himself for two big events during this time. He was engaged to be married to a young woman in Battersea, London, but first the 24-year-old machine-gunner knew he had a role to play in Monash's big offensive.

In the pre-dawn darkness on 8 August 1918, Allen was moving into position, preparing for the attack in front of Villers-Bretonneux, when he was struck, receiving 'nasty wounds' in the arm, which would have stopped other men. But he would be buggered if that scrape was going to prevent him from taking part. He dealt with the pain – 'great pain', it would be said – and 'carried on over an advance of approximately 10 kilometres until orders for his evacuation were received from a medical officer'.

The citation for his Military Medal would document: 'Throughout the operation, he showed an utter disregard for his personal safety, and by his gallantry, self-sacrifice and devotion to duty, he set a splendid example to all ranks. His courage and endurance are worthy of special recognition'. Forty-two days later, while recuperating in England, and with his arm still bandaged, Allen celebrated his marriage to 23-year-old Lillian Gardiner at St Peter's Church, Battersea.

Bertie Southwell was also wounded that day. He was in his mid-thirties now, but had played a role in both the 7th and Pup Battalions. In the years after, he told his children precious little about his time in uniform, but did detail how he came to be hit on 8 August 1918. Southwell was charging when the machine-guns hit him in the middle of the thigh (another report said it was his right hip). He could see the exit wound of the bullet, which came straight through his leg, and it remained a source of amusement in a long, long life. When he was struck, his leg had 'spun around like a top' and he fell instantly to the ground. Southwell always credited that spin with saving his life: if he had remained on his feet, he would almost certainly have been hit again, potentially fatally. Southwell's wound was listed as 'severe' and he was invalided to England. Decades later, as he faced a milestone he never thought he would make, he told a newspaper that he was 'wounded in the stomach in [World] War I and [had] not been expected to live a week'.

That wasn't the case. Southwell got to see many, many more weeks in a long and fruitful life as one of Melbourne's long-serving educators.

Henry Stephens, also struck on the thigh that day, did not get that chance. Wounded for the third time, it was the end of his war. He was dead by the end the next decade, with the repatriation commission saying it was due to his war service.

The 7th Battalion was exceptionally proud to head into battle on 9 August 1918, even if the operational plans and the requirements were not as prosperous as they had been a day earlier. No one in the unit – no matter when they enlisted – needed to be reminded that it marked the third anniversary of the Lone Pine battle, which had brought distinction to the battalion, as well as four Victoria Crosses.

That hot and humid summer's day, men were in their places and ready to attack just south of Harbonnières by 1.30 pm, led by their scouts and accompanied by six tanks. But as the troops began to advance towards Lihons, they came under heavy fire from machine-guns and rifle attack, as well as occasional strafing from German planes which were targeting them from the air. Fire came across two flanks as the lack of artillery support and the sheer expanse of the area needed to advance made for hard work and heavy casualties. Even as it was happening, it reminded some of the veterans of the 7th Battalion's extremely costly advance at Krithia on Gallipoli in May 1915. Bean saw the similarities:

> There was the same long approach over bare, grassy plain, with a few enemy batteries bursting shells over the little columns, then the long advance, without effective covering by artillery in the face of an enemy firing his hardest with rifles and machine-guns . . . the struggle throughout the afternoon . . . as costly as it was valiant, [was] mainly due to a lack of co-operation at Division level, the quick-skittling of support tanks, the flat, open terrain up to the tangle of old earthworks before Lihons Wood, and the stiffening resistance of the enemy to whom our objective meant much.

That made for plenty of casualties and more than a battalion's fair share of heartache.

Take the case of the Harris brothers from Quarry Hill in Bendigo. Battalion Adjutant Oliver Harris and his younger brother Lieutenant Tom had fought almost side by side from the time they had enlisted as Fair Dinkums. That ended on this day. During the assault, there were significant sections of German resistance. One particular group of about fifteen men pocketed in a copse and used the cover to inflict serious damage to the oncoming Australians. Tom Harris could see what was happening and knew he and his men had to silence them before more men were killed. He charged towards them with some of his men in what was a risky but inherently brave move.

The Germans were captured or killed, and four deadly machine-guns silenced. But Tom was critically wounded in the strike. He was whisked away to see if anything could be done for him, but it was all to no avail. He died soon after, the moment made all the more poignant because Oliver Harris had witnessed the incident with Colonel Herrod.

The advance across open ground continued and claimed many of the battalion's best: 52 soldiers as well as six officers. One man who was there, and who contributed much to the legend of the 7th Battalion, Bill Jamieson, wrote: 'Never till then did I realise the cover a tuft of grass could give. Apart from one or two water channels or rain gutters, there was nothing but flat, open country, which afforded Fritz a splendid opportunity for rifle and machine-gun practice at our expense'.

Men were struck down at will, particularly in the legs and ankles, and it was only when the Anzacs pushed closer to the objective that 'the bullets came higher inflicting body and most painful of all, stomach wounds'. The entire battlefront had only short grass as cover, other than the odd copse, and the Germans had some of the old trench lines for their cover. It might have been different with artillery cover, but without any, and against an enemy eager to make a last stand, it made the task all the more difficult for the men.

Lance Corporal Archie Milne was having a busy and bloody afternoon. Sadly, he was used to them. This married member of the Fair Dinkums, who sometimes went by the nickname 'Snowy', had been a butter factoryhand in civilian life. But, as a stretcher-bearer, he was sometimes proving the difference between life and death for men in the frontline. Milne had distinguished himself with great courage at Pozières two years earlier. Back then, after carrying a number of men to safety – many of them much heavier than his 10 stone (63 kilograms) – he collapsed under the strain, without even taking a drink. At around two in the afternoon of 9 August 1918, as sections of the 7th Battalion were close to one of their objectives – a ridge to the left of Lihons – Milne was struck by a sniper's bullet near his heart as a wave of rifle and machine-gun fire exploded across the fields. He was badly wounded, in serious pain, and calling for the stretcher-bearers that he knew could sometimes work miracles. But there were no miracles on this day. Milne was comforted as best as he could by those tending him, and died four hours later, conscious to the end. He was buried the next day with a collective cross for the men of the 7th Battalion who fell in that battle. One of the soldiers nursing him through his final moments expressed sadness, for Milne had been one of the most popular members of the unit, and well remembered and respected for saving many men under fire.

The young man who made a pudding on Gallipoli back in late 1915, which one of his fellow soldiers dubbed the Haslem pudding, Robert Haslem, was also cut down on the pathway to Lihons. The short but stocky labourer from Chiltern was killed and buried in the same spot. It took four more years for his family to organise their own tribute words for his gravestone: 'Time may pass and bring a change fresh with every coming year, but your memory will be cherished by the ones that love you dear'.

Wally Day had a very different experience of the Lihons battle. He had transferred to the battalion transport and was part of a tank crew. It almost cost him his life. The married labourer from Brunswick was operating as a scout for the tank, indicating where it needed to go. But when a shell struck the tank, he knew he had to get out, and fast. Two men in his tank team were killed and another was knocked unconscious. Inexperienced with the operations of the tank, he was unsure how to get in and out of it, but managed to extricate himself. He took with him his knocked-out mate, only to find that they were under serious fire as soon as they emerged.

Taking shelter behind the tank, he heard a strange voice amid the gunfire calling out 'Bill, Bill' in broken English.

Bugger it, he thought to himself, 'I know my name is not Bill, it must be the Germans'.

Day managed to get his mate away, but he was wounded in the back during the process. Having escaped with his life, Day was sent to England for treatment and eventually repatriated home, the bullet in his back accompanying him. He lived to tell the story over and over again, still pointing out the long-healed wound that always reminded him of Lihons, and the difficulties so many of his mates encountered that warm afternoon.

As numerous as the casualties were, the men kept moving forward by whatever means possible. As the battalion's first history recorded:

> By the skilful use of volleys of rifle grenades we got a footing in old gun-pits. Advance over the open was impossible as the Hun was resisting determinedly and his machine guns and snipers were holding us up. Here the old trenches were of some use, and by bombing our way along them we gradually made headway. Eventually, seeing us creeping on, the enemy took fright and bolted. Machine guns were on him in an instant, and many were shot down. With a rush we were up to the last punch, and on our objective and the enemy driven out.

By 6 pm, the red-line objective had been attained. The men held on grimly through more pockets of resistance and a counterattack half an hour later. It had been an extraordinary ordeal. They were relieved from the lines the next day, and the many wounded were taken off for more appropriate treatment. The casualties totalled 238: 58 killed, including six officers.

It had been a tough day, made more so since 'in the eleven nights preceding [they] had had but two nights' rest', and faced a 12-mile (19 kilometres) march before being thrust into battle. The deck was stacked against them. The official battalion report from Colonel Herrod concluded:

The mere statement of facts on paper does not convey any idea of the severity of the task. The position assailed overlooked the whole field of battle, the Battalion advanced and fought over the field in broad daylight, without assistance from other arms of service against an enemy who fought determinedly ... in strongly entrenched positions, with enemy field guns firing over open sights; fought and advanced with an open and exposed flank, against machine gun fire of fierce intensity on a hot day; and at the conclusion of a long, tiring, dusty march ... The 9th August is sacred to the men of the 7th Battalion as the anniversary of their famous Lone Pine fight, and the deeds of that day were worthily emulated by the men of the 7th Battalion.

Bill Scurry followed all the news of the battles with amazement and awe. Of the Australian soldiers whom he had once fought with, and those he had trained, he said: 'Ours are wonderful men, clean built, keen and brainy. They stand very high among the men on the Western Front, both as fighting men and garrison troops'.

But he also knew their laconic, laidback manner:

I think that on my experience of him, the Australian soldier will gauge what you will be satisfied with very quickly, and give you that, and no more. Let him do nothing and he will do thoroughly but once [you] let him know you want a high standard and are strong enough to get it, you can get anything from him.

A student of military history from almost as early as he could remember, Scurry knew the war was rapidly coming to a climax, and could appreciate the Australians were playing a part in history that would last longer than any of their lifetimes.

Scurry knew that if he listened to the doctors and medical boards, he would never see any action again. But in late August, as the Australians continued to push across many fronts, he sensed an opportunity and took it.

When one of his instructional courses was postponed for a week, Scurry had some spare time. Some might have gone sightseeing well away from the guns, but Scurry did the opposite. He sensed a chance to move forward and see some of the familiar faces he had missed from the 15th Brigade and from the Light Trench Mortar Battery he had led before his accident. Scurry travelled to 'the beleaguered city of Amiens' and was able to meet with his old unit and Elliott. He found the brigade headquarters camped in a deep dugout in what used to be the backwood of an old house. It was 'like a meeting of the clan . . . lots of my old friends were there and to see the General's eyes sparkle and hear him laugh when I told him I had come up to spend a few days with him'.

Scurry spent the first day reacquainting himself with men he hadn't seen in some time. 'It did my heart good to see the faces of some of those men again,' he said, then added, with a touch of sadness, 'There were a lot of faces, however, which I did not know.'

The reason for that was clear. Men came and went in the units, depending on how they fared in battle.

Not content with just catching up with some of his old mates, Scurry decided he would stay to witness the battery send off its artillery the next day from the frontline. He thought that night was a spectacular evening – 'a night for anything but war . . . everything was quiet and one could sit outside the posts – there is no continuous line of trenches – and just think, without being disturbed by Fritz, who was not more than 300 yards away, but thoroughly frightened'. He was excited by the opportunity to 'stay and watch the fun' of the movement the next day, and barely slept through the night. Only the occasional crack of rifle fire or machine-gun clatter broke the relative calm.

It would be different – oh, so different – on the morrow, he thought. Around him men slept in 'little bits of trench or holes in the ground' as if they were slumbering in beds in the nearest chateau. Before dawn the next morning Scurry could hear the 'purring' of the tanks moving into position, and the dimly lit forms of Anzacs ready out on the jumping-off tapes, about to go 'right on in to Hunland'.

So much of what happened next was done on a timetable and Scurry, a soldier you could almost set your watch to, was delighted to see such operations. As the sun began to creep into the far-reaching corners of Scurry's good eye, he watched as men bent over their equipment and prepared themselves. Then the countdown started. Two minutes . . . one minute . . . 30 seconds. Scurry watched as men went about their business, his pencil jotting down each of the operations that happened faster than he could possibly set to paper. He would write:

> The gunners are now standing by their muzzles . . . then suddenly from the valley some thousand yards back comes a single flash of a gun, just one flash but before the sound has reached us the long line of ridges behind becomes alive with the bright stunts of flames, while shrieking shells of every calibre fire over us in hundreds. The droning monsters in rear let out full and slide forward like live beasts, low on the ground and seemingly to stalk like pointers in a clover paddock. The mortars in front of and around us put over shells as fast as they can go . . . the machine guns cackle like the laughter of a battalion of school girls in hysterics . . . all of this takes time to write, but . . . imagine it all appearing in the twinkling of an eye out of the silent peaceful twilight before dawn.

Whatever happened in the war next could happen without Scurry feeling the least bit envious of the men who were in the thick of it. He had so wanted to experience that adrenaline rush of being in the frontline one last time, and he had achieved that now. He was grateful for the moment. He was most impressed with how things were working now. If only they had been so systematic two years ago, more of his mates would still be alive.

He sensed that the war was nearly over, that the resolve that had sustained the German Army for so long, and which had still been on display just outside of Lihons a few weeks back when Scurry's old 7th had had such a hard scrap, was almost gone. That brilliant morning, he watched as 'flares and lights of all shapes and colours' were going up in the German lines:

> like a fireworks display, and some shells go over us in the Valley . . . and we see . . . the men [the surrendering Germans] who will stop their fight for the Fatherland that day . . . they trudge along and pass us, disarmed and helpless, but happy to be taken, and so the war goes on.

The war lasted for another ten weeks. Through September and October 1918, the advances continued. There were acts of heroism mixed with some wins and some crushing losses. Two Fair Dinkums were rewarded for their hard work and bravery during this time; two others were killed.

Moyston farmer Frank Vanstan had been inspired to enlist after hearing of the Gallipoli landings through his brother Stan's letters. Three-and-a-half years later, Vanstan, this 'most capable and efficient R.Q.M Sergeant', was doing his best to play a significant part in the end of Australia's involvement in the war. He later won a Meritorious Service Medal for his work around Péronne during September 1918. It was said:

> In the absence of a regular Battalion Quarter Master, this Warrant Officer bore the brunt of the responsibility for regulating the whole supply of the Battalion, and despite many difficulties occasioned by enemy shell-fire and bombing activity, succeeding in the highest degree in maintaining a smooth and efficient service and with a minimum of

inconvenience to the troops . . . [He] has long service both in the line and in the Q.M Branch.

Lieutenant Art Pegler from Mildura should not have had to wait so long to be granted a medal of honour. He had come close a number of times before, but missed out. And even with this one, he wouldn't know about it, or receive it until after the guns had fallen silent. But Pegler's work from 16–17 September through to the day peace was declared earned him a Military Cross. His citation read:

> Lieut. Pegler displayed conspicuous gallantry, power of leadership and devotion to duty. On one occasion whilst in charge of a section advancing with the Infantry an enemy gun opened fire at close range inflicting casualties. Without hesitation and regardless of personal safety, Lieut. Pegler singlehanded rushed the gun and with his revolver forced the crew to surrender. By his initiative and gallantry many lives were undoubtedly saved and his example proved a great incentive to all who witnessed it. At various other times he has displayed remarkable courage.

As Pegler was being recognised for his outstanding service, one of the other men he had enlisted and left Mildura with was killed.

On 21 September 1918, Lieutenant Howard 'Billy' Williams was supervising the firing of the machine-guns when he received a wound just above his ankle. One of the corporals, who happened to come from Swan Hill, went back to assist him and was carrying him down to the trench when a shell smashed into the trench a few feet in front of them. One eyewitness said: 'Poor old Howard got the full force of it right in the small of the back and was nearly cut in two'. The corporal who assisted him didn't have a scratch on him, but 27-year-old Williams was killed instantly. Such are the misfortunes of war.

On the same day, and in the same battle at Péronne, Private Les James, 26, was killed. He had left Melbourne on the *Anchises* with Williams on 26 August 1915 as part of the 8th Reinforcements of the 7th Battalion. Both Williams and James couldn't have known how close they were to going home again, dying just over 50 days before the Armistice was signed.

The men of the 7th Battalion spent 10 November 1918, the last full day and night of the war, resting in billets at Bazieul. Oliver Harris, the adjutant, had been there every step of the way with many of the Fair Dinkums. He had seen good times and bad, and was still mourning the loss of his brother Tom, killed two months earlier. On this chilly, clear night, he sat with the officers around a small stove in the 'roofless estaminet', trying to keep warm from the cold yet fuelled by 'the possibilities of the early ending to the war'. Harris felt he had been away long enough; he wanted to go home to his family and friends in Bendigo.

On that same night Scurry was on leave in Paris, and preparing to leave for Milan. He went out that night to explore the city with three friends – 'we four people owned Paris except for a few policemen here and there' – but 'All the city was absolutely quiet, not a soul was in the streets, but all over was a feeling of expectancy and some of the buildings had already begun to show a few flags in anticipation'. Scurry and his mates called in at the French newspaper, *Le Matin*, 'one of the biggest papers in Paris to see if there was any news of the Armistice discussion', then:

> We went down the deserted streets of the Place de la Concord, now a huge park of captured guns of every calibre. Some were short, little field guns lined in squat ugliness along the edge of the path, while ever and anon, a long tapering snout of some big gun, or the shorter, heavy barrel of a howitzer would tower heavenward. Of mortars and machine guns, there seemed to be thousands, but all silent, and here brooded the same spirit in the streets, that they would be silent forever . . . Further on, we

went up the select Champs-Elysees for a while, and then back again to the hotel. That walk through Paris, I will never forget.

The next day Scurry had confirmation of the 'great news' by midday: war was over.

He explained to his mother:

Did you ever imagine that I would be lucky enough to be in Paris when the news of the 'ceasefire' came through . . . At first it did not make much difference as people in this country have learned to make sure first, but later it got noisier and noisier until the whole place was a swinging mass of people, waving flags, singing and generally appearing very happy . . . But how can we know what it must mean to them [the French], to be sure that there will be no more danger of their homes.

There was dancing in the street and 'girls would kiss the soldiers and on we'd go. I liked that game. It was a glorious picture that it was over, and we had won'.

The 7th Battalion found out around lunchtime that the Armistice had been agreed to, with Harris saying word passed around faster than anything he had seen before: 'The news quickly spread, some believing and some not. It was a sight never to be forgotten to see excited Australians passing that message from group to group'. The men had nothing to toast with, and made do with chlorinated water – a beer would have to wait until later. But the water tasted almost as good as the men celebrated the fact that they had made it through alive, while remembering those mates who hadn't.

Then they celebrated in the only manner they knew how, by lighting a series of campfires, from which Harris said, '[we] sat round them in groups, wondering what they were saying and thinking of the news in far Australia, and how soon we'd be home again!'

The answer wasn't soon. The task of getting home more Australians than had ever been abroad before at the same time took much longer than any of the Anzacs around those camp-fires could have anticipated.

SEVERAL WEEKS BEFORE THE Armistice, Andrew Bellesini was finally told the AIF had agreed to transfer him home for two months' furlough on half-pay for 'family reasons'. It came about after his mother Esther took their case − *her* case − to the Department of Defence in September. This time she enlisted the support of Victorian Member of the Legislative Council, Alfred Hicks, a member of the Nationalist Party, from Bendigo, who wrote to the department:

> I ask to bring under your notice a hard case . . . Mrs. Bellesini, of Victoria St, Eaglehawk, has lost two sons at the front and she has another married son still fighting. She appealed in May to your department for this son to be returned. This son's wife has gone mad and is confined to a lunatic asylum. There are three little children who are being kept by the soldier's mother, this son enlisted in May 1915. Seeing the mother has lost two sons and the wife of another son who is still fighting has gone mad, and their three children left by the mother, it seems to me to be a case that requires immediate attention. Will you kindly see if the son is returning or not, the mother is most anxious.

By 16 October, the department finally recommended that Andrew Bellesini return to Australia. Four days before peace was declared, Bellesini 'reported from his unit in France . . . [and on the 6th] will proceed to No.2 Command Depot, Weymouth to await embarkation'. Having left the Provost Corps, he reverted from lance corporal back to private.

Private Bellesini boarded a ship for his return to Australia on 4 December 1918. That same day, Esther was burying another son, Reverend Father Louis Bellesini, who had died of illness, aged 27. She had now lost three sons in fewer than four years.

PART III

DISCHARGE AND THE DAYS AFTER

18

Surviving the peace

'When it is all over what sad pilgrimage will be made to the last resting place of our poor brave boys who have been killed in battle or have died in exile.'

THE BIGGEST AND MOST destructive war the world had known was finally over. Australia had officially been a part of it for 1560 days. While the men who had fought in the war, including the Fair Dinkums, were relieved the ordeal was over, there were battles ahead for many of them. How could there not be, after what they had experienced, what they had witnessed, and what they had done? There was no precedent in history for what had happened to them, or the tens of millions of other men of so many different nationalities who survived the war. Their lives were altered forever, with many of them left to deal with physical and psychological scars. There was also no template for what they were to do next, or how they were to deal with their families, friends and acquaintances who had lived through the time but not the experience.

How could they understand if they had not been there? The Fair Dinkums sailed to war together, but came home in dribs and drabs rather than as a triumphant force, due to the monumental task of demobilising a vast army of men back from the other side of the world. The process would take more than a year after the Armistice was declared. When the guns fell silent, there were still 92,000 Australian soldiers in France, 60,000 in England, as well as 17,000 in the Middle East.

Some of the men brought home new wives; others were fathers on their return. Some of the marriages were happy ones that lasted the rest of their lives; others were fractured and short-lived. Of the Fair Dinkums, 35 never returned, having made the ultimate sacrifice in the trenches, across French and Belgian fields, in hospitals or casualty clearing stations in France and England, and even one at sea. Another had gone missing in London while on leave; and yet another died in England while on leave shortly after the war.

Cruelly, some Fair Dinkums endured the long years of the war, only to die before the end of the year of peace, 1919. In the intervening years and decades, lives were cut short by wounds, sickness, the lingering effect of poisonous gas on their lungs and hearts, in one case because of the influenza that would ultimately claim more lives worldwide than the 1914–18 war itself, and at least one by his own hand in a place far removed from his family and home.

Some of the men of the 8th Reinforcements of the 7th Battalion survived the first war, only to struggle to survive the peace. Most lived through a second world war, some even serving in it, alongside soldiers from a generation later that saw fighting once more in France and across Europe, and perilously close to Australia's doorstep. One Fair Dinkum would take part in a hat-trick, serving in the Boer War, World War I and World War II, dying during that last conflict.

World War II also brought about the sinking of the *Anchises* after it was twice attacked by air in February 1941, more than 250 kilometres west of Bloody Foreland, off the Irish coast.

Some of the Fair Dinkums were broken by the war and turned to the bottle for solace. A few who had been law-abiding citizens before found themselves on the wrong side of the judicial system in the years after. Others lived long and prosperous lives, making valuable contributions to the country they had fought for, often receiving far less in return than they had given. One even reached his 100-year milestone, receiving a telegram from Queen Elizabeth II, the monarch whose grandfather he had fought for in World War I.

BERTIE HARRIS COULD NOT have been more excited to look around England in January 1919. He had been there a year earlier, but wanted to see more this time. So when he was granted leave from 8–20 January, this one-time miner from Bendigo resolved to make the most of it. After all, the war was over, and a sense of excitement for the future was the overriding emotion. But three days before he was due to report back for his return trip to France, Harris walked into the AIF's administrative headquarters on Horseferry Road and complained of feeling unwell. He was taken to a nearby hospital where he ran a raging temperature. Before long he was transferred to the 3rd Australian Auxiliary Hospital in nearby Dartford and quickly diagnosed with bronchitis – hardly uncommon, given the fierceness of the northern winter. But Harris's condition deteriorated on the second day, to the point where he became delirious and doctors realised he had influenza. He was listed as 'dangerously ill' and his family back in Australia – incredulous that this could happen now that the war was over – were advised of his condition. On the third day, the medical staff knew there was nothing more they could do for him other than to keep him as comfortable as possible. Harris, only 27, passed away at five minutes to eleven, on the night of 22 January 1919. He was accorded a full military funeral at Brookwood Military Cemetery, complete with a firing party and gun salute, a bugler and pallbearers he never knew. His coffin, made of 'good polished elm', was wrapped up in the flag of the country he had served so well. His effects, including his false teeth, a YMCA wallet with photos and cards, and an unloaded revolver, were sent home to his confused, shattered family.

Only a week earlier, Lieutenant Roy Anderson died in the Caulfield Military Hospital of pneumonia and heart failure. He was 24. The last of the five Cobram-Barooga Fair Dinkums to be in the frontline, he had arrived back in Australia the previous October to a hearty reception from his mother Barbara and the rest of the community after his wounding near the Nieppe Forest in April 1918. The wounds that Anderson received – gunshot wounds to the back of the head and contusions of the back – were serious enough to see him sent to England and ultimately home to Australia. But it was thought that he would survive and he was undeniably strong enough to travel from England to Australia in the dying days of the war. When he arrived home, he was in relatively good health. No one, least of all his mother, who finally had her son back after all those years, could have envisaged what would happen next. Anderson took ill suddenly in January 1919, and faded fast when he was in hospital. The young man who had kept a neatly written diary while abroad and who had boasted to his mother eighteen months earlier that 'Should I get back you will never get my mouth shut about it [the experience]' was gone. A train carriage bearing Anderson's casket steamed into the same Cobram station that had previously held his homecoming reception. Mrs Barbara Anderson had her beloved son back for three months, only to lose him all over again.

The three other surviving Cobram–Barooga boys who caught the train in mid-1915 to war all returned to the Murray River region after their early exits from the army. Hugh Knight had to do it without his brother Bertie. He returned to Australia, and married Lillian on 7 August 1918, the day that the 7th Battalion travelled back to the Somme ahead of their forthcoming battle at Lihons. He had four children, worked in a car dealership and garage in Cobram, often having responsibility for driving the new Buicks, Oldsmobiles and Pontiacs from Melbourne, and he worked in the shearing sheds during the season. Knight moved to Melbourne in 1938 where he was a PMG linesman before his sudden death, at 50, in Armadale in 1943. His son was in the RAAF at the time.

Ray Rohner, who enthusiastically wrote a diary of his short-lived time in uniform, and Ray Eaton, who had been sent home due to ill health in 1916, lived the longest of the five local lads, dying within months of each other in 1979. Rohner worked in the Immigration Department and was secretary of the Marine Board of Victoria for 32 years. His crushing disappointment at being sent home meant he was disconnected for a period with the men he had served with, but he was welcomed back in the twilight of his life. He was 82 when he died, during a choral society recital with members of his family. He told those present 'how proud he was of their music-ship when, suddenly in need of air, he slumped and was gone'.

Eaton was also 82, having inherited the role of Registrar of the Births, Deaths and Marriage of the Cobram district from his father. For a time he worked as the local agent for the Vacuum Oil Company and, for 31 years, as officer in charge of the Grain Elevator Board's wheat silo.

Three of the four Mildura Fair Dinkums made it home. Art Pegler came back on the same ship as Italian native Jack Tognola, and soon took over the local butcher business with his brother Gus. It was noted on his return that he looked well, and he remained a prominent Mildura citizen, so much so that the grateful council named a street after him – Pegler Avenue.

His Military Medal came with a letter of congratulations from General Birdwood.

Bert Plant also made it home safely, albeit with a partly amputated right thumb. Just before the end of the war, he became engaged to a young woman in England, having met her at a party of amateur musicians at Salisbury Plains. But the marriage did not proceed and Plant went home and found another sweetheart, Lorna Baker. The pair lived happily in Red Cliffs, just outside of Mildura, managing the local fruit cooperative.

While Plant and Pegler stayed mates in the region, Tognola didn't. He never recovered from his experiences at the front, in particular the gassing he was subjected to. After returning from the war, he went to join his brother in Atherton in north Queensland, where he farmed on the Tablelands for many years. But he couldn't put the past behind him. It came back to him night after night, his lungs so often heaving and his heart weakened due to the heavy gassing in France. He spent the final year of his life in the Greenslopes Military Hospital, dying there on 26 August 1950, 35 years to the day that he waved goodbye to everyone on the pier at Port Melbourne when the *Anchises* took him off to war.

Two older Anzacs who never saw the Western Front also died in Melbourne in 1919. Bill Mudge, who shared a tent with Alf Layfield, the Smiling Boy at Seymour, was sent home before he could get to Gallipoli because of cancer. He died on 18 July 1919 at the Austin Hospital in Heidelberg. His son collected his Victory Medal in 1923 for a war in which his father never got the chance to fire a shot at the enemy.

Irishman Lawrence Flynn outlived Mudge by a little more than four months. He made it to Gallipoli and spent three weeks there, but was sent home before the men left for France. On his return, his tuberculosis flared up and worsened, and Flynn's long battle ended on 24 November 1919, so far away from his native Ireland, and in the same hospital where Mudge had passed away.

Oliver Harris returned to Bendigo in 1919, fittingly, as a hero. He had won a Military Cross, rising from a private to a lieutenant, and received the admiration and gratitude of a proud community for his work with the 7th Battalion. There was sympathy, too, for the family, with the death of Harris' brother, Tom, so late in the war. Harris received a certificate from the Dean of the Faculty of Law, which enabled him to sit his exams early in 1920. He became a prominent member of the Bendigo branch of the Returned Soldiers' Association, and planned to write a book about the 7th Battalion's history at Gallipoli. On his return, Harris married Miss Annie 'Cis' Lienhop from Kangaroo Flat, and the newly-weds lived happily in Hallam Street, Quarry Hill.

All of that changed on 5 April 1920. He awoke that morning, turned to his wife and told her that he felt in 'perfect health'. But within a short time he began to feel faint and the family doctor, Dr Nankervis, was called. Harris was examined and prescribed some medicine. Soon after, he 'succumbed suddenly' in front of his shocked wife. The doctor returned, but it was too late. The man who had survived the worst that war could throw at him died at his home, aged 35. Dr Nankervis certified Harris' death had been 'due to heart failure, supervening on being gassed at the front'. The *Bendigo Advertiser* echoed the thoughts of those who had known Harris before and after the war:

> His ability, courteous manner, and manly bearing made him a favourite with all with whom he came in contact . . . he endeared himself to a large circle of friends of all sections, and among the soldiers, he was a favourite . . . his death will be keenly regretted.

Captain Fred Hoad feared for a time that he would never get out of Germany alive, having been a prisoner of war there in various camps after his capture at Pozières in August 1916. His wounds had been neglected, which affected his health.

But his correspondence with Red Cross agent Miss Mary Chomley connected him to the outside world, and his mood brightened considerably when he was moved to neutral Switzerland in November 1917. Miss Chomley presciently told him that year, 'When it is all over what sad pilgrimage will be made to the last resting place of our poor brave boys who have been killed in battle or have died in exile.'

Hoad's exile was more bearable in Switzerland, where he spent time in Vevey and Interlaken, pining for his wife and children back in Australia, and eagerly awaiting a return home. Three days before the Armistice, he forecast to Miss Chomley 'the day of reckoning has come for such cruel, inhumane beings [the Germans]'. He returned to London as soon as he could manage after the war – and presumably met the woman who had kept him sane with her letters of support and assistance – before boarding the *Orontes* and sailing from Liverpool on Christmas Day 1918, bound for Australia and his family.

Hoad was still troubled by his wounds and health issues in the years after, while never ceasing to point out the mistreatment he received at the hands of the Germans. He even wrote to his former commanding officer, Carl Jess, on his release about his Pozières capture, saying, 'I wanted to write to you to say how sorry I was at not being able to carry on, although, personally, I did all I could up to the time of being knocked out to make the show a success, being only ten yards or so from the German trench when all seemed to be going well.' He returned to work at the Victorian Railways, and gave a series of lectures on his trials, telling a Williamstown Football Club function at the local Mechanics Hall that his food in captivity consisted of 'boiled carrots . . . a menu practically that had little or no variation'. He also detailed an instance where one of the German doctors 'plunged his lance into the swollen limb' of an Allied soldier, 'ripped it up its full length amid the piercing screams of the agonised victim of No Man's Land'. By 1930, the 7th Battalion annual newsletter, *Despatches*, admitted: 'Fred hasn't had much luck since Pozières crippled him; in fact, one word – Ordeal – best describes life as he knew it some of the years following '16'.

Despite his physical issues and advanced years, Hoad signed up for World War II in July 1940, and worked as part of the recruiting staff. He was an area officer in South Melbourne when he took a seizure and died on 2 February 1941. Those Fair Dinkums who knew something of his ordeal of his time as a prisoner of war after Pozières mourned him as a man of character who 'knew his job thoroughly'.

Bill Scurry managed to be transferred back to his battalion in November 1918. This young man, whose drip-rifle innovation had become part of Anzac legend, and whom Pompey Elliott said was 'a military genius of a type unfortunately only too rare', received two life-changing pieces of news that month. The first was that the war was over, finally, and that he could now go home safely, as he had promised his mother he would.

The second, which came towards the end of November, was that his fiancée, Olive, had called off their engagement. He was shocked at the 'unfortunate occurrence . . . my house of cards has tumbled over . . . I cannot understand it . . . all my hopes and ideals centred on to my future with Olive, and I have always considered these things with absolute simple trust'.

All the joy of that month was extinguished, and the news from home left him 'groping in a place of bewilderment'. The only other time he experienced such blackness was at Fromelles on 19 July 1916, when he searched in vain for a friend in the 'awful darkness' of no-man's land before realising that he would never find him. But as he sat down to write one of the most remarkable of his many letters home to his mother, he assured her that he would survive the pain, despite the gravity of the news:

My Mother, do you not worry one scrap for I know the same Power which has guided me through the scrap will see that all is well with me. But what a funny end to my whirl of joy . . . There is still a glow that you and dad will always give to my life, so that you see, I'm not going to be dramatic and commit suicide or anything, but must take it as one of the things that go to make up life.

He implored his mother to not think too badly of the 'poor wee lady'. Besides, he was convinced that the betrothal had kept him pure throughout the war, while other men had been too easily lured into temptation:

> There are many, many dangers here besides death, and wounds, and all of them I have looked upon and fought, but it is to be the thoughts and strength given to me by Olive on the ideals she represented to me, that has enabled me to come back to you as I left. For whatever else happens, we must always thank her for that.

His mother was far less forgiving.

The war may have been over, but Scurry remained busy, helping to prepare some of the men for their return to civilian life. As he mused to his mother, 'If we don't give them anything to do, I think it was you who first told me the old proverb about Satan and idle hands.'

Some of the activities were educational, but there was still plenty of sport. In December, Scurry had another brush with royalty, shaking hands with the Prince of Wales, 'who blew over just before three-quarter-time' at the conclusion of a football match he had played in, despite his eye issues.

'He shook us all very warmly by the hand,' Scurry wrote with a smile. 'He got about half a ton of mud with my lot, as I had spent most of the game on my hands and knees . . . he is a most agreeable chap, but looks very young and frail, and is very nervous at first.'

Just as important for Scurry was the 59th Battalion dinner that ended the year. Elliott spoke, with Scurry following his every word. 'The greatest thing of all to me was the way they drank to the General's health,' he wrote.

The toast was drunk, of course, most enthusiastically . . . at last they let him speak. Then a sight I have never seen before happened. The whole room, without any arrangement, but quite simultaneously got up with one foot on the table and roared: 'For he's a jolly good fellow' and once more drank to the old Pomp's health. Never I think in all the AIF has there been such an outburst of love for one man, and he sat there like an awkward bashful boy . . . And as long as anybody present is alive, it will not be forgotten.

Neither would Scurry's return be forgotten. He sailed back to Australia in May 1919, and on the ship gained an introduction to a nurse from South Australia who had served in the Australian Army Nursing Service in France and Italy. Her name was Sister Doris Barry. They struck up a friendship and maintained contact on their return. His broken heart mended, and the pair were married at St John's in Clifton Hill on 29 January 1920. Ever the gentleman, Scurry presented his new bride with a gold wristlet.

Bunty Lawrence, his one-time schoolmate and the man whose water rations helped to give life to the drip-rifle on Gallipoli, was his groomsman. The reception was held at the Grand Hotel, and as luck would have it, General Birdwood was being entertained at the hotel that day by members of the Army Nurse's Club. Birdwood asked for the bridal party to be presented to him so that he could offer his congratulations. The marriage was a long and happy one, producing four daughters. For a short time, Scurry went back to work in his father's architectural business before his war wounds proved too much; he had to do much of his work with his left hand and his eyesight deteriorated after operations in 1923 where the piece of shrapnel in his right eye shifted to his left eye. It blinded him on the left side and left only 15 per cent vision in the right one.

Scurry moved to Silvan, built a house on the family property, then another after he sold the first one and later still moved to Croydon. In between, he even spent time living in a house at Frankston owned by Elliott. There were some tough times economically for Scurry, though he never complained or bemoaned his lot. On the seventeenth anniversary of the Gallipoli evacuation, the *Argus* reported: 'An heroic Victorian . . . lives in retirement, almost blind, in a quiet house in the Dandenongs'. Two years later he was appointed president of the Lilydale Returned Servicemen's League, and attended a congress in New South Wales on behalf of the branch. Those in attendance stood to their feet in admiration. After the death of his parents and the sale of his father's company, he used some of his modest inheritance to tour Japan with his wife in 1938.

A year later, Australia was at war again, and by December 1941, with Japan. Much to Doris's disappointment, Bill enlisted and, with one lens of his glasses frosted over, spent time at the No. 1 Prisoner of War Camp for Italians and Germans, and later as the commandant of the Japanese Civilian Internment Camp at Tatura. He came to be respected and loved by all who served with him, as well as the Japanese internees, many of whom called him 'Uncle Bill'. He became a major, and that was the name so many people referred to him for the rest of his life. A gentle, compassionate soul, he cared for his wife when chronic arthritis kept her wheelchair-bound, yet still managed to play golf one day a week. On 28 December 1963, he was playing golf at the Croydon Golf Course when he felt faint and rested up against a tree. He then collapsed with a 'coronary occlusion' and was taken home, still having the competitive spirit and humour to tell his wife: 'I was 4 up and now the buggers won't pay me'. He died that day, aged 68.

Scurry outlived his mentor Elliott by 32 years. Elliott's death by his own hand in 1931 caused Scurry untold heartache. He couldn't reconcile the man who had played such a significant part in Australia's war effort by building the character of men ending his life by taking a razor blade to his left elbow. And he never forgave the only newspaper in Melbourne, *Smith's Weekly,* that controversially revealed Elliott's suicide. Elliott's postwar life was plagued by what he had experienced and seen during his four years at war. Family members say Scurry found it difficult to forgive Elliott for what he did.

It wasn't only Elliott who faced such demons. At least one member of the Fair Dinkums, who also happened to be one of Elliott's protégés, took his own life though the circumstances were as mysterious as they were mournful. Clarence Lay should have returned to Australia a hero. He had won a Military Cross. But he joined the Indian Army with his regiment, the 3/23 Sikhs, serving against the Arabs in Mesopotamia, and later was transferred to the Arab and Kurdish Levies in what is now Iraq, which the British Government were putting together. In 1925, Lay was found on his cabin floor with gunshot wounds to his face while aboard the P&O steamer *Moldavia* in Colombo harbour in Ceylon (now Sri Lanka). A gun lay beside him. He had been preparing to board another ship for Bombay, and here he was, dead. Lay's father wrote to the army, asking for details of his son's death to be kept private as 'there is much to be cleared up concerning his death'. One of the men charged with putting Lay's affairs in order back in Australia was Elliott. Elliott and Lay survived war's end, but could not survive what the war had done to them.

Of the three known 'boy soldiers' among the Fair Dinkums, only sixteen-year-old George Yendle never made it back, lost at Fromelles. Bill Wain, who celebrated his sixteenth birthday a few weeks before they sailed to war, went on to be a distinguished soldier in World War II. He enlisted as part of the 2/16th Battalion and after the Syrian Campaign in 1941 became OC of the 2/43rd Battalion, taking part in the Alamein fighting from July 1942, where he was blown out of an observational post, but still refused to stop. He received a Distinguished Service Order for bravery.

'Wain commanded an infantry battalion at Alamein and inspired his men by his determination to close with the enemy and give no ground,' the *West Australian* recorded.

Subsequently, near Sidi Abdel Rahman, his battalion was holding the extremity of a salient on ground vital to ourselves and to the enemy. This position was overlooked by the enemy from two sides and was attacked six times in 14 hours by tanks and infantry with heavy fire support. The battalion stuck to its ground, and Lt-Col Wain directed operations heedless of severe fire. Lt-Col Wain . . . despite the shock and effects of the blast, continued to direct operations and refused evacuation until two days later, when the situation was stablised.

Wain lived to be 80.

The other 'boy soldier', Bruce Murcutt, died in 1936, aged only 38. The gas that poisoned him as a teenager brought a permanent weakness of his heart, and ultimately his demise. A bootmaker by trade, Bruce wore a suit to work every day until the year before his death, when his health seriously deteriorated. He was one of six brothers to either enlist in or train for World War I, and when they all returned alive, their Lincoln Street home in Richmond was daubed with a banner saluting the 'Fighting Murcutts'. But they did not return unscathed. Most of the Murcutt brothers died prematurely in the years after, predominately due to the effects the war had on their health.

Gus Lafargues survived the war on his native soil, but not even the emotional reunion with his mother could convince him to stay in France. He returned to Australia, married, raised a family, and rarely talked of his war experience. He looked forward, not backwards. One of the few stories he told his daughter Avis was how he was wounded one time – maybe it was at Fromelles – and almost left for dead, before an Anzac with German bloodlines came to his aid, put him over his shoulder and took him for treatment.

For a time on his return Gus was a waterside worker and adopted Collingwood as his football team, religiously taking his two daughters each Saturday afternoon to the club's home ground, Victoria Park. He enlisted in World War II, acting as a cook for a time and then as part of the cable station near Apollo Bay, on Victoria's southwest coast. Fittingly, he renewed acquaintances there with one of his mates from the Fair Dinkums, Alf Mercer, who had played a significant part in helping to build and maintain the Great Ocean Road, constructed by returned soldiers from 1919 to 1932.

The 7th Battalion's annual newsletter told its members during the early 1940s:

> Have you ever been to Apollo Bay? If you like a clean beach and babbling streams and the grandeur of the ranges, you'll get them all there. There will be old Sevenths who will be happy to see you: 2618 AW Mercer (and) 2606 AP Lafargues on the No.10 Guard at the Cable station.

Lafargues and his family lived there permanently after the war.

Mercer met his wife, Ada, in England during World War I. After she lost track of Mercer towards the end of the war, she wrote pleadingly to Australian military officials as she was pregnant with his child. They re-established contact and she came out to Australia as a war bride with a child, sharing the boat with a woman who would become the mother of Melbourne footballer Fred Fanning, the only man to kick eighteen goals in a league game. A passion for fishing – with crayfish and couta the prized catch – brought the two old mates even closer together.

They died within a year of each other, in 1956 and 1957 respectively. They had started their lives in different hemispheres; incredibly, they would come to have neighbouring grave plots in the picturesque Apollo Bay Cemetery, forever overlooking the waters that had taken them away to war, and brought them back again.

The wandering barber Lawrence Black came back, too. He had spent more time incarcerated or on the run than he had in the frontline. The recidivist runner was absent without leave on almost ten occasions during his time at war, having also been jailed for desertion. Even when the war ended, it was hard to keep tabs on his whereabouts. On 3 December 1918 he was listed as being illegally absent. But as the Anzacs took their place in the queue to be returned to Australia in the weeks and months after the end of the war, Black took matters into his own hands to get himself home. He stowed away on the transport ship, *City of York,* arriving back in Melbourne on 27 February 1919. In the years after, Black would seek war gratuity for his service as well as any other entitlements, but would be rejected. He pleaded to Victoria Barracks on his return, including a reference from one of the 7th Battalion captains he had served under:

> This man was a member of my command during the latter months of 1917 during which time he proved himself to be a very efficient soldier both in and out of the line. During the Battalion's tour . . . towards the end of December, 1917, he was of a number who volunteered to form a protective patrol along the Battalion front at night . . . the patrol leader had great praise for Black, whose initiative and courage was very marked.

The reference didn't work, and Black was denied.

In 1934, his appeal was once more rejected. Black would, however, come to serve his country once more during World War II, this time staying the course.

Walter Judd left for war as a Salvation Army officer, and returned utterly changed by his experience. He came home to his wife and children the morning after Anzac Day 1918. In the years after, this once respectable man took to the drink to sooth his dark memories from the war, far from the only man to seek solace from a bottle. This led to a short prison term for theft in 1926. As an insurance agent for Colonial Mutual Life Assurance Society, Judd was tripped up by some creative bookwork. When the books were examined, it showed he had not accounted for £34 over a five-month period. When the charge came to court, one of the detectives involved in the investigation confirmed that 'the defendant's lapse appeared to be due to drink. He had previously borne good character. The defendant offered to make restitution. He stated that he had lost the collection book while he was drunk'. At around the same time he had also been 'running a catering establishment . . . [but] was drawing 15/- a week unemployment allowance'. Sadly, Judd's marriage did not survive.

The demon drink also brought about the undoing of another Fair Dinkum at the end of the next war. Like Judd, Dugald Walshe hadn't had an easy war. He had survived that long night at Fromelles on 19 July 1916, with a severely wounded knee, then suffered shell shock after being buried by a shell in the advance at Polygon Wood the year after. He returned home, having been married in England before the end of the war, bringing his bride Rosalie out when it was all over.

But Walshe's demons affected his marriage and his wellbeing. He was under regular treatment for neurasthenia in Adelaide, where he had taken his family to live in the 1920s, and was 'subject to occasional brainstorms and was easily upset'. Still, he enlisted for World War II, as did two of his sons.

But all of his problems came to a head in a court case for assault in November 1945. He had briefly separated from his wife, and they were reconciled. Then he was named as a respondent in separate divorce proceedings: Walshe had been seeing another woman and argued with her, saying, 'if I caught her with another man I would do both of them over'. He had had a few drinks on the night of 8 November 1945 when he met the woman. He thought he saw her with another man on the street and, infuriated, 'hopped into both of them'. The couple fled, but Walshe, then a 49-year-old signwriter, gave chase and caught up to her and continued to assault her. It was a case of mistaken identity. The woman he had been having an affair with came along in the street at that same time, and he exclaimed: 'My God, I have hit the wrong woman, I have done a terrible thing'. He was sentenced to six months imprisonment, with hard labour, his reputation darkened.

Arthur Hart, the man charged with first taking the Fair Dinkums abroad in 1915, remained in touch with many of them over the years. By 1934, the 7th Battalion's annual news-letter, *Despatches,* lamented that Hart was 'looking his years now', though he remained chairman of the Public Service Appeals Board. He was 'AWL' for a few Anzac Day marches at this time, which prompted fears from the men who had served under him. They shouldn't have worried: Hart had taken to visiting the Caulfield Military Hospital and was taking patients or nurses on outings on 25 April, still thinking of others. When he passed away, aged 80, in October 1946, the Fair Dinkum survivors mourned him like an old friend. He had given long and loyal service to the men, and the 7th Battalion. One of those who worked alongside him said on his passing: 'He was senior in years to most of us, and was wise in experience. He was a valued friend, and over the years retained a close association with his former comrades . . . His passing will be greatly mourned'.

Bushmates Peter McLarty and Ron McLean were sons of the soil and took up soldier settlement schemes in the years after, putting in endless backbreaking hours on their allotments for little return. Frank Vanstan also worked the land for many years before becoming involved in the Ararat RSL. His great mate, Daniel Von Ende, would frequently visit him. Their regular reunions over the years were cast as the 'Von-Van Association'. Von Ende changed his name to Ende by deed poll in the years after the war, dropping off part of his German-sounding name.

Bill Campbell started off as a city boy, but came to have an affinity with the land. For a time, he was selling H.V. McKay tractors in Narrandera in New South Wales, before taking up a soldier settlement block at nearby Corobimilla. He raised a family there, and became a well-known and well-regarded Narrandera citizen. When World War II started, he tried to enlist locally, but was not successful; as a farmer, he was deemed too valuable for war service. Undeterred, he packed some clothes, went across the border to Victoria, and signed up. This time, he served only on Australian soil. He was, for a time, at the Myrtleford prisoner-of-war camp, but later sent to Innisvale in Queensland. He died, aged 50, from cancer, leaving behind a wife, four sons and a daughter, a legacy on the land that some of his sons would maintain, as well as a collection of German guns and grenades that he sent to the Narrandera Museum. He had given great service to his family, his community and the country.

So, too, had Bill Batson, the bank clerk who had served much of World War I with the Pay Corps, and made just as significant a contribution in country Victoria to the World War II home front. Batson returned to the Camperdown bank after the war and was there in 1920 when General Birdwood came to the town. He also spent time as bank manager at Nathalia and, finally, Koroit. He tried to enlist in World War II, but was denied because he had 'a soldier's heart' [weakened by war]. He became known as 'the King of Koroit' for the tireless work he made to the war effort, and was looked on as:

a man of outstanding worth ... when the community was plunged into the stress of war, he became Koroit's number one citizen. As secretary of the various patriotic funds, he spent all of his spare time in work for the men and women of the services. The Farewell Committee, the Welfare Committee, Prisoner of War Committee, Waste Products Committee, and War Loans Committee owed practically the whole of their success to his efforts. He was an inspiration. To the men and women of the services, the names of WJ Batson came to mean something big in their lives. Every month for more than five years he sent a news slip and a canteen order to them. As the strain of war eased, and they came home, their first call outside their family circle was Mr. Batson. He was the embodiment of everything that could be expected of a fine, Christian gentleman.

Military Medal winner Alf Honey suffered a badly wounded shoulder late in the war and was returned to Australia along with eleven other Maffra locals to a rousing civic reception in March 1919. The local newspaper recorded:

> Never before in the history of Maffra has there been such a splendid gathering as was witnessed at the Mechanics' Hall ... a galaxy of fighters for freedom, as well evidenced by the decorations well and truly earned. Another matter of congratulation is not only the modest demeanour of these returned men, but the high moral standard set since their return ...

Honey diligently went back to making bread – and friends. He was good at it, and loved by the locals for his bright, cheerful personality and his baking prowess. He became an institution in Maffra, where locals would wait until around morning teatime when the first batch of bread would come steaming out of the ovens before buying a loaf and walking across the road to the dairy for fresh cream. Locals recalled a track worn in the grass between the bakery and dairy.

These war homecomings happened in the big cities and the smallest of towns. At around the time that Maffra got its baker back, Geelong was welcoming Lieutenant Cedric Smith home. He was met at Geelong station by the mayor and driven in a motorcade back to the family home, which was suitably decked out with lanterns and various flags of the Allied nations. A welcome home tea was provided for the young man who had made it through the war almost unscathed.

Percy Brunning, the young man who memorised the eye chart to hide that he couldn't see in one eye, came home and became a builder, working with a company that built the Royal Melbourne Hospital.

Wilfred Williams, who came to call himself Bill Williams, came back in the months after Gallipoli with rheumatism. But he went on to serve two terms as Richmond mayor, as well as 34 years on the council.

A most remarkable reunion of two Fair Dinkum mates came in the sheds of a Riverina shearing station during the 1930s. Wally Day happened to be in the sheds when an outstretched hand came from Hugh McKenzie, who had won a Military Cross, and became a wool merchant in the years after the war. Neither man forgot the dizzying delight of running into an old mate they hadn't seen for years.

George Rae, the hard-nut digger who chastised soldiers who didn't have the mettle required to put their head up and to shoot across the trenches at the enemy, was defiant to the end. While convalescing in hospital in England, he married Laura Cook, one of the young women he met in Manchester. On his return, Rae took on 144 acres (60 hectares) on the Ovens River flat. Having fought with distinction during the war, he fought anything else that defied him – or got in his way – back in Australia. But the Depression was one battle he couldn't win.

It ruined his finances and took his property. As the banks took it over, so did the pressure take a toll on the marriage. Rae's relationship with Laura ended, and he lived the next few years in his 'unique style involved in some well-publicised brawls featured in *The Truth* newspaper twice, once for GBH [grievous bodily harm], having dealt with one man with a tomahawk on the head'. His final years were spent in a Bendigo RSL home. His son would document: 'In his 78th year, he killed a fellow old soldier [at the hospital] with his heavy walking stick. He had clobbered once too often. His own death ensued shortly after'.

Private Andrew Bellesini, whose mother fought so hard to have returned to Australia, lived the long life that Esther had so prayed for, well into his eighties, but it was not a happy one. He outlived most of his family – his two Anzac brothers; his brother, who was a priest; his beloved mother; his wife; and all of his three children. Battalion members visited him at home and when he was permanently residing in a hospital, but lamented after one visit that 'old age, even if painless, can be pitiful'. In his last three years, he was confined to a bed in the Heidelberg Repatriation Hospital, where he found life 'distressing, lonely and empty'. Death came – mercifully – just a fortnight before Anzac Day 1970.

Bertie – never Bert, always Bertie – Southwell had been not expected to live more than a week when he was wounded in the war. The mature-aged student who had gone off to war in 1915 would become one of Victoria's most admired and longest-serving teachers. At war's end, Southwell went to London University to further his education, and while he was there, met and fell in love with a young woman who was doing an arts degree. They became engaged and Elsie Wenden eventually came out to Australia on a ship full of war brides. She married Bertie the day she arrived in Australia, with her new husband's sisters – whom she had never met before – as her bridesmaids. She also went on to become a well-known teacher in Melbourne, as well as an author of several books. They had four children.

Southwell became the inaugural chairman of the 59th Battalion Association – the Pup Battalion he had joined in February 1916 after being transferred from the 7th – in 1929, with the objective to 'keep alive the spirit of comradeship brought into being during active service in Egypt and France'. He taught at Melbourne Grammar from 1921 until his retirement in 1952. But he returned to teaching briefly in 1954 and 1958, covering almost the full gamut of the school, from teacher of the classics to librarian, swimming and lifesaving teacher, coordinator of the Corps Cadets (many of his boys, including two of his sons, fought in World War II) and more. When he was in his mid-eighties, he was fitted with a pacemaker, and another one years later. By the time of his 100th birthday, he was Australia's oldest surviving pacemaker recipient, and made the *Sun News-Pictorial*'s pages. He died, aged 102, eleven days before the 70th anniversary of the Gallipoli landings in 1985, and after a long life exceptionally well lived.

The last of the Fair Dinkums to survive was Harold Grange, a private man who lived quite a solitary existence in the years after the war. He started the war as an apprentice body-frame builder at the Tarrant Motor Company, but took to the hard toil of farming on his return after gaining access to a soldier settlement farm near Lake Bolac in 1921. When he first settled on the block, he lived under a tarpaulin spread over native bushes. He then lived in two huts in those early years (one where he cooked and the other where he slept) before he built his first home on the property. Grange was not married until 1941, and he and his wife never had children. Decades later, he would be the last soldier settlement Anzac to be on his original property. He was a man who preferred solitude to socialising, and let few people into his world, though one was a man who came to work for him – and later help him – over many years, Bryan Park.

The war had not wounded Grange physically, but it changed him. Before Grange died in 1986, he told Park, 'You don't make close friends because you lose them.'

Afterword

THE MEN OF THE 8th Reinforcements of the 7th Battalion are gone, but their stories live on in those who knew them, or those came to know their stories in the decades beyond. Some families kept the men alive in thoughts and prayers; others mourned in silence and spoke little about the soldiers who had gone off to war and either never came back or returned altered.

The five-year-old schoolgirl who had farewelled her brother Alf Layfield in 1915 never understood why he didn't come back. His loss sat with her, as it did with her mother and the rest of the family, just as his piano sat silent as the years went on. His letters home were housed in the same box for decades.

I first met 'Smiling Boy' Alf Layfield when I was about fifteen. By that stage he had been dead for 67 years.

Alf was my great-uncle. I read his letters in 1984 when I started to develop a passion for the Anzacs. I wanted to know more about the young man who wouldn't live to see his twentieth birthday as well as the men he sailed away to war with on 26 August 1915. We shared a birthday, 24 March, and were both extremely fortunate to have our early lives shaped by our remarkable mothers.

Alf's mother was my mother's grandmother. Alf's sister, Pearl, was my grandmother. And on the last night of her life, almost seven decades after they said goodbye, this now great-grandmother, whom Alf used to call 'Little Pearlie', sat down to read the letters her brother had sent home to his loving family. She may even have smiled when she saw one of Alf's descriptions of his mates in one of his letters: 'We are Dinkum soldiers'.

And they were.

The Fair Dinkums

Departed Melbourne on 26 August 1915 aboard the *Anchises*.

2554   ADDISON, Harold George

2552   ALLEN, Albert Edward

2555   ANDERSON, Roy

2556   ANDERSON, William Albert

2551   ATTWOOD, Henry – Killed in action,
21 September 1917

2553   AVERY, George – Killed in action, 25 July 1916

2566   BAKER, Ernest – Killed in action,
25 October 1917

2567   BARBER, George Francis Thomas – Killed in action,
19 July 1916

2569   BATSON, William John

2562   BEATTIE, William Stanley

2563   BELLESINI, Andrew

2669   BELLESINI, Joseph – Died of wounds,
13 March 1917

2560   BELLINGHAM, Phillip John – Killed in action,
19 July 1916

2561	BILLINGTON, Robert Henry
2564	BLACK, Lawrence Joseph
2558	BLAKEY, Harold
2559	BOND, Ralph Richard – Killed in action, 19 July 1916
2565	BRANAGAN, Bernard Francis
2557	BRENNAN, Timothy – Died at sea, August, 1917
2703	BRUCE, Robert
2568	BRUNNING, Percy John
2571	CAMPBELL, James William
2715	CARROLL, Edward
2570	CARTER, John
2719	CLANCY, John Leonard
2572	CLEWS, John Milton – Died of wounds, 19 August 1916
2717	CONGDON, Charles George
2712	CRAVEN, George McEwen
2574	DAVIES, Sydney Daniel
2705	DAY, Walter Clarence . . . enlisted as WILSON, Walter
2576	DICKSON, Henry George
2575	DIXON, Frank Allen – Killed in action, 19 July 1916
2577	EATON, Ray
2710	FAIRBANK, Alfred Edmund
2713	FARRELL, Edward Joseph – Killed in action, 2 October 1917
2579	FLYNN, Lawrence
2578	FRASER, Robert Thomas
2581	GILBERT, Edward
2714	GRANGE, William Harold
2711	HARRIS, John Bertie – Died of illness, 22 January 1919
2583	HARRIS, Oliver John Edward
2720	HARRIS, Victor Thomas – Died of wounds, 9 August 1918
	HART, Arthur George Charles

2585	HASLEM, Robert – Killed in action, 9 August 1918
2588	HAYSEY, Robert Ellesmere
2586	HENDERSON, William
2584	HICKS, Thomas Hector
641	HOAD, Frederick James Sydney
2582	HONEY, Alfred
2709	HOWE, Leslie George
2591	JAMES, George Edward
2592	JAMES, Leslie Gordon – Killed in action, 21 September 1918
2589	JOYNER, Benjamin Boag
2590	JUDD, Walter John Vincent
2593	KENSHOLE, Louis Lennie
2597	KING, Walter Tasman – Killed in action, 19 July 1916
2596	KINKAID, Andrew Thomas
2594	KNIGHT, Bertie Rowbottom – Killed in action, 27 June 1916
2595	KNIGHT, Hugh Menoak
2606	LAFARGUES, Auguste Pierre
2607	LAY, Clarence Walter
2605	LAYFIELD, Alfred Walter – Killed in action, 25 February 1917
2602	LEE, John Edward
2600	LEIGH, Walter James
2604	LEWIS, Leonard
2601	LITTLEMORE, Thomas – Killed in action, 3 November 1916
2598	LIVERMORE, Clement Ross
2599	LOUGHNAN, George Richmond McCrae
2630	McASEY, Walter
2615	McCALLUM, Donald Currie
2633	McCLELLAND, Richard Henry
2614	McEWAN, Edward Ted
2616	McKENZIE, Alexander

2623	McKENZIE, Hugh Wilson
2631	MacKENZIE, Robert Henry – Killed in action, 19 July 1916
2624	McLARTY, Peter
2635	McLEAN, Ronald
2622	McQUEEN, Malcolm William
2628	MAKEPEACE, Ernest William
2625	MANN, Frederick William – Died of wounds, 16 April 1918
2617	MARSHALL, John Strickland
2611	MARTIN, Leslie James
2618	MERCER, Alfred William
2609	MILLS, Gordon Frances – Killed in action, 4 October 1917
2619	MILLS, William
2621	MILNE, Archibald Forrest – Killed in action, 9 August 1918
2634	MOORE, George Merden
2632	MORISON, Lochlan
2627	MORRISON, Rhoderick McKenzie James
2657	MORTENSEN, Waldemar Hendrig . . . enlisted as SHAW, John Sydney – Killed in action, 22–27 July 1916
2610	MUDGE, William
2612	MURCUTT, Bruce Howard Stanley
2613	MURPHY, Thomas Henry
2636	OSTLER, James
2640	PAGE, Ernest Edwin
2641	PALMER, Reginald Wallace – Died of accidental wounds, 2 April 1918
2644	PEGLER, Arthur Richard
2638	PHILLIPS, Eric Woolicott
2642	PLANT, John Bertram
2639	PLUCK, Henry

2645	RAE, George Henry
2652	ROBERTS, George Ernest
2650	ROBERTS, Thomas Matthew – Killed in action, 17 November 1916
2651	ROBERTSON, William Horace
2653	ROBINSON, Arthur
2646	RODRIGUEZ, Paul Carlos
2649	ROHNER, Raymond Sidney
2647	ROYLE, Robert – Killed in action, 3 November 1916
2655	SCOTT, Charles Frederick
2654	SCOWCROFT, Reginald – Killed in action, 19 July 1916
2668	SCURRY, William Charles
2708	SEFTON, William George
2673	SHERIDAN, Donald Leslie
2658	SIMPSON, Frederick Alfred
2660	SIMPSON, Jack – Killed in action, 21 September 1917
2662	SMITH, John Patrick
2666	SMITH, Spencer Stanley – Killed in action, 4 October 1917
2665	SMITH, William Cedric
2664	SOUTHWELL, Bertie Charles Sydney Stedman
2663	SPOONER, Edward Mason – Died of wounds, 31 July 1916
2661	STEPHENS, Henry Thomas
2659	SULLIVAN, Daniel James
2656	SWIFT, Arthur George
2671	THOMAS, Albert William
2672	THOMAS, Michael
2670	TOGNOLA, Giovanni Jack
2718	TRACEY, Walter
2675	UKENA, Frederick

2674	USHER, Forrest William
2677	VANSTAN, Francis Joseph
2676	VON ENDE, Daniel Arthur
2681	WAIN, William John
2692	WALKER, William Ward – Died of wounds, 16 April 1918
2678	WALSHE, Dugald Leslie
2689	WARDROP, Archibald Hastie
2679	WARE, Albert William
2680	WARWICK, David
2695	WATSON, Clarence Alexander
2716	WEARNE, Frank Richard Garfield
2700	WEST, Reginald Henry
2697	WHELAN, Frank Raymond
2687	WILLIAMS, Clarence Stanley
2701	WILLIAMS, Ernest George
2694	WILLIAMS, Howard Ernest – Killed in action, 21 September 1918
2702	WILLIAMS, Wilfred
2686	WINDLEY, Harry – Killed in action, 19 July 1916
2691	WINTLE, Freeman Richard
2685	WOOD, George Clifford
2683	WOOD, Henry Wilfred
2684	WOOD, Leslie Herbert
2682	WOODS, Errol Forster
2698	YENDLE, George – Killed in action, 19 July 1916

Acknowledgements

IF I HADN'T COME to know Alf Layfield and his short
life so well through reading his letters sent back home to my
family from Egypt, Gallipoli and France, this book would never
have been written. I will forever be grateful to a young man
I never met, other than through his letters, but whose decency
in a world gone mad shines through his own words a century
on. Some of the most difficult few paragraphs I've had to write
came in trying to describe Alf's death, but even as I sat at the
keyboard in the early hours of a November morning, I felt as if
he dragged me through. Thanks, mate, and thanks for intro-
ducing me to your Fair Dinkum mates.

This book has been more than twenty years in the planning,
but it's no exaggeration to say that it has been an obsession over
the past three years. The more I delved into the stories of the
152 members of the 8th Reinforcements of the 7th Battalion,
the more fascinated I became with their lives and how the war
affected them. This was never meant to be an intricate military
history, where battles and tactics are dissected and debated.

I wanted to look at the battles at Gallipoli, Fromelles, Pozières, Menin Road, Polygon Wood, Broodseinde Ridge, Nieppe Forest and Lihons, to name a few, within the context of the men's lives and for this book to sit as a social history of a group of young Australians – and a few older ones – who willingly went to war knowing the likely consequences. They were, after all, the Fair Dinkums because you had to be fair dinkum to enlist after it became clear what a mess Gallipoli had become.

Almost a third of the Fair Dinkums never returned; many of those who did bore physical and psychological stains forever. These Anzacs might be seen as part of a microcosm of the young men of Australia from a century ago who were born in the right place but at the wrong time. I would like to thank each and every one of the 152 men, without whom we wouldn't have such a rich tapestry of experiences. In the end, it wasn't only the Smiling Boy who seemed to be guiding me; I'm sure the spirit of the other men also played a role in helping me along the way.

I could never have started or completed this book without the support and love of my family. That goes all the way back to Alf's mother, Ada, whom I never met; to Ada's daughter and my grandmother, Pearl, who was a remarkable lady, and to my own mother, Dawn, who is Pearl's daughter. They have, through the generations, shown us the importance of family. My mum has always been a tower of strength and inspiration for me for as long as I can remember. May she continue to be so for many more years to come. She and my late father, Bob, provided me with a love of storytelling and history, for which I will forever be grateful. It's fair to say that no one was more relieved – with the possible exception of the publishers – than my mother when the full stop went on the last chapter. Thanks a million, Mum. I hope we did your uncle Alf and his mates justice.

My wife Christine has been living with the Fair Dinkums for the better part of our twenty years of marriage. For the past three years, it seemed as if she even shared our house with them.

Her commitment to this book was extraordinary, even when the research and writing interrupted our life almost on a daily basis. Through it all, she provided invaluable guidance, assistance as a sounding board (particularly for medical tips), research and proofreading, often into the early hours of the morning. Importantly, she kept our household – our three children and a sometimes demanding golden retriever – fit, fed and functioning well, even when her husband's head was alternating between 2015 and 1915. I couldn't have done it without you.

To my three amazing kids – Lachlan, Elise and Charlotte – thanks for keeping me sane through the tough times and inspired through the good times. I could not be more proud of you three. Thank you for allowing me to take on this project and for not only understanding its importance to me, but for also embracing the story as well. You are the best kids a dad could ever wish for, and once more, you are living proof of the importance of family. Thanks also for attending the dawn service with me at Watsonia Army Barracks on the 100th anniversary of the Gallipoli landings.

My sister Deb, and brothers Robert and Gary, and the rest of the ever-expanding McFarlane and Craker clans, have always been there for me, and continue to be. Let's hope the end of this book means I get to see all of you a lot more in 2016 than I did in 2015. And yes, Willow and Harper, that means Uncle Glenn is coming to play again soon. Thanks to the rest of my family, including the Hardings, for their support, and also to Howard and Sylvia Leigh for always believing in me. It seems fitting that one of the first expressions Sylvia learnt in English when she came to Australia was 'fair dinkum'.

An item in the *Sunday Herald Sun*'s 'Desperately Seeking' column in late 2013 not only put me in touch with some family members of the Fair Dinkums, it introduced me to one of the greatest assets this book could ever have hoped for. Genealogist Judy O'Neill contacted me with the extremely generous offer to help me locate family members – without charge. I didn't even have a publisher at that stage. Judy was a constant source of information, connection and encouragement throughout this project. Her only request was I tell the stories of the men as they were, and not sanitised to suit modern standards. I hope I've been able to achieve this. I owe so much to Judy for her incredible research in tracking down relatives of the Fair Dinkums.

Many of the family members gave their time, memories, hospitality and sometimes the letters, diaries and photographs of their relatives so willingly. Without them, there would be no book. I'm so appreciative that the Scurry family allowed me to not only read Bill's letters, but to also use excerpts to detail the Fair Dinkums' story. Danny Keane, Janey Runci and Julie Hume were big believers in the project, and could see how excited I was when they produced copies of the many letters Bill Scurry wrote. What a remarkable Australian Scurry was!

Thanks also to Jeanette Robinson and Neil Chisholm for allowing me access to the diaries and letters of their relatives, Ray Rohner and Milton Clews. I was able to chat to Ian King about his relative Wally King and read the letters the four King boys sent home, while Kaye Krohn also assisted. Neil Walker allowed me to look at Bill Walker's letters and provided me with valuable information. I spent a wonderful day in Apollo Bay meeting Avis Coles and Rod Mercer, including visiting the graves of Gus Lafargues and Alf Mercer, resting side by side in one of the most scenic cemeteries in Australia.

Ron McDougall provided information, a great photograph of his relative Reg Scowcroft as well as ongoing encouragement; Joan Batson and Rodney Smallwood helped me find out more about Bill Batson while Rosemary Richardson assisted me from London; Alastair Campbell provided photos and some great stories about his dad, James 'Bill' Campbell. Allan Terrett gave me a detailed history of the Knight brothers and family; Ellen Bunting explained the mystery disappearance of her missing great-uncle, Les Wood, as well as provided a photograph; Allan Day helped me learn more about his father, Wally Day, providing stories and photographs; Stan Murcutt gave me his recollections of his father, Bruce; and Bryan Park produced wonderful background on the longest surviving member of the group, Harold Grange.

David Rae provided an extraordinary memoir from Stanley Rae, the son of that feisty and fearless Fair Dinkum George Rae and offered great encouragement; Alec and Peter Southwell were generous with their time in talking about their father and grandfather Bertie; David and Elizabeth Carrie provided great insight into Bert Plant as well as a wonderful letter that explained his wounds and Fred Hoad's capture at Pozières; while Dianne Pierce kindly provided photographs and information about Spencer 'Gunboat' Smith.

Others to assist in this book included Gordon Dickson (Harry Dickson), James Pegler (Art Pegler), Dorothy Chick (George Yendle), the Bellingham family (Phillip Bellingham), Valerie Pickering (Alf Layfield), Dorothy Warren (Alf Layfield), Fred Meehan (Harry Attwood), Dr Maxwell Lay (Clarence Lay), Norman Finan (John Carter), Ruth Carmichael (Harold Blakey), Ron Stephens (Jack Simpson), Christine Pennell (Walter Judd), Judy Bernstern (Walter Judd), Olwyn Whitehouse (Walter Judd), and Belinda Wallis (Gus Lafargues).

Linda Barraclough (Maffra Historical Society), Bev Hansen (Bendigo/Eaglehawk Historical Society), Julie Hempenstall (Bendigo Historical Society), Lyn Skillen (Leongatha Historical Society), Anne Hayward and Robert Ousley (Richmond Historical Society), Wendy Carter (Koroit Historical Society), and members of the Ararat and Gordon historical societies provided great insight and information. John Foote, Anthony McAleer and Neil Leckie were also important in assisting this project. I would also like to thank the staff of the Australian War Memorial (especially Suzy Nunes and David Gist), the National

Archives of Australia (Gregory Cope), the State Library of Victoria, the Borchardt Library at La Trobe University, and the Bendigo Library for assisting me in my research into the men. Thanks to Donna Bishop, from the *Herald Sun* library, for finding the story on Bertie Southwell of his 100th birthday.

I am indebted to the men who documented the history of the 7th Battalion in many and varied forms, particularly Bill Jamieson, who was, for 60 years, the Honorary Secretary of the 7th Battalion Association and a long-time editor of the annual magazine *Despatches*, as well as Arthur Dean and Eric Gutteridge, who produced the first history of the battalion. Ron Austin's *Our Dear Old Battalion* was a constant source of information and highly recommended reading. Thanks to Sue Austin and Michelle Walters for allowing me to reproduce parts of Ron's wonderful book. Robin Corfield's *Give Me Back Our Dear Old Cobbers* was a strong reference point for information on the 59th and 58th Battalions. Many thanks to Robin's son, Justin, for allowing me to access a few snippets from the book.

The works of Charles Bean were invaluable and enlightening, as always. The quotes taken from the works of Charles Bean are used by permission of the copyright holders, Edward Bean Le Couteur and Anne Marie Carroll.

I was very lucky to catch up for a coffee, a chat and one of those famous South Melbourne dim sims with Lambis Englezos, who assisted me with his exceptional knowledge of Fromelles and encouraged me to preserve the stories of our diggers. The great Les Carlyon gave me some kind words of encouragement when we spoke about my project, almost fittingly at Caulfield Racecourse one afternoon when we were there to see Black Caviar. Ross McMullin also gave me his time during a phone conversation while he was under heavy deadline pressure. His outstanding book, *Pompey Elliott,* was a huge asset in my research and I thank him for allowing me to draw upon parts of his remarkable book.

Acknowledgements

Thanks to the Australian Army History Unit, and in particular Dr Roger Lee, for their great assistance with his project, and to the Australian Red Cross (Dennis Poropat) for providing access to the Red Cross Wounded and Missing Files. Thanks also to the RSL and Claudia Edwards for permission to use material from two Reveille stories.

I would also like to acknowledge the publishers of the books I have referenced during my research and for providing copyright approval at such short notice. I have endeavoured to gain permission for any material I have used, but would be happy to hear from anyone who has not been acknowledged.

Others to provide support and friendship include Michael Rennie, Michael Roberts, Tony De Bolfo and Nick Richardson. I want to thank the *Herald Sun* for their continued support over the past 26 years and for allowing me to take long-service leave to embark on the research. Also thanks to the Greensborough Junior Football Club, particularly the amazing group of boys I coached in 2014 and 2015, for providing me with great distraction during a busy time. The Boro boys proudly used the four pillars of Kokoda – Courage, Endurance, Mateship and Sacrifice – as our values for 2015.

Last, but certainly not the least, I'm forever grateful to Pan Macmillan Australia, and in particular to Angus Fontaine for allowing me to bring the Fair Dinkums to life again after 100 years. Angus was a passionate believer in this project from the moment we spoke. He was exceptionally patient, and a constant source of guidance, support and encouragement. I hope I have rewarded your faith in me. I also want to sincerely thank my outstanding book editor Alex Lloyd and copyeditor Foong Ling Kong for cleaning up some of the rough edges, giving me the confidence to keep on going, and for helping me make this book something I am incredibly proud of writing. Alex was always insightful during the editing process and happily answered my countless queries. I also thank him for helping to secure some text permissions and his overall guidance on copyright, and for encouraging me every step of the way. Also thanks to proof-reader Ron Buck, whose excellent eye for detail picked up some much needed changes we had to make, and to editorial assistant Rebecca Hamilton for being a great help with the picture section.

There were many others who helped me during this time and I thank them. If I have neglected to mention anyone by name, please accept my apologies and sincere thanks.

Endnotes

Epigraph
Page

ix. '"The sort of Australian . . .' Charles Bean, *Letters from France*, Cassell and Company Ltd, London, 1917, p. 224.

Introduction
Page

2. 'He had been . . .': Ross McMullin, *Pompey Elliott*, Scribe, Carlton North, 2008, p. 96.

3. '"a throwback to . . .': Tony De Bolfo, 'How Carlton Helped "Pompey" Through', 2011, http://www.carltonfc.com.au/news/2011-07-14/how-carlton-helped-pompey-through

4. 'The British declared . . .': Ross Coulthart, *Charles Bean*, HarperCollins, Sydney, 2014, p. 37.

4. 'There were unprecedented . . .': 'Scenes in the City', *Argus*, 6 August 1914.

5. 'Prime Minister Joseph Cook . . .': ibid.

5. 'Even before the . . .': 'The Empire's Call', *Argus*, 6 August 1914.

5. 'Then he extolled . . .': C.E.W. Bean, *The Official History of Australia in the War of 1914–18, Story of Anzac*, volume 1, University of Queensland Press, St Lucia, 1981, p. 16.

5. 'By the end of . . .': A. K. Macdougall, *Australians At War: A Pictorial History*, Five Mile Press, Rowville, 2004, p. 30.

6. 'There was a mythical . . .': R. Hugh Knyvett, *Over There with the Australians*, Hodder & Stoughton, London, 1918, p. 96.

6. 'As soldier, politician . . .': Staniforth Smith, *Australian Campaigns in the Great War: Being a Concise History of the Australian Naval and Military Forces, 1914 to 1918*, Macmillan, Melbourne, 1919, p. 42.

7. '"Some days ago . . .': 'Statement in Parliament', *Argus*, 30 April 1915.

8. 'His pen had its . . .': 'Australians at Dardanelles: Thrilling Deeds of Heroism', *Argus*, 8 May 1915.

9. 'The *Age* noted that . . .': 'Returned, Wounded Soldiers', *Age*, 26 August 1915.

9. 'According to the *Age* . . .': ibid.

10. 'The *Age* continued . . .': ibid.

11. 'The letter had arrived . . .': 'Death of Lieutenant Hubert Meager', *Daily Advertiser*, 26 August 1915.

11. 'On reaching Fremantle . . .': 'Men and More Men', *Argus*, 27 August 1915.

1 How far is it to Gallipoli?
Page

15. 'In 1915, almost 98 ...': L.L. Robson, *The First AIF: A Study of its Recruitment*, Melbourne University Press, Carlton, 1970.
16. 'The propaganda espoused ...': 'Submarine Atrocities', *Argus*, 10 May 1915.
16. 'As one report in ...': '100,000 Men', *Argus*, 27 March 1915.
17. 'Madden noted the difficulties ...': 'Every Man Needed', *Argus*, 1 July 1915.
18. 'He described the conflict ...': ibid.
18. 'He relayed a story ...': ibid.
18. 'As former servicewoman ...': Patsy Adam-Smith, *The Anzacs*, Penguin, Melbourne, 2014, p. 208.
19. 'Historian Ernest Scott's ...': Ernest Scott, *Australia During the War*, University of Queensland Press, St Lucia, 1989.

2 Brothers in arms
Page

21. 'He stood before ...': Frederick James Sydney Hoad, series no. B2455, National Archives of Australia, Canberra.
22. 'By February 1915 ...': ibid.
22. 'This dark-haired soldier ...': ibid.
23. 'His medical noted ...': Andrew Thomas Kinkaid, series no. B2455, National Archives of Australia, Canberra.
24. 'As a railway fireman ...': Andrew Bellesini, series no. B2455, National Archives of Australia, Canberra.
25. 'Harry had attended ...': 'School Speech Days', *Bendigo Advertiser*, 15 December 1897.
26. 'In the same week ...': 'The New Soldiers', *Bendigonian*, 22 July 1915.
27. 'Roy Anderson, 21 ...': 'A Cool, Clean Shave', *Cobram Courier*, 14 January 1915.
27. 'All five "striplings" were ...': Seventh Battalion AIF Association, *Despatches*, The Association, Melbourne, 1980.
27. 'The *Cobram Courier* detailed ...': 'Off to the War', *Cobram Courier*, 15 July 1915.
28. 'Pegler's family had originally ...': James Pegler, interview with author, 2014.
28. 'Plant's father was Scottish ...': David Carrie, interview with author, 2014.
28. 'He had arrived in ...': Giovanni 'Jack' Tognola, series no. B2455, National Archives of Australia, Canberra.
29. 'As a young woman ...': Ron McDougall, interview with author, 2014 and 2015.
29. 'When he enlisted in ...': Phillip John Bellingham, series no. B2455, National Archives of Australia, Canberra.
30. 'In the days after ...': 'Recruiting Campaign "Monster Meeting at Leongatha", *Great Southern Star*, 16 July 1915.
30. 'The shire president ...': ibid.
30. 'But his sense of ...': Rodney Smallwood, Unpublished manuscript on Bill Batson's life, Melbourne, 2014.
31. 'Lochlan Morison, a native ...': Lochlan Morison, series no. B2455, National Archives of Australia, Canberra.
32. 'Frank's brother had already ...': 'With the Troops: "Letter from Moyston Boy"', *Ararat Advertiser*, 20 July 1915.
32. 'Was it at all ...': 'Moyston: "From our Local Correspondent"', *Ararat Courier*, 13 July 1915.
32. 'The chairman of festivities ...': 'Harkaway News', *Berwick Shire News*, 18 August 1915.
32. 'In Warragul, 21-year-old joiner ...': Seventh Battalion AIF Association, *Despatches*, The Association, Melbourne, 1976.
33. 'From Gapsted, near Myrtleford ...': Stanley Rae, unpublished memoir, 1989.
33. 'As his son would ...': ibid.
33. 'As one local journalist ...': 'Gippslanders and the War', *Every Week*, 29 July 1915.
34. 'His father, George ...': 'Late George Kenshole', *Geelong Advertiser*, 26 June 1917.
34. 'And when the medical ...': Louis Lennie Kenshole, series no. B2455, National Archives of Australia, Canberra.
34. 'That much was unknown ...': Neil Walker, interview and correspondence with author, 2014.
35. 'Campbell intended to ...': Alastair Campbell, interview and correspondence with author, 2015.

36. 'Scurry was at . . .': Robin S. Corfield, *Give Me Back My Dear Old Cobbers*, Corfield & Co, Lara, 2008, p. 15.
36. 'Elliott had told . . .': Ron Austin, *Our Dear Old Battalion*, Slouch Hat Publications, Rosebud, 2004, p. 9.
36. 'For Elliott, discipline . . .': ibid.
36. 'For a period . . .': W.L. Patterson, 'Captain W.C. Scurry, The Inventor who Saved the Gallipoli Evacuation', *Reveille*, December 1932.
37. 'It was a decision . . .': ibid.
37. 'He had to be . . .': Dawn McFarlane, interview with author, 2014 and 2015.
38. 'Two members of the . . .': Walter Clarence Day, series no. B2455, National Archives of Australia, Canberra.
38. 'So he gave . . .': ibid.
38. 'His was a troubled . . .': Research by Judy O'Neill on Waldemar Hendrig Mortensen, 2014.
38. 'His father, Peter, was . . .': 'News of the Week: New South Wales', *Maitland Weekly Mercury*, 10 October 1896.
38. 'Mortensen owned up . . .': 'Windsor Police Court', *Hawkesbury Advocate*, 9 March 1900.
38. 'He later worked on . . .': Waldemar Hendrig Mortensen (aka John Sydney Shaw), series no. B2455, National Archives of Australia, Canberra.
39. 'He had with him . . .': George Roy Reginald Yendle, series no. B2455, National Archives of Australia, Canberra.
39. 'In chasing his father's . . .': ibid.
40. 'His mother said . . .': 'North Richmond Brothers Defend Empire's Cause', *Herald*, 16 December 1915.
41. 'Their proud parents . . .': ibid.
41. 'Sadly, the Gallipoli . . .': Anne Heywood and Robert Ousley, interview with author as well as research assistance, Richmond Historical Society, 2015; Stan Murcutt, interview with author, 2015.
41. 'His manager wrote to . . .': Harold William Grange, series no. B2455, National Archives of Australia, Canberra.
42. 'So that he didn't . . .': Bryan Park, interview and correspondence with author, 2014.
42. 'He spent a considerable . . .': Alec Southwell, interview with author, 2015.
42. 'His son Alec said . . .': ibid.
43. 'Their father, William . . .': Ian King, interview and correspondence with author, 2015.
44. 'A dental assistant . . .': Harry Windley, Robert Henry MacKenzie, series no. B2455, National Archives of Australia, Canberra.
44. 'Tom was a swimmer . . .': Thomas Matthew Roberts, George Ernest Roberts, series no. B2455, National Archives of Australia, Canberra.
44. 'Just before he went . . .': Harold Blakey, series no. B2455, National Archives of Australia, Canberra.
44. 'Given his background . . .': 'Death of Veteran Stockbroker, Mr W. Forster Woods', *Argus*, 4 December 1942.
45. 'One report said . . .': Seventh Battalion AIF Association, *Despatches*, The Association, Melbourne, 1959.
45. 'Three Fair Dinkums . . .': Eric Woolicott Phillips, Frank Allen Dixon, Clarence Walter Lay, series no. B2455, National Archives of Australia, Canberra.
46. 'A friend recalled . . .': Seventh Battalion AIF Association, *Despatches*, The Association, Melbourne, 1972.
46. 'When faced with . . .': ibid.
46. 'Almost 20 per cent . . .': Joan Beaumont, *Broken Nation: Australia in the Great War*, Allen & Unwin, Sydney, 2013.
47. 'Nearly 700,000 people . . .': J Dawes and L.L. Robson, *Citizen to Soldier: Australia before the Great War, Recollections of members of the First AIF*, Melbourne University Press, Carlton, 1977, p. 63.
47. 'His daughter recalled . . .': Avis Coles, interview with author, 2015.
47. 'Other documents suggest . . .': Auguste Pierre Lafargues, series no. B2455, National Archives of Australia, Canberra.
48. 'He had already shown . . .': Auguste Pierre Lafargues, series no. A659, National Archives of Australia, Canberra.
48. 'The local newspaper . . .': 'About People', *Horsham Times*, 7 July 1915.

49. 'He joined up on . . .': Walter John Vincent Judd, series no. B2455, National Archives of Australia, Canberra.

50. 'He came to board . . .': Neil Chisholm, interview and correspondence with author, 2014 and 2015.

50. 'Bayles, 30, had . . .': Milton Clews, letter to his sister Emily, 20 June 1915.

50. 'A later letter . . .': Clews, letter to his sister Emily, 2 July 1915.

50. 'Clews was presented . . .': Clews diary.

50. 'He had become exceptionally . . .': George Francis Thomas Barber, series no. B2455, National Archives of Australia, Canberra.

50. 'He was believed . . .': Judy O'Neill, research conducted on Edward Mason Spooner, 2014 and 2015.

51. 'He was born in . . .': ibid.

51. 'He was from Annan . . .': David Warwick, series no. B2455, National Archives of Australia, Canberra.

51. 'Donald McCallum was another . . .': Donald Currie McCallum, series no. B2455, National Archives of Australia, Canberra.

51. 'It didn't worry . . .': Timothy Brennan, series no. B2455, National Archives of Australia, Canberra.

52. 'A native of Ireland . . .': Lawrence Flynn, series no. B2455, National Archives of Australia, Canberra.

52. 'The *Sea Lake Times* . . .': 'The Sea Lake Times and Berriwillock Advertiser', *Sea Lake Times*, 15 May 1915.

53. 'Allen, a Cockney lad . . .': The Seventh Battalion AIF Association, *Despatches*, 1980, Australian War Memorial.

53. 'Alf Honey was . . .': Linda Baraclough, research conducted on Alfred Honey at the Maffra Historical Society, 2015.

53. 'But a bout . . .': A.G. Butler, *The Official Australian Army Medical Services in the War of 1914–18*, Volume III, Australian War Memorial, Canberra, 1943, p. 175.

54. 'The official history . . .': Butler, p. 177.

54. 'On his right forearm . . .': Michael Thomas, series no. B2455, National Archives of Australia, Canberra.

54. 'It was a boat . . .': Albert Thomas, series no. B2455, National Archives of Australia, Canberra.

3   Aboard the *Anchises*

Page

56. 'In this twentieth-century . . .': Grenville Tregarthen, *Sea Transports of the AIF*, Naval Transport Board, undated.

56. 'Messrs Alfred Holt . . .': 'New Australian Shipping Service, Launch of New Liner', *Barrier Miner*, 21 November 1910.

56. 'The first was . . .': ibid.

56. 'The three ships . . .': ibid.

57. 'He told those . . .': ibid.

58. 'When Governor-General . . .': 'Seymour Camp, A Splendid Reputation', *Seymour Express*, 23 July 1915.

58. 'The *Seymour Express* claimed . . .': ibid.

58. 'New dinkum Milton Clews . . .': Clews, letter to his sister Emily, 20 July 1915.

59. 'The boredom of camp . . .': Attwood, letter to his family, 15 August 1915.

60. 'He also included . . .': Anderson diary.

60. 'With the large crush . . .': Rohner diary.

60. 'Clews said in a . . .': Clews, letter to his sister Emily, 13 October 1915.

61. 'It was acknowledged . . .': http://anzaccentenary.vic.gov.au/first-shot/3-

61. 'Clews noted in . . .': Clews diary.

61. 'Rohner said after . . .': Rohner diary.

61. 'Anderson was sick . . .': Anderson diary.

61. 'The weather closed . . .': Rohner diary.

62. 'He was back . . .': Anderson diary.

62. 'For a time, Scurry . . .': ibid.

62. 'In a letter . . .': Walter King, letter to his father, undated.

63. 'As such, he added . . .': ibid.

63. 'Layfield wrote to . . .': Alf Layfield, letter to his mother Ada, undated, 'High Seas'.

63. 'Layfield explained their . . .': ibid.

64. 'Rohner recorded with . . .': Rohner diary.
64. 'Anderson wasn't impressed . . .': Anderson diary.
64. 'When the *Anchises* . . .': Clews diary.
64. 'R. Hugh Knyvett . . .': Knyvett, pp. 54–55.
65. 'There was sadness . . .': Rohner diary.
65. 'Ralph Bond, one . . .': Ralph Richard Bond, series no. B2455, National Archives of Australia, Canberra.
65. 'On 14 September . . .': Anderson diary.
66. 'He had left Gallipoli . . .': McMullin, pp. 166–67.
66. 'Elliott wrote to . . .': McMullin, p. 170.
66. 'Rohner noted in . . .': Rohner diary.
66. 'Anderson gave a better . . .': Anderson diary.
66. 'Scurry told his . . .': Bill Scurry, letter to his mother, undated, 'We are now in the Red Sea'.
67. 'On the same day . . .': Harry Bellesini, Red Cross Wounded and Missing File, Australian War Memorial; Harry Bellesini, series no. B2455, National Archives of Australia, Canberra.
67. 'He had only . . .': Died of Wounds, 'Private H. Bellesini', *Bendigo Advertiser*, 6 November 1915.

4   The strange land of the Pharaohs
Page
70. 'After the death of . . .': Seventh Battalion AIF Association, *Despatches*, The Association, Melbourne, 1973.
70. 'Ray Rohner described . . .': Rohner diary.
71. 'Milton Clews knew . . .': Clews, letter to his sister Emily, 13 October 1915.
71. 'Roy Anderson called . . .': Anderson diary; King, letter to his father, 27 September 1915.
71. 'Alf Layfield, who had . . .': Layfield, letter to his mother Ada, 3 October 1915.
72. 'Clews was similarly . . .': Clews, letter to his family, 27 September 1915.
72. 'Ray Rohner was more . . .': Rohner diary.
72. 'Bill Scurry called . . .': Scurry, letter to his mother, undated.
73. 'Scurry mused, part-seriously . . .': ibid.
73. 'Bill Mills had a . . .': Bill Mills letter, 'Gordon Soldier in Egypt', *Gordon & Egerton Advertiser*, 11 November 1915.
73. 'Scurry, as the . . .': Anderson diary.
73. 'The men were . . .': Scurry letter, undated.
74. 'The thing that struck . . .': ibid.
74. 'That afternoon on the . . .': Anderson diary.
74. 'One New Zealand soldier . . .': Second Lieutenant Ormond Burton, *The Auckland Regiment, Being an account of the doings on active service of the first, second and third Battalions of the Auckland Regiment*, Whitcombe & Tombs Ltd, Auckland, 1922, p. 11.
75. 'Wal had seen Henry . . .': Ian King, interview with the author, 2015.
75. 'It was said . . .': ibid.
75. 'He wrote to tell . . .': King, letter to his father, 27 September 1915.
75. 'King told his father . . .': King, letter to his father, 26 October 1915.
76. 'King had no . . .': ibid.
76. 'English-born Barber was . . .': King, letter to his father, 21 November 1915.
76. 'Barber asked King . . .': ibid.
76. 'Rohner noted this . . .': Rohner diary.
76. 'We just get up . . .': Scurry, letter to his mother, 27 October 1915.
76. 'Clews talked of . . .': Clews, letter to his mother, 27 September 1915.
76. 'He figured . . .': Layfield, letter to his mother Ada, 3 October 1915.
76. 'He explained: "We . . .': ibid.
77. 'Layfield recounted to . . .': ibid.
77. 'He explained, writing . . .': Attwood, letter to Bertha, 31 October 1915.
78. 'As he deduced . . .': ibid.
78. 'He was unimpressed . . .': Rohner diary.
78. 'As the *Official History* . . .': Butler, pp. 415–16.
78. 'Clews was disappointed . . .': Clews, letter to his sister Emily, 13 October 1915.
79. 'Layfield might have . . .': Layfield, letter to his mother Ada, 3 October 1915.
79. 'There had been . . .': Layfield, letter to his mother Ada, 29 October 1915.

79.   'The day after . . .': Rohner diary.
79.   'Such was his . . .': ibid.
79.   'He was soon . . .': ibid.
79.   'Several of the men . . .': Butler, p. 485.
80.   'In camp back . . .': William Mudge, series no. B2455, National Archives of Australia, Canberra.
80.   'Layfield alerted his parents . . .': Layfield, letter to his mother Ada, 29 October 1915.
80.   'The doctors noted . . .': Mudge.
81.   'He wrote home . . .': Bill Mills, letter to his father John, 'Gordon Soldier in Egypt', *Gordon & Egerton Advertiser*, 12 November 1915.
81.   'As Layfield explained . . .': Layfield, letter to his mother Ada, 13 October 1915.
81.   'Scurry, too, was . . .': Scurry, letter to his mother, 20 October 1915.
82.   'King was more . . .': King, letter to his father, 16 October 1915.
82.   'He detailed . . .': Scurry, letter to his mother, 20 October 1915.
82.   'Scurry continued with . . .': ibid.
83.   'The first time . . .': Scurry, letter to his mother, undated.
83.   'He was much more . . .': ibid.
84.   'He explained to . . .': Scurry, letter to his mother, 20 October 1915.
84.   'When he was there . . .': ibid.
84.   'Layfield saw some . . .': Layfield, letter to his mother, 29 October 1915.
85.   'He detailed to . . .': ibid.
85.   'He explained . . .': ibid.
86.   'King's company also . . .': King, letter to his father, 26 October 1915.
86.   'He had an enjoyable . . .': King, letter to his father, 7 October 1915.
86.   'The Fair Dinkums . . .': ibid.

5   Off to the front
Page

90.   'Recuperating from minor . . .': Jonathan King, *Gallipoli Diaries: The Anzacs' Own Stories, Day by Day*, Scribe, Brunswick, 2014, p. 176.
90.   'When Australian journalist . . .': ibid.
91.   'The letter, as Les . . .': Les Carlyon, *The Great War*, Pan Macmillan, Sydney, 2006, p. 251.
91.   'Murdoch wrote of . . .': Macdougall, p. 72.
92.   'On 15 October itself . . .': David W. Cameron, *Gallipoli: The Final Battles and Evacuation of Anzac*, Big Sky Publishing, Newport, 2011, p. 185.
92.   'On 2 November 1915 . . .': ibid.
93.   'In a short letter . . .': Layfield, letter to his mother Ada, 6 November 1915.
93.   'The men were afforded . . .': Clews, letter to his sister Emily, 10 November 1915.
93.   'Anderson noted in . . .': Anderson diary.
94.   'He explained how . . .': Scurry, letter to his mother, 13 November 1915.
94.   'Clews noted that . . .': Clews diary.
94.   'The *Royal George* . . .': ibid.
94.   'Clews met someone . . .': ibid.
95.   'Anderson's diary gives . . .': www.wrecksite.eu.
95.   'He wrote . . .': Anderson diary
95.   'Wal King found . . .': King, postcard to his father, undated.
96.   'Major McCrae said . . .': Austin, p. 107.
96.   'On 15 November . . .': Cameron, p. 207.
97.   'He noted in his . . .': Rohner diary.
97.   'It had been an . . .': ibid.
98.   'He wrote home . . .': Robert Haysey, letter, 15 December 1915; 'Our Soldiers', *Essendon Gazette*, 24 February 1916.
99.   'In his last letter . . .': Scurry, letter to his mother, 13 November 1915.

6   The Peninsula
Page

104.   'As one soldier . . .': Knyvett, p. 114.
104.   'Major Alf Jackson . . .': McMullin, p. 80.

105. 'The sea journey . . .': Austin, p. 108.
105. 'But when he filled . . .': Clews diary.
105. 'On that cold, miserable . . .': Austin, p. 108.
106. 'He explained in . . .': Haysey letter.
106. 'Haysey said the group . . .': ibid.
106. 'As one Anzac . . .': Knyvett, p. 114.
106. 'Some of them . . .': Clews diary.
107. 'In a letter he . . .': Clews, letter to his sister Emily, 1 December 1915.
107. 'On the third day . . .': King, p. 271.
107. 'Commander of the Anzacs . . .': Cameron, p. 234.
108. 'For the Fair Dinkums . . .': ibid.
108. 'After the storm . . .': King, p. 274.
108. 'He further voiced . . .': King, p. 272.
108. 'A lack of drinking . . .': Austin, p. 108.
109. 'There was 100,000 litres . . .': Cameron, p. 236.
109. 'The shortage was critical . . .': Clews diary.
109. 'Ever the architectural modeller . . .': Scurry, letter to his mother, undated.
110. 'He managed to make . . .': Rohner diary.
111. 'A history of the . . .': Austin, p. 109.
111. 'While Rohner convalesced . . .': Anderson diary.
111. 'The Unit Diary . . .': Seventh Battalion Unit Diary.
111. 'As historian Ron Austin . . .': Austin, pp. 109–10.
112. 'Alf Layfield settled . . .': Layfield, letter to his mother Ada, 30 January 1916.
112. 'Being at Gallipoli . . .': George Rae, letter to his uncle, 14 March 1916, reprinted in *Myrtleford Mail and Whorouly Witness*, 'On the Sand', 27 April 1916.
114. 'The newspaper described . . .': 'North Richmond Brothers Defend Empire's Cause', *Melbourne Herald*, 16 December 1915.

7 Drip-rifles and departure

Page

115. 'In a letter written . . .': Scurry, letter to his mother, undated.
116. '"I'll give you the . . .': ibid.
117. 'A note thrown . . .': Les Carlyon, *Gallipoli*, Pan Macmillan, Sydney, 2001, p. 517.
117. 'This was heightened . . .': 'His Ghost Rifle Saved the Anzacs', *The Australasian Post*, 6 June 1963.
117. 'What they told Scurry . . .': Cameron, pp. 270–71.
118. 'So, on 24 November . . .': Charles Bean, *Two Men I Knew*, Angus & Robertson, Sydney, 1957, pp. 110–11.
118. 'It was designed . . .': ibid.
118. 'White, it was said . . .': Macdougall, p. 72.
118. 'As Ross McMullin's . . .': McMullin, p. 173.
119. 'On the morning of . . .': ibid.
119. 'By that same afternoon . . .': ibid.
119. 'In his diary . . .': John Monash, *War Letters of General Monash*, Black Inc, Collingwood, 2004, p. 95.
119. 'But the evacuation . . .': Monash, pp. 94–5.
120. 'It also gave . . .': Cameron, pp. 263–64.
121. 'He knew that . . .': Peter FitzSimons, *Gallipoli*, William Heinemann, Sydney, 2014, p. 663.
121. 'This attitude may have . . .': Cameron, p. 264.
121. 'As Elliott's biographer . . .': McMullin, p. 173.
122. 'Elliott later explained . . .': Austin, pp. 109–10.
122. '"It occurred to me . . .': W.L. Patterson, 'Captain W.C. Scurry, The Inventor who Saved the Gallipoli Evacuation', *Reveille*, December 1932.
123. 'Scurry said . . .': ibid.
124. 'He recalled . . .': ibid.
124. 'For a time . . .': ibid.
124. 'Just when Scurry . . .': ibid.
125. 'Elliott was proud . . .': H. Elliott, 'Fooled the Turks'; 'Genius of Youth', *Reveille*, April 1930.

125. 'According to a history . . .':Austin, pp. 110–11.
126. 'While the device . . .': Interview with the Scurry family (Danny Keane, Janey Runci and Julie Hume), 2015.
126. 'Lawrence recalled almost 70 . . .':A. H.'Bunty' Lawrence,'The Last Hours of Anzac:The Gamble of the Evacuation', *Despatches*,The Seventh Battalion AIF Association, 1982.
126. 'The order asked . . .': Cameron, p. 283.
127. 'Birdwood's order continued . . .': Cameron, pp. 283–84.
128. 'As one of the . . .':Austin, p. 112.
128. 'When the Anzacs' . . .': Cameron, p. 293.
128. 'Monash noted . . .': Cameron, p. 294.
128. 'Part of the orders . . .':Austin, p. 111.
129. 'One soldier, casting . . .': Peter Pedersen, *The Anzacs: Gallipoli to the Western Front*, Penguin, Camberwell, 2010, p. 119.
130. 'According to the . . .': Seventh Battalion Unit Diary.
130. 'The 7th Battalion rear . . .': McMullin, p. 176.
130. 'One of the last . . .':Austin, p. 112.
131. 'Seven months later . . .':'Soldiering', *Federal Standard*, 8 September 1916.
131. 'Wally Day never forgot . . .':Allan Day, interview with author, 2015.
131. 'In between departure . . .':Austin, p. 113.
131. 'As *Our Dear Old* . . .': Patterson;Austin, p. 113.
132. 'But there remained . . .': Patterson.
132. 'Lawrence would forever . . .':Austin, p. 113.
133. 'The thing that stuck . . .': Scurry, letter to his mother, 18 December 1916.
133. 'But he said . . .':'His Ghost Rifle Saved the Anzacs', *Australasian Post*, 6 June 1963.
133. 'Within minutes, Scurry . . .': Lawrence, *Despatches*, 1982.
133. 'It was one of . . .': ibid.
134. 'Explosions planted near . . .': Carlyon, *Gallipoli*, p. 524.
134. 'As Carlyon said . . .': ibid.

8   Birth of the Pup Battalion

Page

135. 'After the evacuation . . .': McMullin, p. 179.
136. 'As Charles Bean . . .': Charles Bean, *Anzac to Amiens*, Halstead Press, Canberra, 1968, p. 183.
136. 'Clews wrote to . . .': Clews, letter to his sister Emily, 28 December 1915.
137. 'He relished having . . .': ibid.
137. 'This new dinkum . . .': ibid.
137. 'He wrote to his . . .': Gordon Mills, letter to his father, undated.
137. '"Saw a bit of the . . .":'Australia's Part,"Brothers in Egypt"', *Gordon & Egerton Advertiser*, 10 March 1916; from Lemnos Island.
138. 'His pride was evident . . .':'Pte Bill Mills In The Trenches, "Turks Fair Fighters – But Out For Game"', *Gordon & Egerton Advertiser*, 12 May 1916; Bill Mills letter to a friend, Mr J.T. Ryan, 19 March 1916.
138. 'The death of his . . .': *Gordon & Egerton Advertiser*, 10 March 1916; Bill Mills, letter to his father, undated.
139. 'Derham went down . . .':Austin, p. 115.
139. 'The men were charged . . .': Court martial document involving Harold Addison, Bert Thomas and George Wood, series no.A471, National Archives of Australia, Canberra.
139. 'Each of the men . . .': ibid.
139. 'He documented . . .': ibid.
139. 'All were shattered . . .': Harold George Addison, series no. B2455, National Archives of Australia, Canberra.
140. 'A few of . . .':Austin, p. 115.
140. 'Clews sent season's . . .': Clews, letter to his sister Emily, 28 December 1915.
140. 'Layfield apologised to his . . .': Layfield, letter to his mother Ada, 10 January 1916.
140. 'The men enjoyed Christmas . . .': Clews, letter to his sister Emily, 28 December 1915.
140. '. . . march past General Chauvel . . .':Austin, p. 115.

Endnotes

141. 'The conditions at Sarpi . . .': Lawrence, *Despatches*, 1982.
141. 'One of the chaps . . .': ibid.
141. 'He had been "dumped" . . .': 'Our Soldiers', *Essendon Gazette*, 24 February 1916, undated letter from Robert Haysey.
142. 'Roy Anderson recorded . . .': Anderson diary
142. 'While ambitious, he was . . .': Scurry, letter to his father, 1 April 1916.
142. 'He also sent home . . .': Scurry, letter to his mother, undated.
142. 'Scurry, Lawrence and two . . .': Scurry, letter to his mother, 25 February 1916.
143. '"Very wet," recorded . . .': Anderson diary
143. 'The men went aboard . . .': Austin, p. 115.
143. 'Rohner, thankful to be . . .': Rohner diary.
143. 'There were fears . . .': Scurry, letter to his mother, undated.
144. 'Men with a feel . . .': Austin, pp. 115–16.
144. 'There wasn't much . . .': Wal King, letter to his father, 12 January 1916.
144. 'In the same letter . . .': ibid.
144. 'When noting before . . .': King, p. 176.
145. 'Tel-el-Kabir was hardly . . .': Rohner diary.
145. 'The next month . . .': Layfield, letter to his mother Ada, 30 January 1916.
145. 'On 7 January 1916 . . .': Mortensen, National Archives of Australia, Canberra.
145. 'She followed up . . .': ibid.
146. 'General Birdwood "expected . . .': Pedersen, 2007, p. 122.
146. 'The day before departure . . .': Seventh Battalion Unit Diary.
147. '"My rank is now . . .': Scurry, letter to his mother, undated.
147. 'By the very next . . .': ibid.
147. 'The one thing . . .': ibid.
147. 'In a letter . . .': Scurry, letter to his family, undated.
148. 'Eaglehawk's Harry Attwood . . .': Attwood, letter to his family, March 1916.
148. 'Still, he relished . . .': ibid.
148. 'Scurry looked to the . . .': Scurry, letter to his mother, 1 March 1916.
149. 'He told his sister . . .': Clews, letter to his sister Emily, 14 February 1916.
149. 'He lamented: "All those . . .': Layfield, letter to his mother Ada, 30 January 1916.
150. 'It meant that . . .': Seventh Battalion Unit Diary.
150. 'His solution was . . .': Austin, p. 118.
151. 'It read in part . . .': Seventh Battalion AIF Association, *Despatches*, The Association, Melbourne, 1965.
152. 'The decision to split . . .': Bean, *Anzac to Amiens*, p. 189.
152. 'It was hard . . .': Layfield, letter to his mother Ada, 24 February 1916.
153. '"We got a nice . . .': ibid.
153. 'Clews accepted his . . .': Clews, letter to his sister Emily, 3 March 1916.
153. 'He explained to . . .': Scurry letters, to his parents, 1 March and 9 March 1916.
153. 'And it made it . . .': Scurry, letter to his mother, 1 March 1916.
154. 'Scurry detailed: "Arch came . . .': ibid.
154. 'Wardrop ended up . . .': ibid.
154. 'The young man . . .': ibid.
155. 'In a letter . . .': 'On the Sand', *Myrtleford Mail and Whorouly Witness*, 27 April 1916; George Rae, letter to his uncle, 14 March 1916.

9 Somewhere in France
Page
158. 'Layfield had been . . .': Layfield, letter to his father, 4 July 1916.
158. 'One of the men . . .': Dean and Gutteridge, p. 31.
158. 'Layfield breathlessly sent . . .': Layfield, letter to his mother, 30 June 1916.
158. 'The Prince of Wales . . .': Dean and Gutteridge, p. 32.
159. 'Awaiting them was . . .': http://www.thegreatoceanliners.com/megantic.html.
159. 'The ship "was a . . .': Dean and Gutteridge, p. 32.
159. 'Bunty Lawrence recalled . . .': Austin, p. 123.
159. 'There was, however . . .': Attwood, letter to his family, March 1916.

159. 'He sat on his . . .': ibid.
160. 'In another letter . . .': Attwood, letter to his family, undated.
160. 'Attwood acknowledged: "Almost by . . .': ibid.
160. 'A change came . . .': ibid.
161. '. . . not here for . . .': Dean and Gutteridge, p. 33.
161. 'The men were squeezed . . .': ibid.
161. 'As the 7th Battalion's . . .': ibid.
161. 'One said . . .': ibid.
162. 'As one digger . . .': Knyvett, p. 140.
162. 'Women handed out . . .': ibid.
163. 'What was clear . . .': Dean and Gutteridge, p. 33.
163. 'In their twelve . . .': ibid.
163. 'It was the perfect . . .': ibid.
163. 'Scurry detailed the route . . .': Scurry, letter to his father, 1 April 1916.
164. 'Scurry's difficulties came . . .': ibid.
164. 'Scurry added: "Some . . .': ibid.
164. 'He recalled . . .': Knyvett, p. 132.
165. 'He could not have . . .': Scurry, letter to his father, 1 April 1916.
166. 'Clews enjoyed the anniversary . . .': Clews diary.
166. 'Scurry's thoughts that day . . .': Scurry, letter to his mother, 29 April 1916.
166. 'He sent his ribbon . . .': Scurry, letter to his mother, 11 May 1916.
166. 'In February, a cable . . .': James Ostler, series no. B2455, National Archives of Australia, Canberra.
167. 'At the Melbourne Town . . .': 'Enthusiastic Gathering', 'Rousing Speeches', *Age*, 26 April 1916.
167. 'A "quiet celebration" . . .': ibid.
168. 'One man outside . . .': ibid.
168. 'Reverend Bennett gave . . .': 'The Spirit of Anzac, Service at Methodist Church', *Camperdown Chronicle*, 2 May 1916.
168. 'Former Senator Anthony . . .': 'Anzac Day', *Cobram Courier*, 27 April 1916.
169. 'A chorus of . . .': 'Quarry Hill School', *Bendigo Advertiser*, 22 April 1916.
169. 'Roy Anderson would . . .': 'Letters from our Boys', *Cobram Courier*, 10 August 1916; Roy Anderson, letter to his mother, 18 June 1916.
169. 'On the peninsula . . .': 'In the Desert', *Cobram Courier*, 16 March 1916; Bertie Knight, letter to his family, 2 February 1916.
169. 'In 1916 Keith Murdoch . . .': Keith Murdoch, 'There is a World of Meaning in that Term "Soldiers"', *Herald*, 12 October 1916.
170. 'In a letter back . . .': Roy Anderson, letter to his mother, 9 October 1916.
170. 'On 17 June . . .': Rohner diary.
171. 'Layfield was shaken . . .': Layfield, letter to his mother Ada, 10 May 1916.
171. 'Layfield told his mother . . .': Layfield, letter to his mother Ada, 17 May 1916.
172. 'Writing to a Miss . . .': Donald Sheridan, letter to a friend, 14 June 1916, reprinted in 'Soldiers' Letters', *Horsham Times*, 18 August 1916.
172. 'The first history . . .': Dean and Gutteridge, p. 36.
172. '*Our Dear Old Battalion* . . .': Austin, p. 131.
173. 'Some good news . . .': Seventh Battalion Unit War Diary.
173. 'A few days later . . .': Scurry, letter to his mother, 1 July 1916.
174. 'The *Cobram Courier* . . .': 'For Their Country's Sake', *Cobram Courier*, 20 July 1916.
174. 'The local newspaper . . .': ibid.

10 The ghosts of Fromelles

Page
177. 'In the last letter . . .': George Barber, letter to Wal King's father, 3 July 1916.
178. 'Southampton-born Edward Spooner . . .': Judy O'Neill, research undertaken for author.
179. 'The Spooners were . . .': Patrick Lindsay, *Fromelles*, Hardie Grant, Prahran, 2007, p. 7.
179. '"Pick three officers . . .': Patterson.
179. 'Just four days . . .': Scurry, letter to his mother, 15 July 1916.

180. 'On the morning . . .': McMullin, p. 213.
180. 'The planning for . . .': McMullin, pp. 211–16.
181. 'Lost was the element . . .': Corfield, p. 57.
181. 'When the pair were . . .': McMullin, pp. 210–11.
182. 'While he never . . .': McMullin, p. 211.
182. 'Even so, Elliott . . .': ibid.
182. 'They "manned the sector . . .': Corfield, p. 58.
182. 'The battlefield was described . . .': ibid.
183. 'For seven long hours . . .': McMullin, p. 216.
183. 'The 15th Brigade . . .': ibid.
184. 'One man from the . . .': Knyvett, p. 153.
184. 'Another soldier from . . .': Lindsay, p. 100.
184. 'The 60th Battalion . . .': Corfield, p. 62.
185. 'Clancy, who had been . . .': Robert Mackenzie, Australian Red Cross Wounded and Missing File, Australian War Memorial.
185. 'In 1917, Edwin wrote . . .': Harry Windley, Australian Red Cross Wounded and Missing File, Australian War Memorial.
186. 'His mate, himself dodging . . .': James Spooner, Australian Red Cross Wounded and Missing File, Australian War Memorial.
186. 'Incredibly, he was only . . .': http://www.aph.gov.au/binaries/library/pubs/bn/eco/chron_super annuation.pdf: Chronology of superannuation and retirement income in Australia, 2010.
187. 'One of the scouts . . .': Knyvett, p. 155.
188. 'The citation said . . .': Alfred Honey, series no. B2455, National Archives of Australia, Canberra.
188. 'R. Hugh Knyvett summed . . .': Knyvett, pp. 155–56.
189. 'Wounded, he was seen . . .': King, Australian Red Cross Wounded and Missing File, Australian War Memorial.
190. 'They expressed their grief . . .': 'Loved By All, And Deeply Missed', Great Southern Star, 8 September 1916.
190. 'The identity discs he . . .': Ralph Richard Bond, series no. B2455, National Archives of Australia, Canberra.
191. 'A letter from . . .': Frank Allen Dixon, series no. B2455, National Archives of Australia, Canberra.
191. 'The message was . . .': ibid.
191. 'It read: "War . . .': ibid.
192. 'She fumed: "Why . . .': ibid.
192. 'Scowcroft was officially recorded . . .': Reginald Scowcroft, series no. B2455, National Archives of Australia, Canberra.
192. 'As late as 1920 . . .': ibid.
193. 'Part of Annie's . . .': Death notice, Federal Standard, 20 July 1917.

11   The gates of Hell

Page

196. 'That day, the Fair . . .': Austin, pp. 133–34.
196. 'The base of the . . .': Carlyon, The Great War, p. 127.
197. 'British troops had begun . . .': Austin, p. 135.
197. 'One later said . . .': Macdougall, p. 90.
198. 'The word around . . .': Clews, letter to his sister Emily, 9 July 1916.
199. 'One of the signs . . .': Scott Bennett, Pozieres: The Anzac Story, Scribe, Brunswick, 2011.
200. 'They moved up . . .': Austin, pp. 139–43.
201. 'One who knew him . . .': Seventh Battalion AIF Association, Despatches, The Association, Melbourne, 1962.
201. 'His citation praised . . .': Walter Tracey, series no. B2455, National Archives of Australia, Canberra.
201. 'Maybe it was for . . .': Arthur Conan Doyle, Collected Works of Sir Arthur Conan Doyle, Delphi Classic, 2015.
202. 'By January 1917 . . .': Joseph Bellesini, series no. B2455, National Archives of Australia, Canberra.
202. 'But four days . . .': ibid.

203. 'He had been lucky . . .': 'Bomb Throwing Encounter, "Australians Succeed"', *Bendigonian*, 19 October 1916.
203. 'He explained to . . .': Bellesini, letter to his wife, undated.
203. 'On 1 May 1916 . . .': Mortensen, National Archives of Australia, Canberra.
204. 'Still, there was . . .': ibid.
205. 'There was heavy bombing . . .': Archibald Forrest Milne, series no. B2455, National Archives of Australia, Canberra.
205. 'And through it all . . .': Bill Gammage, *Broken Years: Australian Soldiers in the Great War*, Melbourne University Publishing, Melbourne, 2010.
206. 'Tom Hicks was . . .': 'A Brave Signaller, Officer Pays Tribute', *Bendigonian*, 2 November 1916; Thomas Hicks, letter to his parents, 31 July 1916.
206. 'He was recommended . . .': Thomas Hector Hicks, series no. B2455, National Archives of Australia, Canberra; Australian War Memorial Awards and Honours, Australian War Memorial, Canberra.
207. 'He figured he had . . .': Rae, letter to his family, 7 August 1916.
207. 'Smoke bombs were . . .': ibid.
207. '"We had the pick . . .': ibid.
208. 'Rae was soon evacuated . . .': Alastair Campbell, interview and correspondence with author, 2015.
208. 'Before Rae was whisked . . .': Rae, letter to his family, 7 August 1916.
208. 'Fred Hoad, who had . . .': Austin, p. 142.
208. 'According to the battalion's . . .': Dean and Gutteridge, p. 45.
209. 'The unit diary . . .': Seventh Battalion Unit Diary.

12 Damn Pozières!
Page
212. 'Enemy shelling through . . .': Bert Plant, letter to his family, 19 November 1916.
212. 'Hoad and Plant . . .': ibid.
213. 'This one-time swimming . . .': ibid.
214. 'He spent three weeks . . .': ibid.
214. 'But the image . . .': Frederick Hoad, letter to Miss Chomley, 13 June 1917, AWM 1DRL/0428, Prisoner of War Department, Australian War Memorial.
215. 'Initially, Hoad was . . .': Frederick Hoad, letter to Miss Chomley, 23 February 1918.
215. 'At the first . . .': ibid.
215. 'As punishment for . . .': ibid.
215. 'He battled psychological . . .': ibid.
216. 'His last entries . . .': Clews diary.
216. 'His last postcard . . .': Clews, postcard to his sister Emily, 1 August 1916.
216. 'Oates continued: "He was . . .': Gus Oates, letter to Milton Clews' mother, 21 September 1916.
217. 'Two members of the . . .': Dean and Gutteridge, p. 43.
217. 'He did so under . . .': Hicks.
217. 'The signal lines . . .': 'A Brave Signaller, Officer Pays Tribute', *Bendigonian*, 2 November 1916.
217. 'Hicks's next letter . . .': Hicks, letter to his parents, 27 August 1916.
217. 'Still, he added . . .': ibid.
218. 'Even when the . . .': Peter McLarty, series no. B2455, National Archives of Australia, Canberra; Australian War Memorial Honours and Awards, Australian War Memorial.
218. 'He showed "conspicuous . . .': Milne.
219. 'As his citation noted . . .': ibid.
219. 'After much heated . . .': Austin, p. 151.
219. 'He concluded that . . .': Seventh Battalion Unit Diary.
220. 'Bill Scurry, still . . .': Scurry, letter to his mother, 26 August 1916.
221. 'They were among . . .': Gammage, p. 174.

13 The darkest of days
Page
224. 'He was accused of . . .': Lawrence Joseph Black, series no. B2455, National Archives of Australia, Canberra.
225. 'He had enlisted . . .': Neil Walker, interview and correspondence with author, 2014–15.

225. 'He added that . . .': William Ward Walker, series no. B2455, National Archives of Australia, Canberra.
226. 'Captain Edward Strahan . . .': William Ward Walker court martial, series no. A471, National Archives of Australia, Canberra.
227. 'A return to Etaples . . .': Lawrence Joseph Black court martial, series no. A471, National Archives of Australia, Canberra.
227. 'At his court-martial . . .': ibid.
228. 'The citation, written . . .': Corfield, p. 88.
229. 'As he tried . . .': Scurry, letter to his mother, 9 September 1916 .
229. 'His rationale was . . .': Patterson.
229. 'He apologised to . . .': Scurry, letter to his mother, 9 September 1916.
229. 'He played down . . .': ibid.
230. 'The entire party . . .': Scurry, letter to his mother, 16 November 1916.
230. 'It wasn't until . . .': Scurry, letter to his mother, 5 February 1917.
231. 'The tunnellers were . . .': Seventh Battalion AIF Association, *Despatches*, The Association, Melbourne, 1966.
231. 'Layfield didn't mention . . .': Layfield, letter to his mother Ada, September 1916 (undated).
231. 'Still, Ypres wasn't . . .': ibid.
232. 'To his father George . . .': Layfield, letter to his father George, 19 September 1916.
232. 'He admitted he had . . .': ibid.
232. 'As he proudly penned . . .': ibid.
232. 'Australia's official war correspondent . . .': Bean, *Anzac to Amiens*, p. 287.
233. 'He said the . . .': 'Appeal to Workers', *Bendigo Advertiser*, 21 October 1916.
233. 'He urged Australians . . .': ibid.
234. 'Hughes's plebiscite asked . . .': Carlyon, *The Great War*, pp. 256–57.
234. 'At 50, he was . . .': Austin, p.162.
235. 'As one of . . .': Dean and Gutteridge, p. 62.
235. 'Later he wrote of . . .': Scurry, letter to his mother, 18 December 1916.
236. 'He could barely believe . . .': 'Local news', *Mildura Cultivator*, 16 December 1916; Bert Plant, letter to his mother, 29 October 1916.
236. 'The soldiers' votes . . .': Bean, *Anzac to Amiens*, p. 294.
236. 'Charles Bean noted . . .': ibid.
237. 'The appalling conditions . . .': ibid.
237. 'George Rae described . . .': 'Gapsted Boy's Experiences', *Myrtleford Mail and Whorouly Witness*, 5 October 1916; George Rae, letter to his father, undated.
237. 'The march into . . .': Austin, pp. 164–65.
237. 'Layfield lamented that . . .': Layfield, letter to his mother Ada, 25 November 1916.
237. 'The men took to . . .': Dean and Gutteridge, p. 63.
238. 'They had just got . . .': Robert Royle, Australian Red Cross Wounded and Missing File, Australian War Memorial.
239. 'One of them remarked . . .': Seventh Battalion AIF Association, *Despatches*, The Association, Melbourne, 1966.
240. 'Long after the war . . .': Thomas Matthew Roberts, series no. B2455, National Archives of Australia, Canberra.
242. 'He didn't even know . . .': Ellen Bunting, interview and correspondence with author, 2015.
242. 'A century on . . .': ibid.

14   Mud and blood

Page
244. 'Instead, he recorded . . .': Austin, p. 168.
245. 'As he sat down . . .': Layfield, letter to his mother, 25 December 1916.
245. 'He acknowledged the . . .': ibid.
245. 'They were relieved . . .': Corfield, p. 100.
246. 'The battalion's diary . . .': 59th Battalion Unit Diary.
246. 'He made that point . . .': Attwood, letter to his sister Min, 2 December 1916.
247. '"He replies, why . . .': ibid.
247. 'He was almost intoxicated . . .': Attwood, letter to his family, 18 February 1916.

247. 'Writing home from . . .': Scurry, letter to his family, 25 October 1916.
247. 'To his mother . . .': Scurry, letter to his mother, 18 December 1916.
248. 'He spent Christmas . . .': Scurry, letter to his mother, 31 December 1916.
248. 'He expressed excitedly . . .': Scurry, letter to his family, 25 February 1917.
248. 'All around him . . .': ibid.
249. 'For a time . . .': ibid.
249. 'He felt it was . . .': ibid.
249. 'The ghosts of fallen . . .': ibid.
250. 'The young soldier . . .': Scurry, letter to his mother, 27 February 1917.
250. 'Scurry joked to his . . .': ibid.
252. 'In February 1917 . . .': Hoad, letter to Miss Chomley, 2 February 1917.
253. 'He was grateful . . .': Hoad, letter to Miss Chomley, 13 February 1917.
253. 'The battalion war diary . . .': Seventh Battalion War Diary.
254. '"It's a bit . . .': Layfield, letter to his sister Ruby, 30 January 1917.
254. 'He longed to play . . .': ibid.
254. 'He offered up . . .': Layfield, letter to his mother Ada, 2 February 1917.
255. 'By the time . . .': Austin, pp. 170–74.
255. 'The Australians and British . . .': ibid.
256. 'Witnesses to Layfield's final . . .': Layfield, Red Cross Wounded and Missing File, Australian War Memorial.
256. 'Several of Layfield's . . .': Claude Carpenter, letter to Alf Layfield's mother, 8 March 1917.
257. 'A subsequent letter . . .': Oswald Reynolds, letter to Alf Layfield's mother, 5 May 1917.
257. 'The Huns had withdrawn . . .': Dean and Gutteridge, p. 73.
258. 'One senior military official . . .': Arthur George Charles Hart, series no. B2455, National Archives of Australia, Canberra.
258. 'Hart arrived home in . . .': 'Major Hart's Return, Australian Soldiers Praised', *Bendigonian*, 12 July 1917.
259. '"They did not fight . . .': ibid.
259. 'He told the reporters . . .': ibid.
260. 'One recalled: "Those who . . .': Seventh Battalion AIF Association, *Despatches*, The Association, Melbourne, 1966.
260. 'They spent the day . . .': 59th Battalion Unit Diary.
260. 'There was work . . .': Seventh Battalion Unit Diary.
261. 'When he caught up . . .': Scurry, letter to his mother, 19 March 1917.
261. 'Scurry got word . . .': Scurry, letter to his mother, 11 June 1917.
261. 'On his return . . .': Scurry, letter to his mother, 29 April 1917 .
262. 'He spoke of how . . .': ibid.

15   The push towards Passchendaele

Page
263. 'His sense of . . .': Attwood, letter to his family, 23 July 1917.
264. 'He had the chance . . .': Attwood, letter to one of his sisters, August 1917.
264. 'The next one . . .': Attwood, letter to one of his sisters, 15 September 1917.
265. 'As the *Richmond Guardian* . . .': 'Under the Union Jack', *Richmond Guardian*, 16 March 1918.
266. 'Brennan went to . . .': Timothy Brennan, series no. B2455, National Archives of Australia, Canberra.
266. 'He took delight . . .': 'Lieut. O.J.E. Harris', *Bendigo Advertiser*, 30 June 1917.
267. 'Harris confessed that even . . .': ibid.
267. 'Harris continued . . .': ibid.
267. '"Imagine roads running . . .': 'ibid.
268. 'Gone was the long . . .': ibid.
269. 'Even one of the . . .': Carlyon, *The Great War*, p. 445.
270. 'To which Tubb replied . . .': Austin, p. 189.
270. 'The battalion moved . . .': Dean and Gutteridge, p. 87.
270. 'As *Our Dear Old* . . .': Austin, p. 186.
271. 'There were conflicting . . .': Carlyon, *The Great War*, pp. 452–53.
271. 'The Victoria Cross . . .': Austin, p. 189.

271. 'There were several witnesses . . .': Attwood, Australian Red Cross Wounded and Missing File, Australian War Memorial.
272. 'The precise details . . .': 'Bringing in the Sheaves, Australian Soldiers Assist in French Harvest', *Richmond Guardian*, 3 November 1917.
273. 'An article on . . .': ibid.
273. 'The citation, written . . .': Robert Thomas Fraser, series no. B2455, National Archives of Australia, Canberra.
273. 'One remarked, "If anyone . . .': Seventh Battalion AIF Association, *Despatches*, The Association, Melbourne, 1975.
274. 'He won his citation . . .': Benjamin Boag Joyner, series no. B2455, National Archives of Australia, Canberra.
274. 'Like Joyner, he . . .': Arthur Robinson, series no. B2455, National Archives of Australia, Canberra.
275. 'He was one of . . .': 'Local and General News', *Urana Independent*, 13 September 1915.
275. 'Elliott was impressed . . .': McMullin, p. 305.
275. 'In a letter home . . .': McMullin, p. 304.
276. 'In the lead-up . . .': Bean, *Anzac to Amiens*, p. 368.
276. 'Unlike most commanders . . .': McMullin, p. 327.
277. 'One who was there . . .': ibid.
278. 'Of the 15th Brigade . . .': McMullin, p. 332.
278. 'One who impressed . . .': Seventh Battalion AIF Association, *Despatches*, The Association, Melbourne, 1953.
278. 'According to a history . . .': Corfield, p. 186.
279. 'In July 1917 . . .': Edward Joseph Farrell, series no. B2455, National Archives of Australia, Canberra.
279. 'He and his men . . .': 'Late Corporal Farrell', *Bendigonian*, 5 May 1918.
279. 'One of the men . . .': ibid.
279. 'Farrell's mum, Margaret . . .': Farrell, series no. B2455, National Archives of Australia, Canberra.
280. 'There was an . . .': Seventh Battalion AIF Association, *Despatches*, The Association, Melbourne, 1966.
280. 'As the original . . .': Dean and Gutteridge, p. 92.
280. 'While the battalion . . .': Oliver John Edward Harris, series no. B2455, National Archives of Australia, Canberra.
281. 'Spencer Smith had . . .': Dianne Pearce, interview and correspondence with author, 2015.
282. 'His family regularly . . .': 'In Loving Memory', *Gordon, Egerton & Ballan Advertiser*, 9 August 1918.
283. 'He explained . . .': Bill Batson, letter to family, 10 October 1917.
283. 'When Batson, who . . .': ibid.
283. 'There had been . . .': Dean and Gutteridge, p. 93.
284. 'He was noted for . . .': Robert Ellsmere Haysey, series no. B2455, National Archives of Australia, Canberra.
285. 'Signaller Tom Hicks already . . .': Thomas Hector Hicks, series no. B2455, National Archives of Australia, Canberra.
285. 'In contrast, when . . .': *Argus*, 22 November 1917.
285. 'It was a debate . . .': 'Letters', *Argus*, 4 October 1917.
286. 'General Birdwood visited . . .': Seventh Battalion Unit Diary.
286. 'It was said . . .': Dean and Gutteridge, p. 96.
287. 'Seven officers were . . .': Seventh Battalion Unit Diary.

16   Here comes Fritz
Page
291. 'Anderson remained in communication . . .': Anderson, letter to his mother, 3 August 1917.
292. 'Writing from the Hotel . . .': Hoad, letter to Miss Chomley, 29 November 1917.
292. 'In a letter written . . .': Hoad, letter to Miss Chomley, 14 December 1917.
293. 'Scurry detailed the chance . . .': Scurry, letter to his mother, 9 January 1918.
293. 'Not that he told . . .': Scurry, letter to his mother, 23 March 1918.
293. 'As March turned into . . .': Scurry, letter to his mother, 2 April.
294. 'In the court proceedings . . .': Reginald Wallis Palmer, series no. B2455, National Archives of Australia, Canberra.

295. 'Another witness to the . . .': ibid.
295. 'They placed a notice . . .': 'Death notice', *Argus*, 4 April 1918.
296. 'Russia had been effectively . . .': Macdougall, p. 125.
296. 'The Americans had . . .': ibid.
296. 'A battalion history . . .': Dean and Gutteridge, p. 100.
297. 'The 7th Battalion was . . .': ibid.
297. 'The Fair Dinkums waited . . .': ibid.
298. 'When the Anzacs . . .': Austin, p. 212.
298. 'The Anzacs were shocked . . .': Dean and Gutteridge, p. 102.
298. 'Herrod told his officers . . .': Austin, p. 212.
299. 'One soldier recalled . . .': Austin, p. 213.
300. 'Olive and her children . . .': 'Victory Square, Armadale, Site of the War Widows' Homes', *Malvern Standard*, 21 February 1920.
300. 'Two generations later . . .': Neil Walker, interview and correspondence with author, 2015.
301. 'The men inside . . .': Frederick Mann, series no. B2455, National Archives of Australia, Canberra.
301. 'Mann's wife, Aileen . . .': Death notice, *Argus*, 4 May 1918.
302. 'It was the third . . .': 'Soldier in France', *Myrtleford Mail and Whorouly Witness*, 27 June 1918.
302. 'Even wounded, he sensed . . .': Rae letter, 19 April 1918.
302. 'He told his father . . .': ibid.
303. 'Lieutenant Roy Anderson . . .': Seventh Battalion Unit Diary.
303. 'The house to which . . .': Austin, p. 215.
303. 'One of the men . . .': ibid.
304. 'The *Cobram Courier* . . .': 'The Return', *Cobram Courier*, 31 October 1918.
304. 'Bill Jamieson, who was . . .': Seventh Battalion AIF Association, *Despatches*, The Association, Melbourne, 1982.
305. 'One of the guard's . . .': Macdougall, p. 131.
305. 'According to Elliott's biographer . . .': McMullin, p. 411.
306. 'The 59th Battalion's . . .': 59th Battalion Unit Diary.
306. 'He stated quite clearly . . .': McMullin, pp. 418–19.

17   Saving Private Bellesini

Page
308. 'When pressed to provide . . .': Bellesini, series no. B2455, National Archives of Australia, Canberra.
309. 'That led Dr Green . . .': ibid.
309. 'He concluded . . .': ibid.
310. 'The Australian administrative . . .': ibid.
311. 'Now, as historian . . .': Bean, *Anzac to Amiens*, p. 445.
311. 'In June 1918 . . .': Austin, p. 227.
312. 'Monash, the son of . . .': Monash, pp. 243–44.
312. 'This was used . . .': Macdougall, p. 134.
312. 'French Prime Minister . . .': Carlyon, *The Great War*, p. 646.
313. 'Monash's message read . . .': Monash, p. 254.
314. 'The men resumed their . . .': Dean and Gutteridge, p. 113.
314. 'General Ludendorff would . . .': Monash, p. 254.
314. 'The 59th was able . . .': McMullin, pp. 467–68.
315. 'His biographer said . . .': ibid.
315. 'He dealt with . . .': Albert Edward Allen, series no. B2455, National Archives of Australia, Canberra.
315. 'The citation for . . .': ibid.
316. 'When he was struck . . .': Alec Southwell, interview with author, 2015.
316. 'Decades later, as he . . .': Seventh Battalion AIF Association, *Despatches*, The Association, Melbourne, 1983.
316. 'Wounded for the third . . .': Henry Thomas Stephens, series no. B2455, National Archives of Australia, Canberra.
317. 'Bean saw the similarities . . .': Austin, p. 235.
318. 'But Tom was . . .': ibid.
318. 'One man who was . . .': ibid.

318. 'Men were struck . . .': ibid.
319. 'Milne was comforted . . .': Milne, series no. B2455, National Archives of Australia, Canberra.
319. 'It took four more . . .': Robert Henry Haslem, series no. B2455, National Archives of Australia, Canberra.
320. 'Bugger it, he thought . . .': Allan Day, interview and correspondence with author, 2015.
320. 'As the battalion's . . .': Dean and Gutteridge, p. 122.
320. 'The official battalion . . .': Seventh Battalion Unit Diary.
321. 'But he also knew . . .': Scurry, letter to his mother, 30 July 1918.
322. 'Scurry spent the first . . .': ibid.
322. 'He thought that night . . .': ibid.
323. 'He would write . . .': ibid.
324. 'That brilliant morning . . .': ibid.
324. 'It was said . . .': Francis Vanstan, Honours and Awards, Australian War Memorial.
325. 'His citation read . . .': James Pegler, interview with author, 2015; Arthur Pegler, Honours and Awards, Australian War Memorial.
325. 'One eyewitness said . . .': 'How Howard Williams Met His Death', *Mildura Cultivator*, 28 December 1918.
326. 'On this chilly . . .': Austin, p. 256.
326. 'He went out . . .': Scurry, letter to his mother, 13 November 1918.
326. 'Scurry and his mates . . .': ibid.
327. 'He explained to his . . .': ibid.
327. 'The 7th Battalion . . .': Austin, p. 256.
328. 'This time she enlisted . . .': Bellesini, National Archives.

18 Surviving the peace

Page
334. 'The process would take . . .': Bean, *Anzac to Amiens*, p. 516.
336. 'The young man . . .': Roy Anderson, letter to his mother, 21 August 1916.
337. 'He had four children . . .': Allan Terrett, interview and correspondence with author, 2014–15.
337. 'His crushing disappointment . . .': Seventh Battalion AIF Association, *Despatches*, The Association, Melbourne, 1980.
337. 'He was 82 . . .': Jeanette Robinson, interview and correspondence with author, 2014–15.
338. 'He spent the final . . .': Obituary, John Tognola, *Cairns Post*, 9 September 1950; research by Judy O'Neill.
339. 'Harris received a certificate . . .': Obituary, *Bendigo Advertiser*, 6 April 1920.
339. 'Dr Nankervis certified . . .': ibid.
339. 'The *Bendigo Advertiser* . . .': ibid.
340. 'Miss Chomley presciently . . .': Mary Chomley, letter to Frederick Hoad, 15 July 1917.
340. 'Three days before . . .': Hoad, letter to Miss Chomley, 8 November 1918.
340. 'He returned to work . . .': 'Three Years a Prisoner, Captain Hoad in Germany', *Williamstown Chronicle*, 28 July 1919.
340. 'He also detailed . . .': ibid.
340. 'By 1930, the . . .': Seventh Battalion AIF Association, *Despatches*, The Association, Melbourne, 1930.
341. 'Despite his physical issues . . .': Seventh Battalion AIF Association, *Despatches*, The Association, Melbourne, 1942.
341. 'He was shocked . . .': Scurry, letter to his mother, 28 November 1918.
341. 'But as he sat . . .': ibid.
342. 'Besides, he was . . .': ibid.
342. 'As he mused to . . .': Scurry, letter to his mother, 29 December 1918.
342. 'In December, Scurry . . .': Scurry, letter to his family, 5 January 1919.
343. 'Elliott spoke, with Scurry . . .': ibid.
343. 'Birdwood asked for . . .': Marriage, *The Adelaide Mail*, 28 February 1920.
343. 'For a short time . . .': A. J. McAleer, *The Shrine of Lilydale and its Military Heritage (Volume II), The First World War and its effect on the community*.
344. 'On the seventeenth . . .': 'An Heroic Victorian', *Argus*, 19 December 1932.
344. 'Two years later . . .': McAleer.

344. 'Much to Doris's . . .': Interview with the Scurry family, 2015.
344. 'He came to be . . .': McAleer.
344. 'He then collapsed . . .': ibid.
345. 'He couldn't reconcile . . .': McMullin, p. 655.
345. 'Family members say . . .': Interview with the Scurry family.
345. 'But he joined . . .': Clarence Lay, series no. B2455, National Archives of Australia, Canberra.
345. 'In 1925, Lay . . .': 'A Captain's Death', *Newcastle Morning Herald and Miner's Advocate*, 20 May 1925.
345. 'Lay's father wrote . . .': Lay, series no. B2455.
345. '"Wain commanded an . . .': 'Bravery in North Africa', *West Australian*, 17 May 1944.
346. 'Wain lived to be . . .': Research by Judy O'Neill.
346. 'Most of the Murcutt . . .': Stan Murcutt, interview with the author, 2015.
347. 'One of the few . . .': Avis Coles, interview with the author, 2015.
347. 'For a time . . .': ibid.
347. 'Fittingly, he renewed . . .': Rod Mercer, interview with the author, 2015.
347. 'The 7th Battalion's . . .': Seventh Battalion AIF Association, *Despatches*, The Association, Melbourne.
347. 'Mercer met his . . .': Alfred Mercer, series no. B2455, National Archives of Australia, Canberra.
347. 'They re-established contact . . .': Rod Mercer, interview with author, 2015.
348. 'On 3 December 1918 . . .': Black, series no. B2455, National Archives of Australia, Canberra.
348. 'He pleaded to Victoria . . .': ibid.
349. 'When the charge came . . .': 'Insurance Collector's Theft', *Brisbane Courier*, 21 May 1926.
349. 'At around the . . .': 'False Pretences, Insurance Agent's Trick', *Brisbane Courier*, 17 September 1926.
349. 'But Walshe's demons . . .': 'Sincerely Regrets Assault', *Adelaide Advertiser*, 6 December 1945.
349. 'Then he was named . . .': 'Committed for Trial', *Adelaide Advertiser*, 16 November 1945.
350. 'The woman he . . .': ibid.
350. 'By 1934 the . . .': Seventh Battalion AIF Association, *Despatches*, The Association, Melbourne, 1934.
350. 'One of those . . .': ibid.
351. 'He died, aged 50 . . .': Alastair Campbell, interview and correspondence with the author, 2015.
351. 'He tried to enlist . . .': Joan Batson, interview with the author, 2015.
351. 'He became known as . . .': Seventh Battalion AIF Association, *Despatches*, The Association, Melbourne, 1934.
352. 'The local newspaper recorded . . .': 'Welcome to Our Soldiers', *Maffra Spectator*, 24 March 1919.
353. 'Locals recalled a track . . .': Linda Barraclough interview with author.
353. 'A welcome home . . .': 'Cedric Smith Returns', *Geelong Advertiser*, 8 July 1919.
353. 'Wilfred Williams, who came . . .': Seventh Battalion AIF Association, *Despatches*, The Association, Melbourne, 1977.
353. 'Wally Day happened to . . .': Seventh Battalion AIF Association, *Despatches*, The Association, Melbourne, 1973.
354. 'Rae's relationship with Laura . . .': Rae, unpublished memoir, 1989.
354. 'His son would . . .': David Rae, interview and correspondence with the author, 2015.
354. 'Battalion members visited him . . .': Seventh Battalion AIF Association, *Despatches*, The Association, Melbourne, 1970.
355. 'Southwell became the inaugural . . .': Corfield, pp. 376–77.
356. 'The war had not . . .': Bryan Park, interview with the author, 2014–15.